THE CAMBRIDGE
COMPANION TO
NARRATIVE

EDITED BY
DAVID HERMAN

CAMBRIDGE
UNIVERSITY PRESS

CAMBRIDGE UNIVERSITY PRESS
Cambridge, New York, Melbourne, Madrid, Cape Town, Singapore, São Paulo

Cambridge University Press
The Edinburgh Building, Cambridge CB2 8RU, UK

Published in the United States of America by Cambridge University Press, New York

www.cambridge.org
Information on this title: www.cambridge.org/9780521673662

First published 2007

Printed in the United Kingdom at the University Press, Cambridge

A catalogue record for this publication is available from the British Library

Library of Congress Cataloguing in Publication data

The Cambridge companion to narrative / edited by David Herman.
p. cm. – (Cambridge companions to literature)
Includes bibliographical references and index.
ISBN 13: 978-0-521-85696-6 (hbk)
ISBN 10: 0-521-85696-5 (hbk)
ISBN 13: 978-0-521-67366-2 (pbk)
ISBN 10: 0-521-67366-6 (pbk)
1. Narration (Rhetoric) I. Herman, David, 1962- II. Title. III. Series.
PN212.C36 2007
808 – dc22 2006038545

ISBN 978-0-521-85696-6 hardback
ISBN 978-0-521-67366-2 paperback

CONTENTS

CONTENTS

ILLUSTRATIONS

Chapter 11, "Film and television narrative," contains the following illustrations:

NOTES ON CONTRIBUTORS

H. PORTER ABBOTT is a Research Professor in the English Department at the University of California, Santa Barbara. His central research and teaching interests include narrative, autobiography, modernism, literature and theories of cognition and evolution, and nineteenth- and twentieth-century literature. He is the author of *The Fiction of Samuel Beckett* (1973); *Diary Fiction: Writing as Action* (1984); *Beckett Writing Beckett: The Author in the Autograph* (1996); and *The Cambridge Introduction to Narrative* (2002). In addition, he edited a special issue of the journal *Sub-Stance* titled *On the Origin of Fictions: Interdisciplinary Perspectives* (2001).

TERESA BRIDGEMAN is Honorary Research Fellow in French at the University of Bristol. She has published on stylistics and the pragmatics of narrative and is the author of *Negotiating the New in the French Novel*, as well as many other studies in the linguistics of literature, narratology, discourse analysis, and twentieth-century novels. She is currently working on cognitive aspects of reading contemporary French narratives, including graphic storytelling in *bande dessinée*, with a special focus on the construction of place and space.

MONIKA FLUDERNIK is Professor of English Language and Literature at the University of Freiburg, Germany. She is the author of many studies of narrative, including *The Fictions of Language and the Languages of Fiction: The Linguistic Representation of Speech and Consciousness* (1993) and *Towards a "Natural Narratology"* (1996), which was awarded the Perkins Prize ("most significant contribution to narrative studies") for books published in 1996. She has also written *Echoes and Mirrorings: Gabriel Josipovici's Creative Œuvre* (2000), and edited *Diaspora and Multiculturalism: Common Traditions and New Developments* (2003).

DAVID HERMAN teaches in the English Department at Ohio State University, where he currently serves as Director of Project Narrative (http://projectnarrative. osu.edu), a new interdisciplinary initiative designed to promote state-of-the-art scholarship and teaching in the field of narrative studies. His research focuses on linguistic and cognitive approaches to narratives of all sorts, from stories exchanged in everyday communicative interaction to innovative modern and post-modern literary texts. He is the author, editor, or co-editor of a number of books relevant to these areas of enquiry, including *Universal Grammar and Narrative Form* (1995), *Narratologies* (1999), *Story Logic* (2002), *Narrative Theory and the Cognitive Sciences* (2003), and (with Manfred Jahn and Marie-Laure Ryan) the *Routledge Encyclopedia of Narrative Theory* (2005). He also serves as editor of the *Frontiers of Narrative* book series published by the University of Nebraska Press.

LUC HERMAN is a Professor at the University of Antwerp in Belgium, where he teaches American Literature and Narrative Theory. He is the author of *Concepts of Realism* (1996) and co-author (with Bart Vervaeck) of the 2005 English translation of *Handbook of Narrative Analysis*, which first appeared in Dutch in 2001. He has guest-edited a collection of essays on Thomas Pynchon's *Gravity's Rainbow* for *Pynchon Notes* (1998) and published many essays on the author. His current projects include essays on the typescript of Pynchon's *V.* and on the post-war encyclopedic novel in the United States.

MANFRED JAHN completed studies of English and German Literature at the University of Cologne and SUNY-Buffalo. Based at the University of Cologne in Germany, he has published many articles on focalization, represented speech and thought, and cognitive narratology in such venues as the *Journal of Pragmatics, New Literary History, Poetics Today*, and *Style*. A co-editor (with David Herman and Marie-Laure Ryan) of the *Routledge Encyclopedia of Narrative Theory* (2005), he has also authored a widely used online guide to narratology and narrative theory, freely available at www.uni-koeln.de/~ameo2/pppn.htm.

URI MARGOLIN is a pioneering figure in the field of narrative studies, and has just completed many years of service as Professor of Comparative Literature at the University of Alberta in Canada. Publications include close to sixty essays in numerous collective volumes, as well as in scholarly journals, such as *Language and Literature, Poetics Today*, and *Style*. Professor Margolin is regarded as an expert on the concept of character. The co-editor (with Monika Fludernik) of a special double issue of the journal *Style* devoted to "German Narratology," he has recently published several studies developing a cognitive approach to narrative.

JASON MITTELL teaches American Studies and Film and Media Culture at Middlebury College. He is the author of *Genre and Television: From Cop Shows to Cartoons in American Culture* (2004) and *Television and American Culture* (forthcoming). He is working on a book about narrative complexity in contemporary American television, examining how storytelling has changed in the wake of recent industrial, technological, and cultural transformations.

NICK MONTFORT is a Ph.D. candidate in the Department of Computer and Information Science at the University of Pennsylvania, where he is developing new approaches to natural language generation by exploring areas of intersection among narratology, computational linguistics, and the study of interactive fiction. He is the author of *Twisty Little Passages: An Approach to Interactive Fiction* (2003), the first book-length history of interactive fiction of the text adventure sort, and the co-editor (with Noah Wardrip-Fruin) of *The New Media Reader* (2003), a book and CD anthologizing essays and other writing of historical importance to new media.

NEAL R. NORRICK holds the chair of English Philology (Linguistics) at Saarland University in Saarbrücken, Germany. His research specializations in linguistics include conversation, verbal humor, pragmatics, semantics, and poetics. In recent years, Professor Norrick has focused his research on spoken language, with particular interests in the role of repetition in discourse and verbal humor. He is the author of *Conversational Narrative: Storytelling in Everyday Talk* (2000) and *Conversational Joking: Humor in Everyday Talk* (1993), among many other publications on conversational storytelling and related topics.

RUTH PAGE is Senior Lecturer in the School of English at the University of Central England. The author of studies published in *Discourse and Society, Discourse Studies, Language and Literature*, and *TEXT*, she was recently awarded a grant by the Arts and Humanities Research Council that culminated in the publication of her book *Literary and Linguistic Approaches to Feminist Narratology* (2006). Her ongoing research interests include, in addition to feminist narratology, sociolinguistics, cross-cultural storytelling, critical discourse analysis, and narratives in new media.

JAMES PHELAN is Humanities Distinguished Professor in the Department of English at Ohio State University. A recipient of OSU's Distinguished Scholar Award (2004), he has written about style in *Worlds from Words* (1981), about character and narrative progression in *Reading People, Reading Plots* (1989), about technique, ethics, and audiences in *Narrative as Rhetoric* (1996), and about character-narrators in *Living to Tell about It* (2005). He is the editor of the journal *Narrative* and, with Peter J. Rabinowitz, the co-editor of the Ohio State University Press series on the Theory and Interpretation of Narrative. He has also edited *Reading Narrative* (1989) and, with Peter J. Rabinowitz, *Understanding Narrative* (1994) and *The Blackwell Companion to Narrative Theory* (2005).

HETA PYRHÖNEN is the author of many studies exploring aspects of narrative and narrative theory, including *Murder from an Academic Angle: An Introduction to the Study of Detective Narrative* (1994) and *Mayhem & Murder: Narrative & Moral Issues in the Detective Story* (1999). She is a Professor of Comparative Literature at the University of Helsinki in Finland, and is currently at work on a book-length study titled *Writing a Way Out: The Female Author in Bluebeard's Castle*.

BRIAN RICHARDSON is Professor of English at the University of Maryland. His primary areas of interest are narrative theory, the poetics of drama, and twentieth-century literature. He is the author of *Unlikely Stories: Causality and the Nature of Modern Narrative* (1997) and *Unnatural Voices: Extreme Narration in Modern and Contemporary Fiction* (2006). He is also editor of *Narrative Dynamics: Essays on Plot, Time, Closure, and Frames* (2002), and has guest-edited a special issue of the journal *Style* devoted to "Concepts of Narrative" (2000). Currently, he is finishing a book on modernism and the reader and editing a collection of essays on narrative beginnings.

MARIE-LAURE RYAN is an independent scholar based in the U.S. who has published widely in the areas of narrative theory, electronic textuality, and media studies. She is the author of *Possible Worlds, Narrative Theory, and Artificial Intelligence* (1991), *Narrative as Virtual Reality: Immersion and Interactivity in Literature and Electronic Media* (2001), and *Avatars of Story* (2006). A co-editor (with David Herman and Manfred Jahn) of the *Routledge Encyclopedia of Narrative Theory* (2005), she is also the editor of *Cyberspace Textuality: Computer Technology and Literary Theory* (1999) and *Narrative across Media: The Languages of Storytelling* (2004).

BRONWEN THOMAS is Senior Lecturer in Linguistics and Literature at the Bournemouth Media School at Bournemouth University in the U.K. She is the author of a number of studies of fictional dialogue, published in journals that include *Language and Literature* and *Poetics Today*. Currently she is at work on a book-length study titled *Fictional Dialogue: Speech and Conversation in the Modern and Postmodern Novel*.

MICHAEL TOOLAN is Professor of Applied English Linguistics at the University of Birmingham in the U.K. He is the author of *Total Speech* (1996), *Language in Literature* (1998), and *Narrative: A Critical Linguistic Introduction* (2nd edition, 2001). He has also edited a four-volume anthology of essays on *Critical Discourse Analysis* (2002). The editor of the *Journal of Literary Semantics*, Professor Toolan's research focuses on the linguistic features of narratives and other kinds of texts; his current work explores patterns of coherence and expectation in the reading of narrative fiction.

BART VERVAECK teaches literary theory and Dutch literature at the Free University in Brussels, Belgium. He has published a book on postmodern Dutch literature and has just completed a comparative study of literary descents into the underworld. He also co-authored (with Luc Herman) the *Handbook of Narrative Analysis* (2005).

ACKNOWLEDGMENTS

Many people made this volume possible, and I can single out for explicit acknowledgment only some of the people who have supported the project and helped facilitate its completion. I am grateful to Ray Ryan at Cambridge University Press for believing that this was a book worth publishing and for early discussions that led to my assuming the role of editor. Later, as the project was just getting off the ground, Heta Pyrhönen proactively finished a draft of her chapter on "Genre" and graciously allowed it to be used as a template for the other contributors. Maartje Scheltens, also at Cambridge, provided constant and reliable advice regarding content, formatting, and a host of other issues, and I thank her for her patience in the face of all my many questions regarding the project. During the production process, others at the press, including the copy-editor, Sally McCann, and Liz Davey, have helped make this volume a much better book than it would have been without their assistance and expertise, and I am grateful for all their work.

I owe all the contributors a debt of gratitude for their dedication and patience, and especially for their shared commitment to making this *Companion* a resource for narrative scholars at all levels. The volume aims to be a helpful tool for experts in the field no less than for readers using the book to explore approaches to narrative inquiry for the first time. If the book has met that goal, then this is due to the contributors' deep knowledge of narrative – a knowledge that has enabled them to write about complex ideas in an accessible manner but without in any way "dumbing down" the concepts in question. I should also note how gratifying it has been to work with an international team of experts in the field. With contributors from Belgium, Canada, Finland, Germany, the U.K., and the U.S., the volume itself demonstrates how scholarly interest in narrative cuts across national borders as well as academic disciplines.

Work on this volume began while I was in Raleigh, North Carolina, and was completed in Plain City, Ohio. I am grateful to faculty and students both at North Carolina State University and at Ohio State University for their support and collegiality during this time of transition. My particular thanks go to Barbara Baines, Aman Garcha, Jared Gardner, Esther Gottlieb, Teemu Ikonen, Steve Kern, Kim Kovarik, Valerie Lee, Leila May, Brian McHale, Betty Menaghan, Debra Moddelmog, Don Palmer, Jim Phelan, Laura Severin, Raeanne Woodman, Mary Helen Thuente, Walt Wolfram, and Chris Zacher. I am grateful, too, to have had the opportunity to exchange ideas with many colleagues at workshops and conferences held in recent months. Especially helpful were conversations during meetings at the University of California-Santa Barbara, the University of Louisville, MIT, the Interdisciplinary Centre for Narratology at the University of Hamburg, the University of Helsinki, the University of Connecticut-Storrs, and Georgetown University.

Most of all I thank the family members – in Denver, Colorado; Knoxville, Tennessee; Sanibel Island, Florida; and Johannesburg, South Africa – who have been so supportive, in so many ways, during the time I worked on this volume. My most special thanks go, as always, to Susan Moss, lovely owner of The Golden Beet, and to Tinker, farm cat extraordinaire.

I
Preliminaries

I

DAVID HERMAN

Introduction

In this introduction I seek to provide context for the chapters that follow by addressing questions that many readers of this volume are likely to have – particularly readers coming to the field of narrative studies for the first time. These questions include: Why a *Companion to Narrative*? What is narrative (what are its identifying traits and key functions)? What are some of the major trends in recent scholarship on narrative? What are the distinctive features of this book, and some strategies for using it? My attempt to address the second of these questions (what is narrative?) is meant to be read in tandem with chapter 2, where Marie-Laure Ryan reviews recent suggestions about what constitutes a narrative and proposes her own definition.[1] Conversely, this introduction should afford a sense of the broader research tradition from which attempts to define narrative have emerged.

The working definition that I myself will be using in this introduction, and that I spell out in greater detail below, runs as follows. Rather than focusing on general, abstract situations or trends, stories are accounts of what happened to particular people[2] – and of what it was like for them to experience what happened – in particular circumstances and with specific consequences. Narrative, in other words, is a basic human strategy for coming to terms with time, process, and change – a strategy that contrasts with, but is in no way inferior to, "scientific" modes of explanation that characterize phenomena as instances of general covering laws. Science explains how in general water freezes when (all other things being equal) its temperature reaches zero degrees centigrade; but it takes a story to convey what it was like to lose one's footing on slippery ice one late afternoon in December 2004, under a steel-grey sky.

Yet just as it is possible to construct a narrative about the development of science, to tell a story about who made what discoveries and under what circumstances, it is possible to use the tools of science – definition, analysis, classification, comparison, etc. – to work toward a principled account of what makes a text, discourse, film, or other artifact a narrative. Such an account should help clarify what distinguishes a narrative from an exchange of greetings, a recipe for salad dressing, or a railway timetable. Collectively, the chapters in this book demonstrate how far theorists of narrative, sometimes working in quite different disciplinary traditions, have come in developing a common framework for narrative study. An overarching goal of the book is to enable (and encourage) readers to build on the contributors' work, so that others can participate in the process of narrative inquiry and help create further productive synergies among the many fields concerned with stories.

Why a *Companion to Narrative*?

In keeping with the overall purpose of the Cambridge Companion series, this book seeks to provide an accessible introduction to key ideas about narrative and an overview of major approaches to narrative inquiry. Further, like other Companions, the volume offers a variety of viewpoints on the field rather than an outline or summarization by a single commentator. By registering multiple perspectives on the study of stories, the book not only furnishes a synoptic account of this area of investigation but also constitutes in its own right a unique contribution to the scholarship on narrative. Hence, although it is like other Cambridge Companions targeted at student readers who need a reliable, comprehensive guide – a point of entrance into a complex field of study, as well as a basis for further research – the volume also aims to be a helpful tool for more advanced scholars needing a convenient, affordable, and up-to-date treatment of foundational terms, concepts, and approaches.

Thus far, I have focused on the objectives and design principles of this Companion. But what is the impetus for its publication, the reason for its appearance at *this* moment? The past several decades have in fact witnessed an explosion of interest in narrative, with this multifaceted object of inquiry becoming a central concern in a wide range of disciplines and research contexts. In his contribution to a volume titled *The Travelling Concept of Narrative*, Matti Hyvärinen traces the extent of this diffusion or spread of narrative across disciplinary boundaries, suggesting that "the concept of narrative has become such a contested concept over the last thirty years in response to what is often called the 'narrative turn' in social sciences . . . The concept has successfully travelled to psychology, education, social sciences, political thought and policy analysis, health research, law, theology and cognitive science."[3] The "narrative turn," to use the term that Hyvärinen adopts from Martin Kreiswirth,[4] has also shaped humanistic fields in recent decades, thanks in part to the development of structuralist theories of narrative in France in the mid to late 1960s.

Thus, around the same time that William Labov and Joshua Waletzky developed their model for the analysis of personal experience narratives told in face-to-face interaction, thereby establishing a key precedent for scholars of narrative working in the fields mentioned by Hyvärinen, the literary scholar Tzvetan Todorov coined the term "la narratologie" (= "narratology") to designate what he and other structuralist theorists of story (e.g., Roland Barthes, Claude Bremond, Gérard Genette, and A. J. Greimas) conceived of as a science of narrative modeled after the "pilot-science" of Ferdinand de Saussure's structural linguistics.[5] As I discuss in greater detail below, the structuralists drew not only on Saussure's ideas but also on the work of Russian Formalist literary theorists, who studied prose narratives of all sorts, from Tolstoi's historically panoramic novels to tightly plotted detective novels to (Russian) fairy tales. This broad investigative focus helped initiate the narrative turn, uncoupling theories of *narrative* from theories of the *novel*, and shifting scholarly attention from a particular genre of literary writing to all discourse (or, in an even wider interpretation, all semiotic activities) that can be construed as narratively organized. That same shift helps explain why the present volume is titled A Companion to Narrative rather than A Companion to the Novel – even though Part II of the volume provides a "starter-kit" of terms, concepts, and methods for studying narrative fiction in particular, a major form of storytelling highly developed in the world's literatures.

Taking their cue from the Formalists, and noting that stories can be presented in a wide variety of textual formats, media, and genres, structuralists such as Barthes argued explicitly for a cross-disciplinary approach to the analysis of narrative – an approach in which stories can be viewed as supporting many cognitive and communicative activities, from spontaneous conversations and courtroom testimony to visual art, dance, and mythic and literary traditions.[6] Only after the heyday of structuralism, however, did their call for an interdisciplinary approach to narrative begin to be answered. Although more needs to be done to promote genuine dialogue and exchange among story analysts working in different fields, it is undeniable that the past decade in particular has seen an exponential growth of cross-disciplinary research and teaching activity centering on narrative.[7] International in scope, this activity has also spawned book series and journals in which scholarship on narrative figures importantly.[8] Other manifestations of the way narrative cuts across disciplinary boundaries include initiatives such as the Centre for Interdisciplinary Narratology at the University of Hamburg (www.icn.uni-hamburg.de); the Centre for Narrative Research at the University of East London (www.uel.ac.uk/cnr/); Columbia University's Program in Narrative Medicine (www.narrativemedicine.org/), which aims "to fortify medicine with ways of knowing about singular persons available through a study of humanities, especially literary studies and creative writing"; and Project Narrative at Ohio State University (http://projectnarrative.osu.edu), which brings together folklorists, scholars of language and literature, theorists of storytelling in film, digital media, and comics and graphic novels, and researchers in other fields concerned with narrative. By the same token, over the past decade alone many conferences and symposia have been dedicated to exploring the potential of narrative to bridge disciplines, in ways that may in turn throw new light on narrative itself.[9] The present volume, with contributions by authors in fields that include literature, linguistics, computer science, and film and television studies, can be seen as an outgrowth of this same trend toward interdisciplinarity in narrative research. Collectively, the chapters reveal complex relationships between literary fiction and other kinds of storytelling, and between the analytic frameworks that have grown up around these different modes of narrative practice.

I turn now from the factors contributing to this volume's publication and cross-disciplinary profile to its focal concern: namely, narrative itself.

What is narrative (what are its identifying traits and key functions)?

Consider the following two texts, both of them concerned with human emotions. The first is an excerpt from an encyclopedia article on the topic; the second is a transcription of part of a tape-recorded interview with Mary, a 41-year-old African American female from Texana, North Carolina, who in the transcribed excerpt refers to the fear that she and her childhood friend experienced as a result of being pursued menacingly by a large, glowing, orange ball that Mary characterizes earlier in the interview as "[a] UFO or the devil."[10]

Text 1:
An emotion is a psychological state or process that functions in the management of goals. It is typically elicited by evaluating an event as relevant to a goal; it is positive when the goal is advanced, negative when the goal is impeded. The core of an emotion is readiness to act in a certain way . . . ; it is an urgency, or prioritization, of some goals and plans rather than others; also they prioritize certain kinds of social interaction, prompting, for instance, cooperation, or conflict.[11]

Text 2:
(1) But then . . for some reason I feel some heat or somethin other
(2) and I look back
(3) me and Renee did at the same time
(4) and it's right behind us.

(5) We like . . we were scared and . .
(6) "Aaahhh!" you know
(7) at the same time.
(8) So we take off runnin as fast as we can.
(9) And we still lookin back
(10) and every time we look back it's with us.
(11) It's just a-bouncin behind us
(12) it's NOT touchin the ground.
(13) It's bouncin in the air.
(14) It's like this . . behind us
(15) as we run.
(16) We run all the way to her grandmother's
(17) and we open the door
(18) and we just fall out in the floor,
(19) and we're cryin and we screamin
(20) and we just can't BREATHE.
(21) We that scared.[12]

Text 1 exemplifies what Jerome Bruner calls "paradigmatic" or logico-deductive reasoning.[13] The author uses definitions to establish categories in terms of which (a) emotions can be distinguished from other kinds of phenomena (goals, events, evaluations, etc.), and (b) different kinds of emotions can be distinguished from one another. The author also identifies a core feature (readiness to act) that can be assumed to cut across all types of emotion, and to be constitutive of emotion in a way that other features, more peripheral, do not. In turn, the text links this core feature to a process of prioritization that grounds emotion in contexts of social interaction.

By contrast, text 2 exemplifies what Bruner characterizes as "narrative" reasoning. In this text, too, emotion figures importantly. But rather than defining and sub-categorizing emotions, and explicitly associating them with aspects of social interaction, Mary draws tacitly on emotion terms and categories to highlight the salience of the narrated events for both Renee and herself at the time of their occurrence – and their continuing emotional impact in the present, for that matter. Mary uses terms like *scared* (lines 5 and 21), reports behaviors conventionally associated with extreme fear (screaming, running, feeling unable to breathe), and makes skillful use of the evaluative device that Labov called "expressive phonology,"[14] which can include changes in pitch, loudness, and rhythm, as well as the emphatic lengthening of vowels or whole words (see lines 12 and 20). More than just reflecting or encapsulating pre-existing emotions, the text *constructs* Mary (and Renee) as an accountably frightened experiencer of the events reported. Mary's story provides an account of what happened by creating a nexus or link between the experiencing self and the world experienced; it builds causal-chronological connections among what Mary saw that night, her and Renee's emotional responses to the apparition, and the verbal and nonverbal actions associated with those responses. Text 1 abstracts from any particular emotional experience to outline general properties of emotions, and to suggest a taxonomy or classification based on those properties. By contrast, text 2 uses specific emotional attributions to underscore the impact of this unexpected or non-canonical (and thus highly tellable) sequence of events, which happened on this one occasion, in this specific locale, and in this particular way, on the consciousness of the younger, experiencing-I to whose thoughts and feelings the story told by the older, narrating-I provides access.[15]

Hence, besides using principles of reasoning to develop definitions, classifications, and generalizations of the sort presented in text 1, people use other principles, grounded in the production and interpretation of stories, to make sense of the impact of experienced events on themselves and others, as in text 2. But what are these other principles? Or, to put the question differently, assuming that (as Bruner puts it) "we organize our experience and memory of human happenings mainly in the form of narrative – stories, excuses, myths, reasons for doing and not doing, and so on,"[16] what are the design principles of narrative itself? What explains people's ability to distinguish storytelling from other kinds of communicative practices and narratives from other kinds of semiotic artifacts?

To capture what distinguishes text 2 from text 1, it is important to keep in mind the ideas about categorization developed by cognitive scientists such as George Lakoff and Eleanor Rosch – ideas that Ryan also alludes to in her own proposal for a definition of narrative in the next chapter.[17] This work suggests that at least some of the categories in terms of which we make sense of the world are gradient in nature; that is, they operate in a "more-or-less" rather than an "either–or" fashion. In such cases, central or prototypical instances of a given category will be good examples of it, whereas more peripheral instances will display less goodness-of-fit. Thus, a category like "bird" can be characterized as subject to what Lakoff calls *membership gradience*: although robins are more prototypical members or central instances of the category than emus are, emus still belong in the category, albeit farther away from the center of the category space. Meanwhile, when one category shades into another, *category gradience* can be said to obtain. Think of the categories "tall person" and "person of average height": where exactly do you draw the line? Narrative can be described as a kind of text (a text-type category) to which both membership gradience and category gradience apply. A given text can be a more or less central instance of the category, and less central instances will be closer to neighboring text-type categories (descriptions, lists, arguments, etc.) than will prototypical instances.[18]

Thus, whereas prototypical instances of the category "narrative" share relatively few features with those of "description," more peripheral cases are less clearly separable from that text-type, allowing for hybrid forms that Harold F. Mosher called "descriptized narrations" and "narrativized descriptions."[19] Consider the nursery rhyme "This Little Piggy Went to Market":

Text 3:
    This little piggy went to market.
    This little piggy stayed home.
    This little piggy had roast beef.
    This little piggy had none.
    This little piggy cried "Wee! Wee! Wee!" all the way home.

Recited while one pulls each toe of the child's foot, this nursery rhyme constitutes a playful way to focus attention on and "describe" all five toes by means of a quasi-narrative that groups them together into a constellation of characters, who move along non-intersecting trajectories in a somewhat nebulous space–time environment. The quasi-story is merely a vehicle for the description – that is, the enumeration – of the toes. Conversely, when elaborate descriptions of cultural practices in second-century Carthage encumber but do not completely submerge the plot in Gustave Flaubert's 1862 novel *Salammbô*, the result is descriptized narration. The novel contains many passages where, thanks to provision of elaborate historical details, the forward movement of story time slows without coming to a complete halt – that is, where Flaubert's narrative approaches but does not cross the (porous) boundary separating it from ethnographic description.

But what accounts for where along the continuum stretching between narrative and description (among other text-type categories) a given artifact falls? What are the design principles that, when fully actualized, result in central examples of the category narrative? I suggest that core or prototypical instances of narrative represent or simulate

  (i) a structured time-course of particularized events which introduces
 (ii) disruption or disequilibrium into storytellers' and interpreters' mental model of the world evoked by the narrative (whether that world is presented as actual, imagined, dreamed, etc.), conveying
(iii) what it's like to live through that disruption, that is, the "qualia" (or felt, subjective awareness) of real or imagined consciousnesses undergoing the disruptive experience.[20]

Taking each of these features in turn:

(i) Whereas stories prototypically focus on particular situations and events, scientific explanations by their nature concern themselves with ways in which, in general, the world tends to be. Further, if particularity sets narrative apart from general explanations, narrative's temporal profile helps distinguish the prototypical narrative from many examples of description. Whereas I can in principle describe the objects on my desk in any order (left to right, back to front, smallest to largest, etc.), narrative traces paths taken by particularized individuals faced with decision points at one or more temporal junctures in a storyworld; those paths lead to consequences that take shape against a larger backdrop in which other possible paths might have been pursued, but were not.[21]

Contrast text 2 with text 3 in this connection: transpose any elements of the sequence that Mary recounts and you would have a different story, whereas in text 3 the order in which the little piggies' actions are recounted is a function of the need to rhyme end words and establish logical contrasts, not of any corresponding sequence of actions in a little-piggy storyworld. Meanwhile, insofar as text 1 outlines features of emotion in general, it does not focus on any individualized actors, nor any specific sequence of events.

(ii) But particularized temporal sequences, though necessary for narrative, are still not a sufficient condition. Building on the work of Vladimir Propp, who characterized disruptive events (e.g., acts of villainy) as the motor of narrative, Todorov specified a further test for when an event-sequence will count as a story.[22] Todorov argued that narratives prototypically follow a trajectory leading from an initial state of equilibrium, through a phase of disequilibrium, to an endpoint at which equilibrium is restored (on a different footing) because of intermediary events – though not every narrative will trace the entirety of this path.[23] Todorov thereby sought to capture the intuition that stories characteristically involve some sort of conflict, or the thwarting of characters' intended actions by unplanned events, which may or may not be the effect of other characters' intended actions.

To be categorized as a narrative, an event-sequence must therefore involve some kind of noteworthy (hence "tellable") disruption of an initial state of equilibrium by an unanticipated and often untoward event or chain of events. At issue is what Bruner characterized as a dialectic of "canonicity and breach": "to be worth telling, a tale must be about how an implicit canonical script has been breached, violated, or deviated from in a manner to do violence to . . . [its] 'legitimacy.'"[24] Judged by this criterion, text 3 again would not qualify as a prototypical instance of the category "narrative," even though the contrasts drawn in the first four lines may suggest a rudimentary kind of narrativity, involving a disparity between plenty and dearth, hunger and satisfaction. But Mary's story centers on a strongly (and strangely) disruptive event: the apparition of a supernatural big ball chasing Mary and her friend through the woods in the dark of night. The difference explains why, although text 3 may qualify as a case of narrativized description, Mary's story is a prototypical instance of the category "narrative." For its part, because text 1 does not set up a concrete, particularized situation, there is no background against which a tellably disruptive event might be set off.

(iii) Again, however, whereas disruptive events may constitute a necessary condition for narrative, they do not suffice to make a text, discourse, or other artifact a story. For narrative to obtain, there must not only be a temporal sequence into which events are slotted in a particular way, and not only a dynamic of canonicity and breach, but also a foregrounding of human experientiality, to use Monika Fludernik's term.[25] Narrative prototypically roots itself in the lived, felt experience of human or human-like agents interacting in an ongoing way with their cohorts and surrounding environment. To put the same point another way, unless a text or a discourse encodes the pressure of events on an experiencing human or at least human-like consciousness, it will not be a central instance of the narrative text type.

As an analysis or explanation, text 1 is void of experientiality of this sort. And note the contrast between texts 2 and 3 on this score. Whereas Mary uses emotion discourse to highlight what it was like to experience the frightening events she reports, the closest we get to experientiality in text 3 is the fifth little piggy's cry of "Wee! Wee! Wee!" all the way home.

At this point, readers may wish to turn to the next chapter, where Ryan develops her own proposal for defining narrative and offers a more extensive overview of previous definitions by other narrative scholars. Or, before moving on to chapter 2, readers can continue with my next two sections, where I provide a sketch of recent trends in narrative research and offer a few suggestions about how to take advantage of the distinctive features of this volume.

What are some of the major trends in recent scholarship on narrative?

One way to map out recent developments in narrative inquiry is to draw a distinction between "classical" and "postclassical" approaches to the study of narrative. I use the term *classical approaches* to refer to the tradition of research that, rooted in Russian Formalist literary theory, was extended by structuralist narratologists starting in the mid 1960s, and refined and systematized up through the early 1980s by scholars such as Mieke Bal, Seymour Chatman, Wallace Martin, Gerald Prince, and others. I also include under the rubric of classical approaches work in the Anglo-American tradition of scholarship on fictional narrative; some of these scholars were influenced by and in turn influenced the Formalist–structuralist tradition.[26] *Postclassical approaches*, meanwhile, encompass frameworks for narrative research that build on this classical tradition but supplement it with concepts and methods that were unavailable to story analysts such as Barthes, Genette, Greimas, and Todorov during the heyday of structuralism. In developing postclassical approaches, which does not just expose the limits but also exploits the possibilities of older models, theorists of narrative have drawn on a range of fields, from gender theory and philosophical ethics, to (socio)linguistics, philosophy of language, and cognitive science, to comparative media studies and critical theory. Because of the limited scope of this introduction, the current section focuses mainly on the classical narrative scholarship that has afforded foundations for such postclassical approaches, which are in any case represented by individual contributions to this *Companion* and reflected in the design of the volume as a whole, as I discuss below.

One further comment before my brief survey of contributions to what I am calling the classical tradition of narrative inquiry. Although Labov and Waletzky developed their model for the analysis of narratives told in contexts of face-to-face communication just as structuralist narratologists were proposing their key ideas, and although the Labovian model has been extraordinarily influential in social-scientific research for some four decades, initially there was little interaction between sociolinguistic research on storytelling and other traditions of narrative scholarship. But now there is interest in building an integrative theory that can accommodate both the study of written, literary narratives and the analysis of everyday storytelling.[27] At the same time, among researchers concerned with face-to-face narrative communication, there has been a shift analogous to the one I have characterized as a transition from classical to postclassical approaches. Precipitating this shift is the recognition that the Labovian model captures one important sub-type of natural-language narratives – namely, stories elicited during interviews – but does not necessarily apply equally well to other storytelling situations, such as informal conversations between peers, he-said-she-said gossip, or conversations among family members at the dinner table.[28]

From Russian Formalism to structuralist narratology

The Russian Formalists authored a number of pathbreaking studies that have served as foundations for later research on narrative. For example, in distinguishing between "bound" (or plot-relevant) and "free" (or non-plot-relevant) motifs, Boris Tomashevskii provided the basis for Barthes's distinction between "nuclei" and "catalyzers" in his "Introduction to the Structural Analysis of Narratives."[29] Renamed *kernels* and *satellites* by Seymour Chatman[30], these terms refer to core and peripheral elements of story-content, respectively. Delete or add to the kernel events of a story and you no longer have the same story; delete or add to the satellites and you have the same story told in a different way. Related to Tomashevskii's work on free versus bound motifs, Viktor Shklovskii's early work on plot as a structuring device[31] established one of the grounding assumptions of structuralist narratology: namely, the *fabula–sjuzhet* or story–discourse distinction, that is, the distinction between the what and the how, or what is being told versus the manner in which it is told.

Another important Formalist precedent for modern narrative theory was furnished by Propp's *Morphology of the Folktale*, whose first English translation appeared in 1958.[32] Propp distinguished between variable and invariant components of the corpus of Russian folktales that he studied; more specifically, he drew a contrast between changing dramatis personæ and the unvarying plot functions performed by them (act of villainy, punishment of the villain, etc.). In all, Propp abstracted thirty-one functions, or character actions defined in terms of their significance for the plot, from his corpus of tales; he also specified rules for their distribution in a given tale. Harking back to Aristotle's subordination of character to plot, Propp's approach constituted the basis for structuralist theories of characters as "actants," or general roles fulfilled by specific characters. Thus, extrapolating from what Propp had termed "spheres of action," Greimas sought to create a typology of actantial roles to which the (indefinitely many) particularized actors in narratives could be reduced. Greimas initially identified a total of six actants to which he thought all particularized narrative actors could be reduced: Subject, Object, Sender, Receiver, Helper, and Opponent. Commenting on this model, Greimas remarked "[i]ts simplicity lies in the fact that it is entirely centred on the object of desire aimed at by the subject and situated, as object of communication, between the sender and the receiver – the desire of the subject being, in its part, modulated in projections from the helper and opponent."[33]

I have already begun to discuss how the structuralist narratologists built on Russian Formalist ideas to help consolidate what I am referring to as the classical tradition of research on narrative. Founding narratology as a subdomain of structuralist inquiry, researchers like Barthes and Greimas followed Saussure's distinction between *la langue* (= language viewed as system) and *la parole* (= individual utterances produced and interpreted on that basis); they construed particular stories as individual narrative messages supported by a shared semiotic system. And just as Saussurean linguistics privileged *la langue* over *la parole*, focusing on the structural constituents and combinatory principles of the semiotic framework of language, the narratologists privileged the study of narrative in general over the interpretation of individual narratives.

Indeed, the use of (Saussurean) linguistics as a pilot-science shaped the object, methods, and overall aims of structuralist narratology as an investigative framework. Narratology's basic premise is that a common, more or less implicit, model of narrative explains people's ability to understand communicative performances and types of artifacts as stories. In turn, just as linguists have set themselves the goal of identifying the ingredients of linguistic competence, the goal of narratology is to develop an explicit characterization of the model underlying people's intuitive knowledge about stories, in effect providing an account of what constitutes humans' narrative competence. To be sure, the example of linguistics provided narratology with a productive vantage-point on stories, affording terms and categories that generated significant new research questions – as when Barthes used the concept of "levels of description" to develop a hierarchical model of narrative as clusters of "functions" that are subsumed under the level of characters' actions, which are in turn subsumed under the level of narration; or when Genette drew on the traditional grammatical concepts of tense, mood, and voice to explore types of temporal sequence, manipulations of viewpoint, and modes of narration.[34] Yet narratology was also limited by the linguistic models it treated as exemplary. Ironically, the narratologists embraced structuralist linguistics as their pilot-science just when its deficiencies were becoming apparent in the domain of linguistic theory itself. The limitations of the Saussurean paradigm were thrown into relief, on the one hand, by emergent formal models for analyzing language structure – for example, those proposed by Chomsky under the auspices of generative grammar. On the other hand, powerful tools were being developed in the wake of Ludwig Wittgenstein, J. L. Austin, H. P. Grice, John Searle, and other post-Saussurean language theorists interested in how contexts of language use bear on the production and interpretation of socially situated utterances. In general, the attempt by later narrative scholars to incorporate ideas about language and communication that postdate structuralist research has been a major factor in the advent of postclassical models for research on stories and storytelling.[35]

Anglo-American contributions

I have yet to discuss how Anglo-American scholarship on narrative fiction has contributed to the classical tradition of research on stories. An important figure in this tradition is Percy Lubbock, who took his inspiration from Henry James's novelistic practice as well as his theory of fiction.[36] Lubbock made the issue of "point of view" the cornerstone of his account – to an extent not necessarily warranted by James's own approach.[37] In doing so, Lubbock appropriated James's ideas to produce a markedly prescriptive framework. He drew an invidious distinction between showing ("dramatizing" events) and telling ("describing" or "picturing" events), suggesting that description is inferior to dramatization, picturing to scene-making. As Lubbock put it, "other things being equal, the more dramatic way is better than the less. It is indirect, as a method; but it places the thing itself in view, instead of recalling and reflecting and picturing it."[38] But although he may have been guilty of transforming into hard-and-fast prescriptions ideas that James himself proposed much more tentatively in his own critical writings, Lubbock also drew attention to specific methods or procedures that are at the heart of the craft of fiction.

In response, maintaining a focus on issues of narrative technique, but seeking to restore the complexities evident in James's original statement of his theory (as well as in his novelistic practice), Wayne C. Booth inverted the terms of Lubbock's argument, thereby laying the groundwork for rhetorical approaches to narrative.[39] Instead of privileging showing over telling, Booth accorded telling pride of place – making it the general narratorial condition of which "showing" is a localized effect. Indeed, Booth's brilliant account revealed difficulties with the very premise of the telling-versus-showing debate. He characterized showing as an effect promoted by certain, deliberately structured, kinds of tellings, organized in such a way that a narrator's mediation (though inescapably present) remains more or less covert. Booth also suggested that an emphasis on showing over telling has costs as well as benefits, cataloguing important rhetorical effects that explicit narratorial commentary can be used to accomplish – for example, relating particulars to norms established elsewhere in the text, heightening the significance of events, or manipulating mood.

Furthermore, Booth's wide-ranging discussion of narrative types (ranging from Boccaccio's *Decameron* to ancient Greek epics to novels and short fictions by authors as diverse as Cervantes, Hemingway, and Céline) encouraged subsequent theorists in the Anglo-American tradition to explore various kinds of narratives, rather than focusing solely on the novel. This uncoupling of narrative theory from novel theory – a process that had been initiated independently by the Russian Formalists some forty years earlier – culminated in such wide-scope works as Robert Scholes's and Robert Kellogg's study, *The Nature of Narrative*.[40] Significantly, Scholes's and Kellogg's book was published in 1966. This same year saw the publication of a groundbreaking special issue of the French-language journal *Communications* on "Recherches sémiologiques: L'Analyse structurale du récit" (="Semiological Research: Structural Analysis of Narrative"), which effectively launched structuralist narratology as an approach that likewise applied to narrative in general, not just the novel.

Postclassical approaches: in lieu of a synopsis

I cannot synopsize here the full range of postclassical approaches to narrative inquiry that build on the foundational work just described as well as on other early scholarship on stories.[41] Instead, this *Companion* itself reflects the exciting new developments unfolding in narrative research today. On the one hand, the chapters in Part II of the book all focus on major aspects of narrative identified by earlier theorists: narration and plot; time and space; character; dialogue; focalization; and genre. But the contributors explore these features using ideas that emerged after the pioneering work of the Russian Formalists, structuralist narratologists, and Anglo-American theorists of fiction. On the other hand, Part III and Part IV identify new areas of research for narrative inquiry. The focus of Part III on particular narrative media reflects an emergent concern with how medium-specific properties of stories may require the adjustment and refinement of classical models.[42] Meanwhile, the chapters in Part IV, while continuing to build on classical models, suggest the relevance for narrative study of ideas from fields that did not extensively cross-pollinate with earlier research on stories – fields such as gender theory; philosophical ethics; post-Saussurean linguistics; cognitive science; Marxist critiques of ideology; and the study of postcolonial literatures and cultures.

What are the distinctive features of this book, and some strategies for using it?

As already indicated, this volume is intended to be a resource for readers at all levels, from beginning students to advanced researchers in the field. The following design features are meant to enhance the book's appeal for the broadest possible readership:

- The volume is organized in a "modularized" fashion; that is, readers can focus on particular sections while omitting others, depending on their interests and needs. There are, however, important interconnections among chapters in different sections – for instance, the chapters on "Dialogue" and "Gender," or the chapters on "Time and Space," "Focalization," and "Cognition, Emotion, and Consciousness." Because of these cross-sectional links, even readers focusing on particular parts may benefit from working their way through the volume in its entirety.
- The volume features a glossary containing thumbnail definitions of key terms and concepts. This glossary should help orient readers unfamiliar with the technical nomenclatures that have grown up around the study of narrative, and it may also serve as a "refresher" for more experienced readers.
- Each chapter has been given a simple, keyword-like title. In tandem with four-part division of the volume, this navigational aid will allow readers to zoom in on questions and issues most relevant to them.
- The volume also contains a comprehensive index, which will likewise enable readers to pinpoint the topics and concepts of particular interest to them.

Given these features, the volume should be suitable for courses, at both the undergraduate and the graduate level, in a number of fields, including: literature (History and Theory of the Novel, Studies in Fiction, Critical Theory, Narrative Theory and Narratology, The Linguistics of Literature); comparative media studies (Narrative across Media); communication studies (Narrative Analysis); linguistics (Discourse Analysis: Narrative); medical humanities (Narrative Representations of Illness, Narrative Theory for Clinicians); psychology (Narrative Psychology, Cognitive Psychology and Art, Social Psychology); and philosophy (Aesthetics, Philosophy of Mind), among others.

But whether it is used inside or outside the classroom, by beginning students or narrative experts, in the context of the humanities, the social sciences, or other fields, my chief hope for this *Companion* is that it will help build even more interest in this rapidly developing area of inquiry. Indeed, this book is in essence an invitation. It invites all of its readers to join the growing and increasingly diverse community of scholars engaged in the study of narrative, which can be viewed not just as a means of artistic expression or a resource for communication but also as a fundamental human endowment.

NOTES

1. Readers may be interested in Ryan's debate with David Rudrum concerning attempts to define narrative. The exchange can be found in two issues of the journal *Narrative*, namely, 13:2 and 14:2. Further, Ryan has posted on her website a follow-up to the published exchange: http://lamar.colostate.edu/~pwryan/rudrumresponse.htm. Ryan's and Rudrum's respective positions bear relevantly on the working definition of narrative that I propose in this introduction, where I characterize narrative both as resource for representation and as a mode of communicative practice. See my discussion of sample texts 1, 2, and 3 below; also, for a fuller account of narrative viewed as a discourse practice, see David Herman, "Narrative Theory after the Second Cognitive Revolution." In Lisa Zunshine (ed.) *Introduction to Cognitive Cultural Studies* (Baltimore: Johns Hopkins University Press, forthcoming).

2. Here the term *people* is shorthand for "embodied human or human-like individuals invested with felt, conscious awareness of the situations and events recounted in the narrative."

3. Matti Hyvärinen, "Towards a Conceptual History of Narrative" (http://www.helsinki.fi/collegium/e-series/volumes/volume_1/001_04_hyvarinen.pdf). In Matti Hyvärinen, Anu Korhonen, and Juri Mykkänen (eds.) *The Travelling Concept of Narrative* (Helsinki: Helsinki Collegium for Advanced Studies, 2006: http://www.helsinki.fi/collegium/e-series/volumes/volume_1/ index.htm), p. 20.

4. Martin Kreiswirth, "Narrative Turn in the Humanities." In David Herman, Manfred Jahn, and Marie-Laure Ryan (eds.) *Routledge Encyclopedia of Narrative Theory* (London: Routledge, 2005), pp. 377–82.

5. William Labov and Joshua Waletzky, "Narrative Analysis: Oral Versions of Personal Experience." In June Helm (ed.) *Essays on the Verbal and Visual Arts* (Seattle: University of Washington Press, 1967), pp. 12–34; Tzvetan Todorov, *Grammaire du "Décaméron"* (The Hague: Mouton, 1969). For more on the widespread influence of the "Labovian" approach to narrative inquiry, see chapter 9 of this volume and Michael Bamberg (ed.) special issue on "Oral Versions of Personal Experience: Three Decades of Narrative Analysis," *The Journal of Narrative and Life History* 7:1–4 (1997), pp. 1–415.

6. See Roland Barthes, "Introduction to the Structural Analysis of Narratives." In *Image – Music – Text*. Translated by Stephen Heath (New York: Hill and Wang, 1977), p. 79.

7. See Hyvärinen, "Towards a Conceptual History of Narrative," for arguments that true interdisciplinarity in narrative research has not yet been achieved.

8. Relevant book series include *Frontiers of Narrative*, published by the University of Nebraska Press, *Narratologia*, published by Walter de Gruyter, *Studies in Narrative*, published by John Benjamins, and *Theory and Interpretation of Narrative*, published by the Ohio State University Press. Journals regularly featuring articles on narrative include, among others, *Ancient Narrative*, *Image (&) Narrative*, *Journal of Narrative Theory*, *Language and Literature*, *Narrative*, *Narrative Inquiry*, *New Literary History*, *Poetics*, *Poetics Today*, and *Style*.

9. For example, the symposium on "Narrative Intelligence" sponsored in November 1999 by the American Association of Artificial Intelligence, assembled computer scientists, designers of computer games, philosophers, linguists, and theorists of

literary narrative. For its part, the 2004 interdisciplinary symposium on "The Travelling Concept of Narrative" held at the University of Helsinki sought to connect humanistic and social-scientific trends in narrative research, as did the symposium on "Narratology beyond Literary Criticism" held at the University of Hamburg the previous year.

10. Texana is a small community located in the western, mountainous part of this state in the southeastern region of the U.S.

11. Keith Oatley, "Emotions." In Robert A. Wilson and Frank C. Keil, *The MIT Encyclopedia of the Cognitive Sciences* (Cambridge, MA: MIT Press, 1999), pp. 273–5.

12. In this transcript, I have edited out details important for other kinds of discourse analysis. Also, for ease of reference, I have divided the transcript of the speaker's discourse into numbered clauses. ALL CAPS indicate words that were emphatically lengthened during their production, whereas two dots (. .) mark pauses or hesitations by the speaker. NSF Grant BCS-0236838 supported research on this narrative, and I am indebted to Christine Mallinson for helpful conversations about the story.

13. Jerome Bruner, *Actual Minds, Possible Worlds* (Cambridge: Harvard University Press, 1986). For a critique of Bruner's distinction between paradigmatic and narrative reasoning, however, see David Herman, "Narrative, Science, and Narrative Science." *Narrative Inquiry* 8:2 (1998), pp. 379–90. Also for an argument that Bruner engages in narrative imperialism (whereby the notion of story comes to encompass everything and thereby ceases to be useful), and for a balanced assessment of that argument, see, respectively, Galen Strawson, "Against Narrativity." *Ratio* 17 (December 2004), pp. 428–52, and James Phelan, "Who's Here? Thoughts on Narrative Identity and Narrative Imperialism." *Narrative* 13:3 (2005), pp. 205–10.

14. William Labov, "The Transformation of Experience in Narrative Syntax." In *Language in the Inner City* (Philadelphia, PA: University of Pennsylvania Press, 1972), p. 379.

15. See chapter 17 of this volume for further remarks on the role of emotions and emotion discourse in narrative. On the concept of "tellability," see Neal R. Norrick's discussion in chapter 9. Finally, on the distinction between the narrating-I and the experiencing-I, see Philippe Lejeune, "The Autobiographical Pact." In *On Autobiography*. Edited by Paul John Eakin, translated by Katherine Leary (Minneapolis: University of Minnesota Press, 1989), pp. 3–30.

16. Jerome Bruner, "The Narrative Construction of Reality." *Critical Inquiry* 18 (1991), p. 4.

17. See George Lakoff, *Women, Fire and Dangerous Things* (Chicago: University of Chicago Press, 1987), and Eleanor Rosch, "Principles of Categorization." In Bas Aarts, David Denison, Evelien Keizer, and Gergana Popova (eds.) *Fuzzy Grammar: A Reader* (Oxford: Oxford University Press, 2004), pp. 91–108.

18. Note that stories can contain other kinds of texts, as when a novel portrays two characters arguing with one another. Conversely, people engaging in a debate might use stories to support their positions. Hence, when talking about a text-type category, I am referring to what category the text as a whole can most plausibly be slotted into, though I recognize that there will not necessarily be consensus about how to categorize a given text or artifact.

19. Harold F. Mosher, Jr., "Towards a Poetics of Descriptized Narration." *Poetics Today* 3 (1991), pp. 425–45.

20. For more on the concept of "qualia," a term used by philosophers of mind to refer to the sense of "what it is like" for someone or something to have a particular experience, see Janet Levin, "Qualia." In Robert A. Wilson and Frank C. Keil, *The MIT Encyclopedia of the Cognitive Sciences* (Cambridge, MA: MIT Press, 1999), pp. 693–4, and also chapter 17 of the present volume.

21. In some cases, however, descriptions do involve a time-sequence: recipes, for example, describe a specific sequence of cooking procedures. Hence the need for feature (ii), discussed below.

22. Vladimir Propp, *Morphology of the Folktale*, 2nd edition. Translated by Laurence Scott, revised by Louis A. Wagner (Austin: University of Texas Press, 1968); Tzvetan Todorov, "La Grammaire du récit." *Langages* 12 (1968), pp. 94–102.

23. See Claude Bremond, "The Logic of Narrative Possibilities." Translated by Elaine D. Cancalon, *New Literary History* 11 (1980), pp. 387–411; Emma Kafalenos, *Narrative Causalities* (Columbus: Ohio State University Press, 2006).

24. Jerome Bruner, "The Narrative Construction of Reality," p. 11.

25. See Monika Fludernik, *Towards a "Natural" Narratology* (London: Routledge, 1996), pp. 48–50.

26. For a fuller discussion of this reciprocal influence, and of other aspects of what I am designating the classical tradition of narrative study, see David Herman, "Histories of Narrative Theory (I): A Genealogy of Early Developments." In James Phelan and Peter J. Rabinowitz (eds.) *A Companion to Narrative Theory* (Malden, MA: Blackwell Publishers, 2005), pp. 19–35. Further, for a more detailed account of the distinction between classical and postclassical approaches, see David Herman, "Introduction." In David Herman (ed.) *Narratologies: New Perspectives on Narrative Analysis* (Columbus: Ohio State University Press, 1999), pp. 1–30.

27. See, for example, Monika Fludernik, *Towards a "Natural" Narratology*, and David Herman, "Toward a Transmedial Narratology." In Marie-Laure Ryan (ed.) *Narrative across Media: The Languages of Storytelling* (Lincoln: University of Nebraska Press, 2004), pp. 47–75.

28. For recent work rethinking the Labovian model, see Michael Bamberg (ed.) special issue on "Oral Versions of Personal Experience: Three Decades of Narrative Analysis" and special issue on "Narrative – State of the Art," *Narrative Inquiry* 16:1 (2006); Elinor Ochs and Lisa Capps, *Living Narrative: Creating Lives in Everyday Storytelling* (Cambridge, MA: Harvard University Press, 2001); and chapter 9 of this volume.

29. See Boris Tomashevskii, "Thematics." In Lee T. Lemon and Marion J. Reis (eds.) *Russian Formalist Criticism* (Lincoln: University of Nebraska Press, 1965), pp. 61–95; Roland Barthes, "Introduction to the Structural Analysis of Narrative," pp. 93–4.

30. Seymour Chatman, *Story and Discourse: Narrative Structure in Fiction and Film* (Ithaca, NY: Cornell University Press, 1978), pp. 53–6.

31. Victor Shklovskii, *Theory of Prose*. Translated by Benjamin Sher (Elmwood Park, IL: Dalkey Archive Press, 1990).

32. Vladimir Propp, *Morphology of the Folktale*.

33. A. J. Greimas, *Structural Semantics: An Attempt at a Method*. Translated by Danielle McDowell, Ronald Schleifer, and Alan Velie (Lincoln: University of Nebraska Press, 1983), p. 207. See chapter 13 of this volume for a fuller presentation of Greimas's theory of actants.
34. Roland Barthes, "Introduction to the Structural Analysis of Narrative," pp. 85–8; Gérard Genette, *Narrative Discourse: An Essay in Method*. Translated by Jane E. Lewin (Ithaca: Cornell University Press, 1980).
35. For more details, see Monika Fludernik, "Histories of Narrative Theory (II): From Structuralism to the Present." In James Phelan and Peter J. Rabinowitz (eds.) *A Companion to Narrative Theory* (Malden, MA: Blackwell Publishers, 2005), pp. 48–51. Also, see chapter 16 of this volume for a discussion of how ideas from functionalist linguistics and other approaches to language study are productive for narrative inquiry.
36. Percy Lubbock, *The Craft of Fiction* (London: Jonathan Cape, 1957).
37. See James E. Miller, Jr. (ed.) *Theory of Fiction: Henry James* (Lincoln: University of Nebraska Press, 1972), p. 1; Wayne C. Booth, *The Rhetoric of Fiction* (Chicago: University of Chicago Press, 1961), pp. 24–5. As chapter 7 of this volume discusses, narrative scholars today generally use the term *focalization* rather than *point of view* when analyzing issues of perspective.
38. Percy Lubbock, *The Craft of Fiction*, pp. 149–50.
39. Wayne C. Booth, *The Rhetoric of Fiction* (Chicago: University of Chicago Press, 1961). See chapter 14 of this volume for more on the history and aims of rhetorical theories of narrative.
40. Robert Scholes and Robert Kellogg, *The Nature of Narrative* (Oxford: Oxford University Press, 1966).
41. For fuller accounts, see Matti Hyvärinen, "Towards a Conceptual History of Narrative"; Monika Fludernik, "Histories of Narrative Theory (II): From Structuralism to the Present"; David Herman, "Introduction" to *Narratologies*; Luc Herman and Bart Vervaeck, "Postclassical Narratology." In David Herman, Manfred Jahn, and Marie-Laure Ryan, *Routledge Encyclopedia of Narrative Theory* (London: Routledge, 2005), pp. 450–1; and Ansgar Nünning, "Narratology or Narratologies? Taking Stock of Recent Developments: Critique and Modest Proposals for Future Usages of the Term." In Tom Kindt and Hans-Harald Müller (eds.) *What is Narratology?* (Berlin: De Gruyter, 2003), pp. 239–75.
42. In this same connection, see Marie-Laure Ryan (ed.) *Narrative across Media: The Languages of Storytelling* (Lincoln: University of Nebraska Press, 2004).

2

MARIE-LAURE RYAN

Toward a definition of narrative

In the past fifteen years, as the "narrative turn in the humanities" gave way to the narrative turn everywhere (politics, science studies, law, medicine, and last, but not least, cognitive science), few words have enjoyed so much use and suffered so much abuse as *narrative* and its partial synonym, *story*. The French theorist Jean-François Lyotard invokes the "Grand Narratives" of a capitalized History;[1] the psychologist Jerome Bruner speaks of narratives of identity;[2] the philosopher Daniel Dennett describes mental activity on the neural level as the continuous emergence and decay of narrative drafts;[3] the political strategist James Carville attributes the loss of John Kerry in the 2004 presidential election to the lack of a convincing narrative;[4] and "narratives of race, class and gender" have become a mantra of cultural studies. Gerald Prince regards the contemporary use of the term narrative as a hedging device, a way to avoid strong positions: "One says 'narrative' instead of 'explanation' or 'argumentation' (because it is more tentative); one prefers 'narrative' to 'theory,' 'hypothesis,' or 'evidence' (because it is less scientist); one speaks of a 'narrative' rather than 'ideology' (because it is less judgmental); one substitutes 'narrative' for 'message' (because it is more indeterminate)."[5] Another narrative theorist, Peter Brooks, attributes the surging popularity of the word to a more positive cause: "While I think the term has been trivialized through overuse, I believe the overuse responds to a recognition that narrative is one of the principal ways we organize our experience of the world – a part of our cognitive tool kit that was long neglected by psychologists and philosophers."[6] Whether it is due to the postmodern loss of faith in the possibility of achieving truth or knowledge, or to current interest in the functioning of the mind, the current tendency to dissolve "narrative" into "belief," "value," "experience," "interpretation," "thought," "explanation," "representation," or simply "content" challenges narratologists to work out a definition that distinguishes literal from metaphorical uses. Neither bowing to current fashion nor acting like a semantic police, this definition should prevent the inflation of the term from getting out of hand, but it should also help us understand the mechanisms of this inflation by disclosing the genealogy of the metaphorical uses.

Previous definitions of *narrative*

At first sight nothing seems easier to define than narrative. As the following examples show there is a strong consensus among narratologists on the nature of the object of their discipline:

> Genette: "One will define narrative without difficulty as the representation of an event or of a sequence of events."[7]

> Prince: "The representation . . . of one or more real or fictive events communicated by one, two or several . . . narrators . . . to one, two or several narratees."[8]

> Abbott: "**Narrative** is the representation of events, consisting of *story* and *narrative discourse*, **story** is an *event* or sequence of events (the *action*), and **narrative discourse** is those events as represented."[9]

Looking deeper than events, some authors define narrative in terms of what makes sequence and change possible:

> Ricoeur: "I take temporality to be that structure of existence that reaches language in narrativity, and narrativity to be the language structure that has temporality as its ultimate reference."[10]

> Brooks: "Plot is the principal ordering force of those meanings that we try to wrest from human temporality."[11]

But a temporally ordered sequence of events could be a list rather than a story: for instance, the list of all the patients that a doctor sees in one day. As the next batch of examples shows, many authors feel indeed the need to add something to "representation of a sequence of events" to turn it from a thumbnail characterization into a full(er) definition:

> Prince invokes a certain type of logical relation: "Narrative is the representation of at least two real or fictive events in a time sequence, neither of which presupposes or entails the other."[12]

> Onega and Landa regard causality as the cement that turns sequences of events into stories: "The semiotic representation of a sequence of events, meaningfully connected in a temporal and causal way."[13]

> Bal introduces change, causality, and an experiencing subject: "The transition from one state to another state, caused or experienced by actors."[14]

All of these characterizations provide useful insights, but none offers a complete and self-sufficient definition of narrative, because they depend too much on implicit elements. It is admittedly debatable to what extent definitions should rely on implications. For instance, "event" implies transformation and "action" involves agents; if these agents decide to take actions, they must have motivations, and they must be trying to solve problems. If agents have problems, they must experience some sort of conflict.

A definition should support, even entail, statements like these, but it does not have to spell them out:

Narrative is about problem solving.
Narrative is about conflict.
Narrative is about interpersonal relations.
Narrative is about human experience.
Narrative is about the temporality of existence.

The semiotic status of narrative

Most narratologists agree that narrative consists of material signs, the discourse, which convey a certain meaning (or content), the story, and fulfill a certain social function. This characterization outlines three potential domains for a definition: discourse, story, and use. These domains correspond, roughly, to the three components of semiotic theory: syntax, semantics, and pragmatics.

Syntax is the most problematic area for a definition of narrative, because the concept applies only to semiotic systems with clearly definable units that combine into larger linear sequences according to precise rules. But there is no such thing as clearly definable "narrative units" comparable to the words or phonemes of language. The narratologists who have attempted to divide narrative into constituents have come up with vastly different catalogs of basic elements: for instance, Aristotle's exposition, crisis and denouement; Propp's functions and roles, Greimas's types of actants; Barthes's kernels and satellites, and the more traditional notions of character, action, and setting. If we cannot agree on the basic units of narrative, in the way grammarians (more or less) agree on the syntactic categories of language (nouns, verbs, adjectives, articles, etc.), there is no hope of defining the rules of their combination and of distinguishing well-formed and ill-formed sequences. In narrative matters, there is no equivalent to Chomsky's syntactically grammatical but semantically deficient sentence "colorless green ideas sleep furiously." Eliminating syntax from the definition of narrative means that narrative discourse cannot be described as a specific configuration of purely formal elements.

The second possibility is to define story in semantic terms. In semiotic theory, semantics is the study of the relation between material signs and the states of affairs to which they can refer. But since we cannot isolate a group of properly "narrative" signs distinct from the signs (or sign) of the supporting medium, the standard conception of semantics does not apply to the case of narrative. Or rather, the semantic system that underlies narrative texts cannot be distinguished from the system of the supporting medium: it is because we know what words mean that we can make sense of written or oral stories, and it is because we know what images represent that we can make sense of a comic strip or a silent movie. This is not to say that narrative cannot be defined through conditions pertaining to meaning; I believe indeed that semantics is the most promising avenue for a definition; but for the concept to be operational, it must be redefined as "the type of mental image that a text must evoke as a whole to be accepted as narrative," regardless of the nature of its individual signs. "Narrative semantics," in other words, is not a fixed relation between so-called "narrative signs" and their meanings, but the description of a certain type of cognitive construct.

Is this construct sufficient to categorize a semiotic object as a narrative, or do we need to take into consideration how the object is used? Here we broach key issues in pragmatics, or the study of how signs relate to users and to contexts of use. The proponents of a pragmatically based definition of narrative[15] argue that it is possible to submit a given text to multiple "language games," or textual speech acts. "Narrative" would be one of these games, and there would be others, though it is difficult (or downright impossible) to establish what they might be. According to speech-act theory, you can perform different communicative acts with a proposition like "the cat is on the mat": assert it, ask about it, or make it the content of a command. Now if texts, like propositions, lend themselves to various games depending on the rules selected by their users, it should be possible to read them against the grain, that is, use the texts in games for which they were not necessarily intended. I call this transcategorial reading.

The best candidates for this operation are narrative and recipe, because they both rely on the representation of a sequence of events, the most universally accepted feature of narrative. But consider these instructions: "Beat eggs until they form peaks; pour on fruits; bake 10 minutes until custard is set; cool and serve." To make this text into a story it would be necessary to imagine individuated participants, for instance a chef as agent and the patrons of his restaurant as beneficiary, give the agent a particular goal (acquire a third Michelin star), and assume that the events happened only once, instead of being endlessly repeatable. Conversely, to read a story as a set of instructions, for instance the episode in *The Odyssey* that describes, step by step, how Odysseus builds a boat to escape from Calypso's island, you would have to ignore Odysseus and his goal (return to Ithaca), and extract from the description of particular events a protocol that can be performed over and over again, with you or me or anybody else in the role of agent. In both cases, the transcategorial reading requires the addition and subtraction of so many features that it becomes a demonstration *ad absurdum* of the resistance of content: you just cannot read a text that tells you how to cook a dish as being about an evolving network of human relations – the preferred subject-matter of narrative. The claim that narrative is a particular type of use is further defeated by the fact that narrative itself can be put to many different uses: telling a joke to entertain an audience; reporting current news; confessing one's sins to a priest; testifying in court; reading a story to a child at bedtime, and so on. I am not saying that the same concrete story could be put to all these uses, but rather, that all these communicative situations require a text that fulfills the abstract pattern constitutive of narrativity (= that which makes a text a narrative).

In summary: if narrative is a discourse that conveys a story, this is to say, a specific type of content, and if this discourse can be put to a variety of different uses, none of them constitutive of narrativity, then its definition should focus on story. As a mental representation, story is not tied to any particular medium, and it is independent of the distinction between fiction and non-fiction. A definition of narrative should therefore work for different media (though admittedly media do widely differ in their storytelling abilities), and it should not privilege literary forms.

Narrative, compared to what?

The task of defining narrative – or in fact any concept – will be greatly facilitated if we can situate stories within a class of related entities. But what can we place on the same shelf? In the past few years, many scholars have attempted to capture the nature of narrative through a typology of basic types of text, but there is no consensus regarding what other categories besides narrative should be included in the taxonomy: Chatman opposes narrative discourse to persuasive and descriptive;[16] Fludernik's model comprises narrative, argumentative, instructive, conversational, and reflective discourse;[17] and Virtanen envisions five basic types: narrative, description, instruction, exposition, and argumentation.[18] The lack of agreement concerning what is to be considered a text type – and what, consequently, is narrative – is symptomatic of the unsystematic nature of these typologies: rather than consistently relying on one of the three domains of semiotic theory, they arbitrarily mix semantic and pragmatic criteria. Narrative and description are arguably defined by the content of the text – a changing world for narrative, a static one for description – but categories such as persuasion, instruction, and argumentation are things we do with language rather than what language is about, conversation is a socially defined speech situation, and reflective discourse is a meta-category whose object could be any other text type. As long as the text-type approach remains unable to make a choice between semantic apples and pragmatic oranges, it will not lead to a satisfactory definition of narrative.

An alternative to the text-type approach is to avoid the notions of text and of semiotic artifact altogether, and to conceive narrative as a cognitive style or a mode of thinking. In this view, stories can exist in the mind as pure patterns of information, inspired by life experience or created by the imagination, independently of their representation through the signs of a specific medium. Jerome Bruner suggests, for instance, that "there are two modes of cognitive functioning, two modes of thought, each providing distinctive ways of ordering experience, of constructing reality. The two (though complementary) are irreducible to one another."[19] Bruner calls one mode the narrative and the other the argumentative, or paradigmatic. The narrative mode concerns the particular: it deals with "human or human-like intentions and the vicissitudes and consequences that mark their course."[20] The argumentative mode, on the other hand, "deals in general causes, and in their establishment, and makes use of procedures to assure verifiable reference and to test for empirical truth." It "seeks to transcend the particular by higher and higher reaching for abstraction."

It is easy to recognize the argumentative mode as the scientific and philosophical way of thinking; but the domain of narrative is less clear. When Bruner writes that stories are judged as "good" or "bad," and not by criteria of truth and verifiability, he limits narrative to its entertainment-oriented manifestations, and ignores the vast domain of narratives produced for the sake of information, such as news reports, historiography, courtroom testimony, and to a lesser extent narratives of personal experience. Moreover, the two so-called modes of thinking differ more through their subject-matter – the particular versus the general, the temporal versus the timeless, and the human versus its other, whatever that is – than through the cognitive processes that they bring into play. Both constitute attempts to make sense of the world, and they do this to a large extent through a common pool of mental operations: comparison, distinction, deduction, induction, sequencing (whether events or ideas), and seeking explanation through causal relations. The only significant difference, if indeed the narrative mode specializes in the human, is that narrative involves the reconstruction of minds. But we perform this operation as a normal part of social life. Does it mean that we engage in private storytelling whenever we interact with human beings?

Equating narrative with thought in general, some leading researchers in cognitive science might answer this question in the positive. Schank and Abelson proclaim, for instance, that all of memory consists of stories,[21] while according to Mark Turner, "Narrative imagining – story – is *the* fundamental instrument of thought . . . It is a literary capacity indispensable to human cognition generally."[22] For Turner, noticing objects or events in our perceptual environment amounts to constructing embryonic stories about them: "Story depends on constructing something rather than nothing. A reportable story is distinguished from its assumed and unreportable background. It is impossible for us to look at the world and not to see reportable stories distinguished from background."[23] In this view, the mere action of focusing on a certain tree in the forest is a narrative act, because it makes the tree into the protagonist of a virtual story. But if "thinking about," i.e., distinguishing figure from ground, is always already storytelling, the task of defining narrative becomes both superfluous and impossible: superfluous, because it is no longer necessary to differentiate narrative from any other manifestation of human thought, and impossible, because it is inseparable from a complete theory of mind. We can avoid this impasse, without falling back on a segregationist conception of thinking that distinguishes narrative and non-narrative operations, by regarding narrative as the outcome of many different mental processes that operate both inside and outside stories. The purpose of a definition will then be to delineate the set of cognitive operations whose convergence produces the type of mental representation that we regard as a story.

Narrative: a fuzzy-set definition

Rather than regarding narrativity as a strictly binary feature, that is, as a property that a given text either has or doesn't have, the definition proposed below presents narrative texts as a fuzzy set allowing variable degrees of membership, but centered on prototypical cases that everybody recognizes as stories.[24] In a scalar conception of narrative, definition becomes an open series of concentric circles which spell increasingly narrow conditions and which presuppose previously stated items, as we move from the outer to the inner circles, and from the marginal cases to the prototypes. The proposal below organizes the conditions of narrativity into three semantic and one formal and pragmatic dimension.

Spatial dimension

(1) Narrative must be about a world populated by individuated existents.

Temporal dimension

(2) This world must be situated in time and undergo significant transformations.

(3) The transformations must be caused by non-habitual physical events.

Mental dimension

(4) Some of the participants in the events must be intelligent agents who have a mental life and react emotionally to the states of the world.

(5) Some of the events must be purposeful actions by these agents.

Formal and pragmatic dimension

(6) The sequence of events must form a unified causal chain and lead to closure.

(7) The occurrence of at least some of the events must be asserted as fact for the storyworld.

(8) The story must communicate something meaningful to the audience.

Each of these conditions prevents a certain type of representation from forming the focus of interest, or macro-structure, of a story. This does not mean that these representations cannot appear in a narrative text, but rather, that they cannot, all by themselves, support its narrativity.

(1) eliminates representations of abstract entities and entire classes of concrete objects, scenarios involving "the human race," "reason," "the State," "atoms," "the brain," etc.

(2) eliminates static descriptions.

(3) eliminates enumerations of repetitive events and changes caused by natural evolution (such as aging).

(4) eliminates one-of-a-kind scenarios involving only natural forces and non-intelligent participants (weather reports, accounts of cosmic events).

(5) (together with 3) eliminates representations consisting exclusively of mental events (interior monologue fiction).

(6) eliminates lists of causally unconnected events, such as chronicles and diaries, as well as reports of problem-solving actions that stop before an outcome is reached.

(7) eliminates recipes, as well as texts entirely made of advice, hypotheses, counterfactuals, and instructions.

(8) eliminates bad stories. This is the most controversial condition in the list, because it straddles the borderline between definition and poetics, and because it needs to be complemented by a full theory of the different ways in which narrative can achieve significance. If we accept 8 as part of the definition, then narrativity is not an intrinsic property of the text, but rather a dimension relative to the context and to the interests of the participants. A sequence of events like "Mary was poor, then Mary won the lottery, then Mary was rich" would not make the grade as the content of fictional story, but it becomes very tellable if it is presented as true fact and concerns an acquaintance of the listener.

The eight conditions listed above offer a toolkit for do-it-yourself definitions. When they are put to the question, "is this text a narrative," some people will be satisfied with conditions 1 through 3 and will classify a text about evolution or the Big Bang as a story, while others will insist that narrative must be about human experience, and will consider (4) and (5) obligatory. Some people will regard a chronicle listing a series of independent events with the same participant as a narrative while others will insist on (6). Those who accept recipes as narratives consider (3) and (7) optional; and there are scholars who draw the line below (8), while others may think that a pointless utterance or a boring account of events can still display a narrative structure (this is my own inclination: I regard the "Mary" story quoted above as narrative regardless of context). But if people differ in opinion as to where to draw the line, they basically agree about what requirements are relevant to narrativity and about their importance relative to each other. If we ask: "is *Finnegans Wake* more narrative than *Little Red Riding Hood*?" we will get much broader agreement than if we ask (mindless of the incompatibility of a yes–no question with a fuzzy set): "is *Finnegans Wake* a narrative?"

Through its multiple conditions organized into distinct areas, the definition proposed above not only provides criteria for determining a text's degree of narrativity[25] it also suggests a basis for a semantic typology of narrative texts. While degree of narrativity depends on how many of the conditions are fulfilled, typology depends on the relative prominence of the four dimensions. The Grand Narratives of Lyotard can only be called narrative in a metaphorical sense, because they do not concern individuals and do not create a concrete world, while postmodern novels are often low in narrativity because they do not allow readers to reconstruct the network of mental representations that motivates the actions of characters and binds the events into an intelligible and determinate sequence. Through a structure that I call "proliferating narrativity,"[26] contemporary fiction (especially magical realism and postcolonial novels) may also shift condition (6) from the macro- to the micro-level, becoming a collection of little stories loosely connected through common participants. Among narratives that fully satisfy all the conditions, some emphasize the spatial dimension, others the temporal, and still others the mental. With their detailed construction of an imaginary world, science fiction and fantasy locate interest in the spatial dimension, and these genres often treat the plot as a discovery path across the fictional world. The demand for action and changes of state that makes up the temporal dimension is the dominant feature of thrillers and adventure stories, while the mental dimension, by insisting on the motivations and emotions of characters, rules over tragedy, sentimental romances, detective stories, comedies of errors, and, in the nonfictional domain, narratives of personal experience. In contrast to modernist novels that represent the mind for its own sake, these narrative genres evoke mental processes as a way to explain the behavior of characters.

How important is a definition of narrative anyway?

There may be many different ways to draw the frontiers of narrative, but these differences of opinion do not carry significant cognitive consequences, because when we read a text, we do not ask "is it or isn't it a narrative," nor even "to what extent does this text fulfill the conditions of narrativity," unless of course we are narratologists. Asking people to decide whether or not a text is a story is one of those artificial situations in which results are produced by the act of investigation.

Let me tell a story in support of my claim that judgments of narrativity are variable, and that they are not crucial to understanding. After presenting my definition of narrativity during a lecture, I once asked the audience whether this text, adapted from Brian Greene, qualifies as a story:

> The universe started out as cold and essentially infinite in spatial extent. Then an instability kicked in, driving every point in the universe to rush rapidly away from every other. This caused space to become increasingly curved and resulted in a dramatic increase of temperature and energy density. After some time, a millimeter-sized three-dimensional region within this vast expanse created a superhot and dense patch. The expansion of this patch can account for the whole of the universe with which we are now familiar.[27]

The response was almost unanimously negative, but a few days later, I received an e-mail from an audience member telling me that he had changed his mind: the Brian Greene text was a story after all. No longer under the influence of what was then my personal definition of narrative, this person had decided to evaluate the text according to his own criteria of narrativity. But this does not mean that he had changed his interpretation of the text. Before and after, he probably read it as the representation of a causal chain of extraordinary events that led to a major transformation within the universe.

I can sense at this point disapproval brewing among proponents of a cognitive approach to narrative. But what I am denying is not the importance of narrative for social life, intelligence, memory, knowledge, and our sense of identity, but rather, the importance of *conscious judgments of narrativity* for the processing of verbal or visual information. When we are presented with a text of unknown origin, and asked: "is this or isn't it a narrative" (an exercise occasionally practiced by narratologists),[28] we may diverge in our answers, but this does not mean that some of us are right and some of us are wrong (unless of course we blatantly misread the text), because we apply different criteria of narrativity, and because we can decide whether or not the text fulfills these criteria by paying attention to what it says. If, on the other hand, we are presented with unknown texts and asked: "is this fiction or nonfiction," our answers will be right or wrong, because they will not be an assessment of what the text is all about, but a guess of the author's intent. Fictionality is indeed a type of game that authors invite readers to play with texts: a game variously described as make-believe, suspended disbelief, or immersion in an imaginary world.[29] The same text could, at least in principle, be presented as a creation of the imagination or as a truthful account of facts, and we must be guided by extra-textual signs, such as generic labels ("novel," "short story") to assess its fictional status.[30] Because judgments of fictionality affect what the reader will or will not believe, they are much more important than judgments of narrativity.

"Narrative" is less a culturally recognized category that influences our choices of reading, viewing, or listening materials than an analytical concept designed by narratologists. In everyday conversation we speak about novels (a specific literary genre), about tales (something false or exaggerated), or about stories, meaning compact forms of narrative (gossip, anecdotes, news, folktales, or short fiction) rather than the abstract technical concept that narratologists oppose to "discourse," but we hardly ever use the word "narrative" outside of academic discusssions. Nobody would walk into a bookstore and ask for "a narrative," because what matters to us are individual narrative genres, such as historiography, biography, science fiction, or fantasy, and not the general category that subsumes them all. It was not until the sixties that literary theorists and semioticians began talking about narrative: their predecessors discussed instead folk tales, myth, or the novel. Assessing the narrative status of a text is not a cognitive question that we must consciously answer for proper understanding, but a theoretical question that enables narratologists to delimit the object of their discipline, to isolate the features relevant to their inquiry, and to stem the recent inflation of the term narrative.

If defining narrative has any cognitive relevance, it is because the definition covers mental operations of a more fundamental nature than passing global judgments of narrativity: operations such as asking in what order did the represented events occur; what changes did they cause in the depicted world; what do the events (and their results) mean for the characters; what motivates actions and how does the outcome of these actions compare to the intent of the agent. If a text confronts us with such questions, and if we are able to answer them, we read the text as a story, or rather, we read the story told by the text, whether or not we are aware of what we are doing.

NOTES

1. Jean-François Lyotard, *The Postmodern Condition: A Report on Knowledge.* Translated by Geoff Bennington and Brian Massumi (Minneapolis: University of Minnesota Press, 1984). Grand narratives, also known as metanarratives, are global explanatory schemes that legitimize institutions, such as the practice of science, by representing them as necessary to the historical self-realization of an abstract or collective entity, such as Reason, Freedom, or the State. Hegel's and Marx's philosophies of history are prototypical examples of Grand Narratives. So are the eschatological scenarios of religion.
2. Jerome Bruner, *Making Stories: Law, Literature, Life* (Cambridge, MA: Harvard University Press, 2002), chapter 3.
3. Daniel Dennett, *Consciousness Explained* (Hammondsworth, England: Penguin, 1991).
4. William Safire, "On Language." *The New York Times Magazine* 5 (December 2004), p. 36.
5. Gerald Prince, "Revisiting Narrativity." In Walter Grünzweig and Andreas Solbach (eds.) *Grenzüberschreitungen: Narratologie im Kontext/ Transcending Boundaries: Narratology in Context* (Tübingen: Gunter Narr Verlag, 1999), p. 45.
6. Quoted in Safire, "On Language," p. 36.
7. Gérard Genette, *Figures of Literary Discourse.* Translated by Marie-Rose Logan (New York: Columbia University Press, 1982), p. 127.
8. *A Dictionary of Narratology*, 2nd edition (Lincoln: University of Nebraska Press, 2003), p. 58.
9. H. Porter Abbott, *The Cambridge Introduction to Narrative* (Cambridge: Cambridge University Press, 2002), p. 16.
10. Paul Ricoeur, "Narrative Time." In W. J. T. Mitchell (ed.) *On Narrative* (Chicago: University of Chicago Press, 1981), p. 165.
11. Peter Brooks, *Reading for the Plot: Design and Intention in Narrative* (Cambridge, MA: Harvard University Press, 1984), p. ix.

12. Gerald Prince, *Narratology: The Form and Functioning of Narrative* (Berlin: Mouton, 1982), p. 4.

13. Susana Onega, and José Angel García Landa, "Introduction." In Onega and Landa (eds.) *Narratology: An Introduction* (London: Longman, 1996), p. 3.

14. Mieke Bal, *Narratology: An Introduction to the Theory of Narrative* (Toronto: University of Toronto Press, 1997), p. 182.

15. For instance, David Rudrum, "From Narrative Representation to Narrative Use: Towards the Limits of Definition." *Narrative* 13 (2005), pp. 195–204.

16. Seymour Chatman, *Coming to Terms: The Rhetoric of Narrative in Fiction and Film* (Ithaca, N.Y: Cornell University Press, 1990).

17. Monika Fludernik, "Genres, Text Types, or Discourse Mode? Narrative Modalities and Generic Categorization." *Style* 34:2 (2000), pp. 274–92.

18. Tuija Virtanen, "Issues of Text Typology: Narrative – A 'Basic' Type of Text." *Text* 12:2 (1992), pp. 293–310.

19. Jerome Bruner, *Actual Minds, Possible Worlds* (Cambridge, MA: Harvard University Press, 1986), p. 11.

20. Bruner, *Actual Minds*, p. 13. The next two quotations are also on p. 13 of this text.

21. Roger Schank and Robert P. Abelson, "Knowledge and Memory: The Real Story," in Robert S. Wyer (ed.) *Knowledge and Memory: The Real Story* (Hillsdale, N.J.: Lawrence Erlbaum, 1995), pp. 1–85.

22. Mark Turner, *The Literary Mind* (Oxford: Oxford University Press, 1996), pp. 4–5 (my emphasis).

23. Turner, *The Literary Mind*, p. 145.

24. This idea has been suggested by Fotis Jannidis, "Narratology and the Narrative." In Tom Kindt and Hans-Harald Müller (eds.) *What is Narratology?* (Berlin: Walter de Gruyter), pp. 35–54.

25. Degree of narrativity can be understood in two ways, one pertaining to story (or the "what" of a narrative) and the other to discourse (or the "way" such narrative content is presented). In the story sense, the one I am using here, it means the extent to which the mental representation conveyed by a text fulfills the definition of story. In the discourse sense (developed by Prince in *Narratology*), it means the importance of the story within the global economy of the text and the ease of retrieving it. The same text can present full narrativity in sense 1, but low narrativity in sense 2, when it tells a well-formed story but the progress of the action is slowed down by descriptions, general comments, and digressions. See also the concept of "diluted narrativity" in Marie-Laure Ryan, "The Modes of Narrativity and their Visual Metaphors." *Style* 26:3 (1992), p. 375.

26. Ryan, "The Modes of Narrativity." pp. 373–4.

27. Adapted from Brian Greene, *The Elegant Universe: Superstrings, Hidden Dimensions and the Quest for the Ultimate Theory* (New York: Random House, 2003), p. 362.

28. For instance David Herman in *Story Logic: Problems and Possibilities of Narrative* (Lincoln: University of Nebraska Press, 2002), pp. 87–9.

29. The suggestion that fiction is a game of make-believe is due to Kendall Walton, *Mimesis as Make-Believe: On the Foundations of the Representational Arts* (Cambridge, MA: Harvard University Press, 1990); the formula "willing suspension of disbelief" was coined by Samuel Taylor Coleridge; and the concept

of fictional immersion is discussed in Jean-Marie Schaeffer, *Pourquoi la fiction* (Paris: Seuil 1999) and Marie-Laure Ryan, *Narrative as Virtual Reality: Immersion and Interactivity in Literature and Electronic Media* (Baltimore: Johns Hopkins University Press, 2001). The nature of fiction has inspired many more proposals, which cannot be reviewed here.

30. In *The Distinction of Fiction* (Baltimore: Johns Hopkins University Press, 1999), pp. 109–31, Dorrit Cohn has identified "signposts of fictionality," i.e., features that occur only in fiction. Among these features are, on the discourse level, the description of the private thoughts of characters other than the narrator, which presuppose that the narrator has mind-reading abilities; and on the story level, fantastic themes, such as metamorphosis of humans into animals. (Cohn however restricts her analysis to discourse-related signposts.) But these signposts are optional, and there have been notorious cases of fictional texts being mistaken for biography or autobiography: for instance, the novel *Marbot* by the German author Wolfgang Hildesheimer (1981) was originally reviewed as the biography of a historical individual, though the character of Marbot was invented by the novelist (Cohn, *Distinction*, p. 79). By contrast, one cannot imagine critics mistaking a text for a narrative.

II
Studying narrative fiction: a starter-kit

3

H. PORTER ABBOTT

Story, plot, and narration

One fine summer morning – it was the beginning of harvest, I remember –
Mr. Earnshaw, the old master, came down stairs, dressed for a journey; and,
after he had told Joseph what was to be done during the day, he turned to
Hindley, and Cathy, and me – for I sat eating my porridge with them – and he
said, speaking to his ooon,

"Now my bonny man, I'm going to Liverpool, to-day . . . What shall I bring
you? You may choose what you like: only let it be little, for I shall walk there
and back; sixty miles each way, that is a long spell!"

Hindley named a fiddle, and then he asked Cathy; she was hardly six years
old, but she could ride any horse in the stable, and she chose a whip.

He did not forget me, for he had a kind heart, though he was rather severe,
sometimes. He promised to bring me a pocketful of apples and pears, and then
he kissed his children good-bye, and set off.[1]

This is how the *story* of Emily Brontë's novel, *Wuthering Heights*, begins.
Like most stories, it begins with a beginning. This is a more important point
than it may seem: all stories move only in one direction, forward through
time. If there is a knowable beginning, that's where they begin. If there is a
knowable end, that's where they end. The process of telling is the story's
narration, and at this point Ellen (Nelly) Dean, a servant in the house-
hold, is its narrator. This distinction between story and narration is also
important. It is an implicit acknowledgment that a story is understood as
having a separate existence from its narration. As such, it can be told in
different ways by different narrators. Were Hindley or Cathy our narrator
at this point, the narration of this story would be different, with different
words, different emotional inflections, different perspectives, and different
details. These narrators might even contradict each other. But the usual presumption is that there is a story to be told and that the story itself, going
inexorably through time, can no more correct itself than can events in real
life: Mr. Earnshaw goes to Liverpool and returns with a child he found on
the streets there. The arrival of this child, who will be named Heathcliff, sets

39

off in turn a series of events with even further consequences, none of which can be altered by going back and changing or erasing them.

If you have read *Wuthering Heights*, you know that the novel itself does not start at the beginning of its story, but rather thirty years later with barely a year of the story left to go. There is a different narrator at this point, a vacationing Londoner named Mr. Lockwood, who is renting Thrushcross Grange from Heathcliff and whose narration is not told orally but recorded in his diary. Lockwood enters the novel's storyworld during a pause in the story's action. Through the narration of two visits to his landlord at Wuthering Heights, Lockwood introduces us to four characters and the possible ghost of a fifth, all of them mysteriously miserable and intently at odds. Brontë's decision to redistribute the order in which the story events are told is a *plot* decision. In this instance, it brings us in to a situation that is clearly charged with story, with only the tiniest scraps to indicate what the story is. It was a shrewd bit of emplotment, arousing in the reader, as it does in Mr. Lockwood, a keen desire to know how this bizarre collection of characters wound up together in an atmosphere of such hostility. The management of plot, in this sense of the word, is among other things the management of suspense, which in turn generates the energy that draws us through any well-constructed narrative. We want to know the story, which greatly adds to our pleasure when, after thirty pages, Nelly Dean begins telling the story from its beginning to a bedridden Lockwood.

The distinction between plot and story, like that between narration and story, is an implicit presumption that a story is separate from its rendering. Just as a story can be narrated in different ways, so it can be plotted in different ways. This analytically powerful distinction between story and its representation is, arguably, the founding insight of the field of narratology. If story, plot, and narration can be called the three principal components of the overarching category "narrative," the distinction between story and how it is communicated is so fundamental that scholars of narrative often bring narration and plot together under a single heading, narrative discourse. Over the last seventy-five years, the distinction between story and "story as discoursed"[2] has proven very helpful in understanding how narrative achieves its effects. But nothing is tidy in the study of narrative. This is largely because narrative happens in the mind, with its empirical components – words spoken or printed, pictures on a screen, actors on a stage – transformed by cognitive processes that are still largely mysterious. For this reason, the nature, necessity, and adequacy of these three enduring concepts – story, plot, and narration – have never been completely assured, however fruitful the controversies they have stirred up.

A brief explication of concepts

Of these three key concepts, story is the sturdiest. Scholars may not agree that a story must have a beginning or an end, but there is little dispute that a story is composed of action (an event or events) and characters (more broadly existents or entities) and that it always proceeds forward in time: Heathcliff arrives, Mr. Earnshaw dies, Edgar courts Cathy, Heathcliff disappears, Cathy marries Edgar, Heathcliff returns, he elopes with Isabella, Cathy dies giving birth to Cathy Linton, Linton Heathcliff is born, Heathcliff kidnaps young Cathy, she marries Linton, Hindley dies, Edgar dies, Linton dies, Heathcliff dies. Story was first analytically set off from the manner of its rendering in the wake of Saussure's distinction in linguistics between the signified and the signifier. The spade work for this adaptation was performed by Russian Formalists, who, in the 1920s, introduced the distinction of *fabula* (story) and *sjuzhet* (its rendering). Tzvetan Todorov gave these terms their rough equivalents in French, *histoire* and *discours*, and Gérard Genette greatly elaborated the distinction in his landmark narratological reading of Proust's *A la recherche du temps perdu*.[3] From there, thanks in part to Seymour Chatman's foundational work, the corresponding distinction of story and discourse made its way into English where it is now widely deployed.

Two notable controversies have attended this basic distinction. One is the question of whether it is a real distinction at all since all we ever know of story is what we get through discourse. Story *seems* to pre-exist its rendering (note how often stories are narrated in the past tense) yet, as Culler argues, the rendering also *seems* to generate the story, which would make it follow rather than precede the discourse.[4] The other controversy is closely related to the first and involves the repeatability of story. If a story has a separate existence such that it can be rendered in more than one way and even in more than one medium, how do we know it is the same story when we see it again? What is necessary for us to recognize it as such? Or is it always a new story in every rendering? Some narrative scholars (Barthes, Chatman, Abbott) have attempted to distinguish between those events that are essential for the story to be the story that it is (nuclei, kernels, constituent events) and those that are expendable (catalyzers, satellites, supplementary events),[5] but choosing which events fall in which categories can be a vexed enterprise.

The term narration is a little more slippery than story, having been used in some mutually contradictory ways. It has been used as a synonym for narrative, it has been used more narrowly by some film critics to mean most of the narrative discourse,[6] it has been used still more narrowly to mean the production of narrative by a narrator, and in its most restricted sense it has been used to mean the narrator's words exclusive of all *direct discourse*, that is, recorded speech or thought (dialogue, monologue, interior monologue). Distinguishing the third and fourth of these usages can involve some stubborn entanglement, since direct discourse is often rich with narration. For example, Nelly Dean's narration is, technically, direct discourse, recorded by Lockwood in his journal, yet it bears most of the narration in Brontë's novel. Nelly's narration in turn includes much quoted dialogue and monologue, which in their turn include vital pieces of narration. In short, these two functions are not mutually exclusive. The distinction is still important, but it is a distinction of emphasis: discourse as expression or discourse as narration. In the excerpt above, for example, Mr. Earnshaw's words in quotation are direct discourse, but within them one might focus on the expression of his hearty good nature ("Now, my bonny young man . . .") or on his narration of what will come to pass ("I shall walk there and back").

Two aspects of narration that always have significant consequences are the sensibility of the narrator and his or her distance from the action. Narrators can be brilliant, dumb, deranged, passionate, or cold as ice. They are as various, in short, as we are, and how they are constituted inevitably inflects how they mediate the story. They are also variously close to or distant from the action. In a valuable distinction, displacing the much less useful distinction between first-person and third-person narration, Gérard Genette identified homodiegetic narrators as those who are also characters in the storyworld (or diegesis) and therefore necessarily closer to the action than heterodiegetic narrators, who stand outside the storyworld.[7] The latter tend to have greater reliability, inspiring more confidence in the information and views they convey and often deploying third-person narration throughout. This is not always the case. Some heterodiegetic narrators have clearly developed personalities, refer to themselves in the first person, and even raise suspicions regarding their reliability. But, by and large, heterodiegetic narrators are less personally invested in the story they tell than are homodiegetic narrators, though among these latter, too, personalities and personal investment range widely. Both of the principal narrators of *Wuthering Heights*, Lockwood and Nelly Dean, are homodiegetic, but their personalities and involvement in the action are very different. Lockwood is an imperceptive, shallow, somewhat dimwitted man. And though he is a character in the world of the novel, he comes into the isolated, rural setting of the story from the city and never becomes a part of the action except in one instance and that through sheer inadvertence. Nelly Dean is more perceptive, less self-absorbed, with a good enough heart and a sufficient enough supply of common sense to give her greater reliability than Lockwood. Yet she is much closer to the characters, having lived with them all her life; she has distinct hopes and fears on their behalf and from time to time even plays a role in the action.

Plot is an even slipperier term than narration, both more polyvalent and more approximate in its meanings, indeed so "vague in ordinary usage" that narratologists often avoid it altogether.[8] In common English usage, plot is often identical with story ("it was boring; there was no plot"), yet in the discourse on narrative, the term has been deployed in at least three distinguishable ways. Perhaps most frequently, plot is understood as a type of story – as in E. M. Forster's use of plot to indicate a story that is not merely one thing after another but events connected by cause. Vladimir Propp, Northrop Frye, and Joseph Campbell all developed anatomies of plot types that provide a finite number of story frameworks underlying the infinite variety of narrative. This use of the term, as Hilary Dannenberg has pointed out, also appears in feminist accounts of the ways a culture can limit the roles of women in fiction to certain plot types. All of these usages of plot feature the term as a skeletal story, either universal or culturally fabricated, which performs its psycho-social work while cloaked in a diversity of narrative dress.[9]

Plot is also used to refer to that combination of economy and sequencing of events that makes a story a story and not just raw material. In this sense, it is often used as a value term. Thus Aristotle's concept of "muthos," often translated as plot, is the fashioned story, shaped with a beginning, middle, and end. Brian Richardson has summarized this general usage of plot as "a teleological sequence of events linked by some principle of causation; that is, the events are bound together in a trajectory that typically leads to some form of resolution or convergence."[10] Plot in this sense is a device that brings the story to its fullness and authenticity as story. In Ricoeur's words, plot is "the intelligible whole that governs a succession of events in a story . . . A story is made out of events to the extent that plot *makes* events *into* a story."[11]

A third use of the term plot, modeled on Genette's work and often deployed by narratologists writing in English, features the way plot serves a story by departing from the chronological order of its events, or expanding on some events while rushing through others, or returning to them, sometimes repeatedly. This use of plot is close to the Russian Formalist "sjuzhet" with its analytical attention to the ways in which the plot re-arranges, expands, contracts, or repeats events of the story. By such temporary delays, concealments, and confusions, plot enriches the experience of what would otherwise be just a story. If in Ricoeur's terms the stress is on plot as the artful *construction* of story, in these terms the emphasis is on plot as the artful *disclosure* of story.

Each of these three uses of the term plot can be seen as different perspectives on the same overarching issue of the distribution of narrative parts. As such, these uses are distinguishable from the common use of narration as the manner in which those parts are delivered, the analysis of which tends to feature such issues as voice, focalization, feeling, judgment, mood, distance, and tone. If the first of these uses of plot comes closest to the way in which we use the term in English, the second and third, with their emphasis on the art by which a story is delivered, might more accurately be referred to as "emplotment."

An art of opening and closing gaps

Emily Brontë's plot decision (in the third sense above) to start her narrative close to the end of her story opened up an enormous gulf. The intensity of the characters Lockwood describes and the oddness of their behavior beg for a narrator to recover the story lurking in that gulf and give plausibility to what now looks so strange. Fortunately there is a narrator at hand. But Nelly's narration, like all narration, is only and inevitably a partial recovery. Here is another important point about narrative. It at one and the same time fills and creates gaps. This is an insight that first received extended development by Wolfgang Iser and Meir Sternberg in the 1970s. As Iser wrote, "it is only through the inevitable omissions that a story gains its dynamism."[12] He was thinking particularly of critical gaps, but if you look closely at the sentences of any narrative, you will find gaps everywhere.

One urgent question evoked by the gap Lockwood opens up is what type of story (what plot in the first sense above) is in this gap? Lockwood makes a series of conjectures, all of them, as it turns out, comically in error. But the account he gives of his reading on the night he spends at Wuthering Heights and the fearful dream he has of a waif wandering in exile for twenty years suggest that this plot might at least have something to do with exclusion and punishment. As far as it goes, this turns out to be true, though, as we eventually learn, there are actually two major plots still in progress in this huge gap – a tragic love story (Cathy and Heathcliff's) and a revenge tragedy (Heathcliff's) – and another kind over and done with – that of a girl's entry into society and womanhood (Cathy's) – and still one more – a romance involving young lovers (Cathy Linton and Hareton Earnshaw) – just about to blossom.

In addition, it is important to keep in mind that crowded into the space we are looking into are not just events and the characters involved in them, strung along the armature of their plots, but an entire storyworld, which may, for that matter, even include an entire metaphysical universe. Recent work by Lubomír Doležel, David Herman, Alan Palmer, Marie-Laure Ryan, and others has foregrounded just how much in the way of worlds, inner and outer, actual and possible, material and immaterial, is comprised in a story.[13] Finally, in seeking to fill the gaps of what happens in the storyworld we must cope not only with what is left out of the narration but also with what is given. This is because the narration is inflected everywhere by our sense of who is narrating. We offset for perceived biases – self-interest, love, hatred, envy, fondness, immaturity, personal agenda – that may affect the reliability of the narration, not so often regarding the facts, which we usually (though not invariably) accept, but frequently regarding the emotional and evaluative coloring of those facts.

Plot, narration, and character: trying to understand Heathcliff

Edgar Linton's sister, Isabella, barely two months into her elopement, writes to Nelly asking: "Is Mr Heathcliff a man? If so, is he mad? And if not, is he a devil? . . . I beseech you to explain, if you can, what I have married" (*Wuthering Heights*, 134). A lot in this novel rides on the question of what Isabella has married, but note that our narration in this instance, nested in the more reliable narration of the older and wiser Ellen Dean, is delivered by a passionate, somewhat spoiled, immature, inexperienced reader of popular romances who had, two months before, slotted Heathcliff in the wrong romantic role of the wrong romantic plot, with herself cast as romantic heroine. Later Heathcliff will rub this in: she stubbornly pictured in him "a hero of romance," despite all evidence to the contrary, including his "hang[ing] up her little dog" as they set out on their elopement (*Wuthering Heights*, 148–9). She has in a short time fallen a long way, which no doubt lends its own emotional excess to her narration.

As a plot decision, the narration of Isabella's mistake helps Brontë's readers grasp the originality of her work by helping them to avoid making the same mistake of importing the wrong plot. By way of reinforcement, Cathy has already tried to disabuse her sister-in-law: "don't imagine that he conceals depths of benevolence and affection beneath a stern exterior! He's . . . a fierce, pitiless, wolfish man . . . . and he'd crush you like a sparrow's egg, Isabella, if he found you a troublesome charge" (*Wuthering Heights*, 102). Yet what kind of lover is this, for he is a lover – Cathy's –, and what kind of romance plot is it where the hero can crush young women like sparrow's eggs? Or does the value of this metaphor lie not in its narration of possibilities but in its function as direct discourse, telling us more about Cathy than Heathcliff? For that matter, how reliable is she as a narrator? If what she says turns out to be in part prophetic ("he couldn't love a Linton; and yet, he'd be quite capable of marrying your fortune, and expectations"), the motivation she invokes ("Avarice is growing with him a besetting sin") is paltry, given what we learn.

All of which is to say that determining the character of Heathcliff and what plot he belongs to is at the mercy of a host of conflicting passions and personal agendas. Readers of the 1850 posthumous edition of *Wuthering Heights* would have found the novel framed by a preface written by Emily's sister Charlotte, at that point a respected novelist in her own right. In this paratext they would have encountered a clear and decisive answer to Isabella's question. Heathcliff is "a child neither of Lascar nor gypsy, but a man's shape animated by demon life – a Ghoul – an Afreet." As such there is only one way to read him: "unredeemed; never once swerving in his arrow-straight course to perdition" (*Wuthering Heights*, xxxvi). Yet Nelly, reflecting in the final pages of her narration on what the entire story might say of Heathcliff, provides an eerily proleptic rebuttal to Charlotte:

> "Is he a ghoul, or a vampire?" I mused. I had read of such hideous, incarnate demons. And then, I set myself to reflect, how I had tended him in infancy; and watched him grow to youth; and followed him through his whole life course, and what absurd nonsense it was to yield to that sense of horror.
> "But where did he come from, the little dark thing, harboured by a good man to his bane?" muttered superstition, as I dozed into unconsciousness. And I began, half dreaming, to weary myself with imaging some fit parentage for him . . .   (*Wuthering Heights*, 327)

Though Nelly rejects the idea that Heathcliff is somehow nonhuman, fearful "superstition" prods her to try to narrativize his origins and thus normalize him by establishing his type – a wearying task because of its impossibility. Heathcliff's origins are, in Sternberg's term, a "permanent" narrative gap.[14] All we have to go on are Heathcliff's swarthy complexion, his first appearance alone on the streets of Liverpool, and the "gibberish" he spoke at that time. All three are troubling enough for the characters of this novel and no doubt for much of Brontë's audience. As marks of the invasive non-English "other" they signify mystery and danger. But they could for that matter signify something wonderful, as Nelly suggests to a young, downcast Heathcliff: "You're fit for a prince in disguise. Who knows, but your father was Emperor of China, and your mother an Indian Queen, each of them able to buy up, with a week's income, Wuthering Heights and Thrushcross Grange together?" (*Wuthering Heights*, 57). Yet, again, the same narrator, at another point, could imagine Heathcliff as an "evil beast . . . waiting his time to spring and destroy" (*Wuthering Heights*, 106). To go back to the distinction developed above between direct discourse as expression and direct discourse as narration, what we observe in these instances is reliability in the expression of feelings about Heathcliff but unreliability in rendering what actually constitutes his character.

But what if we looked to Heathcliff's own words for answers to the enigma of who or what he is? After all, there are numerous instances in which he narrates his own actions, as in the following passage: "The first thing she saw me do, on coming out of the Grange, was to hang up her little dog, and when she pleaded for it, the first words I uttered were a wish that I had the hanging of every being belonging to her, except one. . . ." (*Wuthering Heights*, 149). It is hard to see this as a case in which personal feeling undermines reliability of narration, yet the cruelty of the action is so gratuitously excessive that readers have been tempted to put it in brackets by seeing in it, not Heathcliff, but authorial excess. This is basically what Charlotte did when she wrote that her sister, "having formed these beings, did not know what she had done" (*Wuthering Heights*, xxxv). But if you don't finesse the text in this way and read Heathcliff's actions not as the author's loss of control but as the product of her intentions then this preternatural ferocity must be accepted as part of Heathcliff's character.

But what does it tell us? The association of little dogs and Isabella goes way back for Heathcliff, back to the first time he saw her, peeking with Catherine through the window of the Grange.

> Isabella – I believe she is eleven, a year younger than Cathy – lay screaming at the farther end of the room, shrieking as if witches were running red hot needles into her. Edgar stood on the hearth weeping silently, and in the middle of the table sat a little dog, shaking its paw and yelping, which from their mutual accusations, we understood they had nearly pulled in two between them. The idiots! That was their pleasure! To quarrel who should hold a heap of warm hair, and each beginning to cry because both, after struggling to get it, refused to take it! (*Wuthering Heights*, 48)

This is also the moment childhood ended for Heathcliff, when Cathy began to fall away from him, staying for six weeks among the Lintons and returning a young woman with a veneer of new interests and new values. Does this trauma, the greatest of his life to this point, help explain Heathcliff's cruelty toward Isabella's dog? Is the little dog a kind of memorial trigger? If so, such an understanding of Heathcliff might leaven our assessment of his ferocity.

But if we focus on the child Heathcliff's words, not so much as the narration of an event that prepares for and to some extent explains a later event, but rather as the direct expression of his feelings in the moment, there is less to leaven our judgment. The child Heathcliff gives vent to his disgust and the pleasure he took in tormenting these coddled children: "We laughed outright at the petted things, we did despise them! . . . The Lintons heard us, and with one accord, they shot like arrows to the door . . . 'Oh, mamma, mamma! Oh, papa! Oh, mamma, come here. Oh, papa, oh!' They really did howl out, something in that way. We made frightful noises to terrify them still more . . ." (*Wuthering Heights*, 49). For the adult narrator, this is still where the emphasis lies: "I never, in all my life, met with such an abject thing as she is – She even disgraces the name of Linton; and I've sometimes relented, from pure lack of invention, in my experiments on what she could endure, and still creep shamefully cringing back!" (*Wuthering Heights*, 149). Reading Heathcliff's narration thus, it appears that it is Isabella's human weakness itself, "abject" and "cringing," that rouses in him a power of evil that grows more terrible as his victim grows more pathetic: "I have no pity! I have no pity! The more the worms writhe, the more I yearn to crush out their entrails! It is a moral teething, and I grind with greater energy, in proportion to the increase in pain" (*Wuthering Heights*, 150). A demon? Perhaps, but if he is, he is still human enough to wonder, as we do, just what he is.

However great our own wonderment, both the cruel energy of Heathcliff's words and his ability to reflect on that energy are immediate and undeniable. As direct discourse, they give evidence of what constitutes Heathcliff that is more reliable than, say, his description of the Linton children. This difference between direct discourse as personal expression and direct discourse as narration can be critical. Heathcliff, for example, tells how he was once on the point of opening Cathy's coffin when "it seemed that I heard a sigh from some one above, close at the edge of the grave," and then again

> There was another sigh, close at my ear. I appeared to feel the warm breath of it displacing the sleet-laden wind. I knew no living thing in flesh and blood was by – but as certainly as you perceive the approach to some substantial body in the dark, though it cannot be discerned, so certainly I felt that Cathy was there, not under me, but on the earth. (*Wuthering Heights*, 286–7)

Taken by themselves, the words are reliable evidence not of spiritual contact but of Heathcliff's state of mind as it expresses both the recollection of an experience and a conviction about its cause. As to what really happened in the story he tells, well, maybe he heard something, maybe he only imagined it, maybe Cathy was present, maybe she wasn't.

Shortly after Heathcliff himself is buried beside Cathy, Nelly encounters a terrified boy. The narrative shifts for a moment to direct discourse:

Story, plot, and narration

"What is the matter, my little man?" I asked.

"They's Heathcliff and a woman, yonder, under t'Nab," he blubbered, "un' Aw darnut pass 'em."

I saw nothing; but neither the sheep nor he would go on, so I bid him take the road lower down. (*Wuthering Heights*, 333)

The boy's words are the boy's words. They tell us how he is troubled. But as narration, they do not give us enough to rely on them as reporting a real event in the storyworld of *Wuthering Heights*. In this way and a great many others, the narration of Brontë's novel sustains not just Heathcliff but also the world to which he belongs as a collection of narrative gaps.

Adaptation: reconfiguring narrative gaps

In the 1939 film version of *Wuthering Heights*, it is not a little shepherd boy who reports seeing the apparitions of Heathcliff and a woman, but a much more reliable witness, Dr. Kenneth, the man of science. He comes running in, interrupting Ellen Dean who is just concluding her narration to Lockwood. He saw them, he exclaims, "as plain as my own eyes," and points at his eyes for emphasis. As narrator, Ellen (not diminished as "Nelly") is also coded with greater reliability: white-haired and grave, she is played with authoritative dignity by Flora Robson, whose narrowed eyes seem continually to gaze on the unseen. "Under a high rock," she says, and Dr. Kenneth, surprised, confirms. "It was Cathy," she declares. And when Lockwood objects that he doesn't believe in ghosts, she fine-tunes her analysis with the same reassuring gravitas: "Not a ghost, but Cathy's love, stronger than time itself." In short, the metaphysical gap that Brontë's narration and plotting carefully left open is in this version filled decisively. The storyworld of the film includes both this world and the next, so that what looks like an ending is actually the beginning of a whole other life where death doesn't exist. They are "not dead," says Ellen, "not alone. . . . They've only just begun to live."

Of course, when you think about it, there is a puzzle in what Ellen actually means when she says that they are "not dead" or that what Dr. Kenneth saw was "Cathy's love." There's also the question of whether Cathy and Heathcliff constitute a special case, earning a reward that is not open to the rest of us. But the film does not invite the viewer to dwell on such questions. Rather it turns in its final moment to the immediacy of sight and sound. In film, though there are almost always, as above, fragments of verbalized narration scattered everywhere, much of the burden of narration is non-verbal, borne largely by the camera (the angles, duration, and sequencing of what it sees) and not uncommonly by music. Now the scene shifts, the music

49

swells, and the camera reveals a high rock. Charles McArthur and Ben Hecht in their screenplay for the film had at this point prescribed two birds flying off together. But this was not unambiguous enough for Samuel Goldwyn, who replaced the birds with a double exposure of Laurence Olivier and Merle Oberon walking hand in hand under the rock.

In managing the narration and emplotment of the story for film, Goldwyn, his director (William Wyler), and his screenwriters had to deal with constraints that Brontë never had to. They had to deliver an entire story in under two hours; they had to do this clearly enough for a captive audience to grasp it in one sitting; and they had to move the audience sufficiently to bring in enough viewers to cover the film's considerable costs and make a profit. To do this, they pared Brontë's story down, eliminating the whole eighteen-year stretch between Cathy's death and Heathcliff's. With it went Heathcliff's elaborate machinations of revenge and the love story of the second generation. Cathy does not give birth, so there is no Cathy Linton, nor is there Heathcliff's and Isabella's son, Linton Heathcliff, nor does Hindley marry Frances, so she and their son, Hareton, are also gone. The film-makers did keep Brontë's plot decision to begin with Lockwood's visit to Wuthering Heights, but this scene comes, in the adjusted story time, on the heels of Cathy's death and within hours of Heathcliff's. The narrative trigger is Lockwood's dream encounter with Cathy's apparition, and Ellen's voiceover narration follows as an explication of what he saw and what it means. The film was a remarkable feat of restructuring, but the result was a closing of narrative gaps on almost every level – moral, psychological, social, and, as we noted above, metaphysical. It follows a much more conventional romance plot than Brontë did, and Heathcliff plays a more conventional lover, marrying Isabella out of a jealous desire to hurt Cathy, a point he rams home with such plaintive force that the impact appears to be Cathy's deathblow. But this is about as rough as Heathcliff gets in the film, and the fault for this tragic outcome lies clearly with Cathy. The moral is equally clear: don't trade love for wealth and status.

What I hope to have shown in this brief look at the way story, plot, and narration interact is that narrative is an art of the opening and closing of gaps, and that in those gaps lie whole worlds that the art of narrative invites us either to actualize or leave as possibilities.

NOTES

1. Emily Brontë, *Wuthering Heights* (London: Penguin, 1995), p. 36.
2. Seymour Chatman, *Story and Discourse: Narrative Structure in Fiction and Film* (Ithaca, N.Y.: Cornell University Press, 1978), pp. 19–22.

3. Tzvetan Todorov, *Littérature et signification* (Paris: Larousse, 1967), and Gérard Genette, *Narrative Discourse: An Essay in Method*. Translated by Jane E. Levin (Ithaca, N.Y.: Cornell University Press, 1980).

4. Jonathan Culler, "Story and Discourse in the Analysis of Narrative." In *The Pursuit of Signs: Semiotics, Literature, Deconstruction* (Ithaca: Cornell University Press, 1981), pp. 169–87.

5. H. Porter Abbott, *The Cambridge Introduction to Narrative* (Cambridge University Press, 2002), pp. 20–2; Roland Barthes, "Introduction to the Structural Analysis of Narratives." In Susan Sontag (ed.) *A Barthes Reader* (New York: Hill & Wang, 1982), pp. 295–6; Chatman, *Story and Discourse*, pp. 53–6.

6. David Bordwell, *Narration in the Fiction Film* (Madison: University of Wisconsin Press, 1985); Edward Branigan, *Narrative Comprehension and Film* (London: Routledge, 1992).

7. Genette, *Narrative Discourse*, pp. 212–62.

8. Shlomith Rimmon-Kenan, *Narrative Fiction: Contemporary Poetics* (London: Methuen, 1983), p. 135.

9. E. M. Forster, *Aspects of the Novel* (Harcourt, Brace & World, 1955), p. 86; Vladimir Propp, *Morphology of the Folktale*. Translated by Laurence Scott, revised by Louis A. Wagner (Austin: University of Texas Press, 1968); Northrop Frye, *Anatomy of Criticism: Four Essays* (Princeton: Princeton University Press, 1957); Joseph Campbell, *The Hero with a Thousand Faces* (Princeton: Princeton University Press, 1968); Hilary P. Dannenberg, "Plot." In David Herman, Manfred Jahn, and Marie-Laure Ryan (eds.) *Routledge Encyclopedia of Narrative Theory* (London: Routledge, 2005), p. 437.

10. Brian Richardson, "Beyond the Poetics of Plot: From *Ulysses* to Postmodern Narrative Progressions." In James Phelan and Peter Rabinowitz (eds.) *A Companion to Narrative Theory* (Oxford: Blackwell, 2005), p. 167.

11. Paul Ricoeur, "Narrative Time." In W. J. T. Mitchell (ed.) *On Narrative* (Chicago: University of Chicago Press, 1981), p. 167.

12. Wolfgang Iser, *The Implied Reader: Patterns of Communication in Prose Fiction from Bunyan to Beckett* (Baltimore: Johns Hopkins University Press, 1974), p. 280.

13. Lubomír Doležel, *Heterocosmica: Fiction and Possible Worlds* (Baltimore: Johns Hopkins University Press, 1998); David Herman, *Story Logic: Problems and Possibilities of Narrative* (Lincoln: University of Nebraska Press, 2002); Alan Palmer, *Fictional Minds* (Lincoln: University of Nebraska Press, 2004); Marie-Laure Ryan, *Possible Worlds, Artificial Intelligence and Narrative Theory* (Bloomington: Indiana University Press, 1991).

14. Meir Sternberg, *Expositional Modes and Temporal Ordering in Fiction* (Baltimore: Johns Hopkins University Press, 1978), pp. 50–1, 228–41.

4

TERESA BRIDGEMAN

Time and space

Temporal and spatial relationships are essential to our understanding of narratives and go beyond the specification of a date and a location.[1] Flaubert's *Madame Bovary*, the illustrative narrative that I shall focus on in this chapter, is set in the mid nineteenth century in Normandy, France.[2] While this information concerning the *when* and *where* of the novel is important to our cultural understanding of the novel and to our response to Emma's actions and emotions, it is only part of a much wider network of temporal and spatial structures. Narratives unfold in time, and the past, present, and future of a given event or action affect our interpretation of that action, while the characters who populate narrative texts move around, inhabit and experience different spaces and locations, allowing readers to construct complex worlds in their minds.

To read a narrative is to engage with an alternative world that has its own temporal and spatial structures.[3] The rules that govern these structures may or may not resemble those of the readers' world. And while readers do not, on the whole, try to map out hierarchical relations between world levels in the way narratologists do, they nevertheless have a sense that narratives can be divided into different temporal and spatial zones. According to the standard protocols of realist narrative, for example, a narrator looking back on her past life cannot step back in time to intervene in events, any more than a protagonist can know what the author does outside the pages of the text. In each case, access from one "world" to another is blocked by their separation in time and space (in the latter case, access may also be prevented by the fictional status of the protagonist). In non-realist texts, of course, the traversing of spatio-temporal barriers is possible, and is indeed a feature of postmodern narratives where the reader's recognition of the transgression is part of the reading experience. For example, in Paul Auster's *City of Glass* a writer called Paul Auster appears in the fictional world of the story.

Time and space are thus more than background elements in narrative; they are part of its fabric, affecting our basic understanding of a narrative text and of the protocols of different narrative genres. They profoundly influence the way in which we build mental images of what we read.

In what follows, I review key concepts of temporality in narrative, as well as research on narrative representations of space. I then show how these concepts work in more detail, anchoring them in illustrative passages from Flaubert's text. Although I separate time and space for the purposes of discussion, their interaction will become increasingly evident, especially in the discussion of *Madame Bovary*. This novel relates Emma Bovary's boredom with her restrictive provincial existence, her disappointment in her marriage to Charles, a medical officer, and her equally disappointing love affairs with Léon, a clerk, and Rodolphe, a local landowner. Emma eventually commits suicide after falling into debt. The novel offers a detailed and ironic portrayal of provincial life where Emma's foolish romantic dreams, although they are exposed, are treated less harshly than the social aspirations and conformity of those around her.

Key concepts of time and space in narrative

Time has always played an important role in theories of narrative, given that we tend to think of stories as sequences of events.[4] Space has often been set in opposition to time, associated with static description which slows up and intrudes into the narration of dynamic events. However, this opposition fails to recognize how far time and space are bound up with each other in narrative, as Bakhtin has shown.[5] As narratology has come to take account of both possible-world theory and the importance of spatial experience to our understanding, greater attention has been paid to the spatial dimensions of narrative, as will be seen.

Approaches to time in narrative

Theorists posit two basic temporalities of narrative which are generally referred to as "story" and "discourse." The essential distinction here is between the "story" as the basic sequence of events that can be abstracted from any narrative telling and the "discourse" as the presentation and reception of these events in linguistic form (in other words, the act of writing resulting in the written text and the act of reading that text).[6] In oral narratives, the two temporalities can be described as the time of what is told (story), and that of the telling (discourse). In written narratives, where we do not have access to the act of writing and where there is usually little in the text to tell us about the time frame of the narrator's performance, it is the time of *reading* which is the important reference time for discourse.[7] The time of reading clearly varies with different readers, but it can be roughly estimated in relation to the space of the text, the number of pages it takes to treat a particular length of story time. The two temporalities of narrative produce a situation in which the experience of narrative is always linked to temporal relationships. In some texts story and discourse times may roughly correspond, but in most texts they will differ in some way or other as will be shown below.

Whatever the temporal patterns set out within fictional worlds – whether they are those of a nineteenth-century novel that moves toward a defined and anticipated ending, or whether they are those of a postmodern narrative, operating by disjunctions, loops, and effacements – it is inescapable that these patterns will be set against the reader's temporal experience of the text, founded on memory and anticipation. And the reader's attempt to relate these two kinds of temporality will be an important part of the effect of the text.

Genette suggests three main areas in which temporal relationships between story and discourse can produce interesting effects. The first relates to the order of events; the second concerns how long events or scenes last; and the third concerns how often an event occurs. They are known respectively as "order", "duration," and "frequency."[8] In some narratives events are told strictly in the order in which they occur. But they may also be told out of order, for example, using flashback to fill in an important part of a character's past, like Emma Bovary's past life at her convent school. Variations in duration can be used to show which scenes are most important. A scene which is narrated briefly will usually be considered less important than a scene which it takes many pages to narrate, such as the ball scene in *Madame Bovary,* which is the closest Emma comes to entering the world of her dreams and is treated extensively. A scene which is narrated more than once may show a narrator's obsession or it may, in a detective story for example, reveal different views of the same events by different characters.

It is important to consider the effects on the reader of temporal patterns. Sternberg is particularly interested in these, suggesting that we should consider the story–discourse relationship in terms of the universals of suspense, curiosity, and surprise, which are generated by the gaps between story time and discourse time (or communicative time).[9] Suspense arises from the gap between what we have been told so far and what we anticipate lies ahead. Curiosity arises from the gap between what we have been told of the past and what else we imagine might have happened. Surprise arises when a twist in the order of narrative conceals from us an event which is subsequently revealed. For Sternberg, "the play of suspense/curiosity/surprise between represented and communicative time" defines narrativity.[10]

Approaches to space in narrative

As Zoran suggests, spatial relationships can be constructed at a basic and relatively stable topographical level, linking objects and locations, but they can also apply to movements of things and people around a narrative world.[11] We can imagine the layout of Emma's house and garden, we know that Yonville is nearer to Rouen than to Paris, and we can also track the movement of characters around these spaces and between locations, imagining Emma's secret meetings with Rodolphe in the garden, and her journeys to Rouen to meet Léon. Objective spatial relationships between aspects of a narrative are helpful in enabling readers to visualize its contents, but equally important, here, is the way in which characters inhabit the space of their world both socially and psychologically.[12] We do not need to know whether the arbor at the bottom of the garden is on the right or the left, nor how many miles it is from Yonville to Paris, but we do need to have a sense that the arbor is not directly visible from the house, enabling it to be appropriated by the lovers, and that Paris is a distant dream for Emma.

Cognitive theorists have proposed that spatial elements of bodily experience (such as up/down, near/far, inside/outside) are very important for our understanding of both the world around us and of more abstract concepts (including time).[13] Dannenberg, in her work on plot, has shown how useful these core concepts can be in analyzing how space is constructed in different narratives from Sidney's *Arcadia* to Byatt's *Possession*.[14] Of particular importance, she suggests, are Johnson's *path* and *container*, and her own additional concept of the *portal* (whether door or window).

We can conceive of plot as a metaphorical network of paths, which either converge or diverge, of goals which are either reached or blocked. More literally, our image of a work can involve the paths of the protagonists around their world, bringing together time and space to shape a plot.[15] Thus Léon's departure to study in Paris prevents his relationship with Emma from developing further, while his return, and the coincidence of their meeting at the opera in Rouen, triggers its resumption and consummation. Sometimes the plot of a narrative may be even more directly associated with a path, as in pilgrimage narratives. The concept of the container is necessary to our understanding of inside and outside. Containers may be rooms, houses, vehicles, or entire cities and are important factors in the three-dimensionality of narrative space. Whole narratives may be constructed on whether protagonists are inside or outside a container, for example narratives of exile and return (where the country is the container). Dannenberg's portal may be a doorway through which characters can enter or exit a room, or it may be a window through which characters can observe or be observed by others in adjacent spaces.[16] In novels of the fantastic, portals between different worlds, such as mirrors, take on particular significance as privileged sites of power.

The idea of perspective, or point of view, in narratology includes indications in the text of both physical angles of view and the subjective attitudes and emotions of individuals; further, the former can often signal the latter. The physical and psychological point of view of different protagonists can be an important structuring device. In *Madame Bovary* it is largely Emma's point of view which is represented, but sometimes the world is portrayed through the eyes of others, in particular her husband Charles. As readers, we, too, may adopt a perspective suggested by the text and this will affect our attitude towards the world.

Last, when considering space in narrative, we should not neglect how useful spatial information is in keeping track of what is going in. Our association of certain locations with the events that occur in them is particularly strong in our reading of narrative. As a basic mechanism of reading, in texts which develop more than one plot-line at once, location allows us to identify rapidly a return to an already-established ongoing scene ("back in Gotham City"). But the locations of a fictional world can also develop in prominence as they accumulate layers of past history against which we read current activities. The arbor at the end of Emma's garden is such a place. First, she and Léon spend time there; it then becomes the emblematic location for her meetings with Rodolphe, reminding readers that he is not her first lover (II.10). Later, Charles dies there (III.11). Our image of him in death is therefore overlaid by our images of Emma's meetings with her lovers.

Changing conceptions of time and space

Different cultural concepts of both time and space and their interrelationships can influence how narrative is constructed and experienced. For example, in Western writing many nineteenth-century narratives, both fictional and historical, show a strong linear drive towards an ending, whereas modernist and postmodernist narratives tend to perturb this focus on an end point. In modernist fiction, of which *Madame Bovary* is an early example, time becomes subject to personal experience, perceptions, and memories. And, as Heise remarks, in postmodernist fiction, the past and the present become subject to the same uncertainty as the future, and without resolution.[17] Space in nineteenth-century realist novels emerges as a concrete and stable phenomenon, while in modernist fiction it is filtered, like time, through the perceptions of protagonists. In postmodernist fiction, the idea of a "world" is itself destabilized, and different spaces multiply and merge.

A closer look at time

The point in the story at which a narrative begins and ends can have a considerable effect on the reader, as Sternberg emphasizes.[18] Beginnings are where we first encounter the narrative world and establish its key characteristics. And endings are where we move towards our final interpretation of the narrative. Rabinowitz calls these "privileged positions."[19] *Madame Bovary* opens with a scene of schoolroom ridicule, not in Emma's life, but in that of her husband, Charles. It ends, not with her death, nor even with that of Charles, but with the award of the highly coveted *Légion d'honneur* to the local pharmacist, Homais. These choices are highly nuanced in their effect on the reader, but it is obvious that both sideline Emma as the eponymous main protagonist. Further, the opening profoundly influences our view of Charles. Had the novel begun with his early childhood we might have developed an empathy with him, despite his emotional and intellectual simplicity, but this opening enduringly establishes him as an object of scorn.

Order

All reading is a combination of memory and anticipation. Our focus on whatever moment in the text we have reached will invariably be colored by our memory of what has gone before and our anticipation of what is to come. The order in which events are presented in the text is therefore crucial to our temporal experience of narrative.

Many narrative texts employ flashback (*analepsis*, in Genette's terms) as a matter of course, in order to fill in the past history of protagonists while avoiding a lengthy introduction or in order to reveal new facts. At the beginning of *Madame Bovary*, after the scene introducing Charles, there is an analeptic summary of his life until that point. Flashback can be more than textual housekeeping, though. For example, Flaubert uses analepsis in *Madame Bovary* to create an ironic gap between Emma's memory of past events within the main narrative (protagonist analepsis) and the reader's own memory of those events. When Emma looks back with nostalgia on her early life (II.10), the reader remembers her incompetence on her father's farm and her desire to escape by marrying Charles. More generally, the experience of reading calls for us to look back and re-evaluate events in light of current circumstances.

Textually explicit flashforward (or *prolepsis*) is far less common than flashback. Explicit flashforward can establish a narrator's mastery of his or her tale or can generate suspense. In *Madame Bovary*, short-term prolepsis between chapters offers anticipation which is quickly satisfied.

Anticipation is not always produced by prolepsis. The reader's anticipation of what will come next, and indeed what will come at the end of a narrative, is an important part of reading and can be a major motivation for engagement with the text. The strongest anticipatory effects of *Madame Bovary* depend on the creation of situations for which the reader can predict unfortunate if not disastrous outcomes, such as the couple's perpetual borrowing from Lheureux. The knowledge that the latter has brought about the financial ruin of Tuvache sets up a pattern of action which allows the reader to anticipate the same outcome for the Bovarys. By using chronological narration rather than flashforward, Flaubert refuses to give readers a glimpse of the Bovarys' future, thereby disallowing a speedy resolution, drawing out the telling, and increasing suspense.[20]

Readers are accustomed to switching to-and-fro between multiple simultaneous plot strands. One of the most famous scenes in *Madame Bovary* is an exercise in simultaneity, where Emma is seduced by Rodolphe in a room overlooking the square in which the prize-giving at an agricultural fair is taking place (II.8). Our desire to know whether Rodolphe will be successful in seducing Emma is frustrated by the narration of long boring speeches from the prize-giving. The climax of Rodolphe's highly clichéd spiel is intercalated line-by-line with the words of the dignitaries, completing the effect of comic deflation. At the other end of the generic spectrum, in adventure narratives, simultaneous plot lines are used to quite different effect, creating suspense as one narrative line is interrupted by another at a crucial moment.

Duration

It would clearly be a very rare thing for the duration of reading to correspond exactly to the putative duration of events in the story (Genette suggests that dialogue comes closest to this).[21] We do, nevertheless, have a strong sense that the relationship of duration between reading and story-time can vary immensely, and the simplest measure of this variation is the number of words, sentences, or pages it takes to recount a given episode. The main categories suggested by narratologists are descriptive pause (maximum textual space, zero story time), slow-down or stretch (textual space greater than story time), scene (textual space equal to story time), summary (textual space less than story time), and ellipsis (zero textual space, variable story time). The treatment of duration is an important way of foregrounding certain events and reducing the status of others. If an episode is narrated in great detail, this leads us to assume that it is of some significance, for example Emma's death scene in *Madame Bovary*. By contrast, the earlier narration of the death of Charles's first wife occurs with what might be seen as unseemly haste:

> A week later, as she was hanging out the washing in the yard, she had a spasm, and spat blood; and on the following day, as Charles was drawing the curtains, his back turned to her, she exclaimed: "Oh, God!" heaved a sigh and fell unconscious. She was dead! It was incredible!
>
> When all was over at the cemetery, Charles returned home.   (32, I.3)

Not only is the period from first signs of illness to death recounted in two sentences (summary), the social ceremonies attendant on death are completely suppressed (ellipsis). Although Charles devotes some kind thoughts to her, her status is nevertheless reduced by the brevity of the narration, and a potentially significant event is thereby downgraded.

Anticipated norms of duration can be flouted, too, by the extended treatment of an element or event which the reader judges to be insignificant, such as the speeches at the agricultural fair. In such cases, suspense and anticipation can be heightened by the sense that minor matters are delaying the forward movement of the action.

Frequency

The number of times an event is narrated can influence the reader's interpretation of a narrative. *Repetition* involves more than one occurrence at the level of discourse of a single story event, while *iteration* involves the single telling of multiple events.[22] In *Madame Bovary* we have seen how repetition can be associated with the memories of a protagonist as Emma looks back on her past life. Repetition also undermines dramatic impact in Flaubert's use of summary followed by scene. Such events as the wedding and Emma's trip to Rouen with Léon which, through their nature, are logical climaxes in the story, are told twice, the summary serving to deflate and detract from the impact of the subsequent scene, just as a punch-line delivered a second too early detracts from the impact of a joke. Repetition can be used to portray more than one view of events in epistolary novels (i.e., novels told via exchanges of letters between characters), and in modernist stream-of-consciousness novels. In the French *nouveau roman*, events, scenes, and fragments of scenes are repeated in different configurations to far more unsettling effect as the repetitions cannot be attributed to the perceiving eye of a particular protagonist or group of protagonists.

In *Madame Bovary*, the repetitive nature of Emma's life is underlined by the extensive use of iteration, in which repeated actions in the story occur only once in the discourse. This technique is even applied to her two love affairs. For example, Emma's relationship with Léon is not narrated as a sequence of individual and unforgettable moments, but as a set of habitual actions which occur every Thursday (III.5), emphasizing its banality.[23]

A closer look at space

This section first looks at what might be termed measurable and geometric features of the narrative world, while demonstrating how these relate to human experience of that world. It then looks more specifically at how the reader can be positioned in the narrative world.

Dimensions, paths, portals, and containers

The dimensions of narrative worlds can vary. They can range from a single dark space (Beckett *The Unnameable*) to a set of multi-world parallel universes (science-fiction fantasy). The scope of the world can contribute strongly to the effects of a text. Emma feels trapped because the furthest she can escape from Yonville is to the county town of Rouen while she dreams of Paris, Switzerland, and Italy. By contrast, the limits of Charles's personal horizon do not stretch beyond local villages and towns: "He'd be laughed at, talked about! It would spread to Forges, to Neufchâtel, Rouen, everywhere" (196, II.11). It is Emma's lovers, not her husband, who go to Paris.

Proximity and distance between landmarks or humans can be expressed in neutral topographical terms. But their narrative interest lies in their role in indicating how people experience their world. For example, as Emma becomes conscious of her interest in Léon, her acute sensitivity to him is expressed by her attunement to his presence at the limits of her perception. Thus, her heightened awareness of him passing her window (II.4) is expressed through what she can and cannot hear and see: "Twice a day Léon went past from his office to the Golden Lion. Emma heard his step some way off and leaned forward listening; and the young man glided by behind the curtains, always dressed the same, and never turning his head" (110)

The path taken by Emma to La Huchette to meet her lover Rodolphe is described twice in the novel.

> . . . soon she was half-way across the meadow, hurrying along with never a glance behind her.
>
> . . .
>
> Beyond the farmyard was a large building that must be the château itself. She glided in as though the walls had parted magically at her approach. A big

straight staircase led up to a corridor. Emma lifted a door-latch and at once picked out a man's form asleep on the far side of the room. It was Rodolphe. She gave a cry . . .   (176, II.9)

When the cow-plank was not in place, she had to make her way along by the garden-walls beside the river. The bank was slippery and she clung to the tufts of withered wallflowers to prevent herself from falling. Then she struck across ploughed fields, sinking in, floundering, getting her thin shoes clogged with mud . . .   (176–7)

There is a strong contrast in the treatment of Emma's paths. The first follows the principle of the idealized fairy-story approach to an enchanted castle by a favored protagonist. Her orientation is forward, the physical environment parts before her, the staircase is straight and movement is fast and unimpeded. The second represents a quite different situation – she follows an indirect route and physical obstacles produce sideways and downward movements that slow her progress. The contrast between Emma's fantasies and the reality of her life is here expressed in almost entirely spatial terms.

Spatial containment is often associated with the partial access represented by windows in *Madame Bovary*. Both Emma and Charles appear by windows to dream of the places and people beyond them, while the walls of Emma's house serve as the barrier she needs to dream without reality intruding.

The agricultural fair scene, already discussed in relation to time, exploits adjacent spaces with partial access between the bounded space of the room and the open space of the fair. It ends with a shift to the outside, leaving the reader ignorant of the end of the scene between Emma and Rodolphe. Exclusion from a contained space is exploited even more fully in the famous cab scene, where Emma and Léon (we assume) make love as their cab moves around the streets of Rouen. In place of a description of their sexual encounter (made impossible on the grounds of decency), we are presented with a highly detailed topographical account of their route round Rouen. The complete mismatch between external and internal activity produces a comic effect of irony while enabling Flaubert to remain within the proprieties required by nineteenth-century society (although this did not prevent the removal of this passage from the text of the serial publication of the novel in the *Revue de Paris* in 1856).

Such exclusions and inclusions often relate to distinctions between public and private spaces and the manner in which such spaces are constructed and occupied by the protagonists can be revealing. In *Madame Bovary* the deteriorating relationship between the Homais and Bovary households is expressed through the degree of access to each other's private space. At first, the relationship is one of mutual access. Homais invades the Bovary house at all times of the day and evening, while Emma enters Homais's inner sanctum to take the arsenic which kills her. However, after Emma's death, Homais no longer allows his children to play with Berthe Bovary and the two houses are represented as divided by the public space of the street (III.11). This physical opposition rhetorically underlines the contrasts in the fortunes of the two families at the end of the book.

Space, the reader's position, and focalization

In our own worlds, we are physically confined to our bodily experience of the world, but we have the ability to shift this experiencing center to imagine ourselves in other people's places, and in other locations. This ability is constantly utilized in the immersive activity of reading narrative fiction as we shift conceptually from our own reader-centered position to locations in the storyworld. This resembles the changes in camera angle and zoom in cinema, except that the latter must always be explicit, while not all reader positions are clearly cued in a written text.

Fludernik discusses how the spatial indicators of texts can set up an empty space, or "camera position," for the reader.[24] This may coincide with a protagonist's point of vision; it may offer a panoramic panning shot; or something in between. We can have a bird's-eye view or a worm's-eye view; we can find ourselves stationary or in motion; we can be directed along paths followed by a protagonist, as in Emma's visits to La Huchette discussed above, but we can also follow paths around a narrative world with no protagonist present. This is what happens, for example, in the description of Yonville which opens Part II, in which there is no perceiving protagonist to go down the hill with the reader.

When we see through the eyes of a protagonist (who thereby becomes the "focalizer"), his or her location becomes the center of experience. In *Madame Bovary*, surprisingly, Emma does not become the experiencing center until after her wedding but is viewed from the outside by other protagonists. Even when we gain access to her perceptions and thoughts we still often see her from the outside, especially in seduction scenes where her body is described. This restriction of access to her internal states leaves the reader distanced from her emotionally at these moments.

Spatial indicators can indicate a shift in conceptual space from the main storyworld to a sub-world (such as a protagonist's mind). This is often linked to the direction of a protagonist's gaze. Here is a passage which occurs shortly after Emma has realized that she is in love with Léon:

Emma was on his arm, leaning lightly against his shoulder, watching the sun's disc diffusing its pale brilliance through the mist. She turned [her head] round: there stood Charles, his cap pulled down over his eyes, his thick lips trembling, which lent an added stupidity to his face. (114, II.5)[25]

Here, the opening of the first sentence is external narratorial description. The move towards protagonist perception is signalled by "watching" and reinforced by "She turned [her head] round," denoting a shift in the orientation of her gaze. The reader's position shifts from an external view of Emma to a "seeing with" her. In this process, the spatialized indicators of a shift in the experiencing center have an important effect on our interpretation of the text, allowing us to read the critical judgments of Charles in the second sentence as Emma's.

Conclusion: the functions of time and space

On the basis of the above discussion, we can conclude that time and space affect reading at different levels. First, the process of reading is itself a temporally situated experience of the physical space of the text. Although we may temporarily suspend our engagement with our own world while reading, the temporal dimension of reading remains significant, as does the space of the page as the means by which order, frequency, and duration are regulated. Second, time and space are components of the basic conceptual framework for the construction of the narrative world. Much of this chapter has been devoted to demonstrating the mechanisms by which the temporal and spatial aspects of this world can be constructed. While any worlds we construct when reading are only partial worlds, not fully defined in either spatial or temporal terms, they still require a minimal level of spatio-temporal stability. And although postmodern narrative worlds may become quite ragged at the edges and may lose their overall logic of either time or space (but rarely both at once), I would strongly argue that, as readers, we nevertheless continue to require spatio-temporal hooks on which to hang our interpretations. If these are not consistently provided or their uncertainty is highlighted in a given narrative, we experience disorientation and a degree of unease as an essential part of our engagement with that narrative. Third, our immersive experience of narrative has temporal and spatial dimensions.[26] Our emotional engagement with narrative is often linked to temporal parameters (boredom, suspense) or spatial parameters (security, claustrophobia, fear of the unknown), often through empathy with a protagonist's experience of his or her world. Last, our interpretation of narratives, their point, is influenced by temporal and spatial information, both at a local level, and in our overall construction of plot as a mapping in time and space. Our sense of climax and resolution, of complications and resolutions, the metaphors we use for the paths taken by plots are constructed on spatio-temporal patterns. Our awareness as readers of time and space at these four levels is neither equal nor constant. Genres partly determine which level or specific aspect is in focus, but each narrative will have its own internal patterns which foreground certain aspects of time–space. The profile thereby created is a complex structure which is part of our sense of the identity of a given narrative, of what makes it unique.

This chapter has been about written fictional narrative, but many of the complexities in the representation of time and space it has described are to be found in the narratives we tell ourselves and others about our lives, influencing our perceptions of the world and, indeed, our experience of time and space themselves.

NOTES

1. The focus of this chapter is on written narratives. The dynamics of oral narratives, to which I refer where relevant, differ in several respects from these.
2. Quotations are from Gustave Flaubert, *Madame Bovary*. Translated by Alan Russell (London: Penguin, 1950 and all subsequent editions). Part and chapter numbers are indicated for ease of reference to other editions.
3. See Marie-Laure Ryan, *Possible Worlds, Artificial Intelligence, and Narrative Theory* (Bloomington: Indiana University Press, 1991) and Paul Werth, *Text Worlds: Representing Conceptual Space in Discourse* (London: Longman, 1999) for different approaches to fictional-world theory.
4. See E. M. Forster, *Aspects of the Novel* (New York: Harcourt Brace Jovanovich, 1927) and Gerald Prince, *Narratology: The Form and Functioning of Narrative* (Berlin: Mouton, 1982).
5. Mikhail Bakhtin, "Forms of Time and of the Chronotope in the Novel: Notes Towards a Historical Poetics." In Michael Holquist (ed.) *The Dialogic Imagination*. Translated by Caryl Emerson and Michael Holquist (Austin: University of Texas Press, 1981), pp. 84–258. For criticisms of the time/space opposition see Gabriel Zoran, "Towards a Theory of Space in Narrative." *Poetics Today* 5:2 (1984), pp. 309–35, and David Herman, *Story Logic: Problems and Possibilities of Narrative* (Lincoln: University of Nebraska Press, 2002), pp. 266–7 and 298.
6. "Discourse" is a much-used word in cultural and critical theory. In linguistics it refers to interactions in language between language-users. In the story/discourse pair of narratology it refers to the particular "putting into language" of a non-linguistic sequence of events. Film adaptations of books are different discourse representations of what is, supposedly, the same story.
7. For written narrative, "discourse time" is thus the time in which the reader engages with the text (interacts with it), and the "discourse world" is the spatio-temporal domain in which writing and reading occurs (language-use takes place).

8. Gérard Genette, *Narrative Discourse. An Essay in Method*. Translated by Jane E. Lewin (Ithaca: Cornell University Press, 1980).
9. See Meir Sternberg, "Universals of Narrative and their Cognitivist Fortunes (I)," *Poetics Today* 24:2 (2003), pp. 326–8, for a summary.
10. Sternberg, "Universals," p. 328.
11. Zoran, "Towards a Theory of Space in Narrative," pp. 315–19.
12. On the social construction of space, see Michel de Certeau, *The Practice of Everyday Life*. Translated by Steven Rendall (Berkeley: University of California Press, 1988).
13. See, for example, Mark Johnson, *The Body in the Mind: The Bodily Basis of Meaning, Imagination, and Reason* (Chicago: University of Chicago Press, 1987).
14. Hilary Dannenberg, *Convergent and Divergent Lives: Plotting Coincidence and Counterfactuality in Narrative Fiction* (Lincoln: University of Nebraska Press, forthcoming), chapter 3.
15. For approaches to narrative founded on the combination of time and space see Bakhtin, "Forms of Time and of the Chronotope in the Novel," and Mike Baynham, "Narratives in Space and Time: Beyond 'Backdrop' Accounts of Narrative Orientation." *Narrative Inquiry* 13:2 (2003), pp. 347–66.
16. Dannenberg, *Convergent and Divergent Lives*, chapter 3.
17. Ursula K. Heise, *Chronoschisms: Time, Narrative and Postmodernism* (Cambridge: Cambridge University Press, 1997), p. 64. See also Brian Richardson, "Beyond Story and Discourse: Narrative Time in Postmodern and Nonmimetic Fiction." In Brian Richardson (ed.) *Narrative Dynamics: Essays on Time, Plot, Closure, and Frames* (Columbus: Ohio State University Press, 2002), pp. 47–63.
18. Meir Sternberg, "Telling in Time (I): Chronology and Narrative Theory." *Poetics Today* 11:4 (1990), pp. 929–32.
19. Peter Rabinowitz, "Reading Beginnings and Endings." In Brian Richardson (ed.) *Narrative Dynamics: Essays on Time, Plot, Closure, and Frames* (Columbus: Ohio State University Press, 2002), pp. 300–3.
20. See Sternberg, "Telling in Time (I)," for a defence and discussion of the matching of story and discourse orders.
21. Genette, *Narrative Discourse*, p. 87.
22. Genette, *Narrative Discourse*, pp. 113–17.
23. Achieved in French through the use of the imperfect tense. On tense in narrative see Suzanne Fleischman, *Tense and Narrativity: From Medieval Performance to Modern Fiction* (London: Routledge, 1990).
24. Monika Fludernik, *Towards a "Natural" Narratology* (London: Routledge, 1996), pp. 192–201.
25. The English translation omits "her head," which in the original makes the direction of Emma's gaze more explicit.
26. See Marie-Laure Ryan, *Narrative as Virtual Reality: Immersion and Interactivity in Literature and Electronic Media* (Baltimore: Johns Hopkins University Press, 2001).

5

URI MARGOLIN

Character

In the widest sense, "character" designates any entity, individual or collective – normally human or human-like – introduced in a work of narrative fiction. Characters thus exist within storyworlds, and play a role, no matter how minor, in one or more of the states of affairs or events told about in the narrative. Character can be succinctly defined as storyworld participant.

Now, for its part, the storyworld itself divides into the spheres of narration and of the narrated, the telling and what is told about. "Character" in the narrower sense is restricted to participants in the narrated domain, the narrative agents. Characters are introduced in the text by means of three kinds of referring expressions: proper names (including letters and numbers), such as *Don Quixote*; definite descriptions, such as *the knight of mournful countenance*; and personal pronouns (*I, she*). Names and definite descriptions occurring in a given work often originate with it, hence introducing original fictions, or occur already in earlier works by the same author or by others, thereby yielding new versions of the original fiction, or pick out an actual person, thus yielding a literary, sometimes highly fictionalized, version of the real individual.

Characters can be approached from different theoretical perspectives, each yielding a different conception and theory of character. In this chapter, we will concern ourselves with three major ones: character as literary figure, that is, an artistic product or artifice constructed by an author for some purpose; character as non-actual but well-specified individual presumed to exist in some hypothetical, fictional domain – in other words, character as an individual within a possible world; and character as text-based construct or mental image in the reader's mind. Throughout the chapter, Cervantes's *Don Quixote* will serve as our source of illustrations.[1] This classical Spanish novel (published in two parts, in 1605 and 1615, respectively) is the story of a middle-aged impoverished country squire who has been spending all his time reading chivalric romances about the feats of knights errant. He takes it into his head to go into the world as one, achieve fame and glory through adventures, including fighting magicians and monsters, and win the love of a beautiful damsel. But the reality around him is of course quite different, so the novel as a whole becomes the story of the constant conflict between imagination and reality and its consequences, sometimes funny and sometimes moving.

Character as artifice

Don Quixote did not exist before Cervantes invented him; he is precisely the way his author presents him, and could easily have been otherwise. He was born when the text bearing his name was written down, and will go on living as long as at least one copy of it remains and at least one person reads it. And where and how does he exist? In the sphere of our individual imagination as an object of thought, and in the sphere of public communication as an object of discourse. Such, informally, are some of the basic tenets of this approach to character, rooted in contemporary aesthetic theory. Technically speaking, character can be defined from this perspective as a contingently created, abstract cultural entity, depending essentially for its existence on actual objects in space and time and on the intellectual activity of authors and readers.[2] On this view, characters are invented or stipulated by a human mind, and generated in particular cultural and historical circumstances through the use of language, following certain literary-artistic conventions. They are ultimately semiotic constructs or creatures of the word, and it is the socially and culturally defined act of fictional storytelling that constitutes and defines them.[3]

Texts are necessary for characters to exist and subsist; individual minds are needed to actualize them; and the end result is a relatively stable and enduring inter-subjective entity which can be the subject of legitimate public argument about its properties, for example, Quixote as mad, naïve, an idealist, etc.[4] We would thus all agree that, for Quixote to exist in our culture, the text of the novel needs to be available to, and actually read by, people in a given community. These readers then form in their minds text-based images of the Don, which they make available to others by talking or writing about him. The members of the community know they are all talking about the same individual, and when they compare their individual mental images of him they would usually agree about some of his features, thus forming a public image or notion of Quixote that does not depend on any one reader. Accordingly, while literary characters depend for their existence on both physical objects (texts) and individual states of mind, they are not reducible to or identifiable with either.

Characters are abstract in the sense that they do not exist in real space and time, and are more like concepts in this regard. Consequently they are not open to direct perception by us, and can be known only through textual descriptions or inferences based on those descriptions. In fact, they *are* these complexes of descriptions, not having any independent worldly existence. And in order to find out what properties a given character possesses or what claims about him are true, there is only one route to follow: examine the originating text, what is explicitly stated in it and what can be inferred from it according to standard procedures. Since characters are stipulated ("created," "invented"), it makes no sense to ask of their authors how they know that a character is thus and so, or to disagree with them about the makeup of any character. By writing their narratives, authors determine rather than describe the properties of their characters. The semantics of fiction is thus of the say-so variety. X is the case because the text says so.

In fact, the properties ascribed to characters need not even form a logically consistent set, let alone one conforming to actual world regularities. In Voltaire's *Candide* (1759) for example, characters are repeatedly killed off and brought back to life to illustrate various philosophical points raised by the author. While authors can assign their characters any properties they wish, in practice the properties authors assign to their characters are governed by some principle(s) of selection, ranging from lifelikeness (verisimilitude) to an ideological, thematic, aesthetic, or purely inter-literary one, e.g., parody of an earlier text and its characters. The latter is exactly what happens in *Don Quixote*, where the language, actions, and worldview of the chivalric romances are ridiculed and deflated when the Don tries to embody them in the actual world. Since characters are shaped by their authors to attain certain ends and effects, it makes perfect sense to inquire why and to what end they endowed their characters with this particular selection of features.

All texts are finite, while each entity can be specified with respect to an indefinite number of aspects. Consequently, textually created characters are radically incomplete as regards the number and nature of the properties ascribed to them. Generally, which (kinds of) properties are specified or not and how many are a function of the text's length and of the author's artistic method. Some authors are sparing on physical details, while others provide no access to characters' minds. Characters are also usually temporally limited (when we first meet the Don he is already middle aged), and discontinuous, in that not every minute or even year of their lives is presented in the text. Characters are thus partially indeterminate (schematic, not fully individuated), and are technically person-kinds who can be filled in (specified, concretized) in various ways and to different degrees. This is exactly what is being done in literary character analyses, whether undertaken by students or specialists.

Thus any given character may be amenable to a whole range of alternative individuations, all of which are none the less compatible with the original. This one-to-many relation is simultaneously a major source of readerly imaginative re-creation and of endless interpretive controversy. While the stipulative, say-so semantics of character creation may be limited with respect to the amount of information it can provide, it is, by contrast, unrestricted with respect to its nature – hence the incredible variety in the selection and combination of properties one encounters in literary characters such as Don Quixote. In particular, one of the constitutive conventions of literary storytelling provides the option of authoritative portrayal, sometimes in the most direct way, of the working of other minds. The wide use of this totally unnatural access to other minds is one of the hallmarks of literary versus factual modes of characterization, and a major source of readerly interest in, and learning from, what are ultimately "paper people."

Further, literary figures, no less than actual people, beget other people and belong to groups or types. In this case, however, both begetting and affiliation are of course purely verbal and must be mediated through texts created by authors. We have already mentioned that figures with the same name often occur in several texts, by the same or by different authors. Such a succession of same-name figures may extend over centuries, as with Quixote. Viewing characters as historical cultural products, what can we say about the relation between the same-name figures in different texts? Are they the same one, variations on the same, or different alternative versions of the same?

From the perspective of artistic production, a genetic connection between originating and later text(s) is the crucial point. The later text(s) and the original one must be related to each other both historically and intentionally. The author of the later text must be acquainted with the characters in the earlier one, must intend to import one or more of them into his own storyworld, and must intend his readers to recognize their original version. A sequel to *Quixote Part I* (1605) published in 1614 by an anonymous author calling himself "Avellaneda" satisfies all of these conditions. As far as the character's properties are concerned, the original set may be supplemented, reduced, rearranged in terms of relative prominence, or modified, sometimes leading to complete inversion of the original, as when its key features are replaced by their opposites. One amusing example is Byron's *Don Juan* (1824), in which the traditional irresistible and unscrupulous seducer is turned into a shy young man seduced by women. But the shaping principle is always the same: continuity of source, and portrayal in light of the source.

Can the reader carry over the description of a literary figure from one text to another? Can we unite the descriptions of the same-named character in different texts by the same author or by different ones in order to get the complete story of X? While merging information from different texts about an actual individual – who obviously leads a text-independent life – is unproblematic as long as the details are compatible, there is no clear answer when literary figures are involved. One could claim that literary characters are text-bound and cannot be detached from the text or storyworld(s) in which they occur – that they cannot be exported across text and world boundaries. Others would claim, like Cervantes himself, that, as long as texts by the same author are concerned, this is legitimate. And indeed we do so as readers with respect to recurring characters, such as Quixote in parts I and II, or Harry Potter. Quixote in part II, for example, is much less of a fool and more of a reflective and pensive character who speaks eloquently about literature and education and who at the very end renounces the whole chivalric ideal as pernicious nonsense and dies a good Christian. Still others would point out to the undeniable historical process where inter-textual accretion, encompassing numerous works and authors, sometimes leads to the formation in our cultural encyclopedia of a "super" or "mega" character, a generalized literary figure such as Quixote, Faust, or Don Juan, which both synthesizes and transcends any individual figure of this name. Such stereotypes are based on the existence of a set of core properties ascribed to the figure in all of the works in which it occurs and considered essential to it, the sense of its proper name so to speak. In this perspective, the various individual Quixotes are alternative elaborations of one common core.

Finally, most literary traditions and genres have developed a whole array of literary types, that is, limited, fixed sets of co–occurring properties, which can be exemplified with additions and variations by numerous individual figures. To these belong damsels in distress, magicians, picaros, hapless lovers (all of whom occur in *Quixote*, if only in the Don's mind), and many more. In fact, narrative genres are defined in part by their particular stock of such underlying types. Another example would be the detective story with its shrewd private investigator, his sidekick, and the bumbling police inspector.

Character as non-actual individual

The foregoing deflationary view of character as simply a verbal artistic product, a paper person fashioned forth in some artistic-historical context, while probably being the closest to the facts of the actual world, is very different from the way we act when we get lost in a book or immerse ourselves in the world of a work of fiction. As readers, we find it perfectly natural and intelligible to discuss the time and space of Quixote's peregrinations around Spain, we speak unhesitatingly of his looks and behavior, his state of mind, and the radical change in it shortly before his death, all as if he himself and his setting led a text-independent existence. We are willingly engaging in a game of make-believe in which we pretend that there is a spatio-temporal domain in which the Don and his "world mates" exist and act independently of and prior to any narrative about them; that the proper names *Don Quixote*, *Sancho Panza*, and many others do refer to or pick out specific individuals in this domain, while *Dulcinea del Toboso* does not; that some of the claims made by the narrator and the individuals he speaks about are true *tout court* while others are not – in a word, that we are reading a report about what independently and "actually" exists and happens in some domain.

From this standpoint, character can be understood as an individual existing in some world or set of worlds, both individual and world being very close or very far from the actual world in terms of properties and regularities. To the shift in perspective there now corresponds a shift in the kind of issues considered central or crucial. These issues now center on the basic conditions of existence, identity and survival (continuity, sameness) of an individual in a hypothetical domain (= fictional world). In turn, contemporary modal logic, and especially possible-worlds semantics, provide the theoretical foundation for this kind of inquiry. Modal logic is basically the study of what is to be considered possible or necessary in some world; while possible-world semantics is the study of alternative worlds, their governing laws, and the kinds of individuals inhabiting them.

Existence

Once a storyworld is established, one needs to map out its inhabitants by answering the questions who/what exists in this world, and in what mode. Any entity can exist in the fact domain of the storyworld (= the set of facts that make it up) or in any of its subdomains: the beliefs, wishes, intentions, and imaginations of one or more characters, or in a secondary embedded world projected by stories the characters read, plays they watch, etc.[5] In addition, characters form in their minds mental versions of other characters who, like them, exist in the fact domain. The total population of a narrative universe consists of *all* of the above. But how do we know in what sphere(s) a given individual exists, and especially whether s/he exists in the basic fact domain? Ultimately, it is only the authoritative discourse of an omniscient, usually impersonal, narrating voice which can answer this question. If stories are told by a personalized narrator or focalized through characters, some hesitation may remain as to the status of a particular individual. But impersonal narrators too can achieve the same effect by qualifying their existence claims to read "X may have existed" or "some say that X existed." In some postmodern narratives narrators go one step further by first asserting the existence of a given individual in the fact domain and then denying it.

(Lack of) overlap between characters' mental images of the storyworld and its existents and the narrative facts crucially influences the dynamics of the action and its consequences. Evil enchanters exist in the fact domain of the storyworlds portrayed in the chivalric romances Quixote is obsessively reading. The Don believes they exist in his own lifeworld as well, and sets out to fight them. But such agents do not exist in the belief worlds of his world mates, nor in the fact domain as established by the narrator. Sometimes individuals do exist in the fact domain, but their version in the mind of a character is wrong. An unattractive peasant woman by the name of Alonza Lorenzo does exist in Quixote's world, but the Don, needing a lady to adore, represents her in his mind as the beautiful lady Dulcinea. And a belief in some non-existent individual may start from a mere name, and then spread in a community and influence people's behavior. In Iurii Tynianov's story "Lieutenant Salso" (1924), a scribal error, "lieutenant salso" instead of "lieutenants also," creates a non-referring proper name. But people, starting with the Czar himself, begin to believe in the existence of such an individual and this in turn influences their behavior, including devising more and more properties and events for him, building a life story out of thin air.

Identity

Under this term we subsume three questions: what is the given individual like? (possession of properties, predication); what distinguishes it from all other coexisting individuals (singularity, uniqueness, differentiation); what kind of an individual is it (type or category membership, classification).

1. To establish the mere existence of an individual in a storyworld is a necessary but not sufficient condition for its being a full-fledged character, because at this point there is nothing as yet we can say about it. To this end, *individuation*, or the ascription of properties to an individual picked out by a referring expression, is essential. For the purposes of literary analysis it is useful to group the kinds of properties a character can possess into several dimensions: physical; behavioral (action-related) and communicative; and mental, with the latter being further subdivided into perceptual, emotive, volitional, and cognitive. "Character" in the everyday sense refers to one segment of the mental dimension: enduring traits and dispositions to action, in a word, personality. But this is *never* the only aspect of a character's set

of properties, and often is not even the most significant. Quixote's looks, behavior, and modes of communication, for example, are far more significant than any personality model one could attribute to him. The prototypical literary character is an entity with human-like exteriority and internal mental states defined by current cultural concepts. Both exterior and interior components admit of transitory states as well as enduring properties, with the exterior being perceptible by co-agents, while the interior realm is accessible to narrators only, if at all. In fictional worlds, characters can possess any selection and combination of properties one can dream up – not at random, though. The kinds of properties from the three basic dimensions and their combinations any character can possess are constrained in the first instance by what is possible in the given storyworld and, within these constraints, by the individual's role in the story. Some storyworlds, like the Greek epics, possess a dual ontology, whereby the two zones, human and divine, are governed by radically different rules of possibility and probability, and hence are inhabited by individuals with radically different properties (immortality, knowledge of the future, etc.).

Even though we assume in our game of make-believe that non-actual individuals are as complete in their world as we are in ours, only a limited subset of their properties can ever be specified. Since stories by definition involve change, at least some of these known properties of any character are not enduring but time-bound, and the character's total property set inevitably gets modified over time. The standard distinction between static and dynamic characters is based on the (non-)occurrence of major changes in a character's central psychological features. How many and what kinds of properties of an individual need to stay constant to preserve individual identity is once again a function of the nature of the storyworld. As with existence claims, so with predications: only individuation claims made by an authoritative narrating voice are universally valid, and they too can be weakened by modifying them as "possibly" or through an ironic tone.

Endowing a character with simultaneous incompatible properties (tall and short, young and old) turns him into a bundle of mutually exclusive strands which cannot be jointly realized in any narrative universe. Such are the impossible characters of postmodern narrative. Notice also that when one character ascribes properties to another, he himself gets automatically characterized in the process, say as perceptive or obtuse, reliable or not. One of the ways we infer that Quixote's grasp of reality is distorted is through his characterization of the people around him, for example seeing a group of prostitutes as "fair maidens" (I. 3). The ascription of properties, enduring or temporary, to a character yields a cluster of features attached to this existent. But characters seldom exist in isolation in storyworlds, and in addition to being individuated they also need to be differentiated from one another. This leads us directly to the next issue, that of *singularity* or *uniqueness*.

2. How many qualitatively different individuals are there in a given story state, and who is who? To be able to answer these questions unambiguously, any two coexisting characters must differ in at least one property, including the presence of a property in one and its absence in the other. In the case of clones and the like, the only difference would be location in space and time. Science fiction likes to play with such problematic cases, employing both fantasy (teleporting, brain or mind contents transfer), and bizarre natural phenomena such as the bisected brain, where the number of individuals involved depends on the choice of the mental or physical criterion. Further distinctions would be along one or more of the basic dimensions. A situation one often encounters in fiction is that of physical indistinguishability between two individuals coupled with sharp mental or moral contrast (see, for example, Edgar Allan Poe's 1840 short story "Roderick Wilson"). But mental difference is directly accessible to the narrator only, while characters must identify one another by appearance, thereby leading to potential confusion and mistaken identification. Sharp contrast along all three dimensions leads to maximum distinctness and contrast, embodied for example in the traditional comical pair aptly used by Cervantes: the short, fat, happy, and folksy Sancho; and the tall, gaunt, melancholy Don, with his aspirations to nobility and refinement.

3. Once we have established a list of properties for a given character, our next task consists in establishing a general macro-structure or intelligible pattern that will order these properties into a coherent whole. We are, in other words, looking for a general class under which this individual can be subsumed. Such classes are the basis for a system of *categorization* which will enable us to map out the total landscape of the storyworld in terms of the kinds of entities it contains. Obviously, different aspects can serve as a basis for a system of classification, and different aspects will be significant for different kinds of storyworlds. Intuitively speaking, the species category seems to be most basic, as it seems to answer in a fundamental way the question "what kind of individual is it?" on the physical, behavioral, and mental levels simultaneously. Evidently, different storyworlds (science fiction, fantasy, realistic novel) will contain a different assortment of species, which, in some cases, may be quite different from our contemporary actual-world species spectrum. But no matter what the assortment is, a character will always be foregrounded and its category affiliation problematic if it possesses features belonging to different (orders of) species, such as human and animal/vegetable/machine. The problem becomes insurmountable when such a hybrid individual occurs in a realistic setting – which in principle

does not admit the possibility of crossing species boundaries – as in Kafka's stories "Metamorphosis" (1912) and "A Hybrid" (1917).

Beyond the fundamental species categorization, various biological (gender, age), cultural (ethnic), social, actional, and psychological categories can be employed. The most informative or significant dimension of categorization will clearly depend in each case on the key issues or concerns of the narrative world. In *Don Quixote*, for example, social class, especially nobility versus commoner, is a major consideration, as are intellectual and literary attitudes, which in turn determine the characters' systems of values and norms of conduct.

Sameness over time and across storyworlds

The kind and extent of change characters can undergo along any dimension are once again unrestricted in principle, and vastly different in different storyworlds. How much can a character change and still remain the same individual? And who decides and according to what criteria? Very little can be said here that is universally valid. The narrating voice indicates a judgment of sameness in the midst of change by maintaining the same proper name or referring expression for a given individual, and this decision can be supported by the mere fact of the narrator being able to trace a continuous path in space and time for this individual. Normally, characters will identify themselves from the inside (the mental dimension), so that as long as they preserve their memory of past experiences they will think of themselves as the same continuing individual, even if their body is radically transformed. This applies, for example, to all metamorphosis stories from Ovid to Kafka. Their world mates, on the other hand, are limited to judgment on the basis of physical, behavioral, and communicative features, so that a radical change along these lines will lead to the denial of individual continuity/sameness. Dante's characters in the *Inferno* thus judge themselves the same in spite of the incredible change in their body shape and material, which prevents Dante the traveler from recognizing them as the continuants of any this-worldly individual. Conversely, a character with amnesia cannot establish continuity with any previous person stage, while to his world mates his sameness is assured because of physical continuity. Hence decisions about what constitutes sameness of character provide a major source of narrative interest and reader engagement.

Can the same individual exist in different fictional worlds, or is it one version per world, or are there rather one original individual and his counterparts in other worlds? The last view seems the most sensible. According to this view, sameness cannot extend across worlds, but an individual in world B may well be the counterpart in that world of his original name-sake in world A, provided certain conditions of similarity are satisfied. Such conditions would involve key classificatory properties as well as the charac-ter's role in the dynamics of the events. As long as Quixote in any world is an older impoverished country squire who fancies himself a knight errant and who is constantly looking for adventurous engagements, it seems quite natural to consider him a counterpart of the original individual inhabiting the world created by Cervantes. Variation is thus accommodated, but only as long as specific key elements of the original are preserved.

Character as readerly mental construct

Whether characters are considered artifacts or non-actual individuals, we must first form mental images of them in order to be able to make claims about them. The cognitive-psychological approach views characters as just that: text-based mental models of possible individuals, built up in the mind of the reader in the course of textual processing. More precisely, characters are conceptualized here as complex readerly mental representations (con-structs, portraits, mental files). This approach, unlike the previous two, is concerned not so much with the validity and specific nature of any given mental representation but rather with its textual base (cues, sources), the operations involved in its formation, the principles (rules, regularities) gov-erning or guiding these operations, and the architecture of the final construct. Dealing with actual readers and reading, many of the claims made within this framework are at least in principle open to empirical testing. Reading a narrative text is (can be) understood as a complex, multistage activity of information processing, starting with the words on the page and yielding as its final product a representation in our mind of the basic components of the storyworld, in our case character. Reading for character is triggered or initiated by the reader identifying in the text a referring expression and open-ing a mental file bearing this name in which all further information about the corresponding individual will be continuously accumulated, structured, and updated as one reads on, until the final product or character profile is reached at the end of the reading act.

The most basic *operation* of character construction is the formulation by the reader of a text-based, first-order characterization statement ascribing a property of some kind to a character. Direct characterization is a one-step operation, while indirect characterization is multistage. A property (usually mental) is in that case indirectly ascribed to a character as the result of a process of inference starting with a property (usually physical or behav-ioral) directly ascribed to him. Watching a Western (cowboy) movie we can characterize a certain individual directly as wearing a black hat and sporting a facial scar because we perceive these features. On the basis of these perceived features (and a genre convention), we then infer moral attributes and characterize this individual indirectly as a villain.

The *textual database* for reader-formulated characterization statements of either kind is wide and varied. In the first place, literary narrative abounds in direct as well as indirect characterization statements of all kinds (mental, behavioral, etc.) made by narrators and characters about themselves and/or others. The narrator characterizes the Don in detail, the Don does the same, and everybody around him is engaged in drawing conclusions about his mental state from his speech and conduct. But such statements cannot be taken over by the reader as valid and directly incorporated into his or her profile of Quixote. They are just a set of data, which needs to be critically evaluated. It is only through a complex process of computation that the reader can decide which of these claims she will endorse and use in her own character construction of Quixote. As already mentioned, a basic literary convention endows the claims of an impersonal omniscient narrating voice with truth by fiat, while all claims from other sources are fallible. And we also recall that whenever one individual characterizes another (or himself) he himself gets indirectly characterized as regards mental and communicative properties such as knowledge, reliability, honesty, and so on. Most of Quixote's characterizations of himself and of others (as, say, brave knight or evil magician, respectively) are rejected by us, yet they serve as a rich source of indirect characterizations of the Don himself.

Another major, and obvious, source of information for readerly characterization, both direct and indirect, is presented by an individual's actions: physical, mental, and communicative. In literary contexts physical features of an individual's appearance, gestures, mannerism, dress, and natural and human-made environment are indicators for inferences about his or her mental and moral features. Formal elements and patterns are also conventionally assumed to yield information about the individuals involved. Prominent here are character groupings and the parallels or contrasts implied, embedded stories, and how their characters (implicitly) reflect on the characters of the main story, and of course intertextual echoes and allusions, calling to our minds same-named or similar characters in other literary works.

We have repeatedly mentioned the crucial role of readers' inferences for constructing a mental representation of a character. This activity is governed by *rules of inference* of various kinds: those explicitly enunciated by the impersonal authoritative narrating voice, as in Balzac's novels; genre and period conventions (in cowboy movies, scar + black hat → villain); and those based on the reader's general world knowledge. These sets of norms may conflict in a given case, and readers may then prioritize them in different ways, leading to different resultant portraits. Moreover, any individual inference is not a logical necessity: it is merely probable to some degree in the given particular context or situation, given this set of data and using this particular rule of inference.

The account of character construction provided so far has been piecemeal and static. But in reality it is a *process* or continuous mental activity, so one would like to know its major phases or sequence of operations. Recently, scholars studying the cognitive dimensions of narrative have suggested that character as mental model is constructed incrementally in the course of reading on the basis of a constant back-and-forth movement between specific textual data and general knowledge structures stored in the reader's long-term memory.[6] The construction is initiated, as already mentioned, by the reader identifying a referring expression in the text as designating a character. Next the reader establishes a distinct entity in his mental map to which features begin to be ascribed. As one reads on, guided by the "read for character" principle, one proceeds in a step-by-step fashion, making property ascriptions and gathering character-related information, which can in turn serve as a basis for such ascriptions. Once a certain number of properties have been accumulated, they often activate a general knowledge structure stored in long-term memory under which these properties can be subsumed, structured, and integrated into a character model. Detailed information-gathering and the search for an overarching category may well be running concurrently. The character models in question include schemas and stereotypes pertaining to both world knowledge and to the literary encyclopedia, i.e., knowledge about the structure and evolution of the literary system itself. Once a fit between data and category has been established, categorization takes place, and the reader may now proceed top down, integrating all the information available to this point, filling in the mental model, formulating expectations and explaining stored information, for example by relating an individual's action to intentions, beliefs, or dispositions associated with this category. Presumably this is also where one performs second-order characterizations. Such second-order inferences are based on relations between two or more time-frames, such as "character X is inconsistent," or on relations between properties, such as "character Y vacillates between reason and emotion."

As one reads on, additional information comes in which may fall into the established pattern or require its modification/adjustment. In extreme cases, the new information contrasts directly with the defining features of the selected category, causing schema disruption, decategorization of the individual (= we no longer think of him or her as the same "kind of person"), the invalidation of previous inferences and the focused search for a new, better fitting category. This may lead to recategorization or to an inability to do so, in which case one acknowledges encountering a new, hitherto unfamiliar kind of character, which does not match any stereotype in the reader's extant knowledge base. Many innovative writers often seek to create precisely this kind of character. Moreover, since characters exist in temporal frames, a category may apply to one phase of a character's trajectory, whereas a different one is required for a later phase. Quixote thus undergoes a radical change in his beliefs and values towards the end of his life, where he no longer believes in chivalric romances and seeks to live again the peaceful life of the countryside. In such cases one may look for a second-order category to integrate the two phases, such as the rise and fall of a delusional behavioral syndrome. Finally, an individual may display simultaneously radically incongruent category features, preventing any overall integration or closure.

NOTES

1. For a recent English translation see Miguel de Cervantes, *Don Quixote*. Translated by Edith Grossman (New York: Ecco, 2003).
2. See Amie L. Thomasson, *Fiction and Metaphysics* (Cambridge: Cambridge University Press, 1999), pp. 5–14.
3. See Peter Lamarque, *Fictional Points of View* (Ithaca: Cornell University Press, 1996), pp. 7, 12.
4. See Amie L. Thomasson, "The Ontology of Art." In Peter Kivy (ed.) *The Blackwell Guide to Aesthetics* (Oxford: Blackwell, 2004), p. 78.
5. See Marie-Laure Ryan, *Possible Worlds, Artificial Intelligence and Narrative Theory* (Bloomington: Indiana University Press, 1991), chapter 6.
6. See, for example, Jonathan Culpeper, *Language and Characterisation* (Harlow: Longman, 2001); Fotis Jannidis, *Figur und Person* (Berlin: Walter de Gruyter, 2004); and Ralf Schneider, "Towards a Cognitive Theory of Literary Character." *Style* 35:4 (2001), pp. 607–40. For a related approach, see Catherine Emmott, *Narrative Comprehension: A Discourse Perspective* (Oxford: Oxford University Press, 1997).

6

BRONWEN THOMAS

Dialogue

Representing the voices of characters in a story is an effective way of enlivening a narrative. A vital aspect of how we remember and grow close to fictional characters is the way they speak: their accents and dialects place them geographically and socially, while their verbal idiosyncrasies and catchphrases help to make them memorable, even endearing. In an oral narrative, a change in intonation and/or pace may be sufficient to indicate to the listener where the narrator is quoting from another. The process is more complicated when it comes to written narratives, as the writer has to deal with the transition between one channel of communication and another. Nevertheless, the conventions for representing speech have become well established whether the context is a news story, a biography, or a novel, and readers rarely stop to question why speech is laid out as it is. As well as adding variety to a narrative, representing the speech of those who take part in a narrated event, or who are somehow qualified to comment on what takes place, may also contribute importantly to the authenticity and authority of the story, as we appear to be told what happened from "the horse's mouth." It is difficult to imagine a narrative that does not include some kind of representation of speech, but the extent to which this is foregrounded varies considerably. The degree of directness of the report may also vary, but in this chapter I am concerned primarily with what has been termed direct or free direct speech, where the words of the characters appear to be reproduced verbatim and contribute significantly to the central action or plot.

The chapter will begin with a brief historical overview of the devices and conventions developed by novelists for the representation of direct speech. This will be followed by a discussion of issues of realism, and an introduction to some of the key theoretical approaches to the study of dialogue. Finally, I will offer an analysis of Philip Roth's *Deception*, a novel written entirely in dialogue, in order to address and examine issues raised earlier in the chapter.

The historical development of speech representation in the novel

Early novelists in the English tradition honed their techniques in competition with the stage, many even writing for the stage themselves. Thus narrative structure was conceived in terms of set-piece scenes, and novelists developed techniques designed to provide the verbal equivalent of the movements, gestures, and intonations of a live performance. The conventions for representing speech were not fully stabilized until the 1820s,[1] so that, for example, in earlier novels the use of quotation marks is much looser. Norman Page[2] has shown how Jane Austen frequently conflates more than one utterance into a single "speech," while Meir Sternberg[3] has identified ways in which eighteenth- and nineteenth-century novelists used quotation marks for indirect as well as direct forms of speech. Indeed, it is only in the late Victorian novel, Jonathan Ree argues, that quotation marks became "ludicrously fussy."[4] It was during this period that the notion of speech as private property emerged, and Ree claims that earlier novelists may have deliberately left open the attribution of words, rather than merely being inconsistent.[5]

While Austen is usually credited with perfecting the art of conversation and verbal repartee, it is Dickens who is hailed by many as introducing greater variety into the novel in terms of speech. Dickens is responsible for introducing readers to many wonderful dialects and idiolects, and though the chief effect in his time may have been comic relief, since then such voices have increasingly come to dominate narratives and demand our respect. Novelists such as Dickens have stretched every resource of writing and typography to try to capture the sounds of spoken language, such as stammering or lisping, as well as a wide range of accents and dialects. The fact that Dickens often publicly performed scenes from his novels continues the close association between novel and theatre, and Ree has argued that it is likewise impossible for the reader not to approach the novels as "vocal scores" ripe for performance.[6] This would suggest that scenes composed largely of the speech of characters can offer a unique reading experience which blurs the boundaries between novel and drama.

In the early twentieth century novelists continue to introduce new speech varieties, but also experiment with dialogue in a more overtly self-conscious way, making this a key period in the development of the technique. John Mepham argues that it is important to consider dialogue of the Modernist period alongside other stylistic developments, notably the stream-of-consciousness technique, as representing novelists' efforts to put the unspoken into words, influenced as they were by the emergence of psychoanalysis and the "talking cure."[7] Thus James Joyce's preference for dashes rather than quotation marks means that the demarcation between characters' voices, and between characters and the narrator, becomes less rigid. Mepham analyses in depth the technique employed by Dorothy Richardson in *Pilgrimage*, where reported speech is integrated into passages of stream-of-consciousness, ensuring that the boundary between speech and thought remains fluid. Richardson shares with some of the Modernist writers a deep suspicion of talk, and its adequacy for conveying characters' thoughts and emotions.

But the experimentation with dialogue is by no means confined to the avant-garde during this period, and comic writers such as Evelyn Waugh, Anthony Powell, and P. G. Wodehouse continued the tradition of exploiting communicative errors and idiosyncrasies for the reader's amusement and delight. Such writers contributed greatly to the development of dialogue techniques, and were especially sensitive to changes in communicative and cultural practices. Wodehouse continued the tradition of writing for the stage but, like Waugh and Powell, was also influenced by the emergence of new media such as film and radio. Page speculates that it was in response to the new aural culture of broadcasting (first radio, then television), that novelists of this period began to fully exploit the resources available to them for the representation of speech (*Speech*, 318). Mepham, too, notes the influence of film on the development of dialogue technique and argues that in many respects film showed novelists the way in terms of representing the complex and intricate patterns and structures that may emerge in diverse speech situations.[8] Experimentation with dialogue is also a feature of American writing of this period, especially in Hemingway's novels and short stories, resulting in pared-down narratives where there is virtually nothing extraneous to the characters' speech, and where seemingly innocuous, even banal, exchanges merely paper over their insecurities and dissatisfactions.

Readers, too, have had to adapt to the challenges and rewards of novels that rely heavily on direct speech. Where the story unfolds entirely through the utterances of the characters, and contextualization or framing of events is at a minimum, the reader may have to put in a considerable amount of deductive work just to work out who is saying what to whom. For many, narratives with this puzzle-like quality only heighten the pleasure, drawing them in and involving them in the worlds of the characters in a direct, even intimate way. But for others this is a frustrating process, exacerbated by the fact that the author may well be playing games with the reader.

In the so-called dialogue novel, or novel of conversation, experimentation with narrative form goes much further. For writers such as Ivy Compton-Burnett, or Henry Green, the challenge is to compose novels made up almost entirely of dialogue, carefully orchestrated and stylized to produce specific effects. Both these writers are interested in the gaps that exist between what people say and what they mean, and in exploring the consequences of half-truths or outright lies, failures of communication and acts of verbal cruelty. Dialogue novels also tend to be textually distinctive, drawing our attention to the book as a physical object, and to the design of the words on the page. William Gaddis, Nicholson Baker, and Manuel Puig have more recently taken on the challenge of writing novels composed largely of dialogue, often to explore themes of deception, intrigue, or breakdowns in communication. One of the questions such novels raise is precisely where the boundaries lie between such narratives and play or film scripts, and what makes reading a novel composed largely of dialogue distinct from the experience of watching a film or a play. Experimentation with the representation of speech also continues in hypertext fiction and other computer-mediated forms, and it will be interesting to see how writers react to new kinds of "conversation" and "speech" emerging on the web, and to new communication technologies such as cell phones and email. What is certain is that the fascination with trying to capture speech in writing will continue, and that this will remain an important means of opening up narratives to new voices and new rhythms, and to the questioning of cultural practices that comprise the status quo.

Speech and realism: issues and debates

Some writers go further than others in trying to recapture the flavor of the spoken language, perhaps even attempting something close to a phonetic transcription. However, even the most conscientious attempts at recreating a particular sound or dialect in a written medium can only approximate the "real thing." The term "eye dialect" is used to refer to the fact that only very minimal changes in spelling or grammar are needed to signal a shift from standard to nonstandard forms of speech. For other writers, a simple report that something is said "in a Glaswegian accent" may suffice, or they may rely on what Page calls "stage directions" to give the reader an indication of how the words are spoken ("she laughed," "his face crumpled") (*Speech*, 28). Forms such as these are also called *speech tags*, and they play a vital role not only in identifying who is speaking, but also in situating readers in time and place ("she muttered, moving her chair into the evening sunshine") and in evaluating the speech ("he admitted grudgingly"). For dialogue purists, this can be a tedious affair, weighing down the characters' speech and making it predictable. Speech tags also betray the influence and control of the narrator, making them "symbols of the old regime" according to French writer Nathalie Sarraute.[9] However, certain writers (for example

Henry Green) have reacted against this by deliberately foregrounding and ridiculing the banality of the he said-she said formula, while others, most notably Dickens, have experimented with the placement of speech tags to heighten suspense or surprise the reader.[10] One of the skills required of the novelist is to manage what Page calls the "gear shifting" between narration and speech (*Speech*, p. 33), although once again some novelists have chosen to problematize this process: Portugese author José Saramago dispenses both with quotation marks and the line breaks that conventionally distinguish speakers from one another and from the narrator.

Thus although the representation of speech has always been at the forefront of debates about realism, certain limitations and boundaries remain. As Page (*Speech*, 4) puts it, "the whole concept of realism as applied to fictional speech is often based on an inadequate or inaccurate notion of what spontaneous speech is really like" so that what we effectively get is an "idealization of real speech" (*Speech*, 19). Sternberg, too, has attacked the "direct speech fallacy," whereby the effectiveness of a representation is evaluated by its faithfulness to a purported "original," and where the influence of the reporter on what is represented is all too often ignored.[11] It is important to remember that written representations of speech are always "tidied up," and the pressure to attain some level of realism has to be measured against the need to entertain and sustain the reader's interest. Indeed, many of the novels and novelists celebrated for their use of dialogue present us with a version of speech which is heavily stylized and artificial, but whose coinages and curious rhythms may be replicated in other novels or written representations, and even in everyday discourse, demonstrating how complex and paradoxical the whole concept of "realism" is in this regard.

Speech in action and interaction: theoretical approaches to the study of dialogue

It is important to remember that "realism" in dialogue involves much more than accurately recording the surface of talk. Seldom do we see characters in novels interrupting one another, and even rarer are examples of "multi-party talk,"[12] where characters' contributions overlap and clash. In drama there are obvious reasons why this could be problematic, as audiences might struggle to follow what the characters are saying. But it is interesting to consider why novelists who otherwise seem content to challenge every taboo and preconception depict speech situations where characters are astonishingly polite and formal. Peter Burke has shown how the "art" of conversation, far from being fixed or immutable, is subject to cultural change, for instance as notions of politeness or good manners change.[13] A key question for theorists of dialogue such as Lennard J. Davis and Aaron Fogel, therefore, is whether novels help perpetuate an "idealization" of speech and conversation that has far-reaching ideological consequences.[14] Influenced by philosophical traditions of dialogue, these critics look beyond questions of realism to consider the implications that our prevailing "idea of dialogue" has for our understanding of the process of communication and for power relations existing not just between fictional characters but also between author and reader. In this regard, the work of Russian theorist Mikhail Bakhtin is key, demonstrating that the novel is uniquely placed to present a multiplicity of voices competing and clashing with one another, so that even the author's voice becomes just one among many, and no one voice is allowed the "final say."[15] Bakhtin's theories focused attention on the "dialogic principle" as both a structuring device and almost an ethical imperative, and though his work has been criticized by Fogel and others as presenting an overly optimistic view of dialogue, his expansion of the concept, highlighting the intersections between style, meaning, and ideology, has been hugely influential.

What dialogue theorists show us is that we need to uncover the underlying structures governing the speech of characters, and to approach dialogue not with a view to closing off its meanings, but prepared to immerse ourselves in the give-and-take, the nuances, that make dialogue as a stylistic device so exciting. Mepham draws a distinction between "verbal style" and "conversational style" to ensure that these aspects of dialogue are not overlooked.[16] Verbal style, where the novelist represents distinctive speech varieties, has important cultural significance, sometimes bringing to prominence marginalized or unprestigious speech varieties. Mepham argues that it is only in the mid to late twentieth century that novelists experiment with what he calls "conversational style," which is concerned much more with the dynamics and power relations of the talk rather than its surface variations. Most often, Mepham contends, authors use conversational style to expose and explore gender differences, as in William Gaddis's *Carpenter's Gothic*, which charts the troubled marriage of the central characters primarily by means of their tortuous interactions. As Mepham and others have demonstrated, we can learn a great deal about the power relations between characters by analyzing who is control of a conversation, who speaks most, and for the longest amount of time.

Whereas literary historical accounts such as Page's (*Speech*) allow us to identify different varieties, and the techniques and conventions developed to represent them, it has been stylisticians, drawing on linguistic models of speech and conversation, who have largely been responsible for demonstrating the value of analyzing verbal interactions as mini social systems rather than individual sentences thrown together.[17] For example, Grice's "co-operative principle" and its related conversational "maxims" can be used to try to establish the extent to which participants share some common ground in terms of the parameters of the exchange they are engaged in and the direction it takes.[18] Furthermore, Grice's concept of "conversational implicature" allows analysts to explore the important role listeners play in a conversation, and the extent to which participants "read between the lines" and rely on there being a subtext to the talk. Another important strand of this kind of approach is the focus on the "turn taking mechanism" outlined by conversational analysts, which can help identify how the length of turns taken, their frequency, and their distribution may be important indicators of power and control.[19] Stylistic approaches therefore look beyond the individual utterance to consider wider sequences and larger discourse structures, potentially illuminating a great deal in terms of the characters' interrelations and even the wider social and cultural formations in which they participate.

Dialogue in Philip Roth's *Deception*

Deception follows in the tradition of the dialogue novel and explicitly confronts issues of representation and realism.[20] Controversial for both its subject-matter and its technique, the novel centers on an extra-marital affair between a writer, "Philip," and an unnamed Englishwoman. The couple meet occasionally in a room somewhere in London, and the novel traces their relationship entirely via the conversations they have. The only "action" is therefore confined to scenes enacted by the characters in their dialogue, stories they tell, or memories they relive. This immediately highlights the dialogic nature of their talk, in Bakhtin's sense of the term, as we see how their utterances carry within them traces of previous conversations, and echoes of the social and ideological discourses that shape them as individuals.[21] Although many of the conversations have an erotic edge typical of the discourses of romantic love and the illicit affair, the characters seem to be seeking much more than a purely physical intimacy. Philip's Czech friend tells him "men usually talk to women – to get them into bed. *You* get them into bed to talk to them" (*Deception*, 92), and talking is very much at the heart of this relationship. The conversations between the couple are interspersed with other conversations taking place between Philip and various acquaintances of his, including his wife. We only learn this by deciphering the fragments we are offered, as the narrative does not include speech tags to identify the speakers, or any framing commentary.

The novel is structured into seemingly loose arrangements of parts or chapters broken up into smaller sections of varying lengths. Some of these sections consist of self-contained exchanges on a given topic or theme, for example Jewishness or work, while others appear to be fragments from longer conversations. Although the presumption must be that the sections follow some kind of chronological order, this does not entail a clear sense of progression from section to section, and the most we might discern is some loose thematic connection.

A fairly typical exchange from early on in the novel will provide the best illustration of the kind of reading experience we are offered:

"It's very strange to see you."
"Stranger not to, isn't it?"
"No, I usually *don't* see you."
"You do look a bit different. What's been happening to you?"
"That makes me look so different? You tell me what the difference is and I'll tell you what did it. Am I taller, shorter, fatter, wider?"
"No, it's very subtle."
"Something subtle? Shall I be serious? I missed you."   (*Deception*, 16)

With no speech tags to orient us as to who is saying what, and very little in the content of the utterances to offer us clues as to the identities of the speakers, we could be forgiven for sharing some of the frustration hinted at in this exchange. A game-like quality to the repartee is evident, carrying a suggestion of a competitive rather than a co-operative edge, as the speakers echo each other's words, and appear intent on analyzing every nuance. Unusually for this novel, a graphic device is employed to indicate intonation/emphasis (namely, the use of italicized type for "*don't*"), reinforcing the impression of a rather tense encounter in which the first speaker feels the need to assert him or herself. The fact that the speaker of the final utterance has to explicitly signal a change of tone ("Shall I be serious?") conveys the impression that these two have clear boundaries and expectations of the kind of talk that they are going to engage in, and this is very far removed from the kind of script we might expect for a conversation between two lovers who have been apart for some time. How long it has been since they last met is not specified, but the fact that one party comments on the strangeness of their meeting, and the other inquires "What's been happening to you?" suggests that the separation has been longer than they are accustomed to, or had expected, so that they have to re-establish the grounds on which the talk (and the relationship) is to continue.

The section takes us straight to the heart of the conversation, the absence of pleasantries or conventional greetings ensuring that the rather accusatory opening has maximum impact. Although one of the parties seems to be on the defensive, the conversation is soon turned back on to the other as the one who is "different" and the one to whom unspecified things have been happening. This evasiveness and manipulation of the conversation is more typical of the male in the relationship from the conversations we see elsewhere in the novel. The first speaker's anxiety about appearances, and the sudden and unexpected eruption of emotion ("I missed you") might also lead us to conclude that this is the woman, as this is more typical of her conversational behavior. Thus although on the surface the exchanges appear to tell us very little, and seem almost willfully obscure, examining the dynamics and management of the talk offers us an inkling of the tensions and imbalances in the relationship that become more marked and significant later on.

Interventions by an external narrator only occur a handful of times during the novel, so that when they do appear, for example in the stage direction "*laughing*" (*Deception*, 38), the parentheses and italics only add to the incongruity, so accustomed have we become to doing without such narrative props. Playing with notions of identity throughout, Roth's technique forces us to fall back on our preformed scripts about what kind of language different social groupings use. This illustrates the extent to which, as Bakhtin demonstrated, discourses within the novel are in constant dialogue with social and ideological discourses, such as those of gender.[22] For example, the female character talks about domestic concerns and shopping, and is anxious about losing her looks, while the male character's fears are about his sexual performance, and he discloses much less about his feelings and home life. But as much as it trades off these stereotypes, the novel prompts us to question how and why we arrive at them. Moreover, the novel satirizes the impulse for readers to identify characters with their author, as Philip teases us with references to fictional characters constructed by Roth, and berates those critics he feels have misinterpreted his work. The dialogue technique forces us to engage more directly with these questions, given that we are likely to fall into the trap of making these naïve connections as we try to place what is being said into some kind of overarching narrative. As Philip is the only character who features throughout, we look to him for answers to the puzzles the novel sets, but ultimately discover he may be the biggest deceiver of them all. Not only do we have to do without any narratorial evaluations or judgments, therefore, but we also have to continually reassess the assumptions we might tentatively form based on what the characters say.

As the title of the novel indicates, underlying the central relationship is the sense that this is all part of an elaborate game where nothing that is said can be taken at face value. This is set up by the opening scene, where the characters play at devising a questionnaire, and the dialogue technique ensures that we feel part of their games, forced as we are to try to puzzle out who the characters are and what they are doing. Throughout the novel, the characters indulge in role playing or what they call "reality shift" (*Deception*, 105), drawing on, but also parodying, various discourses such as that of the therapy session. Indeed, at the end the entire status of what we have been reading is thrown into question by the appearance of Philip's wife, and her dissection of his excuses and alibis. We are the main victims of "deception" here, it turns out, as the novel toys with our desire to believe in the characters and become immersed in their world, and to search for coherence and consistency in the narrative. The novel ends with the lovers reviewing the "strange story" of their lives, prompting Philip to assert provocatively, "[n]o one would believe it" (*Deception*, 208).

Deception presents a variety of speech styles, contrasting the English-woman's genteel style with Philip's directness, even brashness, and employing broken English for the Czech characters. Moreover, certain verbal mannerisms provide a degree of orientation, such as Philip's tendency to refer to the woman as "my dear," or the woman's frequent references to her drinking. On rare occasions, the dialogue provides us with minimal contextualization. For example, one of the games the characters play involves describing the room in which they meet, allowing us to get some sense of the environment in which the action takes place. In a related technique, we learn that the woman is crying during one of their conversations when she comments that "I've got mascara, I'm afraid, running down my face" (23). Such devices invite us to build a mental picture of the characters and their world, and can be much more involving and moving than a narratorial description. In some instances, this technique provides the verbal equivalent of the "reaction shot" in visual narratives, as the character verbalizes the response he or she is getting: "You are getting more and more resentful with every word I say" (*Deception*, 112). This demonstrates effectively the interdependence of the participants and the dialogic nature of their exchanges as they fine-tune their contributions in anticipation of a response.

But we are never allowed to settle into any kind of pattern for very long. Just as we may feel we are tuning in to the dialogue between the central couple, with its own rhythms and preoccupations, Roth intercuts seemingly unconnected scenes involving the Czech characters, and a former student of Philip's with whom he may also have had an affair, so that our sense of time and place is constantly being disrupted. Occasionally, when the characters take stock of their relationship, we are given hints about the time-frame for events, as in the following exchange between Philip and the Englishwoman:

"How long is it now?"
"Us? About a year and a half." (*Deception*, 23–4)

References are similarly made to precise locations (Notting Hill, the Charles Bridge) and to the ages of the characters, but since these often merely confirm intuitions we have already formed, they may appear rather superfluous.

Roth's technique seems to deliberately thwart any attempt to view the characters as anything other than what Barthes called "paper beings."[23] Although the Englishwoman talks about "my husband" and their troubled life together, he remains a remote figure, and even characters who participate directly in the narrative, such as Olina, or Philip's wife, are only sketched in the broadest of strokes. As a writer, Philip is similarly evasive and suspicious of any attempt at greater depth, reveling in rather than resenting the fact that "where the real exchange ends and the invented one begins I can't even remember anymore" (*Deception*, 181). What the novel hints at, therefore, is that *any* representation of communication between two people must be partial and incomplete, relying on interpretation and guesswork about what the parties may have meant or may have been thinking. This is what appears to fascinate Philip as both writer and lover, and his self-conscious reflections prompt us as readers to look beyond the details of the affair, whatever they may have been, to explore the issues raised by his attempts at representation.

As well as becoming attuned to the different verbal styles and preoccupations of the characters, the reader has to pay heed to the management and organization of the talk to begin to grasp the nature of the central relationships and their dynamics. Philip tends to offer advice to and instruct the Englishwoman, and the age difference between them, revealed in the dialogue but also suggested in the way he addresses her ("my dear"; "my sweet girl"), reinforces the impression that he has the upper hand. The distribution and management of turns at talk is also revealing. At times Philip even appears to direct the exchanges for his own amusement, inviting the woman to "Talk about it. I like to know what's going on in your head" (*Deception*, 20). Cultural differences (he is American, she is English; he is Jewish, she is a Gentile) are explicitly referred to, especially by Philip, often in a confrontational manner. Another interesting feature of the dialogue is the self-consciousness of the characters about their participation in, and co-management of, the talk. This is evident in the way they comment on the direction the talk takes, and make explicit reference to one another's attempts to manipulate the conversation. For example, Philip describes himself as "an écouteur, an audiophiliac" (*Deception*, 44), a description that is heartily mocked by his wife at the end of the novel. As the novel progresses, therefore, our response to the characters, and to their relationship, may shift significantly as we are shown different sides to their characters, or pick up on aspects of their behavior or personalities that they may try to keep hidden.

Philip seems to invite the reader to share in the game-playing, openly declaring his intention to explore various "improvisations on a self" (*Deception*, 98), as though this somehow absolves him of any responsibility to the truth or to the other characters. The whole project, it appears, is concocted as an exercise in writing "shed of all the expository fat" (*Deception*, 189), but while readers might admire Philip's virtuosity, they may also be left feeling uncomfortable because of his rather clinical, self-satisfied tone. Moreover, it may be that one of Philip's main deceptions involves his apparent control of his material. In this respect, it is important to consider the scenes of dialogue in the context of the narrative structure of the novel as a whole, and to consider the ways in which the novel presents us with gaps and silences which may themselves be meaningful and significant.

As mentioned earlier, the novel is structured around fragments of conversations, some more complete than others. However, the way these fragments are juxtaposed, the variations in their length and pace, make us sensitive to the gaps that exist between them. For much of the novel, the elliptical nature of these fragments contributes to the game-like effect, as the reader has to work at piecing them together much in the same way that we work to "get" a joke or puzzle. Some of the segments consist of just one or two utterances:

"That's one of the nicest things that's been done to me all week."
"I liked it too." (*Deception*, 146)

We never learn what has been "done" to the characters here, but in the context of the relationship, and from the nature of the preceding exchanges, we know that this involves something sexual, so that by leaving the detail to the reader's imagination, it both teases us and offers us some illusion of intimacy. But there are gaps and silences that are not so easily explained away. The playfulness is undercut at times by references to the woman's profound unhappiness, but it is the gaps in our knowledge about Philip that are the more intriguing. While he is happy to hold forth about his Jewishness, or his sexual proclivities, he discloses virtually nothing about his domestic affairs or his emotions. Nevertheless, the bitterness he expresses about the reception of his work, and even his need to keep talking (or at least listening), betray a vulnerability and insecurity which are in many ways more fascinating than any of the hang-ups and anxieties the woman parades in front of us. Thus although his evasions and deceptions appear communicatively un-cooperative in Grice's terms, they lead us to search for possible inferences which suggest greater depth to his character.[24]

Such discoveries about the characters, such surprises and reversals, are only made possible by Roth's mastery of the dialogue technique. Readable at one sitting, pared down to the minimum and seemingly content to reproduce the most banal of exchanges, such writing nevertheless makes great demands of the reader. Other kinds of narrative may more overtly dissect the psychologies of the characters, or debate and discuss ethical or philosophical issues. With the dialogue novel, we may initially be seduced by the sheer exuberance of the repartee, by the apparently unashamed playing with surfaces that ensues. But it is the spaces between the utterances and the subtle shifts in the dynamics between the characters that gradually draw us in, usually only on second or third reading. Here we may be not so much "reading for the plot," or even reading for the characters, as we are reading for the spaces in between, so that reading truly becomes an ongoing, even inexhaustible, process where we accept that we may never explore all the possibilities, or be free from the deceptions that this kind of experience may offer us.

NOTES

1. John Mepham, "Novelistic Dialogue: Some Recent Developments." In Zygmunt Mazur and Teresa Bela (eds.) *New Developments in English and American Studies* (Krakow: Proceedings of the 7th International Conference of English and American Literature, 1997), pp. 411–31.
2. Norman Page, *Speech in the English Novel*, 2nd edition (Basingstoke: Macmillan, 1988), p. 28.
3. Meir Sternberg, "Point of View and the Indirectness of Direct Speech." *Language and Style* 15 (1982), pp. 67–117.
4. Jonathan Ree, "Funny Voices: Stories, Punctuation and Personal Identity." In *New Literary History* 21:4 (1990), p. 1044.
5. Jonathan Ree, "Funny Voices," pp. 1039–58.
6. Jonathan Ree, "Funny Voices," p. 1046.
7. John Mepham, "Psychoanalysis, Modernism and the Defamiliarisation of Talk." *Hungarian Journal of English and American Studies*, 4:1–2 (1998), pp. 105–119.
8. John Mepham, "Novelistic Dialogue," p. 429.
9. Nathalie Sarraute, *Tropisms and the Age of Suspicion*. Translated by Marie Jolas (London: John Calder, 1963), p. 112.
10. Mark Lambert, *Dickens and the Suspended Quotation* (New Haven: Yale University Press, 1981).
11. Sternberg, "Point of View," p. 68.
12. Bronwen Thomas, "Multiparty Talk in the Novel: The Distribution of Tea and Talk in a Scene from Evelyn Waugh's *Black Mischief*." *Poetics Today* 23:4 (2002), pp. 657–84.
13. Peter Burke, *The Art of Conversation* (London: Polity, 1993).
14. See Lennard J. Davis, *Resisting Novels: Ideology and Fiction* (London: Methuen, 1987), and Aaron Fogel, *Coercion to Speak: Conrad's Poetics of Dialogue* (Cambridge, MA: Harvard University Press, 1985).

15. Mikhail Bakhtin, *The Dialogic Imagination*. Edited by Michael Holquist, translated by Caryl Emerson and Michael Holquist (Austin: University of Texas Press, 1981).
16. John Mepham, "Novelistic Dialogue," p. 415.
17. See, e.g., Michael Toolan, "Analyzing Fictional Dialogue." *Language and Communication* 5:3 (1985), pp. 193–206, and Geoffrey Leech and Michael Short, *Style in Fiction* (London: Longman, 1981).
18. Paul Grice, "Logic and Conversation." In Peter Cole and Jerry L. Morgan (eds.) *Syntax and Semantics 3: Speech Acts* (New York: Academic Press, 1975), pp. 41–58.
19. Harvey Sacks, Emmanuel Schegloff, and Gail Jefferson, "A Simplest Systematics for the Organization of Turn-taking for Conversation." In Jim Schenkein (ed.) *Studies in the Organization of Conversational Interaction* (New York: Academic Press, 1978), pp. 7–55.
20. Philip Roth, *Deception* (London: Vintage, 1992).
21. Mikhail Bakhtin, *The Dialogic Imagination*.
22. Mikhail Bakhtin, *The Dialogic Imagination*.
23. Roland Barthes, "Introduction to the Structural Analysis of Narratives." *Image-Music-Text*. Translated by Stephen Heath (London: Fontana, 1977), pp. 79–124.
24. Paul Grice, "Logic and Conversation."

7

MANFRED JAHN

Focalization

If narratology – the structural theory and analysis of narrative texts – were to be divided into just two major parts, then *narration* and *focalization* would be very suitable candidates. *Narration* is the telling of a story in a way that simultaneously respects the needs and enlists the co-operation of its audience; *focalization* is the submission of (potentially limitless) narrative information to a perspectival filter. Contrary to the standard courtroom injunction to tell "the *whole* truth," no-one can in fact tell all. Practical reasons require speakers and writers to restrict information to the "right amount" – not too little, not too much, and if possible only what's relevant.

In its original conception, dating back to the late 1960s, narratology is a timeless and culture-independent discipline. Yet narratologists have increasingly become aware of the fact that their seemingly neutral theoretical models may have been shaped by cultural and historical contingencies.[1] This is definitely so in the case of focalization because our present notions about perspectival filtering would hardly exist without the psychological interest that informs Western narrative literature from roughly the eighteenth-century novel onwards. The psychological turn reaches its height with the institution of psychology as a discipline and the flowering of the Modernist literary movement in the period of 1900 to 1950. Let us try to unravel this historical background by taking a brief look at the narrative aesthetics of the Modernist era.

The Modernist roots of focalization

At the beginning of the twentieth century authors such as Henry James, Virginia Woolf, James Joyce, Dorothy Richardson, Katherine Mansfield, Franz Kafka, Arthur Schnitzler, Ford Madox Ford (and many others) perfected a style that came to be called "psychological realism" or "literary impressionism." Just like the French impressionist painters of the 1870s and 1880s, the Modernist writers were not interested in realistic representations of external phenomena but in presenting the world as it appeared to characters subject to beliefs, moods, and emotions. Treating subjectivity not as a distortion to be got rid of in the interest of science and empiricism, the Modernists looked at a world shaped by individual perceptions, and they were fascinated by what they saw. As the psychologist William James (the brother of Henry James, and the person usually credited with coining the term "stream of consciousness"), put it in 1890:

> Let four men make a tour in Europe. One will bring home only picturesque impressions – costumes and colors, parks and views and works of architecture, pictures and statues. To another all this will be non-existent; and distances and prices, populations and draining arrangements, door- and window-fastenings, and other useful statistics will take their place. A third will give a rich account of the theatres, restaurants, and public balls, and naught beside; whilst the fourth will perhaps have been so wrapped in his subjective broodings as to tell little more than a few names of places through which he passed.[2]

Interestingly, James refrained from censuring any of the views he described as inadequate or false (even though the fourth man is clearly "less perceptive" than the other three). Another author who stressed individual perception in her attempt to grasp the essence of literary impressionism was Virginia Woolf:

> Examine for a moment an ordinary mind on an ordinary day. The mind receives a myriad of impressions – trivial, fantastic, evanescent, or engraved with the sharpness of steel. From all sides they come, an incessant shower of innumerable atoms ... Let us record the atoms as they fall upon the mind in the order in which they fall, let us trace the pattern, however disconnected and incoherent in appearance, which each sight or incidence scores upon the consciousness.[3]

Today, Woolf's thoughts read like a program for the Modernist "novel of consciousness." The novel of consciousness was usually cast in the form of what Franz K. Stanzel calls a "figural narrative," that is, a third-person narrative in which the storyworld is seen through the eyes of a character. In his theoretical writings, Henry James called such central perceiving characters "centers," "mirrors," or "reflectors," and to this list narratologists have added a number of variants such as "figural media" (Stanzel), "focal characters" (Genette), "filters" (Chatman), and "internal focalizers" (Bal) – the proliferation of terms clearly indicating the importance of the concept.

A key feature of Modernist narrative technique was to create revelatory reflector characters. These included seemingly ordinary people such as Woolf's Clarissa Dalloway, an upper middle-class mother and wife, and Joyce's Leopold Bloom, an advertisement canvasser. Other popular reflector figures were intellectuals, artists, and children. Henry James's *What Maisie Knew* (1897) covers a girl's development from the age of 5 to 12, while in Richardson's short story "The Garden" (1924) the reflector is an infant who has only just about learned to speak. In Woolf's *Mrs Dalloway* (1925), the reader finds himself in the suicidal mind of a shell-shocked schizophrenic; in Graham Greene's *A Gun For Sale* (1936), the reflector is a murderer; and in Malcolm Lowry's *Under the Volcano* (1947), he is an alcoholic. Anything seems to go in the way of reflectors, be he a Neanderthal man as in William Golding's *The Inheritors* (1955), a dog as in Woolf's *Flush* (1933), or an intelligent robot as in Walter M. Miller's "I Made You" (1954).

The Modernists liked to think of themselves as avant-gardists, and their texts often provoked, challenged, and exhausted their contemporary readers. Because it focuses on a reflector's mind, the figural style tends to avoid exposition of background information, it may restrict itself to recording a reflector's stream of associative consciousness, and often it moves toward an interior moment of "epiphany" (revelation or recognition) rather than reaching a suspense-filled climax. Later, as Modernism became the current tradition, the figural novel made compromises and re-allowed expositions and conflict-oriented plots. Today, the figural style is a staple narrative technique that can be found everywhere, be it in fantasy, romance, the thriller, science fiction, and the journalistic genre called "New Journalism." Let us now see what links the Modernist figural novel to today's theories of focalization.

Theorizing focalization: Genette's model

Bent on "tracing the pattern . . . which each sight or incidence scores upon the consciousness," the Modernists discovered that the best way to achieve directness was to exclude the traditional mediator, i.e., the narrator (or let her or him become as inconspicuous, silent, and "covert" as possible). Normally, the narrator is the functional agent who verbalizes the story's nonverbal matter, edits the verbal matter, manages the exposition, decides what is to be told in what sequence, and establishes communication with the addressee. However, once exposition, comment, and narratorial intervention are dispensed with in the interest of directness, the figural text appears to be determined by the filtering and coloring devices of the reflector's mind, while the reader, seeing the storyworld through the reflector's eyes, becomes a witness rather than the narrator's communicative addressee. Noticing this, many contemporary commentators jumped to one of two conclusions, both equally problematic: either that the narrator was dead and the reflector had somehow absorbed his or her functions (Percy Lubbock); or else that the reflector had become a narrator (Wayne C. Booth). Against this, the general consensus today is that no reflector ever literally *tells* the narrative we are reading. This point is squarely owed to Gérard Genette, who in an often cited statement said,

> most of the theoretical works on this subject [perspective] . . . suffer from a regrettable confusion between what I call here *mood* and *voice*, a confusion between the question *who is the character whose point of view orients the narrative perspective?* and the very different question *who is the narrator?* – or, more simply, the question *who sees?* and the question *who speaks?*[4]

One has to be careful not to take Genette's questions too literally. *Who sees?* aims at identifying a reflector (Genette's "focal character," but not any old seeing character), while *who speaks?* is interested in pinpointing the utterer of the narrative discourse, that is, the narrator (not any old speaking character). Setting his two questions in direct opposition, Genette defuses both the error of declaring the narrator dead and the error of equating focal characters with narrators. More importantly, by prizing apart voice and mood – narration and focalization – he opens the door for focalization to become an independent module of the narratological system. In order to let focalization encompass all narrative forms (not only the Modernist figural novel), Genette stipulates that the overarching criterion of focalization is not (only) "who sees?" but the gradable feature of "restriction of narrative information." Hence, based on a scale of increasing degrees of restriction, Genette distinguishes the following three categories.

A. In the mode of *non-focalization* or *zero-focalization*, events are narrated from a wholly unrestricted or omniscient point of view (as typically in Henry Fielding's *Tom Jones* (1749) and many other eighteenth- and nineteenth-century heterodiegetic [third-person] novels). To get the sound and feel of the style, consider an excerpt from a modern novel, James A. Michener's *Hawaii* (1961):

> Across a million years, down more than ten million years [the island] existed silently in the unknown sea and then died, leaving only a fringe of coral where the birds rest and where gigantic seals of the changing ocean play. Ceaseless life and death, endless expenditure of beauty and capacity, tireless ebb and flow and rising and subsidence of the ocean. Night comes and the burning day, and the island waits, and no man arrives. The days perish and the nights, and the aching beauty of lush valleys and waterfalls vanishes, and no man will ever see them.[5]

This passage exhibits what is commonly called a "panoramic point of view." The narrator has access to (in principle) limitless (i.e., unrestricted) information which clearly transcends what is accessible to ordinary humans (hence "no man will ever see . . ." etc.).

B. In the mode of *internal focalization* the story's events are "focalized through" one or more story-internal reflector characters, and narrative information is restricted to data available to their perception, cognition, and thought. The following excerpt is taken from the beginning of Ernest Hemingway's *For Whom the Bell Tolls* (1943):

> He lay flat on the brown, pine-needled floor of the forest, his chin on his folded arms, and high overhead the wind blew in the tops of the pine trees. The mountainside sloped gently where he lay; but below it was steep and he could see the dark of the oiled road winding through the pass. There was a stream alongside the road and far down he saw a mill beside the stream and the falling water of the dam, white in the summer sunlight.[6]

Hemingway's novel begins *medias in res* (literally, in the middle of things) in the typical fashion of the figural novel, and the passage closely represents the reflector's current perceptions – mainly things he sees, feels, and hears. Perception modes are not only indicated by explicit phrases such as "he could see" but more subtly also by the "pine-needled floor", the "gently" sloping ground, the wind blowing "high overhead." All narrative information in this type of "narrated perception" is strictly aligned with the reflector's current spatial and temporal co-ordinates.

Genette additionally distinguishes three sub-patterns of internal focalization. (1) Texts employing *fixed focalization* are exclusively told from the point of view of a single focal character as in James's *The Ambassadors* (1903), Joyce's *Portrait of the Artist as a Young Man* (1916), and Richardson's *Pilgrimage* (1915–46). (2) *Variable focalization* occurs in narratives that employ more than one reflector. In Woolf's *Mrs. Dalloway*, for example, events are variously seen through the eyes of Clarissa Dalloway, Richard Dalloway, Peter Walsh, Septimus Warren Smith, Rezia Smith, and other characters. (3) Finally, *multiple focalization*, which is a special case of variable focalization, occurs in texts in which the same events are told repeatedly, but are each time seen through a different focal character. An example text is Patrick White's *The Solid Mandala* (1966), to be discussed in detail below.

C. *External focalization* marks the most drastic reduction of narrative information because it restricts itself to "outside views," reporting what would be visible and audible to a virtual camera. Externally focalized narratives typically consist of dialogue and "stage directions" only, as in the following excerpt from Hemingway's "The Killers" (1927), which is often cited as the mode's prototypical case:

The door of Henry's lunch-room opened and two men came in. They sat down at the counter.

"What's yours?" George asked them.

"I don't know," one of the men said. "What do you want to eat, Al?"

"I don't know," said Al. "I don't know what I want to eat."

Outside it was getting dark. The street-light came on outside the window. The two men at the counter read the menu.[7]

As Genette points out, focalization patterns do not necessarily extend across whole texts but may be restricted to "a definite narrative section, which can be very short" (*Narrative Discourse*, 191). Fixed internal focalization is a static pattern by definition (if it weren't static, one wouldn't call it "fixed"), whereas dynamic patterns allow various shifts between patterns. Genette notes that nineteenth-century novelists tend to introduce characters via externally focalized block description before using them as reflectors (*Narrative Discourse*, 190).

Many narratologists have been happy to use Genette's categories, and some have contributed additions and refinements. Genette's allusion to a technique of focalizing through "an impersonal, floating observer" (*Narrative Discourse*, 192) has led David Herman to develop a general theory of "hypothetical focalization."[8] William Nelles has coined useful terms qualifying types of focalization by perception channels, yielding "ocularization" (sight), "auricularization" (sound), "gustativization" (taste), "olfactivization" (smell), and "tactivilization" (touch).[9]

The present author has suggested that all types of real-life perception – or *online perception* as it will be called in the following – need to be complemented by their counterparts in *offline perception* – meaning the imaginary sights, sounds, smells, tastes, and touches that one perceives in recollection, vision, hallucination, and dream.[10] The literary representation of imaginary or offline perception can involve the same styles and techniques that authors use to represent characters' online perception, and occasionally (as in real life) it may difficult to determine whether a character's perceptions are online or offline. On the other hand, imaginary perception can be notably less realistic than online perception; specifically, it easily overcomes real-life constraints when executing spatio-temporal jumps. The following passage from one of the famous childhood recollection sections of Charles Dickens's *David Copperfield* (1849–50) illustrates the phenomenon well:

And now I see the outside of our house, with the latticed bedroom-windows standing open to let in the sweet-smelling air, and the ragged old rooks'-nests still dangling in the elm-trees at the bottom of the front garden. Now I am in the garden at the back, beyond the yard where the empty pigeon-house and dog-kennel are – a very preserve of butterflies, as I remember it, with a high fence, and a gate and padlock; where the fruit clusters on the trees, riper and richer than fruit has ever been since, in any other garden, and where my mother gathers some in a basket, while I stand by, bolting furtive gooseberries, and trying to look unmoved. A great wind rises, and the summer is gone in a moment. We are playing in the winter twilight, dancing about the parlour. When my mother is out of breath and rests herself in an elbow-chair, I watch her winding her bright curls round her fingers, and straitening her waist, and nobody knows better than I do that she likes to look so well, and is proud of being so pretty. That is among my very earliest impressions.[11]

The narrator's mother is here seen in the narrator's selective and mobile recollection. But, an attentive reader of these pages might ask, isn't the passage mainly seen through the child-character rather than through the adult narrator? Indeed, in many first-person (homodiegetic) texts, such as this one, the point of perceptual origin hovers between two co-ordinate systems because first-person narrator and protagonist – also called the "narrating I" and the "experiencing I," respectively – are separated in time and space but linked through a biographical identity relation. This creates an – occasionally unstable – union between the current, remembering self and what French critics term *un autre* (literally, "an other"). (A similar constellation is present in third-person, figural narration where a remembering reflector may also split into a current and a past self. However, only in first-person narration is the past self identical with the text's narrator.) Evidently, in the passage quoted, "now I see" signals focalization through the narrator while "I watch her winding her bright curls" (plus plenty of other detail) is focalized through *both* the child-protagonist *and* the narrator. Bringing the online/offline distinction to bear on the case one recognizes that the child's *online* perception is actually embedded in the narrator's *offline* perception. But, as another attentive reader, mindful of Genette's two questions – who speaks? who sees? – might ask at this point: isn't focalization through the narrator expressly forbidden in Genette's model? Indeed it is, and resolving this problem has resulted in one of the major innovations of post-Genettean focalization theory.

Post-Genettean accounts: Bal, Rimmon-Kenan, and the cognitive approach

Post-Genettean focalization theory has been strongly influenced by Mieke Bal's critique of Genette's model and her introduction of a number of new terms and definitions.[12] Bal specifically points out that Genette's "external" focalization (type C, above) is vague about who sees, what is seen, and how it is seen. She raises a similar objection against the concept of "zero" focalization (type A) because even typical "non-focalized" passages are rarely entirely free of point of view, attitude, restriction of perceptual field, or emotional stance (and the passage from Michener's *Hawaii* quoted above seems to support the point). Bal therefore proposes to subsume Genette's external and zero focalizations under the single category of "external focalization" – external not because things are seen from the outside (as in Genette's etymology of the term) but because they are imaginatively seen by the narrator who, in Bal's definition, is external to the story (in Genette's terms, the narrator would be "extradiegetic"). Bal's narrator now acquires an additional function, namely that of being a possible "external focalizer" (or "narrator-focalizer") systematically opposed to the "internal focalizer" character (a.k.a. reflector etc.) residing within the storyworld. As one can see, Bal's proposal makes it possible to handle the multiple perceiving subjects in the Dickens passage without falling into the trap of the erroneous narrator = character equation. Once having admitted narrator-focalizers, Bal also explores the mechanics of presenting other minds' perceptions, of adopting somebody's point of view, of "delegating" focalization to subordinate focalizers, and of chaining or embedding focalization ("hypofocalization"). Many commentators have applauded the logical and practical gains of Bal's account.

In *Narrative Discourse Revisited*, Genette briefly acknowledges that his own original formula "who sees?" is too "purely visual, and hence overly narrow," and he replaces it by the more general "who perceives?"[13] However, many narratologists have argued for yet a further widening of scope. Shlomith Rimmon-Kenan, in particular, has suggested that the "perceptual facet" should be complemented by two further facets: the psychological facet (subsuming cognition and emotion); and the ideological facet.[14] Although her proposal has not met with general approval (dissenting views have been voiced by Seymour Chatman and Gerald Prince), it is well nigh impossible to deny that psychology, cognition, emotion, and ideology have a direct impact on perception. For this reason, the term *apperception* is often used to designate both the interpretive nature of perception and one's understanding something in "frames" of previous experience. Apperception explains why identical things can be perceived differently by different people, or in other words, why somebody sees X as Y and another sees X as Z, as in William James's four men touring Europe. Obviously, the forms, styles, and rhetorical uses of such "multiperspectivism" are of major interest to literary theory and criticism, but so far only one collection of German essays has been published on the subject, edited by Vera and Ansgar Nünning.[15]

On the cognitive level, perception and apperception (in both real and imaginary forms) affect *all* participants in the game of storytelling, including readers. In the greater picture, the general frame of storytelling contains (1) a narrator who is grounded in the point-of-view co-ordinates of his or her discourse here-and-now; (2) a reader who is situated in a reception here-and-now; and (3) the characters situated in the story here-and-now. But far from fettering the participants to these "home co-ordinates," narrative allows, invites, and possibly even requires "deictic shifts" to imaginary co-ordinates and spaces.[16] Thus narrators may imaginatively transpose to the story here-and-now (the narrator in the passage from Michener's *Hawaii* clearly *sees* that "aching beauty of lush valleys"), or they may adopt a character's view of the current scene; characters freely relocate from online to offline perception and vice versa, while readers can imaginatively hear the narrator speak and let themselves be transported into the world of action (an effect known as "immersion").[17] As can be seen, in this picture, narration and focalization come out as mutually reinforcing and mutually dependent factors of storytelling.

Focalization in Patrick White's *The Solid Mandala*

One of the questions that every narratologist has to decide for himself or herself is whether to stick to Genette's or Bal's model, and whether to use a broad or a narrow conception of facets of focalization. In what follows, Patrick White's novel *The Solid Mandala*, which helped him win the Nobel prize for Literature in 1973, will be analyzed as a case of multiple focalization, and an attempt will be made to treat the narrator's ironical slant as a case of narratorial focalization (external focalization, in Bal's terminology). All broader facets of focalization will be considered (especially psychological, emotional, and cognitive ones), and special attention will be paid to any reading effects caused by focalization.

White's third-person (heterodiegetic) novel, first published in 1966, is set in Sarsaparilla, near Sydney, Australia. It tells the story of unmarried twin brothers, Waldo and Arthur Brown, who never parted company in their lives. There are four chapters. Chapter 1 is a prologue in which the twins, now in their late sixties, slovenly in appearance and failing in health, are seen on their customary morning walk by two ladies on a bus. The narrator's recording device is located very close to the two ladies, registering what they say, perceive, and think. The result is an opportunistic mix of external (in Bal's sense), variable, and collective focalization, often making fun of the characters ("The eyes of the two women followed the tunnel which led inward, through the ragged greenery and sudden stench of crushed weeds.

You could hide behind a bush if necessary").[18] Both focalization and tone stand in sharp contrast to what follows in the next two chapters, entitled "Waldo" and "Arthur," respectively. Chapter 2, by far the longest chapter in the book (63 percent of the text), is focalized exclusively through Waldo, while chapter 3 (26 percent) is focalized exclusively through Arthur. Chapter 4 is a brief epilogue that uses three reflectors for the *dénouement* (resolution of the plot).

In chapters 2 and 3 perception and apperception vary with the different mindsets of the respective reflector characters. Conscious of having descended from upper-class English forebears on his mother's side, Waldo tends to be critical of everything – the Australian environment, the small-town inhabitants, and his brother, whom he considers a half-wit. Entering Waldo's apperceptions and thoughts, the reader soon notices that Waldo's mind is only tangentially concerned with the present because everything he sees in the present reminds him of events that happened in the past: his life with his parents (now long dead), his relations to professional and private acquaintances (among them the girl Dulcie, whom he had once proposed to but was rejected), and growing up and getting old with his brother, Arthur. In fact, around 80 percent of Waldo's chapter is concerned with the offline perception produced by his spontaneous recollections. These passages of retrospection constitute what Genette calls "subjective analepses" – reflector flashbacks – and although they get to us in the associative order of Waldo's consciousness they cumulatively supply the pieces that make up this reflector's biography and personality.

As the psychonarratologists Marisa Bortolussi and Peter Dixon have pointed out, when readers negotiate a reflector-mode text and become privy to the working of a reflector's mind, they have a natural inclination to empathize and identify with the person concerned.[19] True as this may be in general terms and under experimental conditions; in White's novel the reader's relationship to Waldo is anything but harmonious or "consonant." Waldo may be intelligent and erudite, but he is also egoistic, narcissistic (he kisses a mirror at one point), and entirely lacking in humor. His life, as it plays back in his recollections, is a relentless series of professional and personal failures. Symptomatically, the loved girl's features change chameleon-like from attractiveness to ugliness depending on whether Waldo believes she appreciates or scorns him. Because Waldo's outlook on life is so plainly warped and self-deceptive, the reader tends to laugh, with the narrator, at Waldo's unlikely representations and overblown literary aspirations. Referring to one of his "literary notes," Waldo reflects that "[n]ot even Goethe, a disagreeable, egotistical man and overrated writer, whom he had always detested, could have equalled Waldo's *dazzled morning moon*" (*Mandala*, 130). At

the same time the reader is also liminally aware that beneath the text's dissonant humor there lies a serious personality disorder which poses a gathering
threat to the character's environment in general and to his brother in particular. As Waldo's apperceptions become ever more schizoid and addled with
hate, a minor frustration finally precipitates an explosive outburst. Turning
to his brother with the intention to strangle him, Waldo sees Arthur's face
"Opening. Coming apart. Falling" (*Mandala*, 214). Abruptly, chapter 2 ter-
minates at this point.

By this time, the reader has long suspected that Arthur is not the idiot
Waldo takes him to be, and chapter 3, now focalized entirely through Arthur,
gives us an opportunity to see what he is really like. Arthur's mind now serves
as the balancing filter through which the episodes earlier remembered by
Waldo are revisited, and this produces the juxtaposition of contrary apperceptions characteristic of multiple focalization. In a sense, Arthur's outlook
on life is as exotic as Waldo's because Arthur is indeed retarded intellectually and deviant behaviorally. But, unlike Waldo, Arthur has many redeem-
ing qualities: he has a head for figures; he is practical-minded and entrusted
with taking care of everyday chores; and most of the time he has a just
sense of what not to do. Above all, what makes him deviant also makes him
endearing: a "man and child" (*Mandala*, 311), he retains a child-like simple-
mindedness, inquisitiveness, impulsiveness, perceptiveness, and creativeness.
In the storyworld itself, sensitive people are as attracted to Arthur as they
are repelled by Waldo. And while one laughs at Waldo's distortions, Arthur's
strange visions are often oddly appropriate:

> Suddenly Arthur burst into tears because he saw that Waldo was what the
> books referred to as a lost soul. He, too, for that matter, was lost. Although he
> might hold Waldo in his arms, he could never give out from his soul enough
> of that love which was there to give. So his brother remained cold and dry.
>
> (*Mandala*, 284)

Significantly, it is Arthur who sees the mystic pattern of the mandala, which
symbolizes the harmonious union or mingling of opposites, in the speckled
"taws" (marbles) which he likes to give to people he is fond of. Naturally,
critics have also found the mandala pattern in the novel's bonding of the two
unlike brothers.

Waldo's and Arthur's chapters differ in one important technical detail.
While Waldo's flashbacks are linked to the current here and now, Arthur's
chapter represents a single long stretch of subjective analepsis without any
clue as to when or in what situation it unfolds. Compelled to fill in the gap,
the reader is likely to fall back on the conventional motif of a dying (or
possibly dead) man's summary recollection of his life (as used, for instance,

in the film *American Beauty* or in Stevie Smith's poem "Not waving but drowning"). Naturally, it is an assumption that charges the text with emotion and tragedy – and leads to a considerable surprise when it turns out to be false. As the chapter recounts Waldo's mortal attack from Arthur's point of view we learn that it is *Waldo* who dies of a stroke brought on by the exertion of trying to kill his brother. In chapter 4, after Waldo's body has been found by a neighbor, Arthur accuses himself of having killed Waldo, but it is clear that what he means is that he was unable to prevent Waldo from killing himself. At the end of the novel, as Arthur is sent to a mental home, we have a double tragedy on our hands, pitying Arthur for failing to save Waldo, and finally also pitying Waldo because Arthur has taught us how to do so.

The foregoing thumbnail sketch of *The Solid Mandala* illustrates how strategic choices in focalization determine this novel's structure (especially in its counterbalancing or rather contrapuntal chapters), characterization (opening up several viewpoints on the characters), and its surprise outcome.[20] Above all, the novel's strategy of multiple focalization motivates the reader to re-read the text in order to compare the many twice-told events, to reconstrue the personalities of the characters, and to appreciate the many leitmotifs and contrasts. Any reader interested in an in-depth unraveling of these features might wish to consult Gordon Collier's 500-page study of the novel, which is a masterpiece of scholarly analysis and narratological criticism.[21] Collier excellently demonstrates the breadth and variety of reflector-mode narration especially when grounded in focalizers as given to narrativizing their lives as Waldo and Arthur, and he also persuasively demonstrates the merits of a close analysis of focalization. It is along these lines that the following catalog of questions aims at stimulating the reader's further research and exploration.

A task sheet for analyzing focalization

1. Given an internally focalized text, does it use a special reflector or set of reflectors? How accurate are the perceptions and thoughts of the reflectors, and to what extent are they "fallible filters" (to use a phrase of Chatman's)? (In White, we encounter two reflectors whose experiences overlap but whose apperceptions are entirely different. Waldo, of course, is the proverbial fallible filter.)
2. Historically speaking, in what tradition of focalization does the text stand? Is it contemporaneous with or does it predate/postdate the era of Modernism and literary impressionism? Does it anticipate a later style or technique or does it fall back on an earlier style or technique? Does it

use the contrast potential of divergent apperceptions as in William James's four men touring Europe or the unlike brothers in *The Solid Mandala*? (Notable pre-impressionist instances of idiosyncratic apperception occur in the novels of Jane Austen, Gustave Flaubert, and Charles Dickens, often creating a humorous effect similar to that of chapter 2 of *The Solid Mandala*.)[22]

3. In what proportion does the text use ocularization, auricularization, gustativization, olfactivization, and tactivilization? Are the sense data dependent on external circumstances (reflector not able to see anything because it is pitch dark – Molly Bloom in *Ulysses*) or special character traits (the reflector in Patrick Süskind's *The Perfume* [1985] being gifted with an exceptional sense of smell)? Are concomitant thoughts and emotional states represented or left to the reader's empathetic construction?

4. What is the proportion of online to offline perception? What is the relative significance of online and offline segments? (In the two main chapters of White's novel the characters' recollections play a central role. In chapter 3, Arthur's long stretch of floating offline perception serves the purpose of creating a surprise effect.)

5. In which way(s) does the text render a character's perceptions and thoughts? To what extent does it use "interior monologue," "free indirect discourse," and "narrated perception"? Does it use explicit perception indicators (such as "Waldo saw"), or does it leave identification of focalizer and mental process to the reader?

6. If analysis proceeds on the post-Genettean model, which kinds of narratorial offline perception (imaginary perception, recollection, etc.) characterize the narrator's discourse? Do the narrator and the reflector have different degrees of knowledge and different kinds of apperceptions? If so, which concepts best describe the contrasts arising? If the narrator's and the reflector's apperceptions do *not* markedly differ, what are the reasons – narrator restricting him- or herself to what is "public knowledge" in the storyworld? narrator remaining neutral or non-committal? narrator allowing his or her diction to become "colored" by the character's language? Are there specific locations, such as chapter beginnings or endings, that favor expression of the narrator's privileged point of view? Is the degree of consonance or dissonance between the narrator's view and the character's apperception ever treated explicitly? (In White's novel, the narrator's ironical slant initially invites a humorous response but later heightens the tragic effect through contrast and reversal. However, neither in Waldo's nor in Arthur's chapter does the narrator allow himself the freedom of explicit comment.)

7. Is the focalization pattern static (as it would be in a fixedly focalized figural novel) or dynamic (as it would be in variably focalized texts or texts that use both narrator and reflector focalization)? (In White's novel, focalization is highly dynamic, changing from chapter to chapter.)

NOTES

1. Monika Fludernik, "The Diachronization of Narratology." *Narrative* 11:3 (2003), pp. 331–48.
2. William James, *The Principles of Psychology*, Vol. I (New York: Dover, 1950), pp. 286–7.
3. Virginia Woolf, "Modern Fiction." In Andrew McNeillie (ed.) *The Essays of Virginia Woolf*, Vol. IV (London: Hogarth, 1994), pp. 160–1.
4. Gérard Genette, *Narrative Discourse*. Translated by Jane E. Lewin (Oxford: Blackwell, 1980), p. 186.
5. James A. Michener, *Hawaii* (New York: Bantam, 1970), p. 9.
6. Ernest Hemingway, *For Whom the Bell Tolls* (New York: Scribner's, 1943), p. 1.
7. Ernest Hemingway, "The Killers." *The Complete Short Stories of Ernest Hemingway* (New York: Scribner's, 1987), p. 215.
8. David Herman, *Story Logic: Problems and Possibilities of Narrative* (Lincoln: University of Nebraska Press, 2002), chapter 8.
9. William Nelles, *Frameworks: Narrative Levels and Embedded Narrative* (Frankfurt: Lang, 1997), chapter 3.
10. Manfred Jahn, "Windows of Focalization: Deconstructing and Reconstructing a Narratological Concept." *Style* 30:2 (1996), pp. 241–67.
11. Charles Dickens, *David Copperfield* (London: Penguin, 1982), p. 64.
12. Mieke Bal, *Narratology*. Translated by Christine van Boheemen (Toronto: Toronto University Press, 1985); Mieke Bal, "Narration and Focalization." *On Story-Telling* (Sonoma, CA: Polebridge, 1991), pp. 75–108.
13. Gérard Genette, *Narrative Discourse Revisited*. Translated by Jane E. Lewin (Ithaca: Cornell University Press, 1988), p. 64.
14. Shlomith Rimmon-Kenan, *Narrative Fiction: Contemporary Poetics* (London: Methuen, 1983).
15. Vera Nünning and Ansgar Nünning (eds.) *Multiperspektivisches Erzählen: Zur Perspektivenstruktur im englischen Roman des 18. bis 20. Jahrhunderts* (Trier: Wissenschaftlicher Verlag, 2000).
16. Judith F. Duchan, Gail A. Bruder, and Lynne E. Hewitt (eds.) *Deixis in Narrative: A Cognitive Science Perspective* (Hillsdale N.J.: Erlbaum, 1995).
17. On the notions of "transportation" and "immersion" see Richard J. Gerrig, *Experiencing Narrative Worlds: On the Psychological Activities of Reading* (New Haven: Yale University Press, 1993).
18. Patrick White, *The Solid Mandala* (London: Penguin, 1988), p. 14.
19. Marisa Bortolussi and Peter Dixon, *Psychonarratology: Foundations for the Empirical Study of Literary Response* (Cambridge: Cambridge University Press, 2003), chapter 6. The authors define psycho-narratology as the empirical study of narrative reading effects.

20. On cognitive reversal effects see Manfred Jahn, "'Speak, friend, and enter': Garden Paths, Artificial Intelligence, and Cognitive Narratology." In David Herman (ed.) *Narratologies: New Perspectives on Narrative Analysis* (Ohio: Ohio State University Press, 1999), pp. 167–94.

21. Gordon Collier, *The Rocks and Sticks of Words: Style, Discourse and Narrative Structure in the Fiction of Patrick White* (Amsterdam: Rodopi, 1992).

22. For an account of techniques for representing "mind styles," or character-based apperceptions see Geoffrey N. Leech and Michael Short, *Style in Fiction* (London: Longman, 1981), chapter 6.

8

HETA PYRHÖNEN

Genre

In 1926 Agatha Christie published *The Murder of Roger Ackroyd*, dedicating it "to Punkie who likes an orthodox detective story, murder, inquest, and suspicion falling on everyone in turn!" The title signals to readers what kind of book Christie's narrative is, a classification that the dedication reinforces. The dedication specifies the basic components of an "orthodox" detective story: it begins with murder, which is followed by an investigation spotlighting each character in turn as a possible murderer, until the crime is solved and guilt is brought home to a specific character. As if these markers were not enough, the book abounds with references to detective stories: characters discuss their conventions and the book's first-person narrator, Dr. Sheppard, finds himself in the position of a "Watson," the detective's friend and aid. These clues supply readers with a pragmatic user's guide to detective fiction.

This characterization of Christie's book is grounded in the notion of *genre*, grouping texts together on the basis of certain shared features. It suggests that relating a text to a genre may serve a number of different purposes. First, genre helps us to *describe* texts by singling out textual components worthy of attention such as plot structure; in turn, description helps us to *classify* a text by placing it among other similar texts. In this view, genres are principled groupings of texts. Second, genre directs the ways in which we *write*, *read*, and *interpret* texts. Without some shared conception of what, for example, a narrative is, writers would be unable to communicate with readers. A genre functions as a norm or an expectation guiding writers in their work and readers in their encounter with texts. Third, genre *prescribes* artistic practices. Generic conventions are normative, telling authors what they should and should not do. By claiming to have written an orthodox detective story, Christie shows her awareness of genre's prescriptive role. Fourth, genres help us to *evaluate* literary works. Christie's dedication places readers in Punkie's position, inviting them to consider whether she succeeds in her task. Originally her book caused an outcry because readers deemed it unorthodox, complaining that by making the Watson-like narrator the murderer, she had not followed the rules of fair play typical of the genre.

This variety of uses suggests that when we speak of genre we do not speak of it in the same sense each time, because there is no universal pattern in its study that would fit each instance. For example, if textual meaning is thought to reside in authorial intention, then genre functions as a set of prescriptive rules, whereas if it is located in the text, genre is regarded as a pattern of textual features.[1] Each use renders us services, but' we should bear in mind that the terms "genre" and "generic" do not possess the same status and function in all cases.

In order to explore this rich variety, I first briefly delineate the history of the concept of genre, paying attention to major currents of genre theory. I then consider the relevance of genre for the analysis of narrative fiction. Classical genre theory identified narration (*diegesis*) as one of the "natural" forms of imitation; ever since, narrative fiction has had the status of a "super-genre." Here the focus lies on its function in literary communication: generic competence enables readers to decode a narrative, co-creating the story as a meaningful and coherent whole. I illustrate this process by showing how knowledge of generic conventions guides the reading of *The Murder of Roger Ackroyd*. Its unusual solution not only expanded generic possibilities but also, somewhat paradoxically, pointed toward generic dissolution, for the murderer–narrator almost ensured the victory of "evil." Two decades later, the Argentine author Jorge Luis Borges dismantled this crude detective-story morality, heralding a new development that evolved into the so-called *metaphysical detective story*. In conclusion I consider how this offshoot elucidates questions of generic change.

A brief history of the concept of genre

Genre theory began with Plato and Aristotle. Classical genre theory based the existence of genre in the imitative representation of nature. It understood imitation as a natural human instinct. In Plato's *Republic*, Socrates identified three methods of representation: the *diegetic* where poets speak entirely in their own voice; the *mimetic* where they imitate the voices of someone else such as an actor; and the *mixed*, where both methods obtain. Aristotle, however, reduced these methods into two classes – the mimetic and the mixed – but introduced further distinguishing criteria based on subject-matter. Here the basis of separation is the moral or social level of the characters and actions represented that may be either above, below, or equal to us. The prescriptive side of generic classification appeared in the concept of decorum; in other words, Aristotle maintained that certain subjects require appropriate forms and styles. Tragedy, for example, must structurally consist of a single action.[2]

Classical genre theory understood literature as an imitation and emulation of ideal models that were based on stable rules abstracted from exemplary texts. These models were supposed to serve as norms for subsequent literary activity. This theory, explains Jean-Marie Schaeffer, was basically pragmatic, insofar as all of its descriptions could be translated into statements about how a work should be written in order to qualify for inclusion in a genre. Also, it was regulative, for generic notions functioned as criteria serving to judge the degree to which a work adhered to a norm, or a set of rules. Genre resembled a yardstick with which individual works were measured and valorized. It was primarily a criterion for critical discrimination: the theory of genre was where literary criticism and evaluation were carried out.[3]

The classical age distinguished three literary types: *lyric*, *drama*, and *epic* that were for centuries regarded as the natural forms of literature. Aristotle's precepts were reformulated and popularized by the Roman poet Horace in his *Ars Poetica*, which functions as a bridge between classical thought and the Renaissance. Horace reiterated the emphasis on decorum: each genre has a subject-matter, characters, language, and meter appropriate to it.[4] A great deal of experimentation occurred with generic categories during the Renaissance (Rabelais, Shakespeare) and the neo-classical era (Swift), resulting in various hybrid forms such as tragicomedy, but the real point of departure for modern genre theory took place with European Romanticism at the end of the eighteenth century. Associated with such German authors and literary theorists as Goethe, Schiller, and the Schlegel brothers, the Romantics called for a philosophical theory that would explain the existence and intrinsic organization of literature into genres. What was radically new was understanding literature as an autonomous historical entity. Classical genre theory had regarded genres as stable, universal categories. The existence of various hybrid genres and the rapidly growing popularity of the novel, however, called this view into question. The Romantics emphasized that genres are historically determined, dynamic entities whose developmental trajectory may be described with organic metaphors: a genre grows, flowers, ages, and may finally die. This trajectory is, as it were, written into the "genetic" blueprint of a genre that evolves in and through individual texts, creating a textual series and striving towards a genre's historical fulfillment.[5]

Romantic genre theory developed the notion of the triad – lyric, epic, and drama – as a natural generic division by introducing various content elements (such as themes) as defining criteria. This theory led to a number of theoretical knots that Gérard Genette has unraveled.[6] It erroneously linked modes (narration and dramatic imitation) with thematic content, thus confusing *modes* with *genres*. Modes are forms of enunciation that have to do with ways of speaking that people use in contexts of everyday communication. They can be thought of as "natural forms," in the sense that language and its use seem more "natural" to us when compared with the deliberate elaboration of literary forms. We appear to have an innate narrative competence: narration is a mode we learn simultaneously and probably at the same time as we learn our first language. Genres, in contrast, are empirical, historical literary categories. They are always coupled with particular themes and a milieu that together give rise to a specific worldview. Unlike modes, genres are defined by both formal and thematic criteria. Moreover, genres cut across modes; as Genette points out, Œdipus narrated remains tragic. In the classification of genres no class is more natural or ideal than another one; they may simply be more capacious and have a broader and historically longer cultural reach.

The Romantics introduced yet another radical departure from classical genre theory, for in proposing that "every poem is a genre unto itself," they rebelled against the supposed rigidity of traditional generic rules as tyrannical constraints upon an author's individual feeling and sensibility. It was claimed that authors could do without generic doctrines altogether. At the turn of the twentieth century the Italian philosopher Benedetto Croce attacked all notions of genre, and this anti-genre position carried over not only into the aesthetics of Modernism but also into many strands of twentieth-century literary theory. The American New Critics, for example, devalued a text's generic features as extrinsic to its essential literariness. Similarly, poststructuralist theory stresses the indeterminacy of textual meaning, questioning any interpretive privilege or literary authority genres may be said to have.

A work's transgression of generic norms, however, does not mean that the genre does not exist, argues Tzvetan Todorov.[7] On the contrary, artistic violations require a law, one that is to be violated. In fact, norms become visible thanks to such violations. Moreover, a transgressive work such as James Joyce's *Ulysses* initiates new norms, inviting subsequent transgressions (*Genres*, 14–15). Todorov's point is that we cannot do without genres, for they not only ensure intelligibility but also enable us to perceive innovation in literature. David Duff agrees, arguing that genre theory today signals opportunity and common purpose: genre functions as an enabling device for writers and readers, the vehicle for the acquisition of competence.[8] Familiarity with a genre fosters generic competence, that is, an ability (1) to recognize and interpret the codes typical of a given genre; and (2) to perceive departures from it.

Present-day genre theory is anchored in the theory of "speech acts," or what J. L. Austin described as ways of doing things with words.[9] Like speech acts such as questioning and commanding, genres shape literary discourse, ensuring meaningful communication. The Russian literary theorist Mikhail Bakhtin expanded genre theory to encompass the entire field of verbal activity. He maintained that all individual concrete utterances rely on relatively stable types of utterances; these types are speech genres.[10] Bakhtin distinguished between primary (simple) speech genres, familiar from unmediated, everyday speech communication; and secondary (complex) speech genres. The latter are organized, complex forms of cultural communication including, for example, literary and scientific texts. During their formation, secondary speech genres absorb and digest primary ones. In this process, primary speech genres are transformed into literary–artistic components, losing their immediate relation to actual reality. As Todorov observes, this anchoring of secondary speech genres in primary ones abolishes the opposition between literature and nonliterature, giving way to a typology of speech genres. The everyday speech act of telling a story about oneself, for instance, forms the kernel for the literary genre of autobiography (*Genres*, 25). Each literary type of discourse has nonliterary "relatives" that are closer to it than are other types of literary discourse (*Genres*, 11). For example, detective fiction has more in common with (pseudo)scientific treatises of crime such as Cesare Lombroso's phrenology than it has with historical novels of the *War and Peace* variety. Given the intimate bond between primary and secondary speech genres, Todorov rejects the notion of there being either a "natural" or "ideal" ground for genres; instead, he holds that genres are born "[q]uite simply from other genres. A new genre is always the transformation of one or several old genres: by inversion, by displacement, by combination . . . There has never been a literature without genres; it is a system in constant transformation, and historically speaking the question of origins cannot be separated from the terrain of the genres themselves" (*Genres*, 15). One reason for this mobile nature of genres is their intimate link with society, for they are social institutions that always stand in some relation to dominant ideology. In Todorov's words, genres, like any other institution, "bring to light the constitutive features of the society to which they belong" (*Genres*, 19).

The advantage of a model like Todorov's is that it no longer posits genres as the causal principle for the existence of literary texts, as did Romantic genre theory. This theory erroneously held that genres constitute the essence of types of literature, their foundation, and their principle of inherent causality,[11] while present-day genre theory holds that literature does not, and never can, conform to this type of causality. What Jacques Derrida characterizes as "the law of genre" draws attention to the fact that generic designations simultaneously describe a generic reality *and* participate in constructing it.[12] Generic divisions and subdivisions do not simply arise from literature itself, but result from the designations of writers, critics, and theorists. The designation "detective fiction," for example, refers to all the texts that the literary institution, in a given epoch or throughout the ages, accepts as "detective fiction." Moreover, generic definitions extend in two directions, for they not only define what a given genre is but also define what it is not. The setting of these boundaries is always self-referential, for a genre defines a literary phenomenon in terms of itself. What this means is that each time we classify a given text as an instance of a given genre, we cannot help but identify in the text features that this classification deems pertinent. Finally, the law of genre suggests that a generic classification invariably under-determines a text, because it lifts out only some relevant textual traits at the expense of others. A generic classification never covers the global text. *The Murder of Roger Ackroyd*, for instance, could profitably be read as a romance or as a comedy of manners, and not just as a detective story.

The generic writing and reading contract: the case of *The Murder of Roger Ackroyd*

"It is because genres exist as an institution," writes Todorov, "that they function as 'horizons of expectation' for readers and as 'models of writing' for authors" (*Genres*, 18). Genres channel the reader's inferences, help create intelligibility and coherence, and delimit the scope of interpretation. I now illustrate how a reader's knowledge of generic norms and conventions guides the reading of Agatha Christie's classical detective story, *The Murder of Roger Ackroyd*.[13]

The text opens with two deaths: Mrs. Ferrars commits suicide after having confided in Ackroyd that she has previously poisoned her husband and has been blackmailed ever since; immediately afterwards Ackroyd is murdered. The obvious conclusion is that Mrs Ferrars's blackmailer is also Ackroyd's murderer. It is the task of Christie's series detective, Hercule Poirot, to identify the culprit from among many suspects, including Ackroyd's adopted son, Ralph Paton, his niece, Flora Ackroyd, and various friends and dependants. Poirot asks the local doctor, Dr. Sheppard, to act as his "Watson," by helping him with the investigation. Gradually the son emerges as the most likely culprit; his disappearance seems to confirm his guilt. In the novel's surprise ending, however, Poirot shows that Dr. Sheppard, whom no one suspected, actually is the culprit. In Poirot's explanation, moral weakness and greed were his motives. Sheppard has been recording the case with the intention of eventually publishing it as an account of Poirot's failure. Poirot makes him rewrite his manuscript, so that it conforms to generic conventions by narrating Poirot's success.

A detective story like Christie's constitutes an appropriate case study in this context for two reasons. First, by emphasizing narrative sequence, suspense, and closure; by making the hierarchical organization of narrative levels visible; by illustrating the operations of intertextuality; by focusing on characters who are themselves engaged in acts of reading, writing, and interpretation, detective fiction such as Christie's represents the basic components of narrative. Second, it is classified as genre fiction where the fit between generic norms and conventions and a specific text is held to be particularly close. The detective-story genre, however, by no means consists of a group of homogeneous texts. There is, for example, no single archetypal plot, but rather a number of plot schemata and a range of plot conventions. Traditionally, three broad variants are identified as the sub-genres of mass-marketed detective fiction: classical detective fiction, hard-boiled detective stories, and the (police) procedural. Each treats crime and detection differently, for within the relational system of genres, they emphasize shared formal and thematic concerns in diverging ways. Certain features hold a dominant position in one variant but a subordinate one in others. Such features as patterns of plot, modes of narration, character roles, settings, and the author–reader relationship serve as the criteria with whose help distinctions can be made.

Generic competence in classical detective fiction is grounded in a relationship of complicity between authors and readers that resembles a game played according to a set of rules. The fundamental rules of this game comprise the questions "whodunit?" and "who is guilty?" The consequences of a crime are revealed well before the events that led up to it become known. This situation structures this sub-genre – but backwards: the plot strives to establish a linear, chronological sequence of events that eventually explains its own baffling beginning. In the final stage, the detective's reconstruction of the past includes the assessment of how moral responsibility is to be allotted among the suspects. This evaluation highlights the difference between the judicial and the moral codes, which may, but need not, overlap, for an agent may be both legally and morally responsible (i.e., guilty) or one but not the other. The question "whodunit?" is thus not identical with the question "who is guilty?" because the investigation shows guilt to be a more widespread phenomenon than crime. The game-like nature of this sub-genre suggests that to understand the function of textual components and the reading experience, we should understand the rules governing the relationship between author and reader. These rules are grounded in generic practices, although they are not identical with them. Rather, they arise from a conjunction of generic conventions and interpretive strategies, enabling the reader's moves in a game played with and against the author.[14]

In the whodunit a detective such as Poirot functions as a model reader; our own reading mirrors the detective's interpretive activity. Typically, his (and our) murder investigation is obfuscated by minor mysteries such as blackmail, theft, and clandestine marriage, necessitating that he sort out which clues belong to which mystery. Further, he must separate real clues from "red herrings," false fragments, which seem to fit one or more of the existing narrative patterns, but which temporarily invalidate correct hypotheses. Detective-story authors use various strategies when omitting important information at strategic points in the plot: devices of fragmenting information and presenting it in an ambiguous manner; techniques of highlighting insignificant details and of downplaying important ones; and techniques of using the detective to safeguard the solution. Author, detective, and text all play a dual role, for ostensibly their purpose is to enlighten readers, while, in fact, much of the time all three aim at delaying their understanding.[15] The rules of fair play decree that readers be given the necessary facts so that they can succeed in inferring the murderer's identity ahead of the detective. Also, the whodunit's emphasis on narrative construction calls on readers to appraise an author's own storytelling skills.

In *The Murder of Roger Ackroyd* Christie uses two types of clues: material clues such as facts (timing), things (a chair's position), and personal traces (footprints); and immaterial clues such as character traits and behavior patterns (greed, vanity, reticence). Although whodunit authors emphasize ratiocination and logical deduction, readers quickly learn that inference is inherently tied not only to formal generic rules (such as the requirement of a surprise ending) but also to that which is ideologically feasible within this subgenre. In addition to paying attention to formal rules, readers tune into what one might call "middle-class morality" in order to solve detective-story crimes. This fact explains why technical clues in themselves seldom suffice to unravel the case, while clues to personal traits reveal the ideological motivation. This particular case, for example, hinges on Christie's favorite theme, weakness of character and opportunity that together corrupt a person's moral fiber.

The "wavering-finger-of-suspicion" technique spotlights each character in turn as a potential murderer. However, readers can usually disregard some suspects right away, for, contrary to the suggestion of the police, the criminal can neither be an outsider nor the butler. In accordance with this genre's middle-class morality, the culprit is from the same social class as the victim. Therefore, readers retain the housemaid among the suspects, for her lady-like manner suggests she is something other than a servant. Early on most clues point to Ralph Paton, Ackroyd's adopted son. Yet the stronger the case is against him, the more reason readers have to look elsewhere, for Paton's guilt would not supply a satisfying surprise ending. Also, his involvement in the romantic sub-plot gradually speaks against his guilt. One function of the investigation is to establish who has a rightful claim to the fortune everyone hankers after, and the sub-plot helps to identify this person. Poirot correctly guesses that Paton has clandestinely married the maid, a girl of an impoverished, yet genteel, family. When she exhibits moral rectitude, readers can infer that she will steer Paton in the direction of moral probity. The new Mrs Paton proves that the couple can be entrusted with Ackroyd's fortune.

In hiding the murderer under the guise of a "Watson" character–narrator, Christie employs two key strategies of detective-story narration that Donna Bennett calls *confidence* and *confidentiality*. Confidence is the degree to which readers can rely on the truthfulness of the presentation of events; it controls the quality of the information they receive. Confidentiality regulates the quantity of information shared by the detective and readers.[16] There is hardly any confidentiality in this book, for although Poirot draws attention to all clues, he never divulges his conjectures about them to Sheppard or readers. With respect to confidence, Sheppard manipulates our assumptions about a "Watson," for readers assume that despite this figure's limited mental capacities, his moral trustworthiness vouches for his reliability as a narrator as regards the facts of the case. Accordingly, Sheppard's feigned frankness enlists confidence. Yet his narration is thoroughly ambiguous. On leaving from his meeting with Ackroyd, for example, Sheppard states that "[i]t was just ten minutes to nine when I left him, the letter still unread. I hesitated with my hand on the door handle, looking back and wondering if there was anything I had left undone."[17] The ambiguity of Sheppard's narration impedes the perception of the whole by opening up avenues for multiple inferences, and, thus, for the possibility that readers will construct the wrong hypotheses about who is responsible for what. In this instance, they most likely read the lines as a professional confidante's concern for a patient when they in fact refer to a freshly committed murder and its cover-up. Such ambiguously sinister statements pervade Sheppard's narration. If readers catch on to this ambiguity, then early on they will be able to discern the murderer's identity.

Another key clue is Sheppard's sister Caroline's repeated complaints about his reticence, pointing to the discrepancy between Sheppard and Captain Hastings, Christie's "Watson." Hastings is a sentimental, gossiping narrator, while Sheppard's narration is marked by irony, understatement, and detachment. All these characteristics mimic the strategies typical of Christie's authorship. The ironic detachment of Sheppard's narrative voice should alert readers to how this "Watson" narrator not only overreaches the capabilities of his role but also challenges Christie's narrative authority. As was already mentioned, Sheppard's initial intention is to publish an account of Poirot's failure. When she made a murderer the narrator, Christie had to find a way to ensure the detective's definitive victory over evil, a problem that underscores this genre's inherent ties to ideology. Christie solved this clash, argues Carl R. Lovitt, by forcing Sheppard, against his intention and will, into a "Watson's" role. As the murderer, he is privy to the facts of the case, yet Poirot manages to reduce him to a bewildered fool by refusing to divulge his inferences about clues and by finding clues of whose existence Sheppard was unaware. Also, Poirot makes him rewrite his manuscript, so that it respects generic conventions; in fact, the novel we read is this rewritten version.[18]

What does this reading tell us about generic competence? Briefly put, generic competence fluctuates between general fixed interpretive guidelines, functioning as rules of thumb, and the situational judgments of writers and readers about particular texts. These interpretive guidelines are their cumulative summaries of particular decisions, indicating what generic features to pick out as worthy of attention and how to ascribe significance to them. In adopting such rules, we acknowledge that choices of this sort have, with other detective narratives, appropriately reflected the complexities of generic particulars. These rules are plural and occasionally incommensurable: they may conflict with one another. We can and should modify these rules – even disregard them altogether – if they fail to function, following, instead, our intuition about what fits the narrative at hand. In changing the previous conventions pertaining to a "Watson" character–narrator, Christie, for example, challenged readers to do likewise. Generic competence thus consists of an interaction among generic components, conventional rules, and sensibility to particulars. Competence involves our interpretation of what is salient in the genre, and requires that we show our responsiveness and suppleness as writers and readers.

This notion of generic competence is based on understanding genre as a dynamic construct. It is grounded in an interaction among three levels: the level of reader expectations; the body of texts that forms a given genre; and the rules that govern both the interpretation and the production of texts.[19] In this view, a genre continually remakes and reworks its norms, thus extending them. As a dynamic process it is dominated by repetition, but also fundamentally marked by difference and change. Each new instance constitutes an addition to existing corpus and entails a selection from the repertoire of generic elements available at any one time. New novels aim to extend or to modify the repertoire, either by adding a new element or by transgressing one of the old ones. One might thus characterize genre as a plethora of innovations within certain limits.

Genres and historical change

As historical phenomena, genres are subject to changes and modifications, even extinction. Thus detective fiction, as mentioned above, encompasses a number of generic variants such as the hard-boiled detective story that gained ascendancy in the United States from the 1930s onward. Familiar examples are Dashiell Hammett's *The Maltese Falcon* (1930) and Raymond Chandler's *The Long Goodbye* (1953). It evolved as a reaction against the whodunit. Plot structure shows this documentable shift within the genre. The whodunit's mystery motivation is replaced by structures of adventure and the chase that keep the focus on investigative action. Much of the plot deals with an investigator's attempts to fathom what exactly he is to solve, climaxing in a situation demanding a personal, and usually a moral, decision about the criminal's fate.

What accounts for shifts and changes within a genre? The Russian Formalist Iurii Tynianov explained the tradition–innovation process of genres in his essay "The Literary Fact." He calls an *automatized principle of construction* the dominant literary trend at any given time, developed by writers in all its possible variations. He explains that "when we analyze literary evolution we find the following stages: (1) an opposing constructive principle takes shape in dialectical relationship to an automatized principle of construction; (2) it is then applied – the constructive principle seeks out the readiest field of application; (3) it spreads over the greatest mass of phenomena; (4) it becomes automatized and gives rise to opposing principles of construction."[20] Stefano Tani applies these notions to detective fiction, explaining that the hard-boiled narrative took shape dialectically against the whodunit's automatized principle of construction, as seen in its stereotypical use of a detective in one place in the idyllic countryside, and replaced it with an opposite constructive principle, that is, the formula of chase united to a thematic emphasis on the social and existential implications of the urban environment. Subsequently, this new principle was extended to the widest range of phenomena until it got automatized in turn, degenerating into the purely sensational detective story with a mechanical solution as, for example, in Mickey Spillane's Mike Hammer thrillers. It is here that Tani locates the intervention of the metaphysical detective story, a high literary, often parodic and deconstructive, offshoot, which structures itself on another opposite constructive principle: the suspension of the solution.[21]

Hard-boiled and metaphysical detective narratives, however, do not enjoy the same standing within detective fiction. Todorov maintains that in genre fiction such as the detective story changes do not concern the way a story is told but rather the *form of interest* that motivates it. The whodunit, for example, thrives on curiosity, whereas the hard-boiled narrative feeds on suspense. These divergent interests explain the different thematic concerns of these two subgenres, which, in the case of the whodunit, reinforce its puzzle-like nature, while the hard-boiled narrative emphasizes violence, sordid crime, and amorality.[22] Although the changes the hard-boiled authors introduced presented a complex, ambiguous, and relativistic reality alien to the whodunit, they nevertheless still operated *within* the genre. Todorov's point is that even radical alterations in a genre's thematics do not threaten its fundamental assumptions. Rather, in Tani's words, hard-boiled authors innovated the rules of the game "by making them more credible and by tuning them up with that sense of uneasiness and relativism that all gifted modernist writers experienced in the same period" (*Doomed*, 24).

The metaphysical detective story, in contrast, represents a more radical departure from the mainstream generic repertoire. Jorge Luis Borges's "Death and the Compass" (1942), Umberto Eco's *The Name of the Rose* (1980), Vladimir Nabokov's *Pale Fire* (1962), and Thomas Pynchon's *The Crying of Lot 49* (1966) are well-known examples. The metaphysical detective story scrutinizes the very ideas of mystery and crime, especially the possibility of creating enigmas through narrative and linguistic means. The interest lies in the meta-textual and meta-narrative processes of creating and sustaining a sense of a crime and an investigation. The text itself now becomes the mystery to be solved. The plot manipulates temporal and causal relations without establishing a basis for organizing the elements of the story into a coherent whole. It parodies the notion of solution as closure, either by supplying inconclusive solutions or by refusing to provide any solution whatsoever. Further, metaphysical detective fiction uses the conventions and the settings of the mainstream variants in order to textualize reality, drawing attention to its constructed nature. Through these measures it calls on readers to act as co-creators of the text, for our reading and interpretation are the major, often even the only, means of lending coherence to the narrative. The intention is to make us examine more closely these acts and generic conventions. Metaphysical detective stories play with the rules, techniques, and conventions of mainstream detective fiction from *without*, pushing against the confines of its mass-marketed cousin. Tani argues that it negates, even destroys, the fundamentals of detective fiction; while Merivale and Sweeney see this relationship as marked by a flamboyant self-reflexiveness: "these stories apply the detective process to [detective fiction's] own assumptions about detection."[23]

These notions about generic change are partly grounded in the idea of a continuously changing hierarchy of genres. The Russian Formalists argued that in each literary epoch different literary schools and literary genres compete with each other: it is this competition that brings about change. The generic system is, as it were, in a state of permanent revolution. When an old form has used up its possibilities, it gives way to new ones. "Serious novelists do not even try to 'improve upon' detective fiction," Tani writes, "but rather use the form as a scrapyard from which to dig out 'new' narrative techniques to be applied to the exhausted traditional novel" (*Doomed*, 34). What happens here is a process called "the canonization of a junior branch," which takes place when a previously minor or marginal genre such as detective fiction acquires a new position of literary dominance. Literary evolution, however, does not run a smooth course from one stage to the next, but is, rather, discontinuous in nature. The Formalists maintained that in the history of literature the legacy is not transmitted from father to son, but from uncle to nephew. The questions the metaphysical detective story takes up, for example, can be argued to owe much more to the tradition of the philosophical tale such as Voltaire's *Zadig* than to the mainstream detective story.

In insisting that the metaphysical detective story negates its mainstream cousin, Tani combines Formalist views with another conception of generic change. Not all generic change can be explained by referring to the process of the dialectical self-creation of new forms within the literary system. Change is also motivated by a genre's immersion in a particular socio-cultural context. This emphasis is familiar from Bakhtin's work. He argued that genres are not only formal but also *socio-historical* entities. They are ways of seeing and interpreting particular aspects of the world, strategies for conceptualizing reality. Genres have this function of representing changing conceptions of the world, thanks to their status as "transmission belts" between social history and linguistic history.[24] Accordingly, the metaphysical detective story – also known as the postmodern detective story – is thought to reflect the wider alterations in the socio-cultural climate of the twentieth century. "The shift within detective fiction," claims Tani, "corresponds perfectly to a shift without, in the general literary and cultural atmosphere" (*Doomed*, 38). In particular, it dramatizes postmodernism's lack of a center (absence of a goal and of a solution), as well as its refusal to posit any unifying system – including, paradoxically, genre.

The *feminist detective story* further emphasizes how generic development is always fundamentally tied to extra-literary contexts. In fact, from Edgar

Allan Poe's first detective stories onward, the genre was inimical to women. Feminism as a socio-political movement made possible the generic variant of feminist detective fiction. Some of its key conventions, such as the focus on friendship, derive from feminist discourse. What these observations underline is that explanations of generic change need to account both for modifications within the literary system and for the impact of the larger sociocultural context.

NOTES

1. Thomas O. Beebee, *The Ideology of Genre: A Comparative Study of Generic Instability* (University Park, PA: Pennsylvania State University Press, 1994), p. 3.
2. Heather Dubrow, *Genre* (London: Methuen, 1982), pp. 46–8.
3. Jean-Marie Schaeffer, "Literary Genres and Textual Genericity." In Ralph Cohen (ed.) *The Future of Literary Theory* (New York: Routledge, 1989), pp. 167–87.
4. Dubrow, *Genre*, pp. 49–52.
5. Schaeffer, "Literary Genres," pp. 171–2.
6. Gérard Genette, *The Architext: An Introduction*. Translated by Jane Lewin (Berkeley, CA: University of California Press, 1992).
7. Tzvetan Todorov, *Genres in Discourse*. Translated by Catherine Porter (Cambridge: Cambridge University Press, 1990).
8. David Duff, "Introduction." In David Duff (ed.) *Modern Genre Theory* (Harlow: Longman, 2000), pp. 1–24.
9. J. L. Austin, *How to Do Things with Words* (Cambridge, MA: Harvard University Press, 1962).
10. Mikhail Bakhtin, "The Problem of Speech Genres." In David Duff (ed.) *Modern Genre Theory* (Harlow: Longman, 2000), pp. 82–97.
11. Schaeffer, "Literary Genres," p. 171.
12. Jacques Derrida, "The Law of Genre." In Derek Attridge (ed.) *Acts of Literature* (New York: Routledge, 1992), pp. 221–52.
13. Agatha Christie, *The Murder of Roger Ackroyd* (London: Fontana, 1957).
14. Heta Pyrhönen, *Mayhem and Murder: Narrative and Moral Problems in the Detective Story* (Toronto: University of Toronto Press, 1999).
15. Donna Bennett, "The Detective Story: Towards a Definition of Genre." *PTL: A Journal for Descriptive Poetics and the Theory of Literature* 4 (1979), pp. 233–66.
16. Bennett, "The Detective Story," pp. 250–7.
17. Christie, *Murder*, p. 39.
18. Carl R. Lovitt, "Controlling Discourse in Detective Fiction, or Caring Very Much Who Killed Roger Ackroyd." In Ronald G. Walker and June M. Frazer (eds.) *The Cunning Craft: Original Essays on Detective Fiction and Literary Theory* (Macomb: Western Illinois University Press, 1990), pp. 68–85.
19. Stephen Neale, *Genre* (London: British Film Institute, 1980); Thomas J. Roberts, *An Aesthetics of Junk Fiction* (Athens, GA: University of Georgia Press, 1990).
20. Iurii Tynianov, "The Literary Fact." Translated by Ann Shukman. In David Duff (ed.) *Modern Genre Theory* (Harlow: Longman, 2000), pp. 29–49.

21. Stefano Tani, *The Doomed Detective: The Contribution of the Detective Novel to Postmodern American and Italian Fiction* (Carbondale: Southern Illinois University Press, 1984), pp. 36–8.
22. Tzvetan Todorov, "The Typology of Detective Fiction." In *The Poetics of Prose*. Translated by Richard Howard (Oxford: Basil Blackwell, 1977), pp. 42–52.
23. Patricia Merivale and Susan Elizabeth Sweeney, "The Game's Afoot: On the Trail of the Metaphysical Detective Story." In Patricia Merivale and Susan Elizabeth Sweeney (eds.) *Detecting Texts: The Metaphysical Detective Story from Poe to Postmodernism* (Philadelphia: University of Pennsylvania Press, 1999), p. 3.
24. Bakhtin, "Problem," p. 88.

III
Other narrative media (a selection)

9

NEAL R. NORRICK

Conversational storytelling

Introduction

Conversation is the natural home of narrative, and the most familiar context of storytelling for most of us. Storytelling is a common part of conversation between friends and family members. We tell stories to make a point, to catch up on each other's lives, to report news, and to entertain each other. And one story opens the floor to other participants for stories of their own. Our conversational stories are embedded in their local contexts, their forms and functions developing from and reflecting these contexts.

Conversational storytelling is not simply oral storytelling. Much of the research on *oral* narrative is based on stories from *non-conversational* contexts. Research on oral storytelling began with monologic stories explicitly elicited in interviews, and much recent work maintains this tradition, while other scholars have investigated narratives produced as retellings of films, picture stories, or stories previously read.[1] Stories in everyday conversational contexts share some but clearly not all characteristics with these other oral genres. Genuine conversational storytelling is always interactive, negotiated, and not simply designed for a particular audience by a single teller; indeed, it is often hard to determine even who is the primary teller, especially when the events were jointly experienced or the basic story is already familiar. Conversational stories may be deeply contextualized, diffuse, and not easily detachable from the local conditions that occasion them or understandable outside of them. Further, there are many kinds of conversation from family dinner-table talk, to self-revelation in troubles talk between women friends, to talk between guys in a sports bar meeting for the first time; each context may have its own characteristic conditions on storytelling rights and tellability, and engender stories of different kinds. Finally, in everyday conversation, stories are told for a reason and they fulfill multiple simultaneous functions: sharing personal news, entertaining listeners, revealing attitudes, constructing identity, inviting counter-disclosure, etc.

Distinguishing story from narrative, event, and performance

In the study of conversational storytelling, a distinction is sometimes drawn between story and narrative: a *narrative* is any representation of past events, but for a text or discourse to qualify as a *story* proper it must be a narrative with a point in context.[2] Narratives may include travelogues, project reports, and comparable kinds of texts with no evaluation by the narrator, but a story will always possess personal and contextual relevance and contain evaluation by the teller. We can further distinguish event, story, and performance. The story can be separated from the past events narrated, but also from the performance, so that we can be said to be retelling a single story in separate performances.[3] The bare narrative of temporally ordered clauses, or small fragments of discourse such as *Sue closed the door*, constitutes the substratum of any particular performance, which will generally flesh the story out with a preface, background information, dialogue, evaluation, and a closing. The same real-world events may provide the stuff for several stories, just as the "same story" will receive different narrative treatments from different tellers; indeed, even a single teller will vary the narrative form to fit the particular occasion. But the variation of story in performance is probably most obvious in cases of "polyphonic" or many-voiced narration in natural conversation, where no single participant can control the course of the story, and multiple voices vie for the right to formulate its point.

Cues to narrative structure

According to Labov, narration is a method of recapitulating past experience by matching a verbal sequence of clauses to the sequence of events reported.[4] Thus, a narrative consists of a sequence of past tense clauses sequentially ordered with respect to each other, as in:

> so he get all upset.
> then I fought him.

Reversing the order destroys the sequence as a narrative proper – or changes it into a different story:

> then I fought him.
> so he get all upset.

Beyond the skeleton of temporally ordered narrative clauses, other "free" clauses are typically found in stories. These free clauses can be moved or eliminated without destroying the basic narrative structure. For instance, in the story excerpt below, the narrative clauses (lines 1–4 and 6) describe an irreversible series of events, while the free, non-narrative clauses provide orientation (line 5) and evaluation (lines 7–8). In this story excerpt, a woman is describing the first time she was sent in to play in a league basketball game.

1 so I went I went in
2 and I had the ball,
3 and I just like turned around
4 and I shot it–
5 didn't even look
6 and it like hit off the backboard
7 so hard.
8 it was so bad

Labov assigns both narrative and free clauses to specific function elements, namely:

Abstract: answers the question "what was this about?"
Orientation: answers the questions "who, what, when, where?"
Complicating action: consists of sequentially ordered narrative clauses
Evaluation: answers the question "so what?"
Resolution: answers the question "what finally happened?"
Coda: puts off any further questions about what happened or why it mattered.

To illustrate, in the conversational story below, where two women are talking about their first jobs, the *abstract* is a joint accomplishment by both women, identifying what the story will be about in lines 1–3, namely April's first job at a fast-food restaurant. *Orientation* appears in background information such as that the incident took place the summer after April's sophomore year in high school (lines 14–16) and that there was so much to learn (lines 10–11), and in the narrower frame of the crucial event, namely "learning the drive-through" (line 18). Lines 25–8 contain the irreversible narrative clauses of the *complicating action*:

and the *first* time I had to do it
I said "welcome to McDonald's may I take your order?"
and everybody just *laughed* at me

Evaluation occurs first in line 5, "the most embarrassing moment of my life happened then," and again in lines 8–9, "I can't believe I did this, but–um I was really nerv–," and line 24, "and, and I was so embarrassed." The *resolution* comes in lines 29–31, as the listener and teller again jointly determine that April did not "try and pull it off like a joke." Finally, line 34 ("yeah, that was my very first job") constitutes the *coda*.

FIRST JOB

1 Ellen: what was YOUR first job?

2 April: first job um

3 oh : that was at the Halsted Burger King in Halsted Illinois.

4 and I remember

5 the most embarrassing moment of my *life* happened then. {laughs}

6 Ellen: {laughing} what does that *mean*? {laughing}.

7 April: {laughing} um no this is just–

8 I can't believe I did this

9 but– um I was really nerv–

10 and there's so much to learn.

11 I mean y'know there's so many things at Burger King

12 you have to [make and uh–]

13 Ellen: [how old were you?]

14 April: I was like a sophomore in high school.

15 Ellen: okay.

16 April: yeah, [the summer after my sophomore year.]

17 Ellen: [you were young,] okay.

18 April: and um we were learning the drive-through

19 and just the thought of speaking on–

20 into that microphone

21 and y'know into outside–

22 Ellen: yes.

23 April: and you have to pretend to take orders

24 and, and I was so embarrassed.

25 and the *first* time I had to do it

26 I said "welcome to McDonald's [may I take your order?"]

27 Ellen: [oh *no* {laughing}.]

28 April: and everybody just *laughed* at me {laughing}.

29 Ellen: {laughing} did you try and pull it off like a joke

30 like you meant to say that?

31 April: no. {laughing}

32 Ellen: no.

33 {laughing} good job.

34 April: yeah, that was my very first job.

In this transcript, "disfluencies" flourish, such as false starts with abrupt cut-offs and restarts or self-corrections and repetitions. False starts and pause-fillers like *ah*, *um*, along with the discourse markers *but* and *well*, cluster especially in the introductory section immediately following the initial evaluation in lines 4–5, "I remember the most embarrassing moment of my *life* happened then," itself a partially formulaic introduction. Disfluencies are also prominent just before the climax in lines 25–8, which – we should note – are delivered without a hitch. This pattern is characteristic for conversational stories. Even experienced storytellers performing narratives they have told before typically embed false starts, repetitions, and corrections in introductory materials. Such disfluencies give the listeners a chance to attune themselves to the coming narrative; they encourage audience attention and participation.

As this example demonstrates, the basic internal structure of conversational stories is much the same as other oral narratives, but conversational stories contain incomplete elements and extraneous bits, so that they require regularization, to be comparable to the monologic, practiced narratives of interview subjects and exemplary storytellers. The process of regularization involves the elimination of false starts, repetitions, and digressions by the teller as well as attention signals and comments from listeners, and the integration of pieces from both teller and listener into complete clauses.[5] Nevertheless, the elements characteristic of conversational (by contrast with monologic, practiced) storytelling are important features of the performance for both tellers and listeners.

Storytellers deploy discourse markers like *well* and *though*, along with related cues to organize telling into coherent form and chronological order, and to navigate around contextual disruptions. Discourse markers signal how utterances are related to foregoing talk and how they are to be understood. Thus, *oh* typically introduces an utterance expressing surprise, as in "oh, I didn't realize," while *though* often closes an utterance expressing something negative, as in "it never really mattered though." Discourse markers correlate with expectations that participants are likely to have about how a story should be structured and told. For example, *well* and *anyway* initiate and conclude narrative action, guiding listeners back to the main sequence of narrative elements following interruptions and digressions. Listeners key on discourse markers, attention signals (like *m-hm* or *wow*), comments, details, and co-telling to reconstruct chronological sequence, causal connections, and evaluation, and to streamline the telling performance into a consistent story.

In oral storytelling, specialized formulas and repetitions of various kinds cluster around openings and closings, transition points, and climaxes. In marking story sections, formulaic speech, repetition, and dialogue provide special windows on narrative organization. In storytelling, we find not only stock formulas but also rephrasing and parallel structures to organize the story performance and to heighten dramatic effect. All these rhetorical devices signal teller attitudes and serve as guides to listeners.

Finally, notice that all the verbs in the story FIRST JOB are in the past tense, except for those representing the narrator's own speech in line 26.

This pattern is common, but by no means essential. Indeed, conversational narrators may use what is sometimes called the conversational historical present tense throughout a story; alternatively, they may begin in the past tense and switch to the present for special emphasis at the climax or may switch between the past and present tenses for varying effects during the course of telling.[6]

Openings and closings

Conversationalists who want to gain the floor to tell a story must signal their intention to the other participants. They must enlist the interest of these potential auditors to engage their active listenership. Further, they must signal the ends of stories, so that their listeners may respond appropriately, perhaps with stories of their own. Tellers have various standard ways of prefacing their stories to obtain the floor and to cue their closings and secure proper uptake as well. Formulaic story prefaces often seek to justify tellability, as in "You'll never believe what happened . . . ," though it sometimes suffices for a prospective teller to say simply, "I remember this one time." One participant may also select another as storyteller with various elicitation techniques used to justify tellability or confirm someone else's telling rights: "tell the funny story about you and Judy."

Storytellers generally clearly mark story closings, too, so that listeners can co-ordinate their responses. Tellers of funny stories must be particularly careful to set up their "punchlines" to elicit laughter. Tellers deploy characteristic closing formulas like "and I lived to tell about it" to link the story back to the present time, but they also frequently produce a summary of the action or formulate the point of a story with relation to the current topic of conversation, as with "yeah, that was my first job" in the excerpt above.

Constructed dialogue in conversational narrative

In line with our understanding of tellers reconstructing a story for a particular context and audience, we must recognize that tellers construct dialogue for their purposes rather than simply reproducing speech from memory verbatim.[7] Much of what speakers construct as direct speech – that is, the direct quotation of someone else talking versus an indirect summary or paraphrase of their words – is simply not meant to, indeed cannot, represent recall of real talk: tellers produce as direct speech utterances never actually spoken ("and I almost said"), general observations ("everybody says"), talk they cannot have observed, say by multiple speakers ("so the voters are saying"), and so on. At least half of "direct quotations" are not authentic; they lie along a continuum, ranging from possible to impossible as real quoted speech. Moreover, direct speech often has a symbolic meaning for evaluation, as when a narrator says, "and I said to myself, 'this is it.'"[8]

We can distinguish the speech being reported from the telling frame, which introduces and sometimes comments on the dialogue. The telling frame typically sets off speech with verbs of saying – most frequently the verb *say* itself and verbs suggesting voice qualities like *whisper* and *yell* – but other words are used to mark direct speech as well, such as *go*, *like*, and *all*:

> she goes "so just wait till I get back."
> and we're like "well maybe we will."
> and she's all "whatever."

However, in conversational storytelling the reporting frame may also mark speech with bare *and* or without any lexical signal at all, as in:

> when my grandmother BROKE in on us
> and SHAMED me for life.
> and "JIM what are you DOing."
> "GIRLS go home."

The flexibility of the human voice allows conversational storytellers to clearly mark speech by different characters with voice shifts alone. When speakers construct dialogue with no explicit marker of direct speech, they often suggest quoted talk with terms of address (like *Jim* and *girls* above) and discourse markers (like *so* and *well* in the previous example).

Storytelling rights

The right to tell a particular story in a given context may be a matter for negotiation between the participants. Storytelling rights are generally related to personal knowledge of the events reported. We can distinguish *A-events* known only to the primary storyteller from *A–B events* known to the teller and one other participant, and further distinguish both from *O-events* known generally to members of a group or culture at large.[9] We can extend this list to include *F-events*, those shared by the members of a family, or, since any close-knit group will share events constitutive for their identification as a group, *G-events* can serve to denote the more general category.[10] Thus, children may tell an oft-heard anecdote about their parents' meeting, getting married, and so on, just as any new member will begin to absorb and participate in the telling of stories about the origins and history of the group. These vicarious G-events are often the material for repeated co-narration in groups. Furthermore, groups may narrowly constrain storytelling rights. Only those individuals personally involved in the events reported generally possess the right to tell or co-tell the story: if a girl who had a fight is present, the story is hers alone to tell; but if she is not, another girl who experienced the fight may tell the story.[11]

Tellability

The tellability of a story is also something conversationalists negotiate in the given context, though in earlier approaches it was often viewed as an inherent property of the (detached) content of a story. According to this earlier tradition, a story must be "reportable" or "tellable": A would-be narrator must be able to defend the story as relevant and newsworthy to get and hold the floor and escape censure at its conclusion. Labov essentially builds a specific version of tellability into his corpus by requesting stories on specific topics like near-death experiences. But tellers do not simply relate the seemingly fatal events step by step; they characteristically stop the action at the climax for an evaluative comment, typically something like "and I said to myself, this is it." Consequently, Labov focuses on the importance of evaluation in determining reportability. Telling a story without evaluation or without a currently relevant point can lead to a loss of face for the teller, especially when the story is received with a scathing "what's the point?"[12]

Tellability is often equated with "local news" by tellers and listeners, in so far as their stories generally begin with some reference to a new or unexpected event, e.g., "the most gosh-awful wreck on the Ventura Freeway." They also characteristically end with some final reference to the reportability of the story, as in the closing "It wasn't in the paper last night. I looked."[13] The sort of news that makes a story salient today will no longer make it salient tomorrow. If you see a person every day at work, the sorts of news which count as tellable need not exceed the sort of thing one might hear on the evening news, but this same material will not suffice for a story to tell someone you see only every six months. Stories about potential local news events seen or heard recently tend to be told first, then stories of personal accomplishment and experience since the last meeting occurred. Even when interlocutors run out of news, they can reminisce, telling old stories not for the sake of their content but for other reasons. A primary reason for telling a particular story in reminiscence is the opportunity for co-narration and laughing together.[14]

According to more recent research perspectives, tellability depends not only on the (detached) content of a narrative but also on the contextual (embedded) relevance of the story for the participants involved. Thus, family dinner-table talk reveals children routinely telling familiar stories and relating unnewsworthy tales at the request of their parents as a part of the socialization process.[15] Indeed, conversationalists often tell stories familiar to some or even all their listeners, and it is precisely the familiarity of story content which influences participation rights, since it presents the opportunity for significant co-narration. Familiar funny stories are typically prefaced in ways which label them as unoriginal (e.g., "remember the time we . . .") and yet these signals animate participants to involvement rather than cuing them to question the relevance and tellability of the stories. The tellability of familiar stories hinges not on their content as such but on the dynamics of the narrative event itself, and humor makes co-narration desirable.

In fact, it is not really very difficult to get the floor to tell a story in interaction among family and friends; indeed, storytelling is a central, desirable ingredient of such interactions. There are standard ways of moving from topical talk, where everyone takes turns speaking, into the storytelling mode, where a single teller is the primary speaker while the others become listeners. One participant may elicit a story from another in various ways ("Tell the one about you and Judy"), and a simple "I remember one time" is enough to gain the floor and the attention of other participants – or, in the case of "remember the time we . . . ," to enlist them as co-narrators. Moreover, storytellers and recipients deploy various "contextualization cues"[16] to ensure smooth transitions from topical talk into the narrative mode and back. These contextualization cues are words like "okay" and "so" or prosodic features of talk such as tempo, volume, and intonation. Conversationalists share expectations not only about relations between the elements of a narrative like the climax, resolution, and coda but also about story patterns themselves, such as how a travel story will progress or how a personal anecdote will end. They are attuned to typical signals like "when I was a kid" to introduce personal narratives; they recognize the typical formulas like "that was that" to end a story; and they prepare to respond in appropriate ways – for example, by telling apposite stories of their own. Of course, they also recognize standard justifications for tellability like "the most embarrassing moment of my life" in the conversational story excerpt above.

The dark side of tellability

Some stories, though eminently tellable in their extra-ordinary content, are not tellable for many tellers under most circumstances, because they are too personal, too embarrassing, or obscene. Some newsworthy personal experiences are for that very reason untellable, because they would be embarrassing to the teller, the listeners, or both. The details of illness and medical procedures, or sexual behavior and fantasies, have no place in stories told in polite conversation for many people. Stories should report events outside everyday experience, but they should not stray too far from community standards. Furthermore, stories about infidelities and crimes may be outright dangerous to tell – for fear of affected persons or the authorities finding out and seeking retribution.

Even if tellability is often equated with local news, and a story about "the most gosh-awful wreck on the Ventura Freeway" is tellable as news, at some point the gruesome details of the wreck with the dead and injured, the blood and guts may go beyond the tellable into the area of the no longer tellable. Conversationalists may tell transgressive stories "in the pursuit of intimacy," pushing the envelop of propriety in order to modulate rapport, attending to cues like laughter to avoid rushing beyond acceptable standards.[17] In relating a transgressive experience, the teller risks rejection on two levels: the other participants may refuse to listen to the offensive story; and they may negatively judge the teller for the behavior reported. On the positive side, the teller may gain the listener's admiration for the experience reported, may modulate intimacy through self-disclosure, and may inspire the listener to reply with similar self-disclosure.

Tellability is, then, a two-sided notion: Some events bear too little significance to reach the lower-bounding threshold of tellability, while others are so intimate (or frightening) that they lie on the dark side of tellability.[18] The conversational narrator navigates the path between these two boundaries in various ways. Storytellers may worry about the "scathing 'so what?'" following a story with no clear point or significance, but there is often more shame in transgressing norms than in telling a boring story. The societal sanctions for obscenity are more immediate and obvious than those for telling pointless stories: responses to the former are immediate and unmistakable reprimands like "You can't talk like that here!" while responses to the latter are ambiguous long-term behaviors such as avoidance. Within the scope of expectations about appropriate experiences to relate and appropriate ways of telling, narrators and their audiences co-construct their individual personalities through their negotiation of the upper boundary of tellability and their joint evaluation of the characters and events described.[19]

Audience response and co-narration

Even as a teller works to design a story appropriate to the local audience and context, the audience is already imposing a designing of its own: interrupting, correcting, co-narrating. Conversational narrative is always interactive telling, more or less polyphonic, but necessarily negotiated among participants. Listenership is not a passive state, but an active involvement in the storytelling process.

Short of becoming ratified co-narrators, the audience acts as co-author of the story and helps determine the trajectory, structure, and point of a narrative through questions and comments like those in the sample excerpt FIRST JOB above. Attention to audience response underscores the nature of telling as a *narrative event*, a speech event among others with its own characteristic norms governing the scene, participation rights, message content, message form, and rules of interpretation.[20] Listeners may engage in byplay during narrative, producing observations, details, and dialogue designed to comment on the ongoing story for some sub-group of listeners.[21] "Heckling," by contrast, addresses the primary teller directly and is heard as negative commentary on the telling or content of the story in progress. Byplay is apparently more likely to attract the attention of a primary teller and thereby to assume center stage in an interaction, when both the byplay and the primary narrative are oriented toward humor.[22]

In full-fledged collaborative co-narration, all co-tellers have had access (at least vicariously) to some common previous event, so that there is no need to establish common experience and no competitive "story topping," though participants may still vie for the right to tell. Co-narration of this kind provides participants with a resource for saying "we two" to each other or portraying their togetherness for an audience. Indeed, differing expectations about what counts as a story can lead to dissonance between co-narrators.[23] Participants use various strategies – both supportive and antagonistic – to become co-narrators. Two co-narrators may produce a "conversational duet," presenting a single shared story for a third party; such collaborative telling affects turn-taking and related matters such as simultaneous speech.[24] For example, co-narration can be a genuine team performance with the co-tellers subordinating their personal identities to the success of the performance.[25]

Response stories

Response stories are produced in reply to foregoing stories by other participants in a conversation. They may be second stories, responding thematically to the immediately foregoing story, or responses to various preceding stories, perhaps in a longer series of related stories. Response stories either seek to establish common experience, saying "the same thing happened to me . . ."; or they competitively seek to "top" previous stories in some way, saying, for instance, "an even funnier thing happened to me." Either way, response stories attest to attentive listenership, ratify foregoing stories, and provide

participants with a resource for saying "me too." They allow conversationalists to expand on a particular theme in narrative form, recording similar
experiences and their personal reactions to them.

In response to a story told in the third person ("she went to X," "he did
Y"), a potential teller can follow up with a story about the same topic or
the same characters, thus building thematically on a previous story. Moreover, there are global telling contexts such as "flash bulb memory" stories
in response to "where were you when . . . ?" and "eulogies" at birthday
parties, roasts, and funerals, built around "I knew her when." Finally, two
tellers may team up to perform related personal narratives as sequential
stories with common characters and events, where the second presents a
continuation of the first, say because the outcome of the first set of events
involving one set of people affected what happened to their friends right
afterwards. Such *interlaced* stories represent a resource for conversational
narrative performance, ranging between first story–second story organization, where separate storytellers relate similar experiences, and collaborative
narration of an experience the two tellers shared.[26]

Retelling and retold Stories

Retellings make a story generally familiar in a group: "what becomes increasingly important is not the news itself, but the way of telling it."[27] Stories
help define and ratify group goals and values; co-narration of familiar stories demonstrates membership and contributes to group cohesion. Research
on retelling was initially a matter of defining what was meant by "the same
story" in one theoretical framework or the other. Then as real data became
available and research began to focus on them, other questions became
important: e.g., about when and how tellers repeat stories; the effects of
retelling on telling rights, tellability, co-narration, and on the internal form
of the narrative.[28]

Focusing on narrative events in which tellers reconstruct a story for separate audiences yields a clearer view of what tellers repeat, which makes it
possible to recognize separate performances as versions of the same story.
Comparing two natural occurrences of a story told for different audiences,
one sees the teller expanding or suppressing particular scenes, even as the
two versions maintain a shared underlying plot, the same primary foci of
interest, substantial overlap in narrative statements concerning what happened, and even wording repeated more or less verbatim. Of course, each
audience shapes the trajectory of the story as well. Storytelling is more than a
process of retrieving information from memory, selecting from it, and verbal-
izing it in serial, narrative form; the conversational storytelling performance

requires contextually appropriate reconstruction rather than simple recall of ordered events. Tellers become caught up in a dynamic context and in their own performance, even as they tailor a basic story to fit the current thematic needs of the interaction. In telling our personal stories, we create and recreate our past in light of our present needs and concerns, instead of simply recapitulating stored experience.

Interactional functions

Stories fulfill many functions in conversation. They allow participants to share news, to catch up with each other's lives, to entertain each other, to ratify group membership, to modulate group rapport, and to present an individual personality within the group. Response stories contribute directly to the coherence of conversation and they reflect shared experiences and attitudes on the part of participants. Especially the retelling of familiar tales and the reformulation of common experiences over time serve to get a group story straight and to convey or ratify group values.

In recent years, much has been written about the narrative construction of identity: the way narratives constitute one's individual identity, especially within the (peer) group.[29] Narrators construct identity through their choice of certain personal experiences to relate and their way of presenting these experiences to the current audience in the current context. They negotiate the perspective and trajectory of the story with their listeners, based on the present setting, type of interaction, and foregoing talk as well as the history of interaction the teller shares with these interactants. All these decisions reflect the sort of identity a teller hopes to convey in the given context.

A two-sided notion of tellability, encompassing both the familiar lower-bounding side of tellability and the often ignored upper-bounding dark side, sees identity construction as taking place between these two bounds. Even safe and impersonal stories do much work in social identity construction, by demonstrating recognition of, and respect for, standard group norms, but transgressive ones accomplish a different kind of identity work, due to the higher risk factor. Narrators ensure that their stories bear enough general significance to engage the interest of listeners, but usually avoid transgressing the boundaries of propriety and intimacy, unless they seek to approach or traverse these boundaries – with the cued approval of their recipients – in order to present special facets of their personalities in the pursuit of increased intimacy. It is within this framework of expectations about stories that tellers work to ratify their membership in the group even as they construct an individual personality through a conversational performance attuned to the dynamic, ever-shifting contexts of talk.

NOTES

1. For a foundational study on stories elicited in interviews see William Labov and Joshua Waletzky's "Narrative Analysis: Oral Versions of Personal Experience." In June Helm (ed.) *Essays on the Verbal and Visual Arts* (Seattle: University of Washington Press, 1967), pp. 12–44. Charlotte Linde continues this tradition in *Life Stories* (New York: Oxford University Press, 1993), whereas a number of scholars examine oral retellings of filmed events in Wallace Chafe (ed.) *The Pear Stories* (Norwood: Ablex, 1980).

2. Livia Polanyi, *Telling the American Story* (Norwood: Ablex, 1985).

3. Richard Bauman, *Story, Performance, and Event* (Cambridge: Cambridge University Press, 1986); Shoshana Blum-Kulka, " 'You Gotta Know How to Tell a Story': Telling, Tales, and Tellers in American and Israeli Narrative Events at Dinner." *Language in Society* 22 (1993), pp. 361–402.

4. The name Labov, with no further specification, refers to the work of Labov and his co-workers, as described in: Labov and Waletzky, "Narrative Analysis"; William Labov, "The Transformation of Experience in Narrative Syntax." In *Language in the Inner City* (Philadelphia: University of Pennsylvania Press, 1972), pp. 354–96; and William Labov and David Fanshel, *Therapeutic Discourse* (New York: Academic Press, 1977).

5. According to methods described in Polanyi, *Telling the American Story*, pp. 26–33, and Neal R. Norrick, *Conversational Narrative* (Amsterdam: Benjamins, 2000), pp. 29–38.

6. On the conversational historical present see Nessa Wolfson, "The Conversational Historical Present in American English Narrative." *Topics in Socio-Linguistics* 1 (Dordrecht: Foris, 1982); Barbara Johnstone, " 'He says . . . so I said': Verb Tense Alternation and Narrative Depictions of Authority in American English." *Linguistics* 25 (1987), pp. 33–52; and Joanna Thornborrow, "The Construction of Conflicting Accounts in Public Participation TV." *Language in Society* 29 (2000), pp. 357–77.

7. See Deborah Tannen, "Introducing Constructed Dialogue in Greek and American Conversational and Literary Narratives." In Florian Coulmas (ed.) *Direct and Indirect Speech* (Berlin: Mouton, 1986), pp. 311–22, and Patricia Mayes, "Quotation in Spoken English." *Studies in Language* 14 (1990), pp. 323–63.

8. Labov, "The Transformation of Experience in Narrative Syntax," p. 37.

9. Labov and Fanshel, *Therapeutic Discourse*, pp. 62–4.

10. On F-events see Shoshana Blum-Kulka and Catherine E. Snow, "Developing Autonomy for Tellers, Tales, and Telling in Family Narrative Events." *Journal of Narrative and Life History* 2 (1992), pp. 187–217. On G-events see Neal R. Norrick, "Twice-told Tales: Collaborative Narration of Familiar Stories." *Language in Society* 26 (1992), pp. 199–220.

11. See Amy Shuman, *Storytelling Rights* (New York: Cambridge University Press, 1986), pp. 29–38.

12. See Livia Polanyi, "So What's the Point?" *Semiotica* 25 (1979), pp. 207–41.

13. Harvey Sacks, *Lectures on Conversation*, Vol. II. Edited by Gail Jefferson (Oxford: Blackwell, 1972), pp. 3–16.

14. See Neal R. Norrick, "Humor, Tellability and Conarration in Conversation." *TEXT* 24 (2004), pp. 79–111.

15. See Elinor Ochs, Ruth Smith, and Carolyn Taylor, "Detective Stories at Dinnertime: Problem Solving through Co-narration." *Cultural Dynamics* 2 (1989), pp. 238–57; Blum-Kulka, "'You Gotta Know How to Tell a Story,'" pp. 374–83; and Blum-Kulka and Snow, "Developing Autonomy," pp. 187–9.

16. John J. Gumperz, *Discourse Strategies* (Cambridge: Cambridge University Press, 1982), pp. 131–40.

17. See Gail Jefferson, Harvey Sacks, and Emanuel Schegloff, "Notes on Laughter in the Pursuit of Intimacy." In Graham Button and John R. E. Lee (eds.) *Talk and Social Organisation* (Clevedon: Multilingual Matters, 1987), pp. 152–327.

18. Neal R. Norrick, "The Dark Side of Tellability." *Narrative Inquiry* 15 (2005), pp. 323–43.

19. See Michael Bamberg, "'I know it may sound mean to say this, but we couldn't really care less about her anyway': Form and Functions of 'Slut-bashing' in 15-year Olds." *Human Development* 47 (2004), pp. 331–53.

20. As described by Dell Hymes, *Foundations in Sociolinguistics: An Ethnographic Approach* (Philadelphia: University of Pennsylvania Press, 1974), pp. 52–3.

21. For more on these interactional dynamics of conversational storytelling see Marjorie H. Goodwin, "By-play: Negotiating Evaluation in Story-telling." In Gregory R. Guy, John Baugh, Deborah Schiffrin, and Crawford Feagin (eds.) *Towards a Social Science of Language: Papers in Honor of William Labov*, Vol. II. (Philadelphia: Benjamins, 1997), pp. 77–102. Goodwin's account builds on Erving Goffman's *The Presentation of Self in Everyday Life* (Garden City: Anchor Books, 1959), pp. 174–86; see also "Footing" in Goffman's *Forms of Talk* (Oxford: Blackwell, 1981), pp. 124–57, on types of participation frameworks.

22. See Neal R. Norrick, "Contextualizing and Recontextualizing Interlaced Stories in Conversation." In Joanna Thornborrow and Jennifer Coates (eds.) *The Sociolinguistics of Narrative* (Amsterdam: Benjamins, 2005), pp. 107–27.

23. As demonstrated by Deborah Tannen in "The Effect of Expectations on Conversation." *Discourse Processes* 1 (1978), pp. 203–9.

24. See Jane Falk, "The Conversational Duet." *Berkeley Linguistics Society: Proceedings of the Sixth Annual Meeting* (1980), pp. 507–14.

25. Norrick, "Humor, Tellability and Conarration in Conversation," pp. 99–104.

26. Norrick, "Contextualizing and Recontextualizing Interlaced Stories in Conversation," pp. 107–10.

27. Tannen, "The Effect of Expectations on Conversation," p. 261.

28. See Wallace Chafe, "Things we Can Learn from Repeated Tellings of the Same Experience." *Narrative Inquiry* 8 (1998), pp. 269–85; and Neal R. Norrick, "Retelling Stories in Spontaneous Conversation." *Discourse Processes* 25 (1998), pp. 75–97.

29. Bamberg, "'I know it may sound mean to say this, but we couldn't really care less about her anyway,'" pp. 332–5.

10

BRIAN RICHARDSON

Drama and narrative

From the outset, theories of drama and theories of narrative have been closely linked. Aristotle's *Poetics*, still the starting-point for any narrative theory, devotes more space to drama than to epic. The topics he covers, including character, plot, beginnings and endings, poetic justice, and the goals of representation, are as relevant to narrative theory as to a poetics of drama. Classic statements about these and other aspects of narrative, whether from the Renaissance, neo-classical, or Romantic periods, are likewise filled or even dominated by references to drama, as a look at the critical work of Castelvetro, Sidney, Dryden, Samuel Johnson, and Coleridge makes clear. Quite simply, if you are going to discuss plot and character, you must take drama and its theorists into account. Furthermore, performed stories, whether in drama, film, ballet, or video, have an additional enacted dimension that can interact with many of the other elements of narrative, particularly in the cases of character, time, and space. Strangely, while cinema was quickly brought into the fold of narrative theory, most notably in Seymour Chatman's *Story and Discourse*,[1] drama has lagged behind, leaving a number of important theoretical contributions in the wings, as it were. Some recent theorists, following Genette, restrict the definition of narrative to stories that are told or narrated rather than enacted (though even in this limited case, as we will see, drama has important contributions to make). Many if not most theorists, however, follow Roland Barthes, who stated that "narrative is present in myth, legend, fable, tale, novella, epic, history, tragedy, drama, comedy, mime, painting (think of Carpaccio's *Saint Ursula*), stained glass windows, cinema, comics, news item, conversation."[2] I will be using this broader conception of narrative in the pages that follow.

Non-Western traditions of narrative theory also focus on drama: Bharata's third-century treatise, the *Natyashastra*, centers on classical Sanskrit drama. Likewise, classical Japanese poetics is available in the treatises of Zeami, a seventeenth-century Noh playwright and performer. Samuel Beckett, author of some of the most innovative works of narrative fiction in the twentieth century, also constructed plays that are remarkable for the innovative ways in which they represent events on stage; in both genres, Beckett challenges the basic elements of conventional representation. His dramatic work, especially *Endgame*, is thus a natural focus for this chapter. Below, I outline the major categories of narrative analysis and show their relevance for drama in general and Beckett's work in particular, paying particular attention to the distinctive differences that performance involves.

Character

The most comprehensive theories of character emphasize its multiple facets: fictional characters have a *mimetic* relation to the individual human beings and recognizable types of human behavior they are modeled on: braggarts or misers on stage are deemed "realistic" in so far as they resemble braggarts or misers in life. Meanwhile, at a *formal* level, characters can also be functions or part of an abstract design that constitutes the plot or forms a symmetrical pattern: Restoration comedy typically pairs the amorous adventures of a romantic couple with those of a more practical or sensual couple as the two co-plots reflect each other in both analogous and opposed manners. Characters can represent ideas or embody *ideological* positions (including positions the playwright may be unaware he or she is endorsing): characters in medieval or Brechtian allegories represent easily identifiable concepts of Christian or Marxist doctrine, and an author like George Bernard Shaw reinscribes patriarchal values even in plays that purport to do the opposite.[3] Finally, performed narratives like drama also contain an *enacted* "fourth dimension" where the physical body of the actor may alter the status of the character he or she portrays: in dramas where one actor plays different roles, such as King Duncan and Macduff in the first productions of *Macbeth*, the characterizations are thereby transformed and we can perceive another, somatic reason for Macbeth's horror over his situation. A more extreme example can be found in Caryl Churchill's *Cloud Nine*: the cast list for this play states that a man should play the female role of Betty in the first act since "she" is entirely the creation of the dominant male Victorian sensibility. There is no precise equivalent for this unique feature in written narratives, and it deserves to be incorporated into our theories of character.

For the most part, theater of the absurd seems to depart radically from mimetic conventions, as unusual figures say and do outlandish things.[4] But one cannot escape entirely from a mimetic framework: even if there is no discernible psychology in place, in every instance there are always crucial points of congruence: one readily perceives the systematic miscommunication between many married couples in the preposterous dialogue between

Mr. and Mrs. Martin in Ionesco's *La cantatrice chauve (The Bald Soprano)*. The gradual display of very general representations of key aspects of human behavior is no doubt why *Waiting for Godot* received such a sympathetic reception when it was performed at the penitentiary at San Quentin in 1957. Likewise, the central figures of *Endgame*, Hamm and Clov, are engaged in an exaggerated but ultimately psychologically accurate relation of co-dependency. Hamm acts as a man who loves displays of his own power, while Clov exhibits a dependence that will not allow him to escape his servitude even though he may be physically able to do so. The other two characters, Nagg and Nell, are aged, legless grotesques living in ashcans. Nagg's character is deliberately inconsistent as his speech alternates between puerile whining and the eloquence of a seasoned raconteur. Here again we see Beckett creating seemingly impossible individuals only to reveal their uncomfortable similarity to all-too-human models.

At the *formal* level, we may see the largely supernumerary characters Nagg and Nell as slightly distorted mirror images of the main characters' relations.[5] Just as Clov threatens to but cannot leave Hamm, so Nell threatens to but cannot leave Nagg. Their physical dependence on Hamm parallels Clov's psychological subordination to him. Finally, their pathetic existence further exemplifies the larger theme of the futility of generation that runs throughout the play. There will be no new life, new cycle of births, or vernal renewal; "there's no more nature" (*Endgame*, 11).

At the ideological level, it is widely affirmed that Hamm and Clov are personifications of Hegel's "Master–Slave dialectic"; recent criticism further postulates that the two protagonists are part of a national allegory and stand for England and Ireland. This last interpretation would be underscored in performance if the actor playing Clov were to give an Irish lilt to his pronunciation (to accompany his more Hibernean vocabulary) while the actor portraying Hamm spoke in upper-class British intonations. The difference that enactment can make on characterization is evident when one considers the different effects that actors of difference races or genders would produce on stage; this is why Beckett and Beckett's literary executors are keen on policing such possible stagings. Another effect of enactment is triggered by the sudden appearance of two actors hidden in standard-sized ashcans, which always startles the audience and make the physical component of their desperate situation painfully evident.

Plot

Aristotle argues for a concept of plot that is unified, an "imitation of one action and that a whole, the structural union of the parts being such that, if any one of them is displaced or removed, the whole will be disjointed and disturbed."[6] Yet he also acknowledges that some authors erroneously present several largely unrelated episodes from the life of a man, and therefore falsely assume that since Heracles was one man, the story of Heracles must also be a unity. Many modern theorists, building on a story grammar derived from Vladimir Propp, likewise aver that "the *fabula* that constitutes the global structure of the drama is a dynamic chain of events and actions," and that "the series of distinct actions and interactions of the plot are understood to form coherent *sequences* governed by the overall purposes of their agents."[7] This approach to plot lends itself best to classical tragedy, which typically builds toward a single resounding conclusion. This model is implicit in Chekhov's famous pronouncement on the inevitable narrative economy of drama, that is, his assertion that if a pistol is introduced at the beginning of a play, it must be fired by the fourth act. The sequences of events that occur in non-tragic dramatic forms and genres, however, are rather less tightly conjoined. Elizabethan histories, Brechtian epic theater, many types of comedy (especially Aristophanic), and symbolist, avant-garde, and Modernist plays (including Chekhov's own) all employ a differently coherent structure of events, often replacing causal connections with thematic or metaphorical ties. Perhaps the most thoroughgoing negation of the Aristotelian concept of plot is the kind enacted in the theater of the absurd.

In *Endgame*, there is no single, unified action, no dynamic chain of events, but merely a series of largely gratuitous doings. The play is rather an assault on the teleology implicit in much traditionally plotted drama than an embodiment of it. As one arbitrary or meaningless event follows another, the question is not how tightly they are all connected, but whether there is any connection there at all. To interpret this play, one does not follow the trajectory of its plot but attempts to determine whether it has any semblance of plot. Early on, Hamm asks Clov whether or not he has "had enough." Clov responds he has always had enough, to which Hamm responds, "then there is no reason for it to change" (*Endgame*, 5). With this, Beckett seems to be challenging the basic premise of drama, transformation, and instead constructs a static drama, devoid of all that makes a story "narratable," or worth telling. There is a disequilibrium, even a conflict – Clov's continued subservience to his blind, immobile master. But, as we quickly realize, this too will not change. When Hamm asks, "Why do you stay with me?" Clov replies, "There's nowhere else" (*Endgame*, 6), a statement that may just be literally true, as we will see. For characters and audience, this amounts not to a plot but to a refusal of plot. Despite repeated claims that "We're getting on" (*Endgame*, 9) and "Something is taking its course" (*Endgame*, 32), there is no unified, coherent aggregation of events, but rather an avowedly arbitrary conglomerate of random actions that lead nowhere. In this respect, *Endgame* is a defiantly anti-Aristotelian drama. The play frequently alludes to Shakespeare's *The Tempest*, but even these allusions and re-enactments do not provide an alternative pattern for the unfolding of this set of events.

On stage, the audience can also interact with the represented events in certain limited cases, as when in an experimental work the audience votes to determine which direction the plot will take (Michel Butor's libretto, *Votre Faust*), an earlier version of a strategy that later would appear in hypertext fictions. Another distinctively theatrical form of interaction appears at the end of a Renaissance masque (or Amiri Baraka's "Slave Ship"), where the characters are joined by the audience in a final dance. When performed in a small space, the audience can likewise feel part of the storyworld, especially if, as is sometimes the case, the spectators walk out of the theater a few feet away from Hamm, who remains on stage and in character.

Beginnings and endings

For the most part, beginnings and endings occupy privileged positions in drama. A compelling beginning is often a practical necessity to keep spectators in their seats, while an unsatisfactory ending can bring on boos and catcalls after the performance as well as negative reviews by theater critics. Aristotle sensibly defined the beginning as "that which does not itself follow anything by causal necessity, but after which something naturally is or comes to be" (*Poetics*, section 7, 52). Beginnings in drama are often abrupt, plunging the audience into the middle of the action ("Who's there?" in *Hamlet*). Other times, the first words are devoted to exposition, as in Sheridan's *The Rivals* where a servant and a coachman meet up and one asks the other how it is that he has come to Bath. In a few cases, one finds deceptive beginnings, as in Jean Genet's *Les Bonnes* or Tom Stoppard's *The Real Thing*, in which the audience believes it has entered the storyworld only to learn that it is observing a fictional play enacted by the characters within the storyworld.

As is only to be expected given Beckett's rejection of traditional plot, beginnings and endings are similarly skewed in his work. *Endgame* commences, rather than begins; there is no action initiated and no resolvable disequilibrium is announced. Instead, Hamm's first speech announces not a beginning but an ending: "Enough, it's time it ended, in the shelter too. (Pause.) And yet I hesitate, I hesitate to . . . to end. Yes, there it is, it's time it ended and yet I hesitate to – (he yawns) – to end" (*Endgame*, 3, Beckett's ellipsis). The play, that is, begins with the announcement of its impending end, and then continues more or less statically until Clov packs his bag, stands near the exit, and refuses to respond to Hamm. At this point the play ceases. Clov has not left the room; nothing is resolved; there is no closure; there is no reason why the entire play might not begin again at its starting-point, as happens in Beckett's *Play* and seems to be the likely future of the characters in *Waiting for Godot*. As Hamm states, "The end is in the beginning and yet you go on" (*Endgame*, 69). This refusal of beginnings, development, and closure is emblematized in the discussion surrounding the earlier ringing of the alarm clock: Clov states, "The end is terrific!" while Hamm states, "I prefer the middle" (*Endgame*, 48). Of course, there is typically no variation in the sound of an alarm clock; at one point it simply slows to a halt, as does this play. Aristotle described what he felt were the best and worst kinds of ending, denigrated the *deus ex machina*, and observed that "many poets tie the knot well, but unravel it ill" (*Poetics*, section 18, 59). Beckett here refuses to untie his minimal knot. In so doing he further extends the common Modernist literary strategy of the open ending, as pioneered by Chekhov and praised and practiced by Virginia Woolf. The performative nature of the theater also offers unique kinds of closure, as in Sam Shepard's play *Mad Dog Blues*, where the play ends with the actors walking offstage, through the audience, and out of the exits, thus bringing into collision the world of the audience and the storyworld of the play. Some productions of *Endgame*, as discussed in the last section, can achieve a comparable fusion.

Time

The starting-point for most theories of time in narrative is Genette's account of the categories of order, duration, and frequency. Order is the relation between the chronological events of the story and the sequence in which those events are presented to the audience. Thus, a novel might begin with an account of a funeral and then work backwards in its presentation of the major incidents in the life of the person; it might scramble the order of the presentation of those events (Faulkner's *The Sound and the Fury*, for example); or it might start with the character's birth and proceed in a linear fashion to the end. Although there are frequent and notable exceptions across the world's narrative traditions, many stories are presented in a largely chronological fashion along with regular flashbacks ("analepses") and a few occasional "flashforwards" ("prolepses"). Genette's concept of duration attempts to measure the relation between the time represented in the narrative and the time it takes to read the representation of those events. Genette also uses the idea of frequency to measure how many times the same event or set of events is narrated in a text. Each of these categories can be applied to drama, though we will see there are some interesting differences between narrated and enacted stories.

In most plays, there is no significant difference between the sequence of events in the story (*fabula*) and the sequence in which they are performed on stage (*sjuzhet*). Gaps between events, however, can be prominent, as when a figure representing Time enters the stage between the third and fourth acts of *The Winter's Tale* to announce to the audience that sixteen years have just elapsed. More serious discrepancies between the order of the story and its presentation, or what Genette calls "anachrony," can also occur, as when the narratorial Voice of Cocteau's *La Machine infernale* announces at the end of the first act: "Spectators, let us imagine that we can wind back the last few minutes and relive them elsewhere . . ."[8] More extreme cases are also possible, as in Armand Gatti's *La Vie imaginaire d'eboueur Auguste G* (1962), in which the protagonist's life is presented in a series of interpolated scenes from several different time periods.

In narrative fiction, temporality is largely a fabricated construct; the timeline and presumed duration of events have to be constructed during the process of interpretation. The reader can often only estimate the time that elapses as events unfold and dialogues are spoken, and the time of reception will vary considerably from reader to reader. In drama, however, things are rather different. The entire length of a performance can be clocked, and the duration of specific scenes can be measured with precision. The typically linear trajectory of the play can be directly compared to the time experienced by the audience. Aristotle famously noted that the amount of represented time in Greek tragedy rarely exceeded a day; this comment was hypostatized by neo-classical critics into a powerful injunction. Many playwrights, such as Ben Jonson or Jean Racine, worked comfortably within these parameters; in *Volpone* or *The Alchemist*, there is a complete correspondence between the time that is represented and the time it takes to enact the play. Historically, this injunction has proven to be a most compelling challenge to the playwright; even after its authority was overthrown by a series of commentators beginning with Samuel Johnson, the most unlikely constellation of playwrights continued to work within its parameters, including Lord Byron (of whom Goethe said he broke every other rule of society except the unities of time and space in his plays), Oscar Wilde, and numerous absurdist and *avant-garde* writers, including Beckett: the story of *Endgame* is entirely coextensive with its enactment. Curiously, however, time is seemingly unknowable or irrelevant in this play. Near the beginning, Hamm asks what time it is, to which Clov responds dubiously, "The same as usual" (*Endgame*, 4); later on, "yesterday" is oddly defined as "that bloody awful day, long ago, before this bloody awful day" (*Endgame*, 43). Where *Waiting for Godot* offers contradictory temporal indicators between its two acts, *Endgame* simply presents continuous events in an indeterminate temporal setting.

Frequency is another category usefully applied to modern dramas that retell or re-enact the same scene several times. The first is apparent in the repetitious narration of Mouth in Beckett's "Not I"; the second in Beckett's *Play*, in which the entire drama is repeated verbatim immediately following its first performance.

Despite the many strictures imposed on playwrights over the centuries, many have manipulated neo-classical conventions to suit their own ends. Corneille's *L'Illusion comique* presents the events of many years through the medium of a magic mirror that is observed by the main group of characters in a single continuous sitting. Byron's *Cain* travels around the universe in a strangely dilated, alternative temporality as the simultaneous events on earth take up only a few hours. Shakespeare often creates thematically apposite temporal contradictions in his works, as the time in the magical forest passes at a different rate of speed than it does in the corrupt city. Even in the one mature play that seems to conform to neo-classical strictures, there is some interesting play with time: at the end of *The Tempest*, the boatswain discloses that the events have taken only three hours to transpire – and not the more that four hours Prospero had earlier reckoned on (1.ii.240). More extreme is the final soliloquy of Marlowe's Dr. Faustus, in which an hour is said to pass while the protagonist speaks uninterruptedly and without any temporal elision for fifty extremely dramatic lines.[9]

Space

Space is especially interesting in drama. As in narrative fiction, the area represented on stage may be a nearby locale, a distant realm, or an entirely fictitious world. More intriguingly, a stage may represent a stage; in which case of course it is presenting, rather than representing, fictional space; it shows you a real stage, with real chairs and real doors. Sabine Buchholz and Manfred Jahn[10] propose further distinctions in this connection, noting that there are: (1) texts containing contiguous sub-spaces, where characters freely move from one space to the next (England and France in *Henry V*); (2) texts with discontinuous, ontologically distinct spaces that can only rarely be crossed (Eden and distant planets in Byron's *Cain*); and (3) works that project different kinds of spaces on different narrative levels (the teller's world and that of the tale in Brecht's *The Caucasian Chalk Circle*).

Beckett rarely changes scenes, but the single space presented to the audience is rarely an unproblematic one. The space presented on stage in *Endgame* is particularly curious since it refuses nearly all the differentiations outlined by narrative theory. Its nature is so ambiguous that an investigation of the setting is an essential component of any interpretation of the work

and a central interpretive drama in itself. At different points in the play Clov goes up a ladder to look out of each window; his reports on what he has seen and what lies outside the room are always ambiguous. At some points the play seems to be set in a part of the world where places are three days away by horseback; at other times we seem to be in a postapocalyptic version of this world, or a representation of purgatory, or even a different, parallel, world where there is no nature.

With Beckett, there are always other possibilities as well. It has frequently been remarked that the shape of the room, with its two high windows, suggests the outlines of a human skull, in which case the "space" would be a mental rather than a physical one. A postcolonial reading would suggest that the area on stage is also an allegorical space that represents Ireland under British rule. Finally, we can also note that the space is also explicitly affirmed to be a stage, as when Hamm knocks on the wall and says, "Do you hear? Hollow bricks" (*Endgame*, 26) or, still more flagrantly, when Clov trains his telescope on the audience and says he sees "a multitude ... in transports ... of joy" (*Endgame*, 29, Beckett's ellipses). We might further observe that, since the play has no intermission, the audience can easily feel enclosed within the same compressed space as the characters, especially during a production in a small theater. Here, too, we see how analysis of drama can enhance or extend basic concepts of narrative theory.

Beckett thus evokes all of the possibilities of represented space, as well as the physical place of the performance. By refusing to indicate which of these usually mutually contradictory spaces is the "correct" one, he maintains a multifaceted yet indeterminable spatial setting. He suggests multiple possible worlds without having to indicate which is the actual world of the play.[11]

Cause

Just as every play has a temporal and a spatial setting, so too does it have canon of probability to which it adheres. The causal laws governing the storyworld represented on stage may be: (1) supernatural, subject to divine forces (*Oedipus Rex*); (2) naturalistic, obeying ordinary patterns of natural law and human psychology (*Miss Julie*); (3) chance, with an unlikely number of coincidental or chance happenings (*Rosencrantz and Guildenstern are Dead*); or (4) metafictional, where the events of the play can be altered by an authorial agent (*The Beggars' Opera*). In many cases, determining the nature of the causal laws governing the world is a central concern of the characters. In *Oedipus Rex* both Laius and Oedipus believe that they can elude fate through will and planning, while Jocasta asserts at one point that chance rules all. Obviously, these interpretations are proven false by the end of the play as fate is shown to be inescapable. The causal laws governing the world of *Endgame* are never fully spelled out; like its temporal and spatial setting, its causal laws remain vague and largely unknowable.

Narration

For many years, it was widely assumed that fiction was narrated, while drama was merely enacted; or, to use Genette's terms, that narrative fiction was fundamentally diegetic (though it might contain mimesis in the form of quoted dialogue), while drama was fundamentally mimetic (though it likewise might contain diegesis in internal narrations). The twentieth century, however, is filled with compelling examples of narration in drama, both on and offstage. One of the most exciting current approaches to dramatic theory focuses on narration in drama.[12] Building on the recent work of Seymour Chatman, Manfred Jahn has argued that every film and play has a narrator; this is the "agent who manages the exposition, who decides what is to be told how it is to be told, . . . and what is to be left out."[13] Jahn goes on to postulate further that "the enunciating subject of the stage directions is not (or is not initially) the playwright but a narrator."[14] Such a concept is readily applied to the agent behind *Endgame*.

There are several types of narration in drama. The simplest case is when a character in a play tells a story or recounts a group of events to other characters. This can be part of a theatrical convention, as in Greek drama, which precludes the enactment of death and thus makes its narration essential (typically at the end of the play). In *Endgame* Hamm narrates several events, including the arrival of Clov in his domain – a narrative that evokes Prospero's account to his daughter of how the two arrived on the island in *The Tempest*. The history of drama also provides a number of other possibilities. Many traditional dramas from antiquity to the eighteenth century employ a "frame narrator" or speaker of the prologue who introduces the play that is about to be performed (*Romeo and Juliet*). It is not uncommon for a modern drama to consist entirely of narrations by characters (Harold Pinter's *Landscape*, Conor McPherson's *This Lime Tree Bower*). There is also the genre of the monodrama, a narrative of the thoughts and experiences of a single character on stage. This rare form emerged briefly during Romanticism and has been reinstituted and transformed by Beckett. His play "Not I" is a powerful narration spoken by an illumined mouth that keeps telling the same story about another individual and who keeps insisting, increasingly unconvincingly, that it is not the story of herself. We are presented with, that is, a "pseudo-third-person" narration.

More daring is the "generative narrator," the character who comes on stage and narrates events which are then enacted before the audience. We may differentiate two types of generative narrator: one who is part of the story world he or she describes, as in Tennessee Williams's memory play *The Glass Menagerie*; the other more closely resembles a third-person narrator and exists outside (or above) the storyworld that the narration creates (the offstage voice in Simone Benmussa's *La Vie singulière d'Albert Nobbs* [1977], or the storyteller in Bertold Brecht's *Caucasian Chalk Circle*). Postmodern variants are also possible: Tom Stoppard's *Travesties* is an utterly unreliable memory play and Beckett's "Cascando" employs a generative narrator who is exhausted and defeated by his narration; he cannot control the voice and music he conjures up.

Frames and reflexivity

Most drama of the last two centuries is unframed; that is, presented without any introductory material such as prologue or a voice or text that sets the scene, and the demands of exposition are taken care of in the dialogue. Looking at the history of drama, however, we find that the storyworld of a play can be framed in a number of ways, many of them presented or enacted on stage. These include the introduction by the chorus in Greek drama, the summary in Plautine comedy, and the formal prologue of Restoration and eighteenth-century drama, spoken by an actor who is not yet in character. Framing devices can also be miniature plays in themselves, as in the frame play that circumscribes the main drama (Christopher Sly's scene at the beginning of *The Taming of the Shrew*), or the kind of dramatized introduction in the theater that appears in some Elizabethan plays (the "inductions" to Ben Jonson's comedies) and classical Indian theater (also used in Goethe's *Faust*), as characters such as the poet and the director discuss the play that is about to be performed. In some modern dramas, the narrator or an offstage voice performs the function of the traditional prologue: "I give you truth in the pleasant disguise of illusion. To begin with, I turn back time. I reverse it to that quaint period, the thirties . . . I am the narrator of the play and a character in it."[15] Beckett tends to avoid framing devices, preferring instead to plunge his audience into a maelstrom of words and acts that the spectators must contextualize themselves.

A comprehensive theory of narrative in general should include a space for reflexivity, or works that consciously reflect on their own status as fiction or drama. This is true of the poetics of drama in particular, where framing slides easily into issues of reflexivity. Considerable work has been done on the subject of metadrama, or drama about drama, in recent years.[16] There are a number of ways a play can refer to itself or its status as a play; as might be expected, Beckett employs a wide range of self-referential styles, from the representation of the rehearsal of a scene ("Catastrophe") to dramas involving the production, repetition, and rewriting of a basic narrative ("Cascando"). We may also note that Hamm is a kind of playwright figure, that he directs the events and characters around him, and generally dramatizes his existence as an actor: "Me – to play" are his first lines (*Endgame*, 2); appropriately, his name suggests a performer who craves the spotlight.

Another type of reflexivity is simple frame-breaking, a dramatic analogue of Genette's notion of "metalepsis," or the intrusion of one story level onto another. This occurs when the characters recognize they are figures in a play, as when Clov trains the telescope on the audience or, when moving toward the door, he announces like a vaudeville actor, "This is what we call making an exit" (*Endgame*, 81). There is also the question of Clov, "What is to keep us here?" which Hamm answers, "The dialogue" (*Endgame*, 58). Near the end of the play Hamm states that he is "warming up for" his "last soliloquy" (*Endgame*, 78).

Still another type of reflexivity occurs when characters' dialogues refer both to what the characters are experiencing and to the play as a play. We find this in Nell's lament, "Why this farce, day after day?" (14), which could refer to the meaningless actions repeated over and over or the daily repetition of the actors' performance. We find in addition what is called the *mise en abyme*, or miniature reproduction of the central situation dramatized in the play, here presented in a narrated story:

> I once knew a madman who thought the end of the world had come . . . I used to go and see him in the asylum. I'd take him by the hand and drag him to the window. Look! There! All that rising corn! . . . All that loveliness! (Pause) He'd snatch away his hand and go back to his corner. Appalled. All he'd seen was ashes.   (*Endgame*, 44)

As Hamm goes on to remark, this case is not unusual, which suggests a complementarity between this narrated vision and the many attempts Clov makes to see something other than the "corpsed" world outside the room (*Endgame*, 30). Finally, we may point to the text's sustained rewriting (and negating) of *The Tempest*, another play that contains embedded dramas and a playwright figure as protagonist, and where minor scenes are staged to produce specific effects on the characters who observe them. When Hamm says, "Our revels now are ended" (*Endgame*, 56), it carries resonances of Prospero's famous metadramatic continuation of those lines in *The Tempest*: "These our actors, / As I foretold you, were all spirits and / Are melted into air, into thin air . . . We are such stuff / As dreams are made on, and our little life / Is rounded with a sleep" (IV. i. 148–58).

Conclusion

It is evident that drama provides a great number of compelling examples that can greatly enrich our understanding of key elements of narrative theory. Specifically, the presence of human bodies performing on a physical stage would seem to require an expanded conceptualization of space and closure, and enactment gives the concept of character a "fourth," performed dimension. Live performance also shows how audience members can enter the storyworld and participate (more or less briefly) in the plot of the play. Finally, these examples show how dramas employ familiar concepts like narrative time in a distinctive manner. That is, the works discussed above, especially those by Beckett, reveal that specific categories of narrative theory need to be expanded or modified to encompass the many salient examples from drama and how still others, though fundamentally unchanged, can be given fresh and illuminating applications. Like Aristotle, we would do well to analyze drama side by side with the narrative practice of Homer and his descendants. Such a move would allow the complementary aspects and distinctive differences of drama to move to the foreground, particularly those that involve performance. A narratological analysis is especially useful for comprehending the dramatic work of Beckett, many of whose innovations in fiction also appear in his plays, and whose challenges to familiar conventions of representation are perhaps even more powerful when presented on the stage.

NOTES

1. Seymour Chatman, *Story and Discourse: Narrative Structure in Fiction and Film* (Ithaca: Cornell University Press, 1978).
2. Roland Barthes, *Image Music Text*. Translated by Stephen Heath (New York: Hill and Wang, 1972), p. 79. For a sustained discussion of the relations between drama and narrative see Ansgar Nünning and Roy Sommer, "Diegetic and Mimetic Narrativity: Some Further Steps Toward a Naratology of Drama." In John Pier (ed.) *New Essays in Narratology* (Berlin: de Gruyter), forthcoming.
3. James Phelan, for example, uses this model (the terms of which he calls "mimetic," "synthetic," and "thematic") in *Reading People, Reading Plots: Character, Progression, and the Interpretation of Narrative* (Chicago: University of Chicago Press, 1989), pp. 1–14. For a study that applies this model to drama and includes a fourth, "enacted" category see Brian Richardson, "Beyond Poststructuralism: Theory of Character, the Personae of Modern Drama, and the Antinomies of Critical Theory." *Modern Drama* 40 (1997), pp. 86–99.

4. The theater of the absurd was inaugurated by the earlier plays of Eugene Ionesco and Beckett, and was adopted by or influenced a large number of subsequent playwrights, including Arthur Adamov, Harold Pinter, Jean Genet, Vaclav Havel, Edward Albee, Maria Irene Fornes, and the early Tom Stoppard. This kind of drama features inconsequential dialogue and general miscommunication, preposterous sequences of events, and unusual or impossible settings.
5. Samuel Beckett, *Endgame* (New York: Grove, 1958), p. 19.
6. Aristotle, *Poetics*. Translated by S. H. Butcher. In Hazard Adams (ed.) *Critical Theory Since Plato* (New York, Harcourt Brace Jovanovich, 1971), section 8, p. 53.
7. Keir Elam, *Semiotics of Theatre and Drama* (New York: Methuen, 1980), pp. 120, 123.
8. Jean Cocteau, *The Infernal Machine and Other Plays*. Translated by Albert Bermel et al. (New York: New Directions, 1963), p. 33.
9. For a fuller account of time in drama see Brian Richardson, "'Time is Out of Joint': Narrative Models and the Temporality of the Drama." *Poetics Today* 8 (1987), pp. 299–309.
10. Sabine Buchholz and Manfred Jahn, "Space in Narrative." In David Herman, Manfred Jahn, and Marie-Laure Ryan (eds.) *The Routledge Encyclopedia of Narrative Theory* (London and New York: Routledge, 2005), pp. 551–5.
11. For a fuller discussion of space in *Endgame* see Brian Richardson, "Theatrical Space and the Domain of *Endgame*." *Journal of Dramatic Theory and Criticism* 14:2 (Spring 2000), pp. 67–76.
12. An important account of Brechtian "epic" narration in drama has been provided by Manfred Pfister in *Theory and Analysis of Drama*. Translated by John Halliday (Cambridge: Cambridge University Press, 1988), pp. 71–6, 120–31. See also Brian Richardson, "Point of View in Drama: Diegetic Monologue, Unreliable Narrators, and the Author's Voice on Stage." *Comparative Drama* 22 (1988), pp. 193–214 and "Voice and Narration in Postmodern Drama." *New Literary History* 32 (2001), pp. 681–94; Monika Fludernik, "Narrative and Drama." In John Pier (ed.) *New Essays in Narratology* (Berlin: Mouton de Gruyter), forthcoming; and Ansgar Nünning and Roy Sommer, "Diegetic and Mimetic Narrativity: Some Further Steps Toward a Naratology of Drama."
13. Manfred Jahn, "Narrative Voice and Agency in Drama: Aspects of a Narratology of Drama." *New Literary History* 32 (2001), p. 670.
14. Manfred Jahn, "Narrative Voice and Agency in Drama." p. 672.
15. Tennessee Williams, *The Glass Menagerie* (New York: New Directions, 1970), p. 23.
16. For a good overview of the subject and its theories see Richard Hornby, *Drama, Metadrama, and Perception* (Lewisburg PA: Bucknell University Press, 1986).

JASON MITTELL

Film and television narrative

Narrative theory is a flexible tool, useful for analyzing elements of story-telling common across a wide range of media. A detailed vocabulary for the mechanics of plotting or elements of characterization can help us understand a novel, television show, comic book, videogame, film, opera, or any other form of storytelling. Although the concepts explored in this collection can be applied productively to any medium, we must also be aware of the ways that any specific medium creates particular storytelling parameters, constraining some options while enabling others. Thus the goal of this chapter is to out-line some of the specific narrative facets that are common to moving-image storytelling as found within film and television, and to explore how these two media function as major narrative forms in contemporary culture.

Film and television share a common visual and aural form, and thus many of their specific storytelling practices are similar; however, the two media diverge in crucial ways, with sufficiently different structures that we cannot analyze film and television narratives identically. By examining these media comparatively, we can see how film and television differ from literature in areas such as narration, perspective, temporality, and comprehension, and diverge from each other regarding plot structures and viewer engagement. To explore aspects of moving-image narration and to exemplify the particular ways that film and television narratives function, this chapter explores two popular examples: the film of *The Wizard of Oz*; and the television series *Lost*.

Moving-image narration and *The Wizard of Oz*

It can be difficult to notice how a given medium tells stories on its own terms – we are so used to specific norms associated with the media of literature, film, and television that we often do not dwell on their particular attributes. A useful way to notice a medium's unique properties is to compare it to another form. So let us compare examples of a familiar novel and its film adaptation, not to judge the faithfulness of the adaptation or to explore creative choices, but to understand how the basic mechanisms of storytelling function within literary versus moving-image narratives.

Quite early in L. Frank Baum's novel *The Wonderful Wizard of Oz* (originally published in 1900), we get this account of Dorothy's first glimpse of Oz:

> The little girl gave a cry of amazement and looked about her, her eyes growing bigger and bigger at the wonderful sights she saw. The cyclone had set the house down very gently – for a cyclone – in the midst of a country of marvelous beauty. There were lovely patches of greensward all about, with stately trees bearing rich and luscious fruits. Banks of gorgeous flowers were on every hand, and birds with rare and brilliant plumage sang and fluttered in the trees and bushes. A little way off was a small brook, rushing and sparkling along between green banks, and murmuring in a voice very grateful to a little girl who had lived so long on the dry, gray prairies.[1]

Although it is impossible to reproduce the corresponding moment from the film *The Wizard of Oz* (MGM, 1939) on the printed page, the film presents the same basic content using a completely different grammar of storytelling within a 90-second sequence. Dorothy opens the door to reveal the lush landscape of Oz in a sequence comprised of four edited shots. The first, most famously, is taken from within the house as Dorothy opens the door – the interior is filmed in black-and-white (like the previous 15 minutes of the film), while Oz itself is in glorious Technicolor and accompanied by swelling music. Before we see much detail of Oz, we cut to a medium-shot of Dorothy and Toto (now outside in color) surveying the wondrous landscape with wide-eyed amazement. The film then cuts to a shot starting behind Dorothy and slowly rotating and rising in a minute-long 180° panoramic crane motion that presents a leisurely vista of Oz. Finally we cut to a shot of Dorothy over some bushes, who offers her quotable line, "Toto, I have a feeling we're not in Kansas anymore."

So what can we learn from comparing these two ways of telling the same basic narrative content, Dorothy landing in an unknown but beautiful place? The modes of conveying this information are quite distinct, pointing to the storytelling strategies and possibilities available to literature versus moving images. In the novel, Baum uses vocabulary which, today at least, might be called "cinematic," with language that evokes visual and aural details while explicitly alluding to the motion of the birds and brook. When reading this passage, it is hard not to visualize the landscape described, creating an imaginary vista that begs to be captured on film. Baum does not employ many of the techniques that literature offers to convey emotion, like first-person

1

2

1 and 2 Dorothy's expression of awe guides our own emotional response to the lush Technicolor land of Oz as seen in successive shots, providing the cinematic parallel to Baum's descriptions.

narration, portrayals of interior states of mind, or freezing story-time to explore particular dimensions of a situation. We recognize Dorothy's emotions not from interior monologues or access to her thoughts, but through descriptions of her exterior behavior – wide eyes and amazed cry. Still, the value-laden descriptions he provides ("wonderful," "marvelous beauty," "stately") seem to be Dorothy's own judgments – we are seeing these sights for the first time along with her, and we appreciate her own wonderment at the contrast between Oz and her "dry, gray prairies," even if we are not privy to her innermost thoughts. Thus stylistically Baum's account of Dorothy's first glimpse of Oz seems less consistent with the tradition of nineteenth-century novels than with the medium of cinema that had yet to be fully realized when the novel first appeared.

Even the most cinematic of literary texts, though, uses a different narrative grammar than that used in the film version of Oz, which exemplifies the unique possibilities as well as limitations of moving-image storytelling. Baum tells us that Oz is a "country of marvelous beauty" and the flowers were "gorgeous" – we then imagine our own vision of a landscape warranting that praise. In contrast, filmmakers must start with a visualization, presenting a set of moving images that they invite viewers to evaluate as beautiful and wondrous. This sequence from Oz does suggest some of the specific ways that film can convey an emotional reaction without using the explicit evaluative and descriptive vocabulary that literature offers, as there are no adjectives in cinema. Like Baum's prose, the film allows Dorothy's external reactions to cue viewers' responses – the 8-second shot of Dorothy's reaction to Oz shows her cycle through emotions of confusion, trepidation, wonderment, and joy, all wordlessly conveyed through Judy Garland's performance via facial expressions and gestures. We never see a shot from Dorothy's actual point of view, but film conventions have taught us that a sequence alternating between shots from over a person's shoulder and her facial reactions (termed "shot/reverse shot") will be interpreted as conveying her perspective. Just as Dorothy's reactions in the prose version cue readers to visualize a scene provoking cries of amazement and widening eyes, Garland and the camera guide our own judgments of the film's pre-visualized world of Oz.

Other cinematic techniques lack such direct literary parallels. Notably this sequence utilizes the rare and powerful device of shifting from black-and-white to color cinematography, a move that would have been especially powerful upon the film's debut in 1939, when black-and-white films were much more commonplace than those shot in color. It is hard to imagine how a novel might accomplish such a dramatic shift in texture – perhaps a notable shift in type font or page layout might highlight a transformation in the formal means of storytelling, although it is unlikely any such shift could be as powerful and noteworthy. This visual shift operates at the level of storytelling discourse, or the way a story is told, rather than the level of story itself – we assume that Dorothy doesn't literally notice the change from black-and-white to color, but that this transformation is a strategy of narration used to convey the distinction between the vibrancy of Oz and Kansas's "dry, gray prairies."

Most films lack the narrative voice used in literature to convey attitudes toward the action, such as Baum's witty aside "for a cyclone." Instead, film-making techniques such as camera angles and movement, editing, music, and unusual tricks like the shift to color all function to guide viewer comprehension and emotional response to the story represented on screen. A crucial distinction here is between diegetic and non-diegetic elements of a narrative. The diegesis refers to the storyworld which the characters experience, whether we witness it or not – even though we do not see Dorothy's house land on the Witch of the East, it is a diegetic element of the film's narrative, later recounted by the Witch of the North. Oz's lush vegetation and architecture, Dorothy's comments and gestures, and the special effects of the tornado are diegetic elements that have clearly occurred within the film's fictional universe. By contrast, non-diegetic elements are used to tell the story, but do not actually appear within the film's internal storyworld. Typically, films employ non-diegetic techniques such as camera movements, edits, and soundtrack music to represent aspects of the storyworld and guide our reactions to onscreen events. The minute-long crane around Oz portrays diegetic elements of landscape, character, and setting, but the actual viewpoint presented is outside the world of the narrative, mirroring the way a literary extradiegetic narrator presents a scene to readers; the shot invites viewers to share in Dorothy's emotional state of awe at her new surroundings. Devices like this crane shot and the switch to color are extravagant moments of moving-image storytelling asserting a distinctive narrative voice, but nearly every edit, camera shot, and musical score functions similarly to convey a particular perspective on the diegesis and to establish an emotional tone.

Just as moving-image storytelling lacks literature's ability to describe and evaluate elements of the storyworld via adjectives and narrative voice, except via the "literary" device of voice-over narration, films are also limited as to how much of the diegetic world can be presented or withheld. In Baum's narration, he tells us enough to paint a vivid picture in our minds, but leaves out many potential details. For instance, is there anything floating in the brook's water? That detail is absent from the book, and isn't really necessary to convey the sense of Oz's lushness. Or Baum could have wanted to withhold this detail until later, when he might mention a flock of ducks in the water. Filmmakers cannot choose to leave visual details ambiguous, however; if a film shows a scene, all elements in the storyworld must be included in the image or they will be assumed not to exist in the diegesis. A film must typically represent every last detail within the portion of the storyworld that is visually presented – the film of Oz clearly shows that the water is dotted with lily pads and flowers, consistent with, but not included in, Baum's accounts of lush foliage. Thus a film's visual and auditory representation of a storyworld generally contains all of the elements that comprise that setting, while a novel will selectively present details that convey necessary narrative information and set an effective tone. But if novels can be more ambiguous in the details of a setting, they can also effectively highlight particular details deemed relevant, like the sound of the brook. For a film to highlight a detail, especially within a crowded and elaborate setting like Oz, the filmmaker must consciously focus upon it via devices like close-ups or having an actor refer to it; thus cinematic representations of setting simultaneously present more complete but less highlighted details than literary narration.

Finally, this segment of Oz also illustrates differences in the way litera-ture and film treat time. We might consider three different temporal streams within all narratives. Story-time is the time-frame of the diegesis, how time passes within the storyworld. Story-time typically follows realist conven-tions of straightforward chronology and linear progression from moment to moment, with exceptions like science-fiction time-traveling or magical clocks freezing temporal progression. Discourse-time is the temporal struc-ture and duration of the story as told within a given narrative. Narratives often reorder events through flashbacks, retelling past events, repeating story events from multiple perspectives, and jumbled chronologies – these are manipulations of discourse-time, in so far as we assume that the charac-ters experienced the events in a linear progression. Genres such as mysteries play with discourse-time to create suspense concerning past events, waiting until the end of the narrative to reveal the inciting incident that diegetically occurred near the beginning of the story, and more experimental narratives manipulate discourse temporality to promote ambiguity or aesthetic reflec-tion. Finally, there is narration-time, the temporal framework involved in telling and receiving the story. For literature, this is quite variable as every-one reads at a different pace – for example, we might read a book in install-ments over a period of days or weeks. For film and television, however, narration-time is strictly controlled, given that a 2-hour film has the same duration for all viewers, while television restricts narration-time even further through its schedule of weekly installments and commercial breaks.

Temporally, the example of *Oz* appears quite straightforward, but even this simple example highlights some key medium differences. This film sequence clearly takes 90 seconds of narration-time, and since it presents a continuous chronology, both discourse- and story-time share the same temporal flow. The book is less clear in this respect – reading the sequence probably would take most readers less than a minute, but there are no indications of how much time is passing as the narrator describes Dorothy's first impression of Oz. Literary narrative has the temporal freedom to freeze story-time to indulge in detailed descriptions or asides; likewise it has the ability to be ambiguous with temporality, offering no markers of time passing within the narration. This does not mean that no story-time passes as we read about Oz, but it is left vague as to how long Dorothy marvels at the landscape before encountering the Munchkins, an ambiguity typically unavailable to filmmakers. Moving-image media can mark temporal shifts through devices like editing, dissolves, and flashbacks, but it is quite rare that a film pauses to describe a scene or delve into a thematic diversion. Thus film can be much more precise with its temporal continuity, but it lacks the the ambiguity and temporal play often employed in literary narratives.

What do these comparative possibilities and limitations of film and television versus literature mean for our understanding of narrative? It is crucial that we grasp the medium-specific particularities that make moving-image media distinct in their ability to tell stories. According to some dismissive critics, film and television cannot achieve the narrative depths and complexity of great literature, and thus are condemned as inherently inferior media. While certainly film and television cannot successfully mimic literature's unique strengths, an understanding of the medium-specific potentials of moving-image storytelling allows us to appreciate what they offer on their own terms. Through their use of visual details, temporal construction, and presentational mode, film and television can offer particular pleasures and aesthetic achievements unique to their media. The rest of this chapter examines one particularly innovative, accomplished, and extremely popular example of moving-image storytelling to explore how television narrative operates: the television series *Lost*.

Television's narrative forms and *Lost*

At first glance, it might seem that television narratives would be less demanding and complex than movies or literary texts: television has long been dismissed by its critics as a low-quality and creatively bankrupt medium. But in terms of narrative structure and comprehension, television offers a set of challenges and possibilities that complicate how stories are told and understood, and numerous programs have strategically played with story-telling techniques to create unique, innovative narratives. Most films and novels are self-contained, creating a storyworld that is unique to that par-ticular book or film. There are ongoing series of books or film sequels, but typically each individual entry in the series is self-standing, like the James Bond books and films; series that require readers or viewers to follow the story sequence in order, like the Harry Potter series, are exceptional cases typical of genres like science-fiction and fantasy. Historically, the serialized narratives of nineteenth-century fiction have given way to stand-alone nov-els, and even in their own time such texts were usually released as singu-lar narratives upon completion. For television, this tendency is reversed: the exceptions are stand-alone television narratives, like made-for-TV movies or anthology series that offer a new storyworld with each new episode, such as *The Twilight Zone*. Most narrative television offers ongoing storyworlds, presenting specific opportunities and limitations for creating compelling narratives.

Television series typically follow either episodic or serial structures. Episodic series present a consistent storyworld, but each episode is rela-tively independent – characters, settings, and relationships carry over across episodes, but the plots stand on their own, requiring little need for con-sistent viewing or knowledge of diegetic history to comprehend the nar-rative. In American television, this has been the most common model for primetime television; hence, situation comedies and dramas have followed episodic norms in crafting a familiar storyworld with plots that commence and resolve within each episode. Often the only chronological markers in episodic series are the birth and growth of children and additions or sub-tractions to the cast of characters – we can place the episodes of *Bewitched* in a rough order based on Tabitha's age (as well as its shift to color and recasting of Darrin's character). Yet there are minimal narrative differences between these various episodes: we do not need to know Tabitha's infant back-story to appreciate her toddler mishaps. Likewise, many episodic dramatic programs follow a procedural structure, where each episode follows the process by which a self-contained narrative enigma is solved through detec-tive work, legal maneuvers, or medical investigation, typified by contempo-rary dramas like *CSI*, *Law & Order*, and *House*. Episodic programs offer a compact violation and restoration of the underlying situation's equilibrium; further, although the narrative disruption's specific form depends on genre conventions – crimes on cop shows versus family squabbles on sitcoms – the basic structure of episodic programs transcends genre. The conclusion of any episode returns the characters to the equilibrium of their given situation – any lessons learned or characters changed will likely be forgotten or ignored in subsequent episodes.

Alternately, serial narratives in American television were for many years confined to the genre of the daytime soap opera, although primetime serials have been more common in other countries, such as Latin American *telenovelas* or British "kitchen sink" shows. By the 1980s serial form entered primetime in America, through family dramas (*Dallas* and *Dynasty*, so-called primetime soaps), crime shows (*Hill Street Blues*), and medical dramas (*St. Elsewhere*). Serial narration features continuing storylines traversing multiple episodes, with an ongoing diegesis that demands viewers to construct an overarching storyworld using information gathered from their full history of viewing, which for some soap operas can go back decades. As Robert Allen and others have explored, serial narration is not simply a matter of continuing stories, but offers its own set of narrative norms.[2] Soap operas, both daytime and their primetime progeny, prioritize relationships over events; even when a major event happens in a soap opera, the question of "what happens?" is often secondary to "how does it affect the community of relationships?" Hence, events are narrated to audiences with a great deal of redundancy, not only to ensure that all viewers share sufficient story knowledge but also to explore how the retelling of an event impacts the web of relationships that comprise any soap opera's storyworld. Even if viewers are witnessing the seventh retelling of the previous week's key narrative event, they are gleaning information about how this event impacted each character who learns about it, accumulating nuance in direct proportion to the amount of long-term backstory knowledge any viewer possesses to make sense of these ongoing tales. As such, the narrative events of serial dramas traditionally focus more upon relationship changes than the chains of cause-and-effect actions that are typical of episodic procedural dramas or sitcoms; when soap operas do feature narrative events like murders, accidents, and schemes, they are typically narrated so that viewers focus upon the ripple effects any given event has upon the community more than suspense over what may happen next.

The main structural difference between episodic and serial narratives is the status of events at the end of a given episode. Serial programs refuse full resolution of plots, typically ending episodes with an unresolved cliffhanger designed to stimulate viewers to tune in for the next episode. When serial storylines do resolve, they are often replaced with even more suspenseful or engrossing narrative enigmas to keep viewers watching. In contrast, episodic programs typically wrap-up major plot points by the end of each episode, enabling them to be viewed in any order. Core narrative conflicts that define the series usually remain across episodes – for instance, *Bewitched* never resolves the underlying conflict between Samantha's witch powers and her human assimilation – but the particular plots that such situations create are introduced and wrapped up within the confines of a single episode. A mixture of serial and episodic forms results in narrative arcs, multi-episode plotlines that run across a series, but eventually are resolved. Arcs can be as brief as two episodes, in the common formulation of a "two-parter" in a typically episodic series, or might run throughout an entire season or beyond. One of the many innovations of *Buffy the Vampire Slayer* was its use of singular arcs for each of its seven seasons, structured around a specific villain threatening the town of Sunnydale. In contemporary programming, story arcs are a common storytelling device for television narratives, with even procedural dramas and conventional sitcoms incorporating minor arcs concerning character relationships or ongoing problems.

Television storytelling is faced with many specific structural limitations when compared to the more flexible formats of film or literature. There are few mandates for how long a book should be, how to structure chapter breaks, or how characters might evolve over the course of a story. Although films generally run around 2 hours, any film's exact length and story pacing are flexible. Commercial American television is far more structurally constrained – programs are almost always designed to fit precisely into 30 or 60 minute schedule blocks, and networks demand regular commercial breaks that segment programming (and reduce actual running times to 22 or 45 minutes). Television programmers have established narrative norms that use commercial breaks to structure plots, providing markers for suspenseful moments and signaling act breaks within the story. Thus television's institutional constraints structure how stories are narrated, forcing creators to follow strict guidelines and narrative routines. The realities of producing an ongoing narrative through the collaborative enterprise of creating television programming can also force unplanned story developments: when an actor dies, leaves a program, or gets pregnant, as with John Spencer's sudden death midseason in *The West Wing* or Jennifer Garner's pregnancy during *Alias*, writers must restructure narrative arcs and story plans accordingly, a practical reality that a serial novelist like Dickens never had to cope with. Likewise, network mandates to boost ratings or fan reactions to particular characters or stories can alter long-term plans for a series, underscoring how television storytelling must juggle numerous pressures to maintain an ongoing storyworld while attempting to craft coherent and consistent episodes comprising a larger narrative arc.

These institutional pressures on television storytelling constitute extrinsic norms that range beyond any one program; the entire television medium follows certain norms such as series format and regular scheduling. Other extrinsic norms are restricted to particular genres, such as the soap-opera norm of repeating story material across episodes and even between scenes, or crime procedurals presenting and resolving a given case over the course of one episode. While these rules can be broken, audiences will notice when the story deviates from such narrative norms. All narrative forms can establish intrinsic norms as well, storytelling practices that get established as typical within that particular narrative. For example, the presentation of Kansas in black-and-white and Oz in color is an intrinsic norm for *The Wizard of Oz*, but irrelevant for any other film. For self-contained stories like those presented in most films and literary texts, intrinsic norms only apply to that particular narrative, although film series can establish ongoing intrinsic norms, such as opening all James Bond films with a pre-credit action sequence or all Harry Potter books with a scene at Privet Drive. For television, series narration lends itself to establishing intrinsic norms typical to a given program that will repeat across episodes. For instance, *Six Feet Under* begins every episode with a "death of the week" to be handled by the family's funeral home. Intrinsic narrative norms allow a series to establish its own style and train viewers to comprehend patterns – as *Six Feet Under* progressed, the show misdirected viewer expectations as to who would die in the initial segment, creating a spectatorial pleasure unique to the long-form series narrative typical of television.

Few shows exemplify the storytelling possibilities unique to the television medium more dramatically than the innovative and popular program *Lost* (ABC, 2004). The show's premise – a plane crash leaves a group of strangers stranded on a mysterious island in the South Pacific – might appear at first glance to restrict narrative options, limiting action to one setting, few long-term plot options, and a narrow cast of characters. But both the show's content and its form significantly expand the palette of narrative techniques. From the first episode it becomes evident that there is more to the island than a deserted wilderness, as polar bears, other inhabitants, and an unseen monster all threaten the castaways. *Lost*'s central narrative questions and pleasures might appear to be predicated on the suspense of what will happen to the survivors: will they get off the island or will the "Others" (the island's mysterious inhabitants) get them first? But the show has created equally compelling narrative enigmas in the backstory of each character: what were Kate's criminal acts and motivations? Why was Claire told that she must raise her own baby? What happened to the previous crash victims decades before? And were these people brought together on this airplane and then spared in the crash by random accident or something more significant? In probing these past and future mysteries, *Lost* balances notions of fate and randomness, overdetermined causality with blind chance, generating a thematic richness that also keeps viewers guessing.

Lost's storytelling scope is carried out in a truly innovative discursive style, with nested flashbacks structured into each episode as an intrinsic norm. Every episode foregrounds one character's backstory, interweaving past events with the challenges of island life to create parallel narrative threads interrelating in often surprising ways. *Lost*'s formal complexities offer intricately crafted puzzles which partially reveal themselves each week while adding new wrinkles and mysteries to the richly drawn characters and the snapshots of their pre-crash lives. Additionally the flashbacks allow for a degree of misdirection and formal play. For example, the second season debuted with a close-up of someone's eye, which had been established as an intrinsic norm to signal flashbacks. We then see a sequence of someone exercising to a 1970s song and using an old computer, signaling that we are in the midst of a flashback and leaving viewers to deduce which character it is. The scene is interrupted by an explosion, followed by the character manipulating mirrors to peer through a series of shafts. What he sees offers a narrative twist: this scene is happening within the diegetic present and he is actually in the island's secret hatch that provided an earlier mystery. By establishing and manipulating intrinsic norms, *Lost* offers narrative pleasures that motivate, or even require, viewers to learn the show's unique storytelling strategies, a process of narrative comprehension that necessitates a great deal of cognitive energy.

It might appear that popular film and television, as mainstream mass media, require little effort to comprehend the stories they tell; after all, they are typically designed for millions of viewers as an entertaining diversion. But while most films or programs may not require a great deal of conscious effort for comprehension, the basic mechanisms of following a story are not "natural" or simply automatic. We must learn how to process the fragmented camera shots, multiple streams of auditory material, and conventions of visual composition, turning them into a story that typically appears "realistic" even though we never experience the real world through such devices. David Bordwell outlines the process of narrative comprehension of film using research in cognitive sciences to explain how watching a film, and television by extension, draws upon mental processes and frameworks to facilitate understanding.[3] Viewers learn to comprehend media by building mental schemata, or cognitive patterns, that process visual and aural information into recognizable conventions that can be applied to any moving-image example. These range from simple schemata, like viewing a discontinuous edit between two shots as continuous action, to more specific and conscious conventions, such as understanding a dissolve into another scene that occurs while a character narrates to signal a flashback. Cognitive schemata are used, often without conscious awareness, to collect bits of information presented in a film and construct it into a seemingly naturalistic narrative world; viewers strengthen comprehension and acquire new schemata through the repetitive act of viewing media and becoming more skilled as spectators.

Cognitive schemata are the means by which we construct a narrative in our minds. A film's story seems to be occurring in the diegetic world portrayed on screen, but it actually is a mental construction we create – *Oz* never shows Dorothy's house land on the witch, but in our cognitive assembly of the story this event has clearly happened. How do we know? We witness evidence of the event (the witch's legs sticking out from under the house), see reactions to the event ("Ding Dong, the witch is dead!"), and are told it happened by reliable characters. Despite not explicitly representing the event, the film offers enough material that it would be considered a misunderstanding of the narrative to believe that this key narrative event did not occur. Other narrative information might be more ambiguous – the conclusion to the film of *Oz* leaves it unclear whether Dorothy's adventures were real or a dream. The characters disagree on the status of Dorothy's claims, and it is left to viewers to process events as real or a dream. We can draw upon schemata from real life (talking scarecrows and flying monkeys cannot be real) and film genres (in fantasy stories and musicals anything can happen) to generate a hypothesis for what really happened to Dorothy. A key aspect of narrative comprehension is that we tend to notice ourselves making such inferences and hypotheses only when narration is ambiguous or mysterious, as typical narrative connections and assumptions that we make from moment to moment, like the witch's death, are processed nearly automatically following learned schemata at a cognitive level that we are barely aware of.

Lost's first season episode "Walkabout" exemplifies these cognitive processes, as we learn about the character John Locke both through his efforts to hunt boar on the island and flashbacks that show him as an office drone planning to do a rugged Australian wilderness walkabout. We comprehend information that the show presents using hypotheses and schemata: in island scenes, we twice see Locke view his barely moving feet after physical accidents, which we comprehend as an attempt to establish his own well-being in a post-traumatic daze. Likewise in the flashbacks, Locke repeatedly rebuffs people telling him that he is not fit to do the walkabout by exclaiming, "don't tell me what I can't I do!" – a sentiment that we read as responding to concerns about his age or lack of experience. But in the episode's final flashback

3

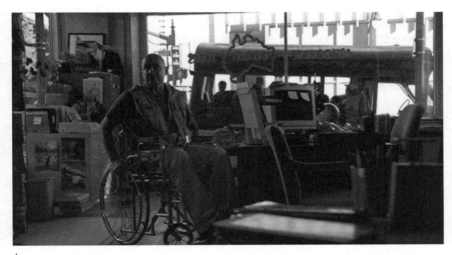

4

3 and 4 Both characters realize that Locke is in a wheelchair, but the audience is not provided with this crucial information until the camera angle shifts in the scene's final shot. Such twists cleverly exploit the camera's ability to present details of the diegetic world in a selective way.

sequence, it is revealed that Locke was in a wheelchair prior to the crash; this new information forces us to rethink hypotheses made earlier, and recall unnoticed details such as how flashbacks strategically showed Locke sitting without moving to obscure this information. Such narrative deceptions use viewer tendencies to fill in narrative gaps with the most likely assumptions and follow typical schemata: if a character is walking in the narrative present, we assume he could always walk even when we don't see it. Once revealed, it makes sense within *Lost*'s quasi-mystical storyworld that Locke's paralysis would be cured by the crash, but the show uses our own learned patterns of comprehending narrative gaps to "trick" us into assuming that Locke could walk during the flashbacks. This episode demonstrates how watching a narrative is an active ongoing process of comprehension, as viewers make and revise cognitive hypotheses and assumptions to create their own version of the storyworld. Films and television shows train their viewers to follow particular processes and schemata, allowing for more complex and sophisticated narratives to emerge and achieve mass popularity.

This sequence, and the subsequent reflection that viewers must go through to process what they have just seen, highlights the importance of point of view or focalization in moving-image storytelling. Literary narratives can signal focalization through pronoun usage and other techniques. For example, a first-person narrator will be indicated through the use of "I" and commentary on the action, which can tend toward either a present experience or distanced reflection of events. Films and television can offer similar first-person perspectives, as in voice-over narration typical of *film noir* crime dramas or films told through a narrator's explicit recollection of earlier moments. Furthermore, character-based perspectives in moving-image narration can slide along the same continuum that stretches between the older, narrating-I and the younger, experiencing-I in first-person literary narratives. Yet they can also take advantage of the credibility or authority with which viewers tend to invest scenes represented on screen. Thus, in Locke's flashback, Locke himself clearly knows that he was paralyzed and cured, but the show withholds this information. It thereby causes the audience to recategorize these scenes (retrospectively) neither as full interior views of Locke's memories, nor as completely external views of Locke and his experiences, but rather as a complex, mixed mode in which the narration strategically manipulates Locke's firsthand memories to heighten viewers' cognitive and emotional involvement in the storyworld.

The internal norms of *Lost*'s complex chronology and focalization require a highly active mode of cognitive engagement to comprehend its long-form narrative, as each episode adds new revelations to the show's central enigmas while opening up new mysteries concerning both past and future events. Viewers are expected to pore over minutiae from each episode to piece together clues about larger narrative mysteries and conspiracies. By establishing a constantly expanding, complex storyworld, *Lost* invites viewers to actively decode the show's narrative enigmas; one result has been the formation of a participatory online fan community offering theories and compiling evidence in a collaborative effort to parse the program. While other media offer narrative twists and techniques that drive viewers to reflect on storytelling mechanics, the ongoing continuity of television series requires a level of investment and immersion not available within a 2-hour film. Thus at their most complex, television narratives like *Lost* counter the stereotype of the television audience as passive couch potatoes. Instead, such narratives help create highly engaged, participatory viewers.

Nearly all of the specific techniques used by film and television explored in this chapter have parallels in other media, but there remain important lessons to be learned by taking any medium seriously and analyzing how it tells stories in a distinctive fashion. Viewers learn the particular codes and patterns that comprise the norms for film and television, as the popularity of complex stories like *Lost* attests. Although it has become a critical cliché to decry how moving-image adaptations can never surpass the quality of their literary sources, we cannot judge a film or television narrative using the same criteria established for print narratives. Rather we should engage these media on their own terms, keeping in mind the robust repertoire of narrative strategies and possibilities that can offer unique compelling storytelling experiences distinct from those afforded by literary fiction.

NOTES

1. L. Frank Baum, *The Wonderful Wizard of Oz* (New York: Dover Publications, 1960), pp. 19–20.
2. Robert C. Allen, *Speaking of Soap Operas* (Chapel Hill: University of North Carolina Press, 1985).
3. David Bordwell, *Narration in the Fiction Film* (Madison: University of Wisconsin Press, 1985).

12

NICK MONTFORT

Narrative and digital media

The computer can be used to extend or demolish traditional narrative concepts in all sorts of ways, but its ability to combine narration and simulation has been particularly significant in digital art, electronic literature, and video games. In narrating, computers represent events either by directly outputting narrative text, graphics, and sound or by generating this from some underlying representation of what has happened. In simulating, computers determine what happens in some model world, using a system of rules. Approaches developed by narrative scholars can provide specific insights into how simulation and narration function and interrelate in digital works.

Consider this excerpt from a transcript of interaction with Steven Meretzky's 1985 interactive fiction *A Mind Forever Voyaging* – input from the user, also known as the interactor, is shown in italics:

>*go northeast*
Church Lobby
The regional central headquarters of the Church is an architectural splendor; light spills down from above, giving the illusion that the countenance of God is gazing down upon a visitor in full force and fury. A huge image of a radar dish, symbol of the Church, hangs above the inner sanctums to the east, and impressively tall arched doorways lead out to the northwest and southwest.

A wooden rack in the lobby, for the purpose of distributing literature about the church, contains one pamphlet.

WARNING: Record buffer full. Auto-deactivation of record feature.

>*exit simulation mode*
Aborting to Communications Mode.

– SIMULATION TERMINATED –

>*PEOF*
Dr. Perelman's Office
This is the office of your creator, Dr. Abraham Perelman. It is cluttered and disorganized. Overstuffed bookshelves line the room. Perelman's desk is covered

with a number of items, including a decoder, a map of the city, a ball-point pen, and a printout of a magazine article. Steam from a cup of coffee is fogging the lens of your visual unit.

Doctor Perelman is sitting at his desk, reading through stacks of papers and occasionally typing on his desk terminal.

>*perelman, look at the record buffer*
Perelman looks intrigued. "You've recorded something interesting, eh? Let me get a few of my colleagues together, and we'll view the buffer. I'll let you know when we're done, okay?" He leaves the room.

This bit of interaction with a rather venerable computer game may be puzzling, not least because it begins in one simulated world (where the church lobby exists) and ends in another (where Dr. Perelman's office exists). In this interactive fiction, the user or interactor directs two different manifestations of a "player character" (roughly similar to the "man" or "ship" of classic arcade games, but with qualities of a character in a narrative) through a world, or possibly multiple worlds – ones that join the rich qualities of textual worlds[1] that are seen in novels with computer-simulated worlds. The interactor can go beyond exploration to influence these worlds, in a mode that has been called *ontological*.[2]

This chapter first identifies several important dimensions of digital works, using those dimensions to explore ways in which such works can differ and to examine *A Mind Forever Voyaging* in greater detail. After this, the chapter draws on the idea of *narrative levels* as described by Gérard Genette to deal with levels of simulation and narration in this particular *potential narrative,* this space of possibility within which many different narratives can be realized. This concept applies to several other sorts of digital literary and gaming experiences as well, including multimedia and multi-player digital systems. The chapter concludes by considering several other sorts of digital works and briefly describing how theories of narrative can help illuminate them.

The nature of digital works

A digital work may consist only of data or it may be better understood as a program; furthermore, programs may be interactive or non-interactive, and those that are interactive may be for single users or multiple users. Independently, a digital work may use a single channel of output or it may provide a multimedia experience. Looking at these dimensions of digital systems makes it easier to see how narrative on the computer can function in different ways.

Data/Programs: a deep understanding of computers may not be necessary in appreciating or studying all sorts of digital works. Many digital works can be characterized quite well on the level of data. The category "data" can easily hold a digital facsimile of the First Folio, an electronic text of *Moby Dick,* and a DVD of *Casablanca* – all of which are formally the same as pre-digital works but have a different material nature, using a digital rather than an analog system for representation. A new film or book that is originally created for digital presentation and distribution, but which is formally the same as these, is in the same category as these new editions of pre-existing works. Such digital representations allow for works to be manipulated and processed in new ways, since data can be used as a component of some more complex digital system. But, by themselves, these sorts of digital media works are not computer programs. They are better viewed as "documents," or as part of the broader category of "data."

Some digital data can be quite expressive and interesting to consider as narrative. Interesting new examples include some Short Message Service (SMS) stories (which are written to fit the 160-character limit of cell-phone text messages) and textual Flash animations by Young-Hae Chang Heavy Industries, including *Dakota,* which plays on Pound's first and second cantos. While these works relate to the material nature of digital technologies in particular ways, and while they fit interestingly into the contexts of digital communication, it is nevertheless important to notice that they do not use the computer's processing abilities to do anything formally new: an SMS story is a very short textual story, and *Dakota* is a motion picture with a soundtrack, albeit one that is legible and easy to distribute. Studies of the material aspects of these works would have to consider their digital nature and their digital contexts, but pre-digital narrative theory does not need to be extended to explain anything about how they actually function.

There are a huge number of digital works – popular, literary, artistic, and other – that cannot really be approached as data, however, and cannot be well understood in pre-digital terms. Some computer works take input from one or more users, or from other sources, and use that input in some way to determine how they operate. Such works may be rather computationally simple, but however complex they might be, they function in some way as interactive computer programs. To understand them, it is necessary to take an approach that is appropriate for systems that compute as well as narrate.

For instance, consider a classic, popular system: the arcade game *Ms. Pac-Man.* There is a joystick that allows user input; the direction of the joystick controls the Ms. Pac-Man figure during the main play sequence; dots disappear when Ms. Pac-Man intersects them, causing the player's score to increase; the four ghosts do different things depending upon what Ms.

Pac-Man does, generally pursuing her but running away and blinking for a short time after Ms. Pac-Man intersects a "power pill"; a ghost intersecting Ms. Pac-Man when the ghost isn't blinking causes play to end unless there is another "life" in reserve; and so on. To pretend that *Ms. Pac-Man* is a novel or a motion picture, discussing only the text this system displays or the moving images it presents, would be to overlook important, fundamental aspects of this digital work.[3] People do not appreciate *Ms. Pac-Man* simply as a reading or viewing experience. They enjoy playing it – or, to use terms that are not restricted to games, they enjoy interacting with it and operating it. At the same time, even *Ms. Pac-Man* is an expressive digital system which suggests a narrative (however unimportant this narrative might be to the player's experience of this particular game) through its system of rules, through the signs that are associated with different elements of the game, and through cut scenes – the three animated mini-movies that appear between levels, and that portray some romantic encounters between Pac-Man and Ms. Pac-Man.

Non-Interactive/Interactive: in computing, the term "interactive" refers to any program that accepts input from a user while it executes, using this input in some way as it runs. (Traditionally, the alternative was a "batch" program which would go through a stack of punched cards without waiting on a person's reply.) There are digital works that do not use direct input from the user, instead employing news feeds, network traffic data, or other sources such as a user's hard disk or a set of old emails. For these and other reasons, the data/program distinction is not the same as a "non-interactive/interactive" distinction.

Single Interactor/Multiple Interactor: a digital system may take input from a single user or it may allow communication and interaction involving several people, either remote or co-present. At one extreme, a work may be almost impossible to share with others, for instance, because the single interactor might have to put on a virtual reality helmet. At the other extreme, a system for multiple interactors may be useful only for communication, and may have no "content" independent of what users put into it; telematic art, which connects people in distant locations, provides an example.[4] Digital work with narrative aspects usually does not lie at either extreme. Most "single-player" systems allow for multiple people to observe, offer advice, and even take turns using the one interface. Conversely, many systems that are set up mainly for multi-user communication, such as chat-centered virtual environments, acquire persistent objects and simulated characters ("bots"), meaningful room descriptions, and other "content" apart from person-to-person communication.

Just as people can tell conversational stories over the telephone, using directly connected teletypes, or by post, they can also tell stories by communicating through some multi-user digital system. The digital medium and particular digital environments certainly influence the way storytellers communicate in conversation, offering rich opportunities for narrative studies of multi-user systems.

Single-Channel/Multimedia: distinguishing data from programs and interactive from non-interactive work does not say anything about whether textual, visual, musical, or other channels are being used in the program's output. Complex, interactive computer programs can use a single channel of input and output – a single "medium" rather than "multimedia" – while a pre-computer Futurist film, on the other hand, can use many semiotic channels.

These particular dimensions are certainly not the only ones that can be used to analyze different digital works; other ways of characterizing the digital can provide different insights. Espen Aarseth described seven dimensions of dynamics, determinability, transiency, perspective, access, linking, and user functions, a typology which Aarseth developed to characterize any sort of "cybertext" or text machine but which has been particularly useful in considering digital works.[5] Janet Murray described how the digital medium is essentially procedural, participatory, spatial, and encyclopedic.[6] Lev Manovich considered the important qualities to be numerical representation, modularity, automation, variability, and transcoding.[7] Most recently, Marie-Laure Ryan considered the "most fundamental" qualities of digital media to be their reactive and interactive nature, multiple sensory and semiotic channels, networking capabilities, use of volatile signs, and modularity.[8] This chapter's four dimensions of difference suggest that the distinction between programs and data (which parallels Murray's account of the "procedural" nature of digital media and Manovich's discussion of "automation") is most fundamental, with the most far-reaching implications for computer-mediated forms of narrative.

In terms of these four dimensions, *A Mind Forever Voyaging* is a program (rather than data), is interactive, is single-user, and is single-channel. The essential innovation that computing brings to narrative is neither the ability to communicate narratives to distant story recipients nor the ability to convey narrated content through multiple media. As the other chapters in this volume suggest, print narratives migrate far beyond the original place and time in which they were produced, and film and TV narratives, not to mention stories told face-to-face, have long exploited multiple semiotic channels. What *is* innovative about the computer is its ability to define a complex, formal program, governed by rules and algorithms, and to allow a user's interactions to influence the workings of this program. The analysis of *A Mind*

Forever Voyaging that follows aims to show that even non-networked, all-text programs relate to narrative in new and interesting ways.

Interactive fiction and *A Mind Forever Voyaging*

Interactive fiction is a particular form of digital work, most popular in the 1980s, that is especially rewarding to consider from a narrative standpoint. While some interactive fiction has graphics and sound, the essence of this form is the textual exchange between the interactor and the computer program. The initial text provided by the computer, and the texts that the computer provides after this, describe existents and events in the simulated world. Input – commands to a character – influences events. Interactive fiction pieces may be visually unspectacular, but they are complex computer programs that are both potential narratives (different things can be narrated depending upon the interactor's input) and simulated worlds (not just "settings," but complete environments that have their own simulated natural laws, sometimes strange ones).

Video games (originating, according to many, with *Spacewar* in 1962) pre-date interactive fiction, but interactive fiction also has a rich history. The first work in the form was *Adventure,* created by Will Crowther around 1975 and expanded by Don Woods in 1976. *Adventure* accepted simple one- or two-word commands and simulated a real cave in Kentucky with added magical elements and puzzles. Other "mainframe" games soon followed, including *Zork* (1977–9) at MIT, called *Dungeon* for a short time and inspiring the first multiple-user generalization of interactive fiction, the MUD (Multiple-User Dungeon). Interactive-fiction-producing companies (including Infocom, Level 9, Melbourne House, and Magnetic Scrolls) formed an important part of the entertainment software industry in the 1980s. Commercial projects involved the conversion of existing books and collaboration between programmers and established authors, including Douglas Adams, Robert Pinsky, and Tom Disch. As the 1990s began the commercial prospects for interactive fiction did not look so good. But while companies left the interactive fiction business, the availability of free and inexpensive tools for interactive fiction development (including Text Adventure Development System [TADS] and Inform) allowed individual authors to create interactive fiction easily focusing on particular qualities of the world and the narration of it rather than requiring that an author/programmer rebuild the whole system from scratch each time. In consequence, innovative interactive fiction development continued though the 1990s and into the first decade of the new millennium. Authors almost always offered their work for free online, just as the early authors of *Adventure* and *Zork* did.[9] Modern-day interactive fiction can be found at the IF Archive,[10] which is easily accessible through Baf's Guide,[11] a site offering search capabilities and capsule reviews.

A Mind Forever Voyaging, developed at, and published by, Infocom in 1985, is a product of the commercial era of interactive fiction; it was written and programmed by a single "implementor," Steven Meretzky. The game is a dystopia, and a departure from the humorous interactive fiction Meretzky is best known for. *A Mind Forever Voyaging* was not a commercial success, and its textual output is not always, by itself, wonderful reading. But many have found the experience of this interactive fiction piece to be very compelling, and have been impressed by the way it simulates a future city and calls upon the interactor to figure out its main puzzle. It was one of the first works in the form to show interactive fiction's potential for political critique and engagement with culture. Finally, its use of different levels of simulation makes it the ideal example of how the study of narrative can inform our understanding of complex digital works.

By typing commands, the interactor controls a player character, an entity that is a character in the narrative sense (that is, an anthropomorphic existent within the story) and also within the simulation (rather than just being mentioned, the player character participates in the simulated world to whatever extent other simulated existents do). The player character is distinguished from other characters because it is directly commanded by the interactor. In *A Mind Forever Voyaging* the player character is PRISM, a conscious computer program, gendered male, who exists in March 2031 on the outskirts of Rockvil, an American city. PRISM's abilities in this "reality" of 2031 are limited: he can read a few files in library mode, watch TV news, or flit about the complex where his hardware is housed, peeking through video cameras and listening through microphones. There is not much to hear or see, but he can chat with his creator, Dr. Abraham Perelman, revealing more about the project and the political climate. A few other manipulations are possible (PRISM can change maintenance settings in the complex, for instance), but the typical abilities of a player character – to walk around a space and move objects about – are missing from this first level of simulation.

PRISM has another special capability, however. He can enter "simulation mode" and become part of a hypothetical future, as the character Perry Simm. PRISM is called upon to explore the future to see what the effects of the right-wing "Plan for Renewed National Purpose" are likely to be. The following transcript shows another small snippet of interaction with *A Mind Forever Voyaging,* which takes place entirely in this simulated future, the Rockvil of 2041.

Rockvil Centre
The name of this plaza tells it all. The well-maintained portico of City Hall
stretches along the west side of the plaza, and Dunbar's lies on the southeast
corner. Park Street leads north and south. Main Street and Centre Street both
begin here, leading eastward and northeastward, respectively.

>*go west*
City Hall
The city's seat of government is an old concrete-slab building dating back to
the late twentieth century. The only exit is east.
A government official is sitting on a bench in the center of the lobby, eating a
snack.

>*record on*
Record feature activated.

>*talk to the official*
You have a brief chat with the government official, who cheerily comments on
how well things in the city are running, and how rewarding his job has been
lately. Suddenly he glances at his watch, mumbles a polite parting message,
and hurries away.

>*quit*
Do you really want to quit? (y/n) >*y*
[The game has finished]

These exchanges between the human interactor and the computer took place
in less than a minute, while the processing of solving the game takes at least
several hours, often spread over several days.

The first input from the player, "go west," was a *command* to Perry Simm,
and resulted in Perry walking into city hall, where he sees a government
official. After this, the player typed "record on" to instruct PRISM to record
Perry's sensations. This allows PRISM to show Dr. Perelman later what he
has seen and experienced. This "record on" is a command as well, but of
a different sort – it is directed at PRISM in the "frame world" of Rockvil
in 2031, not to Perry in the simulation. Presumably, the government official
has no idea that the record feature is being activated, and recording does not
influence anything in this simulated future Rockvil that contains city hall.
After this, the next input, "talk to the official," is an ordinary command to
Perry, just like the earlier "go west." The final two inputs, "quit" and "y" (to
confirm quitting the game) are of yet another sort. They are neither directed
at the simulated Perry in 2041 nor at PRISM in 2031, but at the computer, in
2005, that was running *A Mind Forever Voyaging* when this transcript was
being generated. These inputs are called *directives* rather than commands;

they pertain to the game itself and not what it simulates.[12] The question "Do you really want to quit?" is of course not being posed to PRISM or Perry Simm, but to the interactor.

These levels of simulation correspond to diegetic levels in a narrative – the extradiegetic level at which the narrator relates a story, the diegetic level where the characters and setting are, and the hypodiegetic level that is introduced when a character in the story herself tells a story.[13]

Level	Extradiegetic	Diegetic	Hypodiegetic
	Interactor	Player Character (PRISM)	Player Character (Perry Simm)
Input	*Directive*	*Command (1)*	*Command (2)*
e.g.	quit	enter simulation mode	close fridge
Output	*Report*	*Reply (1)*	*Reply (2)*
e.g.	Do you really want to quit?	This simulation is based 10 years hence.	Okay, the refrigerator is now closed.

In *A Mind Forever Voyaging* hypodiegetic and diegetic commands can be intermingled, and there are many worlds available. (After returning from a rather cheerful 2041, PRISM gains access to a simulated 2051, where things are worsening; future Rockvils become accessible later in the game.) But the basic distinction between the "out-of-game" directive and report and the "in-game" command and reply holds for practically all other sorts of digital media work. In classic arcade video games, for example, the score is shown to the player (not the "ship") in a "out-of-game" report; a player who gets to enter his initials after getting a high score is issuing a directive that does not influence the world of the game, just the high-score list. The score display and the high-score interaction take place on the extradiegetic level. In contrast, moving a ship or a character around in such a game occurs on the diegetic level.

In *A Mind Forever Voyaging* the interactor can command Perry, in the 2041 Rockvil, to enter a Joybooth, a sort of coin-operated (actually, card-operated) virtual reality station:

>*put card in slot*
A wave of warm contentment washes over you as the joybooth, and the world, recede. You barely notice as the headset probes the pleasure and imagination centers of your brain, and you feel yourself moving down a tunnel of swirling colors and lights, a warm breeze blowing in your face.
The roller coaster whooshes out of the tunnel, and you scream, not from fear but from the exhilaration of the experience. Rav, scrunched next to you in the seat, laughs and laughs and laughs and Frita laughs and laughs and hands

you some cotton candy and suddenly the roller coaster is gone and the park is
gone

In terms of the generated narrative, Perry Simm manages here to enter yet
another reality – a simulation *within* the simulated Rockvil of 2041, which
returns him to some early twenty-first-century memory:

> Interactor & Program
> > PRISM & Dr. Perelman (Rockvil 2031)
> > > Perry Simm (Rockvil 2041)
> > > > Perry & Rav & Frita (Childhood, within the Joybooth)

However, there is an important difference between this lowest level and the
one above. The lowest level is narrated, but not simulated. This childhood
memory is told in a single "dump" of text; the interactor's next chance to
command Perry is back in the Rockvil of 2041. Perry cannot be commanded
to talk to Rav, to go on particular rides at the amusement park, or to do
anything else in that childhood world. Rav and Frita are not even characters
in the sense in which Perry and Dr. Perelman are, in interactive fiction or
ontological terms, because they are not existents in the simulation.

Likewise, characters who appear only in video cut scenes or in the introductory sequence differ from those who exist as part of the simulated world,
participating in this simulation with the interactor's player character. Since
the combination of simulation and narration can be compelling, a rather
"flat" or sketchy character who is both simulated and narrated may be more
meaningful than one that has no in-game existence, but only appears in cut-
scenes, even if the non-simulated character is very well developed in narrative
terms. In early interactive fiction, the thief from *Zork* and the robot helper
Floyd from *Planetfall* (another of Meretzky's games) are flat but compelling
characters who play important roles in the simulation.

A character who exists in *A Mind Forever Voyaging* in several of the
simulated future worlds is Perry's wife, Jill, a painter who appears in this
transcript, from a 2051 simulation:

Living Room
    This is the large living area of your apartment, with a bedroom to the north
    and a kitchen to the east. The front door of the apartment, next to the couch
    on the south wall, is open. A huge window provides a panoramic view to the
    west.
    Jill's current artistic endeavor, an acrylide painting, is on her easel, near the
    entrance to the kitchen. In one corner is the old word processor where you do
    your writing.
    Jill is standing at the easel, working on her current painting.

A thin partition separates Mitchell's sleeping area from the rest of the living room.

>*look out the window*
The panoramic view overlooks the suburbs of Westwood and Brentwood, as well as extensive woodlands. The forests, as a result of increasingly acidic rain, are thinner and browner each year.

You hear a commotion in the hallway and then a half-dozen Border Security Force officers storm in, rifles ready. You freeze as they tramp about the apartment wielding Rad-Detectors. After a few nightmare minutes, they seem satisfied and begin to file out. The apparent leader turns to you. "Sorry for the inconvenience," he says apologetically. "You know how things are. We're only doing it for your own protection." He closes the door behind him. You hear sobbing and turn to see Jill crying in the corner of the living room.

>*comfort jill*
As you hug her and stroke her back, Jill calms down noticeably.

While Jill is not a very round character in *A Mind Forever Voyaging*, her existence as someone who is both simulated (she can be comforted, spoken to, etc.) and narrated (she is represented as painting, as reacting to the raid, etc.) helps to intensify the emotional tenor of the BSF search, showing it as an event with human consequences.

The urban planning simulation *SimCity*, published in 1989, led to a popular series of games and offered new ways for players to think about systems and relate to their urban environments. But even a bit of interaction with *A Mind Forever Voyaging* should show that this piece's dual nature as simulation and potential narrative allow it to offer a very different, powerful perspective on the future of cities. This interactive fiction achieves its effect by simulating a city that is the player character's home, that the interactor must explore and understand, and that can be seen to change and worsen over time. The main puzzle that the interactor must figure out to set things right back in the "reality" of 2031 is an intriguing one as well, and relies on a nuanced understanding of the game's levels of simulation. While *A Mind Forever Voyaging* throws light on the way in which levels of simulation and narration can work, it also shows that even mainstream commercial computer games have the potential to suggest compelling dystopias.

Digital forms, genres, and threads of practice

Interactive fiction, as engaging and influential as it is, occupies a small niche in today's universe of digital practice. This chapter closes with a look at a range of expressions of computer creativity and with some consideration of how narrative approaches can be used to understand them.

Video games: current commercial video games are characterized by 3D computer graphics, by the use of full-motion video cut-scenes and pre-recorded soundtracks, and by the market dominance of a small number of blockbusters. Some of these games – for instance, the popular ones that simulate sporting events – rely on the engaging simulation of a non-digital game and on licensing deals that connect the game to "real" sports franchises. It is unclear how the narrative analysis of such video games will be useful. Abstract games such as *Tetris* also form an important part of the history of computer gaming, but they have no meaningful narrative dimension, and it is not clear that any narrative ways of thinking are involved in playing them. Even in these cases, there are levels of simulation ("in-game" and "out-of-game" reports), but perhaps not an interesting interplay of simulation and narration.

There are many modern-day video games, however, including the infamous *Grand Theft Auto* series by Rockstar Games, that actually do simulate a world and present a space of possible narratives, much as a piece of interactive fiction does. Although other sorts of game experiences (a driving simulation, for instance) are part of the *Grand Theft Auto* games, the distinctions here between what is simulated and what is narrated, but not simulated, apply directly. Status information such as the current "warrant level" is related out-of-game, for instance, not as part of the representation of the rich simulated environment. Characters in cut-scenes cannot be interacted with, although some of those in cut-scenes correspond to characters who are also simulated in the interactive world. Turn-based graphical adventure games (including *Myst, Maniac Mansion,* and games in the *King's Quest* series) are even more similar to text-based interactive fiction, although they provide graphical output and usually don't accept typed text.

MUDs, MOOs, and other virtual environments: many shared virtual environments are accessible online; these range from all-text MUD and MOO (MUD Object Oriented) systems to graphically rich MMORPGs (Massively Multiplayer Online Role-Playing Games) such as *Everquest, Ultima Online,* and *World of Warcraft.* In a sense, these are multi-player interactive fictions, but the presence of other players can fundamentally change the way that players approach the system, causing social interactions to take precedence over interactions with simulated world. Players can tell and act out stories on their own in these worlds, and "event teams" (employees of the company that runs the MMORPG) can also cause things to happen in the guise of characters.

Blogs, newsgroups, chatspaces, and messaging systems: the Internet has afforded many new modes of communication. In this category are social systems that lack the simulated virtual environments discussed previously, but which still offer interesting new twists on communication. The weblog or blog, for instance, can be formally characterized as a reverse-chronologically-ordered set of postings on the Web, but it is typically a forum for one or more people to post texts and images dealing personal matters, or to link to other pages on the Web for purposes of critique or discussion. The blog is a nonfiction form, but just as Daniel Defoe took the nonfiction form of the travelogue and the nonfiction form of the journal and used these as the basis for two early English novels, *Robinson Crusoe* and *A Journal of the Plague Year*, some bloggers, such as Rob Wittig, are fictionalizing the form of the blog for novelistic purposes. Such projects, along with the SMS stories mentioned earlier, show that recent digital communication systems will support not only personal and conversational stories but also more self-consciously literary sorts of narratives.

Other digital art and electronic literature: computer creativity seems to be almost as old as computing itself. Some early systems involving narrative included poetry generators, story generators (James Meehan's 1976 TALE-SPIN being the most famous example), and conversational characters or "chatterbots" (such as ELIZA, developed by Joseph Weizenbaum in the 1960s). The development of story-generating systems, which are run with a certain set of parameters and generate a story based upon them – without user input along the way – shows that non-interactive systems can do interesting things as programs. Creative text-generating systems and chatterbots continue to be developed today.

Networked texts provide another form for computer creativity. Hypertext and hypermedia literature of note includes Michael Joyce's *afternoon: a story*; Stuart Moulthrop's *Victory Garden*; and Shelley Jackson's *Patchwork Girl*; along with more recent Web fictions such as the collaborative novel *The Unknown*. Many of these can be read in many different ways and are hard to fathom as a whole; they contain self-referential and sometimes even contradictory texts. This led Murray to describe early works of this sort as "privileging confusion,"[14] and Ryan to suggest that the reader's activity in encountering a hypertext is not a radically new process of connecting narrative fragments but is more like that used by someone assembling a jigsaw puzzle.[15] These works showed, however, that hypertexts did not have to conform to any "Choose-Your-Own-Adventure" template, and they also raised questions interesting to narrative theorists. Since the coming of the Web, digital narratives have been deployed in fragments not just in hypertext poems and novels but also in location-aware systems (which use the Global Positioning System [GPS] or some other means to make the user's physical location a factor), augmented reality games (which lace the network and parts of the "real world" with clues and narrative fragments), and various other pieces involving computation and animation.

Narratives of digital experience: considering simulation and narration together, as in the exploration of *A Mind Forever Voyaging,* seems a very fruitful way to approach digital work from a narrative standpoint. Still, it is only one way. There are clearly other ways in which people use narrative to organize and express all sorts of computer-mediated experiences. Players of *The Sims,* to mention just one example, post screen captures and tell stories online about what their characters did in the game. There are many ways that narrative fragments and suggestions exist in virtual spaces, in games, and in other digital contexts that are not themselves narratives or simulations.

The workings of computers and narratives

A close look at *A Mind Forever Voyaging* reveals a complex play of levels, a play that may seem surprising in a stand-alone, vintage computer game that lacks graphics and sound. But *A Mind Forever Voyaging* shares an important quality with digital work before it, such as TALE-SPIN, and more recent digital work, such as *Half-Life* 2. It is an interactive computer program, capable of both simulation and narration. By considering exactly how this program and other digital works function, it is possible better to understand how the symbol-manipulating machines that have been around for half a century can engage with people, stories, potential stories, and people's narrative capabilities, and how they can become machines for making meaning.

NOTES

1. See Marie-Laure Ryan, *Narrative as Virtual Reality: Immersion and Interactivity in Literature and Electronic Media* (Baltimore: Johns Hopkins University Press, 2001), pp. 90–3.
2. Marie-Laure Ryan, "Beyond Myth and Metaphor: The Case of Narrative in Digital Media." *Game Studies* 1:1 (July 2001), <www.gamestudies.org/0101/ryan/>.
3. On the dangers of exclusively "narrativist" approaches to video games see, for instance, Jesper Juul, "Games Telling Stories?" *Game Studies* 1:1 (July 2001), www.gamestudies.org/0101/juul-gts/, and Espen J. Aarseth, "Computer Game Studies, Year One." *Game Studies* 1:1 (July 2001), <www.gamestudies.org/0101/editorial.html>.
4. Roy Ascott, *Telematic Embrace: Visionary Theories of Art, Technology, and Consciousness.* Edited by Edward A. Shanken (Berkeley: University of California Press, 2003).
5. Espen J. Aarseth, *Cybertext: Perspectives on Ergodic Literature* (Baltimore: Johns Hopkins University Press, 1997), pp. 62–4.
6. Janet Murray, *Hamlet on the Holodeck: The Future of Narrative in Cyberspace* (New York: Free Press, 1997), pp. 71–90.

7. Lev Manovich, *The Language of New Media* (Cambridge: The MIT Press, 2001), pp. 27–8.

8. Marie-Laure Ryan, "Will New Media Produce New Narratives?" In Marie-Laure Ryan (ed.) *Narrative Across Media: The Language of Storytelling* (Lincoln: University of Nebraska Press, 2004), p. 338.

9. Nick Montfort, *Twisty Little Passages: An Approach to Interactive Fiction* (Cambridge: MIT Press, 2003), pp. 65–221.

10. IF Archive <http://ifarchive.org>

11. Baf's Guide to the Interactive Fiction Archive <www.wurb.com/if/>

12. Nick Montfort, "Toward a Theory of Interactive Fiction" (2003), <http://nickm.com/if/toward.html>

13. Gérard Genette, *Narrative Discourse: An Essay in Method*. Translated by Jane E. Lewin (Ithaca: Cornell University Press, 1980), pp. 227–34. Genette calls the hypodiegetic level "metadiegetic," a term avoided here because this use of "meta-" conflicts with the way it is used in philosophy, computer science, and even interactive fiction development.

14. Murray, *Hamlet on the Holodeck*, p. 133.

15. Ryan, "Beyond Myth and Metaphor."

IV

Further contexts for narrative study

13

RUTH PAGE

Gender

Over the last twenty years, the role that gender might play in the analysis of narratives has emerged as an important area of consideration. *Feminist narratology* is the umbrella term which covers the many different ways in which gender-related aspects of narratives and the models used to analyze them may be interrogated from a feminist point of view. The integration of insights derived from gender studies incorporates a range of distinctive approaches including feminist perspectives along with neighboring areas of inquiry, such as queer theory.

Warhol characterizes feminist narratology in useful, broad terms as "the study of narrative structures and strategies in the context of cultural constructions of gender."[1] These cultural constructions of gender are significant because narrative analysis does not take place in a context-free vacuum. Rather, the models of narrative theory have been derived from the study of actual texts. Feminists would argue that the telling as well as the analysis of narratives are human activities – activities that necessarily entail gendered assumptions and practices.

Critics working within feminist narratology have asked questions about gender and narrative that cover a range of topics and embrace a variety of perspectives. These critics take both narrative texts and narrative theory as their object of study and reflect different stages and debates in feminist theorizing. In its diversity, feminist narratology does not represent a unified "school" or "discipline," but there are common themes that run throughout. To begin, I provide a brief outline of the key developments and issues in this sub-field of narrative theory. I then turn to Angela Carter's *The Passion of New Eve*, using that text to illustrate how the principles and practices of feminist narratology may be put to work.[2] My discussion raises questions about the limits as well as the possibilities of feminist narratology. I therefore conclude by offering some cautionary notes that should be taken into account when embarking upon the study of narrative and gender.

A brief history of feminist narratology

The term feminist narratology first came into use in the mid 1980s. The work of Susan Lanser has been credited as the main impetus for inaugurating the project, which took rise in 1986 with the publication of Lanser's "Toward a Feminist Narratology."[3] Lanser argued for the mutually beneficial integration of narratology and feminist criticism. She pointed to the androcentric bias in the corpora upon which the classical models of narrative theory had been founded, and suggested that despite their claims to gender neutrality narratological models were in fact gender-specific, focusing primarily on texts by and about men. In order to remedy this, she proposed that existing narratology be re-examined and, if necessary, revised in order to deal more adequately with narratives told or read by women, as well as stories representing female characters. In turn, narratology offered feminist criticism a useful toolkit of replicable parameters which could elucidate the forms and functions of women's narratives, for example, in pinning down the ways in which they might (or might not) differ from men's. Since then, a sizeable body of research has flourished that followed the dual directions laid out by Lanser. On the one hand, a whole spectrum of concepts from narratological theory have been scrutinized for their potential alignment with male-centered or "masculinist" values, including plot structure, the status of the narrator, characterization, reader response, and more. On the other hand, a great many literary narratives, especially those by British or American women, have proved fertile ground for the kind of close reading that feminist narratology promotes. A useful collection which brings together many such studies is *Ambiguous Discourse*, edited by Kathy Mezei.[4]

Some twenty years on, feminist narratology is recognized as a significant sub-domain within narrative theory. However, the field is highly complex where critics have varying emphases and use terms in differing ways. In part, this is a result of the language used to discuss "gender," which can encompass a variety of meanings that are interrelated but separable. Because of the confusion that can arise between them, I will clarify four terms – namely, *gender*, *sex*, *sexuality*, and *feminist* – that commonly appear in feminist narratology.

Early feminist narratology was eager to recoup the value of women's texts. The distinction between women and men implies a distinction based on *sex*, which is taken as the biological categorization of an individual. Usually, this invokes the associated terms "male" and "female," but as postmodern feminist theorists have gone on to point out, further possibilities exist, too, as in the case of intersexed or transgendered individuals. In contrast, the term *gender* is often used to refer to the socially constructed norms, practices, and codes which facilitate the identification of an individual or his or her behavior as "masculine," "feminine," "butch," "sissy," androgynous, and so on. Within literary criticism, and certainly some parts of feminist narratology, *gender* has also been used interchangeably with *sexuality*. However, the two have separate meanings, where *sexuality* is understood as referring to specifically erotic relationships of desire and to the sexual "orientations" by which people express their desires. Again, though, the terminology needs to be refined to accommodate distinctions between lesbian, gay, straight, and bisexual possibilities. Finally, the modifier *feminist* is used as a political label to reflect an ideological position. While by no means unified in actual usage, *feminism* is a theoretical position and a practice that seeks not just to expose gendered inequalities but also to change them.

The meanings of each term have also undergone radical change in recent years and this too has implications for feminist narratology. Feminist narratology began as a result of what has come to be known as second-wave feminism, which began in the West in the 1960s. Second-wave feminism focused on the oppression of women as a group, demanding equal treatment for women and men. The academic application of this within narratology tended to emphasize binary categories and assume patterns of difference between "men" and "women" and the stories they might tell. During the 1990s and onwards those working in postmodern gender theory began to reconceptualize the way terms like sex and gender could be used. The work of Judith Butler moved feminists to consider gender in more plural terms as a fluid performance rather than a fixed given. The impact of this on feminist narratology is that scholars now try to ask a more diverse range of questions that take into account the shifting and localized ways in which gender might be of importance to particular narratives, and might intersect with other influential factors like race, class, sexuality, or cultural context. In line with this diversification, feminist narratology has also become increasingly integrative, incorporating queer theory, linguistics, and postcolonial perspectives.[5] Recent work has gone on to show the relevance of feminist narratology for folklore, popular culture, and visual arts.[6]

Despite its diversification, however, feminist narratology has retained the two main functions outlined in Lanser's inaugural paper. First, it serves as a means of clarifying the interpretation of narrative texts, especially where that interpretation is concerned with gender-related matters. Second, it has provided the means for reflecting on, and in some cases reformulating, narrative theory itself. I will explain and illustrate these functions in further detail with reference to Angela Carter's novel *The Passion of New Eve*.

The Passion of New Eve

Angela Carter's fiction has been recognized as feminist in so far as it challenges gender norms and rewrites patriarchal myths, being innovative in its content as well as its manipulation of narrative forms. As such, her work provides an appropriate starting-point for considering the ways in which feminist and narratological perspectives can be combined productively.

The central theme of *The Passion of New Eve* (henceforth, *New Eve*) foregrounds the status of gender, exploring this in biological, social, and theoretical terms. *New Eve* is the story of an English man, Evelyn, who travels to New York. On arrival, Evelyn becomes involved with a prostitute, Leilah. After impregnating her, he abandons her and escapes into the desert. He is then captured and taken to Beulah, an enclosed community of women who serve the multi-breasted fertility goddess, Mother. Mother performs surgery on Evelyn, transforming him biologically into a woman, Eve, whom she plans to impregnate with Evelyn's sperm and so begin a new social order. Eve escapes from Beulah but is captured once again, this time to be taken to the masochistic world of one-eyed Zero, where she is forced into submission as one of Zero's wives. Zero has a vendetta against Tristessa, a film star who had been the object of Evelyn's erotic desire. In order to destroy Tristessa, Zero and his wives attack her. Here it emerges that Tristessa is in fact a man, and s/he and Eve are married and escape from Zero back into the desert. But Eve and Tristessa are attacked by another band of revolutionaries and Tristessa is killed. Eve is ultimately found by Leilah, now identified as Lilleth, who takes her to a cave where Eve seeks reunion with Mother, but ultimately sets sail upon the ocean.

Carter's novel has already attracted interest within feminist narratology.[7] In the following discussion, I build on this previous work, highlighting the narratological features which help interpret the disturbing ways in which Carter destabilizes the concept of gender in this novel.

Feminist narratology in application

In this section, I seek to show how ideas from feminist narratology can be used to generate productive interpretations of texts like Carter's. The interpretation sketched below includes elements "outside" the text, such as the reader's response to the narrative. Similarly, Monika Fludernik examines the strategies readers use to interpret ambiguous representations of gender in works by contemporary women writers.[8] Her work is a good example of feminist narratology's increasing interest in narratives where the correlations between gender, sex, and sexuality are exposed as fluid, multiple, and socially constructed. As the earlier plot summary suggests, the content of *New Eve* similarly destabilizes gender identity, particularly through the two main characters that change sex. Analyzing character thus stands at the heart of *New Eve*'s thematic concerns.

In itself, exploring character is a wide-ranging area in narrative theory that can employ a plethora of models and perspectives. I will look first at a "bottom up" approach which traces how a character's traits are established. Toolan points out that fictional characters are created from words in the narrative, from which the reader as a "creative accomplice" can build a mental picture of what that character is like.[9] These mental pictures are influenced by the reader's "real-world" knowledge of sex, gender, and sexuality, which in their various manifestations perform crucial roles in establishing identity. The textual evidence that the reader might use to demarcate sex includes words indicating biological status (*male, female, man, woman*) as well as, in English, third-person pronominal expressions such as *he* and *she*. Both sex and gender can be implied, too, by ways in which characters orient themselves to social codes (such as dress), or even terms of description which carry gender-specific connotations (*handsome* versus *beautiful*). The role of sexuality is intertwined with this. In her paper, Fludernik indicates the power of heterosexuality as a default interpretation, such that if the object of erotic desire is marked as female, then the desiring subject is automatically assumed to be male. In *New Eve*, these means of identification are used as textual clues which confound the reader's attempt to establish a consistent gender identity for the two main characters, Eve(lyn) and Tristessa. The confusion created as the reader encounters apparently conflicting information exposes the bases from which definitions of gender and sex are derived and points to the collapse of a fixed, binary system of difference. The opening sentence of *New Eve* contains the first signal of Evelyn's sex.

> I took some girl to the movies and, through her mediation, I paid you a little tribute of spermatozoa. (5)

Evelyn's ability to produce "spermatozoa," followed by numerous references to his "cock" and "erection" seem fairly unequivocal indications of his male status. His gender is constructed as masculine through references to male-dominated sports like rugby, football, and cricket. Evelyn's erotic desire for women marks him as heterosexual; his love interests include the film star Tristessa (when assumed to be female) and Leilah. Tristessa also appears to be unproblematically female and feminine in the first part of the novel. She is described as "The most beautiful woman in the world" (5), who stars in female film roles, functioning as an example of "the mode of femininity" (71). However, even before Carter spells out in detail the surgery that physically transforms Evelyn to Eve, there are hints that biological sex is an unstable category. Only a few pages into the first chapter, Evelyn refers to "the black lady ... [who] fitted me with a uterus of my own" (9), throwing into question Evelyn's status as biologically male. These disruptions to the norms of sexed identity lead to narrative surprise, especially in the case of Tristessa's secret identity. While the reader has been prepared for Evelyn's physical transformation, which is described in detail, there are only sparse, indirect hints that Tristessa is not a woman. Indeed, the revelation of Tristessa's "true" sex as biologically male is narrated as a shock to the other characters. Eve mirrors the first-time reader's reaction: "I could not think of him as a man; my confusion was perfect" (128).

The force of this narrative surprise exposes and disrupts real-world notions of gender. Indeed, disrupting the biological sex of these two characters enables Carter to separate biological, social, and psychological elements of gender. Gender becomes plural, fluid, a changeable process rather than a stable attribute. Thus even when Eve is coded as biologically female through body parts (vagina, breasts, and clitoris), named as "woman," and referred to with feminine pronominal expressions, the narrator makes it clear that the psychological transformation into womanhood is separate from this. In Zero's harem, the narrator relates the transition thus: "I had become almost the thing I was. The mediation of Zero turned me into a woman. More. His peremptory prick turned me into a savage woman" (108). Social markings such as dress are proved to be unreliable indicators that result in gender confusion. Eve is dressed as a dandy in "*his* evening clothes" for "*her*" marriage to (male) Tristessa in a form of "double drag" (131–2, emphasis added). The narrator goes on to say, "I had become my old self again in the inverted world of mirrors. But this masquerade was more than skin deep ... I was a boy disguised as a girl and now disguised as a boy again" (132). In *New Eve*, the textual information that a reader might use to ascribe male or female identities to characters uncouples sex from gender and in so doing begins to deconstruct the binary categorization of people into men versus women.

The traits that indicate what a fictional character is like are not the only aspect of characterization relevant for feminist narratology. Relationships between fictional characters are important too. One approach that explores this is the model proposed by Greimas.[10] He argued that a character's status was determined by his or her function within the plot, proposing just six roles (which he termed *actants*) that form three pairs:

Giver	+	Receiver
Subject	+	Object
Helper	+	Opponent

The relationship between the six roles is usually represented in diagram form:

Sender   –   object   →   receiver
(Superhelper)
                                  ↑
Helper   →   subject   ←   opponent

This model fits many traditional fairy tales. The Disney version of one such fairytale, *Aladdin*, provides a simple example. Aladdin, a young man (Subject), seeks marriage to the beautiful Princess Jasmine (Object). In his attempt to achieve this he is helped by his friend Abu, the monkey (Helper), opposed by the Sultan's wicked adviser (Opponent), but rescued by the Genie with his magical powers (Superhelper). Here is the diagram again, annotated with the characters filling the roles. The role of Receiver is left empty, because at these initial stages in the narrative, Aladdin has not actually achieved his objective of marrying Jasmine.

Genie   –   Jasmine
                       ↑
Abu   →   Aladdin   ←   Sultan's evil advisor

Greimas's model is not in itself gendered, but certainly within the corpus of folk and fairytales from which it is derived, there is often (although not exclusively) some correlation between actant role and the gender of a character. Typically, the area of interest for feminists focuses on the central pair Subject/Object and reinforces gender stereotypes of an active, desiring male hero (the Subject) and a passive heroine who is the object of his desire. Within *New Eve*, multiple configurations of this pattern are possible. Given the importance of erotic desire in the content of *New Eve*, establishing the relationship between Subject and Object is of particular interest. Eve(lyn) as Subject is related to various objects of desire. Some of these are abstract, like freedom from captivity. Others are concrete, such as other characters in the story. Where this desire is expressed in erotic terms, Greimas's paradigm becomes the means of interpreting sexuality in this novel. In the first chapter, Evelyn remembers and re-enacts erotic desire for the screen icon, Tristessa (who, we are led to believe, is female). Evelyn's later pursuit of Leilah is described in terms of unambiguous heterosexual desire. Both pairs set up an initial relationship between male Subject (Evelyn) and female Object (Tristessa, Leilah).

As the story progresses, and Evelyn becomes Eve and Tristessa is revealed as biologically male, this relationship becomes more complex. Superficially, heterosexuality is maintained, but the gendering of the actants is reversed so that the female character now in the Subject role is able to express sexual desire. But, as we have seen, the biological identification of Eve as female can still entail the memories and sexual responses of (male) Evelyn. The female Eve surveys herself saying, "I had become my own masturbatory fantasy. And – how can I put it – the cock in my head, still, twitched at the sight of myself" (75). This duality confuses the gendered status of the Subject and Object roles when occupied by Eve and Tristessa and the subsequent interpretation of the sexual desire between them as heteronormative or homoerotic.

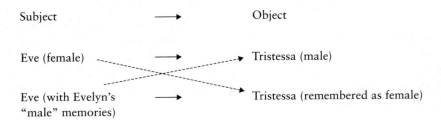

The diagram shows that the ambiguous gendering of Eve and Tristessa opens up at least two ways of interpreting the relationships of sexual desire between the two characters. One possibility is that readers may interpret the relationship between female Eve and male Tristessa as following a heterosexual paradigm, echoed in reverse by the retrospective pairing of male Evelyn's desire for Tristessa (perceived to be female). Alternatively, the representation of both characters as simultaneously male and female means that readers may infer homoerotic desire between the Subject and Object. The dotted lines in the diagram indicate the potential desire between female Eve and female Tristessa or male Evelyn and male Tristessa.

The narrative does not resolve whether or not Eve's relationship with Tristessa is homoerotic. Instead, heterosexual and homoerotic interpretations coexist. Significantly, this analysis of Subject and Object points once again to the separable but intertwined categories of sex and sexuality. On the one hand, the desire between Eve(lyn) and other characters is expressed in explicitly sexual terms, but this sexuality is not tied to sex or gender unequivocally and can be realigned in plural combinations. On the other hand, desire does not have to be erotic at all, as Wallace points out.[11] For example, desire for riches or possessions is not sexual in nature. So whereas feminist narratology is interested in the ways that the concept of actants might throw light on representations of sexuality in texts like *New Eve*, it is important to remember that this does not imply that all characters in the Subject role are gender-specific or all desire sexual.

Feminist revisions to narrative theory

We have seen how the analysis of character traits and character roles can be useful in helping to interpret the complex and sometimes skewed relationships between gender, sex, and sexuality in *New Eve*. However, early critiques of feminist narratology argued that feminist (re)interpretations of particular texts did not really contribute to a revision of narrative *theory*, as such.[12] Yet later work, such as Lanser's recent research on narrative voice,[13] suggests that these early critiques were misplaced.

Lanser builds on Genette's distinction between narrators who are part of the story they are telling and those who are not, establishing sex as a significant feature that correlates in different ways with the narrator, or the source assumed to be responsible for "who speaks."[14] Narrators who are also characters in the storyworld are termed *homodiegetic*. An example of this is Lockwood in *Wuthering Heights*. Homodiegetic narrators can also tell their own stories, such as Jane's first-person narration in *Jane Eyre*. These are labeled *autodiegetic* narrators. Finally, the narrator may not be a participant in the story at all, but appear to stand apart from this, as in the case of the narrative voice in Jane Austen's *Pride and Prejudice*. These narrators are *heterodiegetic*. Lanser points out that narrators can be represented in more or less detail within the story, which can be exploited to reveal degrees of information about the narrator, including their sex. Heterodiegetic narrators are typically the least represented of the three, leading Lanser to argue that, normatively, these kinds of narrators are not marked for their sex. In contrast, because of their participation as characters within the story they are narrating, homodiegetic and autodiegetic narrators *are* usually marked for their sex, by virtue of the same kinds of textual clues that establish a character's traits as male or female, for example. Lanser's observation is significant in two respects. First, these normative patterns can be exploited or disrupted in experimental narratives where the gender of the narrator is obscured, ambiguous, or shifting. Second, readers may bring gendered assumptions with them that influence their interpretation of narrators, even when the heterodiegetic narrator is unmarked for sex (for example, employing a default interpretation of the narrator as male).

New Eve has an autodiegetic narrator, where the speaker referred to by the pronoun "I" also corresponds to the protagonist, Eve(lyn). Thus when the reader begins the novel for the first time, he or she may initially transpose the cues which characterize Evelyn as male onto the narrating voice, too. But it is also clear that the narrating voice is recounting events retrospectively. Once the reader is alert to Evelyn's future change in sex (from the reference to having a "uterus" onwards), there is a fissure between the autodiegetic narrator (whom we then interpret to be female) and the character Evelyn, who is still signaled as male. As a result, the narrative voice in the first half of the novel contains a dual aspect where the "I" simultaneously represents both the male character Evelyn and voice of the older female Eve.

The gender ambiguity created by the unfolding revelations of Eve(lyn)'s sex has implications for the narrative analysis of narrators. Most importantly, it points to the significance of grounding our understanding of voice in the study of actual texts, for the capacity to construct this dual or ambiguous narrative voice is medium- and language-specific. The gender ambiguity of interpreting the speaking "I" of *New Eve* is possible because first-person pronominal expressions in English do not inflect for gender, and so can refer to either or both male and female characters simultaneously. Languages which inflect more extensively for gender (for example, Romance languages) would have to indicate Evelyn's female sex from the outset of the narrative, rather than progressively revealing this transition. Likewise, audio or film versions of the text would have to code the speaking voice of the narrator as female, again denying the narrative suspense entailed by the progressive journey towards Evelyn's sex change.

In general, feminist revisions of narrative theory have led some theorists to argue for an alternative system of female or feminist models. Debates about plot structure formed an early focus for exploring the apparent differences between narratives by, or about, women versus men; in this research, the patterns associated with different plots have been given gendered labels. An influential example is the "male plot of ambition" described by Peter Brooks.[15] This plot is characterized by a quest-like progression that moves in a chronological sequence from a perceived beginning to a conclusion where obstacles have been overcome and goals achieved. It is labeled "male" on the basis of the sex of the fictional hero, although this often correlates with the biological status of the author. In addition, the pattern often reinforces masculine behavior (for example, undertaking quests would be socially proscribed for women in certain contexts), and in psychoanalytic terms mirrors a male, heterosexual pattern of erotic desire, typified as a move towards climax and release of narrative tension.

The issue of closure is particularly important in distinguishing between plot-types. Brooks describes the male plot's drive towards closure in terms of the death instinct. Other literary critics have noted the ideological significance of closure, as demonstrated, for example, in the marriage that completes social plots like the romance. Rosalind Coward points out that both marriage and the silencing of death are ambivalent from a feminist point of view, at least as expressed in many nineteenth-century novels.[16] Margaret

Homans goes on to conclude that many critics working in early feminist narratology (such as Susan Winnett, Rachel Blau DuPlessis, and others), took this association one step further and transferred social and psychological values onto structure (rather than content alone).[17] The outcome of this is that narrative form itself becomes the site of feminist struggle. The "male" plot is not only masculine in terms of its content but also patriarchal in its ideology. The alternative patterns which "break the sequence," to borrow Virginia Woolf's much-cited phrase, contrast with this as a means of emancipation for women writers.

The characteristics of feminist fiction that uses "alternative patterns" include fragmentation of narrative sequences, along with a sense of open-endedness, or lack of defined narrative outcome. Typical examples include the work of Virginia Woolf and Angela Carter.[18] In feminist narratology, the repetition of narrative climaxes or unconcluded sequences are often described in contradistinction to more linear plot-types. A notable example is Susan Winnett's essay where she makes use of breastfeeding and childbirth as analogies for the female plot, mapping narrative features onto specifically female experience.[19] This kind of feminist narratology has been heavily influenced by psychoanalytical theory, often operates at a metaphorical level, and derives the status of the form (male or female) from the content of the narratives in question. It has continued to resonate through narrative interpretations up to the present, but it is by no means uncontroversial. The relationship between structural characteristics such as linearity or closure and ideology (here, ideologies specifically related to gender) has been fiercely debated by Richardson and raises serious questions for this aspect of feminist narratology.[20]

These debates about the relationship between narrative form (specifically, linearity, and closure) and ideology are pertinent to *New Eve*. However, linearity is itself a diffuse concept that can consist of semantic elements (inferred meaning), along with linguistic features (such as syntax), and textual forms (sequences of pages). Feminist narratology has tended to focus on the representation of time as a form of linearity. Honor Wallace's critique of feminist narratology contains a useful discussion of this.[21] She summarizes the contrast between Kristeva's psychoanalytic notion of lyric timelessness and the "linear time" of narrative (p. 177). The distinction between time and stasis does not deal with textual features or a discussion of language itself (such as uses of tense or finiteness). Instead, it operates at a highly metaphorical level, equating the contrast between time and timelessness with narrative and non-narrative genres, respectively. Kristeva's work (upon which Wallace bases the contrast) explicitly describes lyric timelessness in psychoanalytic and biological language that is connected to "women's bodies" (177), imposing gendered values on the stasis of forms like the non-narrative lyric.

The imagery used to describe time in New Eve emphasizes the gendered contrast between masculine time and feminine stasis, at least at the surface level. For example, in Beulah, Eve(lyn) is indoctrinated with the following lecture,

> Proposition one: time is a man, space is a woman.
> Proposition two: time is a killer.
> Proposition three: kill time and live forever. (New Eve, 53)

From a narratological perspective, the ordering of events in New Eve deviates from the unidirectional nature of "masculine" time; the straightforward, chronological sequence is disrupted by flashforwards and flashbacks, challenging the singular temporality of Eve(lyn)'s history. The flashforwards and flashbacks also function to destabilize the reader's perception of Eve(lyn)'s sex, either alluding to Evelyn's future sex change or referring back to Eve's earlier (male) memories as Evelyn. These temporal displacements subsequently blur the interpretation of other narratological features such as narrative voice. However, the resulting gender confusion is an effect specific to New Eve, and it is worth noting again that it is not that linearity as it is expressed through narrative time as a formal feature is inherently gendered. Indeed, to claim that non-linearity and temporal displacements are in themselves feminist features is too strong, and overlooks the fact that a great deal of New Eve's narrative follows a relatively straightforward time sequence and that textually, the novel follows a linear sequence of pages which the reader experiences with a clear sense of beginning and ending.

More generally, the metaphorical equation of (non)-linearity with gender ideology is open to far-reaching critique. Homans discusses the abstract nature of the equation and argues that it cannot account for narratives by women outside of the Euro-American tradition.[22] Richardson demonstrates the importance of looking at empirical evidence, showing that feminist writers often cited as "breaking the sequence" in fact employ considerable quantities of linearity in their writing.[23] Similarly, I have argued elsewhere against positing an indissoluble connection between narrative form and ideological valence.[24] While texts like New Eve manipulate narrative forms to exploit feminist interpretations, it is too strong to claim that any one of these stylistic features, be it characterization, voice, or linearity, is typical of all narratives written by women or can be treated as the basis for an alternative narrative system.

Conclusion

My analysis of *New Eve* has indicated some of the ways in which gender can be an important factor to consider in the study of stories, both generating productive interpretations and clarifying the limits of narrative theory itself. But, in line with feminist narratology's emphasis on context, it is important not to impute universal, context-free meanings to textual features that in some narratives bear significantly on issues of gender. Those working in the wider field of feminist linguistics have cautioned against the assumption that any linguistic form (including those used in narrative) can be correlated with gender in a simplistic fashion. As Cameron puts it, it remains crucial not to impose stereotypical concepts of gender on the analysis of data, even though "where the object of observation and analysis has to do with gender it is extraordinarily difficult to subdue certain expectations."[25] Likewise, rather than assuming that women's narratives will be different than those told by men, feminist narratology now seeks to come to terms with shifting, variable relations between gender and narrative. Instead of assuming that gender will always be the bedrock explanation for any particular narrative feature or effect, feminist narratologists have increasingly come to recognize that gender is itself interconnected with a range of influential factors. This means that gender might not be the bottom-line explanation for the use of any particular narrative feature or effect, but can be interrelated with a range of other factors such as race, historical context, and so on. As both narrative analysis and feminist theory continue to diversify, understandings of the relationship between gender and narrative will no doubt continue to evolve in more fluid, plural directions, extending the impact of feminist narratology across disciplinary boundaries to incorporate narratives by, about, and for women in many different cultural and sub-cultural settings.

NOTES

1. Cited in Kathy Mezei (ed.) *Ambiguous Discourse: Feminist Narratology and British Women Writers* (Chapel Hill and London: University of North Carolina Press, 1996), pp. 6–7.
2. Angela Carter, *The Passion of New Eve* (London: Virago Press, 1982).
3. Susan Lanser, "Toward a Feminist Narratology." *Style* 20 (1986), pp. 341–63.
4. Mezei (ed.) *Ambiguous Discourse*.
5. On queer theory see Susan Lanser, "Sexing the Narrative: Propriety, Desire and the Engendering of Narratology." *Narrative* 3 (1995), pp. 85–94; on linguistics see Ruth Page, *Literary and Linguistic Approaches to Feminist Narratology* (Basingstoke: Palgrave, 2006); on postcolonialism see Margaret Homans, "Feminist Fictions and Feminist Theories of Narrative." *Narrative* 2 (1994), pp. 3–16.
6. For applications to folklore see Susan Lanser, "Burning Dinners: Feminist Subversions of Domesticity." In Joan Newlon Radner (ed.) *Feminist Messages: Coding*

in Women's Folk Culture (Urbana: University of Illinois Press,1993), pp. 36–53. Meanwhile, interventions in the study of popular culture and the visual arts are exemplified by Robyn Warhol and Mieke Bal, respectively, in *Having a Good Cry: Effeminate Feelings and Pop-Culture Forms* (Columbus: Ohio State University Press, 2003) and "Close Reading Today: From Narratology to Cultural Analysis." In Walter Grünzweig and Andreas Solbach (eds.) *Transcending Boundaries: Narratology in Context* (Tübingen: Gunter Narr Verlag Tubingen, 1999), pp. 19–40.

7. Alison Lee, "Angela Carter's New Eve(lyn): De/En-Gendering Narrative." In Kathy Mezei (ed.) *Ambiguous Discourse: Feminist Narratology and British Women Writers* (Chapel Hill and London: University of North Carolina Press, 1996), pp. 238–49.

8. Monika Fludernik, "The Genderization of Narrative." *GRAAT* 21 (1999), pp. 153–75.

9. Michael Toolan, *Narrative: A Critical Linguistic Introduction*, 2nd edition (London: Routledge, 2001), p. 80.

10. A. J. Greimas, *Structural Semantics: An Attempt at a Method*. Translated by Danielle McDowell, Ronald Schleifer, and Alan Velie (London and Lincoln: University of Nebraska Press, 1966), pp. 196–221.

11. Honor Wallace, "Desire and the Female Protagonist: A Critique of Feminist Narrative Theory." *Style* 34 (2000), pp. 176–87.

12. Nilli Diengott, "Narratology and Feminism." *Style* 22 (1988), pp. 42–51.

13. Lanser, "Sexing the Narrative," pp. 85–95.

14. Gérard Genette, *Narrative Discourse*. Translated by Jane E. Lewin. (Ithaca: Cornell University Press, 1980), pp. 33–85.

15. Peter Brooks, *Reading for the Plot* (Cambridge, MA: Harvard University Press, 1984), p. 39.

16. Rosalind Coward, "How I Became my Own Person." In Catherine Belsey and Jane Moore (eds.) *The Feminist Reader: Essays in Gender and the Politics of Literary Criticism* (London: Macmillan, 1989), pp. 35–47.

17. Homans, "Feminist Fictions," p. 6.

18. Several contributors to Kathy Mezei (ed.) *Ambiguous Discourse* discuss these authors.

19. Susan Winnett, "Coming Unstrung." *PMLA* 105 (1990), pp. 505–18.

20. Brian Richardson, "Linearity and its Discontents: Rethinking Narrative Form and Ideological Valence." *College English* 62 (2000), pp. 685–95.

21. Wallace, "Desire and the Female Protagonist," p. 177.

22. Homans, "Feminist Fictions," p. 8.

23. Richardson, "Linearity and its Discontents," p. 685.

24. Page, *Literary and Linguistic Approaches to Feminist Narratology*.

25. Deborah Cameron, "Performing Gender Identity: Young Men's Talk and the Construction of Heterosexual Masculinity." In Jennifer Coates (ed.) *Language and Gender: A Reader* (Oxford: Blackwell, 1998), p. 270.

14

JAMES PHELAN

Rhetoric/ethics

The rhetorical approach conceives of narrative as a purposive communicative act. In this view, narrative is not just a representation of events but is also itself an event – one in which someone is doing something with a representation of events. More formally, the rhetorical theorist defines narrative as somebody telling somebody else on some occasion and for some purpose(s) that something happened. This conception has several significant consequences for the kinds of knowledge about narrative the approach seeks. It gives special attention to the relations among tellers, audiences, and the something that has happened. The focus on purposes includes a recognition that narrative communication is a multi-layered event, one in which tellers seek to engage and influence their audiences' cognition, emotions, and values. Moreover, the approach recognizes that, in telling what happened, narrators give accounts of characters whose interactions with each other have an ethical dimension and that the acts of telling and receiving these accounts also have an ethical dimension. Consequently, the rhetorical approach attends to both an ethics of the told and an ethics of the telling.

In this chapter, I want to elaborate on these points and to demonstrate what rhetorical interpretation of narrative looks like. Therefore, I will first offer a brief, partial analysis of Edgar Allan Poe's "The Cask of Amontillado,"[1] and then turn to a short account of the approach's historical evolution. From there I will go on to elaborate its main underlying principles, a move that will also prepare the way for a return to Poe's story and a completion of the rhetorical analysis.

One Text, two audiences, multiple purposes

In "The Cask of Amontillado," Poe's narrator, Montresor, tells a friend why and how he took revenge upon his rival, Fortunato. Montresor seeks revenge because Fortunato has injured his pride by insulting him, and Montresor's method is to take advantage of Fortunato's own pride. Montresor lures

Fortunato, a wine connoisseur, into his cavernous wine cellar on the pretext of needing Fortunato's opinion of a new shipment of Amontillado. Once in the catacombs, Montresor chains Fortunato to a wall and buries him alive by building a tomb of bricks around him. Montresor ends his telling this way:

> I thrust a torch through the remaining aperture and let it fall within. There came forth in return only a jingling of the bells. My heart grew sick – on account of the dampness of the catacombs. I hastened to make an end of my labour. I forced the last stone into its position; I plastered it up. Against the new masonry I re-erected the old rampart of bones. For the half of a century no mortal has disturbed them. *In pace requiescat!* (366)

This passage highlights one of the especially salient features of narration in fiction: the same text is used for two distinct acts of telling with two distinct purposes, one act and purpose involving the narrator (Montresor) in relation to his audience (called, in a term coined by Gerald Prince, the narratee);[2] and the other act and purpose involving the author (Poe) and his audience. Since the author's telling contains the narrator's, Poe's rhetorical task here is simultaneously to create the illusion that Montresor's telling is wholly motivated by his character, his situation, and his relation to his narratee, and to use that telling to convey to his (that is, Poe's) audience his quite different purposes. Before we look at the relation between the two acts of telling in this passage, we need a little more context.

In the story's first paragraph, Montresor identifies his narratee as someone "who so well know[s] the nature of [his] soul" (360). Montresor also articulates the conditions for a successful revenge: "I must not only punish, but punish with impunity. A wrong is unredressed when retribution overtakes its redresser. It is equally unredressed when the avenger fails to make himself felt as such to him who has done the wrong" (360). Because Montresor recites these conditions so coolly and confidently, we infer that he is telling the story as a way of boasting to his friend about his successful revenge. Moreover, this inference gains further support as the story develops and Montresor recounts with apparent satisfaction how effectively he manipulated Fortunato.

In the final paragraph, however, a new note creeps into Montresor's telling when he reports "my heart grew sick" (366). Although Montresor quickly supplies the cause – the dampness of the catacombs – we are likely to doubt his explanation. He defines his heartsickness as a physical reaction to his immediate environment, but Poe, by placing the report at the moment when Montresor realizes that Fortunato has stopped struggling, invites us to understand the heartsickness as a metaphorical one. Fortunato's resignation brings

Montresor face-to-face with the enormity of what he is doing: murdering a man as a response to being insulted by him. No wonder his heart grows sick.

This conclusion leads us to look even more closely at the relation between Montresor's telling and Poe's telling, and, in order to do that, we need a brief overview of how rhetorical theory distinguishes between reliable and unreliable narration. As I have argued in *Living to Tell about It*,[3] narrators perform three main functions: they report about characters and events; they interpret those reports; and they ethically evaluate those reports and/or interpretations. Authors can signal either that they endorse or depart from these reports, interpretations, and evaluations; endorsement signals reliable narration and departure unreliable narration. Furthermore, narrators can be unreliable either through distortion or through not going far enough. Thus, they can be unreliable in six ways: they can underreport or misreport; they can underread or misread (underinterpret or misinterpret); and they can underregard or misregard (underevaluate or misevaluate).

The discrepancy between Montresor's explanation for, and our understanding of, his heartsickness shows that he is a reliable reporter (his heart did grow sick) but, at least in this utterance, an unreliable interpreter and evaluator. He misinterprets the reason for his heartsickness because he misevaluates his own character, regarding it as more cold and calculating than it actually is. Poe also implicitly invites us to consider whether Montresor knows that he is being a misinterpreter and misevaluator: does Montresor sincerely believe that his heart grew sick because of the dampness of the catacombs, or is he too proud to admit what he recognizes as the real reason? At this point, Poe's telling does not point us to a clear answer. However we answer that question, we can see that Poe uses Montresor's unreliable narration to indicate that he has not fully succeeded in carrying out the revenge according to his code: the heartsickness is evidence that he has failed to punish Fortunato with impunity. Again, at this point, Poe's telling does not allow us to decide whether Montresor is aware of the gap between the code and the execution of the code, or whether his denial of the reason for his heartsickness protects him from that awareness.

The relation between Montresor's telling and Poe's telling becomes more complex with the story's final two sentences. Montresor's comment that Fortunato's grave has not been disturbed for fifty years links up with the revelation of his heartsickness to shed new light on the purpose of his telling. Why tell the story fifty years after the event and why tell it to one "who so well know[s] the nature of [his] soul" (360)? Because the heartsickness Montresor felt at the climactic moment of his revenge has lingered for fifty years, motivating him now to seek some relief through confessing to one whom he regards in much the way that a regular penitent regards his priestly confessor. To be sure, Montresor remains too proud to confess outright (doing so would be a frank admission that he has failed to punish Fortunato with impunity), but we can now infer his purpose: to confess under the guise of boasting. I will defer a discussion of Poe's purpose until the final section of this chapter except to say that it is in part to move us by involving us in the gradual discovery of Montresor's purpose.

These conclusions can be further refined by a closer look at the final sentence. Montresor's "*In pace requiescat!*" (366), the prayer uttered at Christian funerals for the repose of the deceased's soul, represents a covert communication of a very different attitude toward Fortunato than Montresor has previously expressed. Overtly a formulaic recital consistent with his boasting, the prayer covertly expresses a sincere desire by a remorseful Montresor. This inference in turn allows us to recognize the difference between Montresor the narrator and Montresor the character. At the time of the action Montresor the character completely denies the implications of his heartsickness and so "hasten[s] to make an end to [his] labor" (366). But fifty years later Montresor the narrator ends his telling with this prayer. Poe's signalling this difference suggests that Montresor is now, at least at some level of his consciousness, aware of the cause of his heartsickness. Similarly, he also must be somewhat aware that he has not lived up to the code of revenge and that he is telling the tale more for the relief of confession than for the pleasure of boasting. Indeed, the prayer follows from that purpose: now that he has confessed, he can pray for the repose of Fortunato's soul.

Within Poe's telling, the prayer has further effects, including some that Montresor is not aware of. First, it underlines the enormity of Montresor's crime: Fortunato most likely has not had a proper funeral, has not previously had anyone pray for the repose of his soul. Second, the prayer calls attention to Montresor's own lack of peace for the last fifty years. Consequently, Poe invites his audience to infer that Montresor, who must now be not far away from the time of his own death, utters his *requiescat* with both Fortunato and himself in mind. Poe communicates, in other words, that with the prayer Montresor ends his telling by expressing a subconscious desire to have in death what his act of revenge has taken from him in life.

There is a lot more to say about "The Cask," especially about its ethical dimension, and I will say some of that more as this chapter proceeds, but for now I turn to an account of the evolution of the rhetorical approach to narrative.

From poetics to rhetoric

The rhetorical approach to stories and storytelling has its roots in Aristotle's *Poetics* with its definition of tragedy as the imitation of an action that arouses pity and fear and leads to the purgation of those emotions.[4] Although Aristotle's treatise is appropriately called *Poetics* because he is primarily concerned with identifying and analyzing the principles of construction underlying effective tragic drama, his definition makes rhetoric part of poetics by linking tragedy to its effect on its audience. Aristotle's most significant twentieth-century followers, the first-generation neo-Aristotelian critics at the University of Chicago, who published their manifesto in 1952,[5] also made rhetoric part of poetics in much the same way. R. S. Crane's influential essay "The Concept of Plot and the Plot of *Tom Jones*"[6] assumes that the key to the form of Fielding's novel is its emotive effect, specifically, the pleasure the audience experiences in seeing Tom move to the brink of fulfilling the prophecy that he was born to be hanged only to escape from the noose and be happily married to his beloved Sophia Western. Crane reasons back from this emotive effect to its causes in Fielding's specific choices about the sequence of the events and about his disclosures of who has the true knowledge of Tom's parentage. Crane's analysis of those choices, in turn, provides the basis for his definition of plot as a synthesis of character, action, and thought designed to affect the audience's emotions in a particular way.

Crane's student, Wayne C. Booth, in his groundbreaking 1961 book, *The Rhetoric of Fiction*,[7] inverted the relation between poetics and rhetoric within the neo-Aristotelian approach. In so doing, he paved the way for the rhetorical approach I am describing in this chapter. *The Rhetoric of Fiction* starts out as a defense of certain narrative techniques that had fallen out of favor in the mid twentieth century, particularly the use of overt authorial commentary such as that employed by Fielding, Dickens, Eliot, and other eighteenth- and nineteenth-century novelists. Booth does not assume that such commentary is always effective but instead argues that any judgment of effectiveness should depend on the relation between the commentary and the novel's overall purpose of affecting its audience in a particular way. If the commentary advances the purpose, it is effective; if it detracts from the purpose, it is ineffective.

In advancing this case, Booth argues that any technique will produce some effects on its audience rather than others and that, therefore, any technique is fundamentally rhetorical. Consequently, Booth's case about overt authorial commentary becomes just one part of his larger argument about the relation between rhetoric and fiction. The choice for the novelist is not *whether* to use rhetoric but rather about *which kind* to use – that associated with overt commentary or with the withholding of commentary, with the presentation of dramatic scenes or summaries of events, and so on.

This conception of narrative as fundamentally rhetorical influenced Booth's attention to the relations among authors, narrators, and audiences. The most important relation is that between the author, or to use the term Booth coined, "the implied author," and the implied audience. (By the implied author, Booth means the version of himself or herself the author constructs in writing the narrative.) The implied author's communication can be direct or indirect, depending on the kind of narrator employed; reliable narration goes hand-in-hand with direct communication, unreliable with indirect. As we have seen with "The Cask of Amontillado," a narrator may reliably perform one function (e.g., reporting) while unreliably performing another (e.g., interpreting).

Booth's attention to the rhetorical exchanges among authors, narrators, and readers led him at the end of *The Rhetoric of Fiction* to make an early foray into ethical criticism. He explores the ethical consequences of what he calls "impersonal narration," when employed in the representation of ethically reprehensible characters. By "impersonal narration" Booth means both narration by a character (first-person narration, or, more technically, homodiegetic narration) and center-of-consciousness narration. Booth notes that the very act of following a character's inner life typically generates at least some sympathy for that character, and he worries that such sympathy may override authorial signals about a character's ethical deficiencies. This portion of Booth's argument received the most resistance from his own audience in the 1960s, and, as he notes in his Afterword to the second edition (1983), he himself soon felt that it was inadequate – though he always maintained his conviction that ethics is an integral component of rhetoric. In 1988 Booth returned to this general thesis in *The Company We Keep*.[8] He argues that because the rhetorical construction of a narrative invites its audience to follow a certain trajectory of desire, narrative inevitably has designs on its audience's values, if only to influence us to desire some things rather than others. More generally, Booth develops his concern with the complex exchanges between author and audience into the metaphor of books as friends – friends who can be either beneficial or harmful. *The Company We Keep*, along with Martha Nussbaum's *Love's Knowledge*,[9] J. Hillis Miller's *The Ethics of Reading*,[10] and other works on ethical criticism in the late 1980s and early 1990s, effected an "ethical turn" in the study of narrative that itself has moved in a variety of directions, only some of them rhetorical. Lisbeth Korthals Altes gives a very helpful account of this turn.[11]

The evolution of rhetorical narrative theory from *The Rhetoric of Fiction* to the present day is a complex story involving much more than Booth's writing *The Company We Keep*. That story would need to account for (a) further work by neo-Aristotelians, including Booth's contemporaries, Sheldon Sacks[12] and Ralph W. Rader,[13] and the next generation, including David Richter,[14] Peter J. Rabinowitz,[15] and myself;[16] and (b) intersections between this work and many other developments in narrative theory, especially Gérard Genette's structuralist approach to narrative discourse,[17] Mikhail Bakhtin's ideas about the novel as the site for dialogue among different sociolects, each entailing its distinctive ideology,[18] and developments in various contextualist narratologies that seek to link questions of technique and structure to questions of politics and culture. But I can give a clearer picture of the rhetorical approach if I shift from the story of its evolution to a discussion of the key principles that underlie my own practice of the approach.

Six principles of a rhetorical theory of narrative

The first and most overarching principle has been the focus of the early part of this chapter: narrative is a rhetorical action in which somebody tries to accomplish some purpose(s) by telling somebody else that something happened.

The second principle involves the relationship among the three main components of the rhetorical communication, what rhetorical theory calls the points of the rhetorical triangle: speaker, text, and audience. The approach postulates a recursive relationship among authorial agency, textual phenomena (including intertextual relations), and reader response. Texts are designed by authors in order to affect readers in particular ways; those designs are conveyed through the words, techniques, structures, forms, and intertextual relations of texts; and reader responses are a function of and, thus, a guide to how authorial designs are created through textual phenomena.

Methodologically, the recursive relationship among author, text, and reader means that the rhetorical critic may begin the task of interpretation from any point on the rhetorical triangle, but that task will require considering how each point both influences and is influenced by the other two. With "The Cask of Amontillado," I started with a textual phenomenon – the new note in Montresor's narration in his final paragraph – and moved from there to its effect on readers and to Poe's agency. I could have started with other details, such as the audience's feeling ethically distant from Montresor, or Poe's strategies of characterizing the narratee with just one phrase and of placing that phrase in the story's second sentence. But either of those starting-points would have eventually led to the other two components of the communication.

The third principle concerns audience. Peter J. Rabinowitz has argued for the existence of four distinct audiences in fictional narrative,[19] and in re-examining Rabinowitz's model, I have suggested the need to distinguish one of those audiences from the narratee.[20] That modification leaves us with five audiences:

- the flesh and blood or actual reader: each of us with our glorious (or not so glorious) individuality and common human endowments.
- the authorial audience: the author's ideal reader. The rhetorical model assumes that the flesh and blood reader seeks to enter the authorial audience in order to understand the invitations for engagement that the narrative offers. It is for this reason that I refer to what "we" do as members of Poe's authorial audience. The rhetorical model also assumes that individual readers will then assess those invitations and accept or reject them in whole or in part. I will return to this point when discussing the ethical dimension of Poe's story.
- the narrative audience: the observer position within the narrative world that the flesh and blood reader assumes. In fiction, we are in this observer position when we respond to characters as if they were real people. Our ability to enter the narrative audience is one important reason why we respond affectively to fictional narratives such as "The Cask of Amontillado."
- the narratee: the audience addressed by the narrator. As flesh and blood readers of "The Cask," we do not, at the beginning of the story, know the nature of Montresor's soul, so we recognize that he is addressing someone distinct from us.
- the ideal narrative audience: the narrator's hypothetical perfect audience, the one he expects to understand every nuance of his communication. The ideal narrative audience may or may not coincide with the actual narratee, and it may or may not be an important part of a rhetorical interpretation. Montresor's ideal audience would recognize that he is confessing under the guise of boasting; the actual narratee may or may not have that recognition.

The fourth principle is about the nature of readerly interests and responses. As flesh and blood readers enter the authorial and narrative audiences, they develop interests and responses of three kinds, each related to a particular component of the narrative: mimetic, thematic, and synthetic. Responses to the mimetic component involve an audience's interest in the characters as possible people and in the narrative world as like our own, that is, either our actual world or one that is possible given what we know and assume about the actual world. Responses to the mimetic component include our evolving judgments of characters and our subsequent emotions, desires, hopes, expectations, satisfactions, and disappointments. Responses to the thematic component involve an interest in the characters as representative of classes of people, e.g., Montresor as emblematic of the corrupt aristocracy, and in the cultural, ideological, philosophical, or ethical issues being addressed by the narrative, e.g., the story's interest in pride, revenge, and guilt. Responses to the synthetic component involve an audience's interest in, and attention to, the characters and to the larger narrative as a made object.

The rhetorical approach recognizes that different narratives establish different relationships among these interests, and these different relationships in turn can help us recognize different narrative purposes. Some narratives are dominated by mimetic interests, some by thematic, and others by synthetic, but as a narrative develops, it can generate new relations among those interests. In most realistic narratives, for example, the audience has a tacit awareness of the synthetic while it focuses on the mimetic and the thematic components. In "The Cask of Amontillado," our main interest is in Montresor as a possible person and in the thematic issues his story raises, even as we retain our awareness that we are reading fiction. Metafictional narratives, however, have shown our covert awareness of the synthetic can become overt. For example, when the narrator of John Fowles's *The French Lieutenant's Woman* says at the beginning of chapter 13 that "the characters I create never existed outside my own mind," he breaks the mimetic illusion that those characters are people who are acting of their own accord and calls attention to their status as artificial constructs.

The fifth principle involves the significance of narrative judgments for the multilayered nature of narrative communication. The approach assumes that readers make three main types of narrative judgment, each of which has the potential to overlap with or affect the other two: interpretive judgments, ethical judgments, and aesthetic judgments. Interpretive judgments are about the nature of actions or other elements of the narrative; for example, we interpret Montresor's showing his mason's trowel to Fortunato as Montresor's private joke at Fortunato's expense. Ethical judgments are about the telling and the told, that is, the motives and actions of characters and the values implicit in the narrator's relation to the tale and the audience, and about the underlying value system of the author and the way her relation to narrator, tale, and audience relates to that value system. For example, we judge Montresor's code of revenge as ethically deficient (among other things, the victim becomes an object to be manipulated), and Montresor the narrator's attitude toward Fortunato as cold and dismissive until the end of the tale. By contrast, Poe's relation to his audience is more ethically satisfying because of the way he invites us to co-operate with him in our understanding of Montresor's telling. Aesthetic judgments are about the artistic quality of the narrative and of its parts. As we co-operate with Poe, we recognize the skill behind his communication.

The rhetorical approach also notes that individual narratives explicitly or implicitly establish their own ethical standards and, therefore, it seeks to make narrative judgments from the inside out (that is, on the basis of those standards) rather than the outside in (on the basis of a some ethical system that the interpreter brings to the narrative). When Montresor begins his telling by claiming that Fortunato's unspecified insults are sufficient cause for his act of revenge, Poe communicates the discrepancy between his values and those of Montresor. The rhetorical theorist does bring values to the text, but she remains open to having those values challenged and even repudiated by the experience of reading. A rhetorical theorist with deep religious beliefs will be likely to feel a strong challenge to those beliefs when she enters the authorial audience of Albert Camus's existentialist novel *The Stranger*.

The sixth principle involves the importance of narrative progressions. A narrative's movement from its beginning to its end is governed by both a textual and a readerly dynamics, and understanding their interaction provides a good means for recognizing a narrative's purposes. On the textual side narratives proceed by the introduction, complication, and resolution (in whole or in part) of two kinds of unstable situations. The first kind exists on the level of story, that is, the events and existents, including character and setting, of narrative, and I call them simply *instabilities*: they involve relations within, between, or among characters and their situations. The progression of "The Cask" is generated in part through the unstable relations between Montresor and Fortunato. The second kind exists at the level of discourse, that is, the narration and its techniques, and I call them *tensions*: they involve relations among authors, narrators, and audiences, and they include gaps between tellers and audiences of knowledge, beliefs, opinions, and values. Unreliable narration involves a progression by tension. The progression of "The Cask" is also generated by the tension resulting from Montresor's unreliability and from his initially undisclosed motive for telling the tale. On the readerly side narrative progression includes the trajectory of our developing responses to the pattern of instability–complication–resolution. Surprise endings are evidence of the way textual and readerly dynamics interact: the surprise depends on the textual dynamics leading the audience's responses in one direction and then suddenly taking them in a quite different one.

This account of progression also implicitly reinforces the significance of narrative judgments and the connection between rhetorical form and rhetorical ethics. In "The Cask," for example, our interpretive judgments about Montresor and Fortunato are crucial for our recognition of instabilities and tensions, and our ethical judgments of both characters are crucial for our readerly responses, because they deeply influence our emotional reactions to them. More generally, we can be moved to tears by the suffering of characters whom we regard as ethically admirable, even as we can take satisfaction in the punishment of characters whom we regard as ethically deficient. With these principles in mind, let us return to Poe's story.

Progression, judgment, and ethics in "The Cask of Amontillado"

Poe's first paragraph is worth another look because it introduces the story's main instabilities and tensions and invites an abundance of narrative judgments.

> The thousand injuries of Fortunato I had borne as I best could; but when he ventured upon insult, I vowed revenge. You, who so well know the nature of my soul, will not suppose, however, that I gave utterance to a threat. *At length* I would be avenged; this was a point definitively settled – but the very definitiveness with which it was resolved, precluded the idea of risk. I must not only punish, but punish with impunity. A wrong is unredressed when retribution overtakes its redresser. It is equally unredressed when the avenger fails to make himself felt as such to him who has done the wrong.   (360)

The main instability is the relation between Montresor and Fortunato, but an almost equally important one is between Montresor and himself, or more specifically, his code of revenge: the forward movement of the narrative is generated in large part by our double interest in what will happen between the two characters and whether what happens means that Montresor executes the revenge according to the code. The forward movement is also influenced by our awareness of the tensions generated by Montresor's unreliability as an ethical evaluator. To assume that insults are not only worse than injuries but also cause for carrying out an elaborate revenge is to reveal a seriously deficient value system, one that places personal pride above the value of human life. On the readerly side, consequently, our interest in the progression involves not just whether Montresor will succeed with the revenge but our sense that, if he does, he will prove himself to be an extremely cold, cruel, and clever individual – simultaneously fascinating and repulsive. At the same time, this paragraph begins our engagement with Poe as the creator of this extraordinary character, and it raises questions about the ethical value of that engagement.

Between the first paragraph and the last, the progression of the action proceeds very smoothly, as Montresor recounts all but the last step in his successful execution of his plan for revenge. Poe uses dialogue to carry the middle of the progression, dialogue that tacitly shows how brilliantly and with what great enjoyment Montresor manipulates the inebriated Fortunato. Poe does have Montresor linger over the details of the final steps of the revenge in order to show that Montresor is on the verge of fulfilling the requirements of his code. Fortunato sobers up and becomes acutely conscious of Montresor as Avenger. Fortunato lets forth a "succession of loud and shrill screams" (365), so loud that they unnerve Montresor. But the thickness of the catacomb's walls reassures Montresor that he is the only one who will ever hear Fortunato's screams, and so he mocks Fortunato by echoing those screams. In short, it appears as if he will be able to punish with impunity.

But Fortunato's last plea, which Montresor also echoes, is of a different kind: "*For the love of God, Montresor!*" (366). Because this plea links up with the other religious language in the story – Montresor's early reference to his soul and his final prayer – Poe invites us to see the final plea as contributing first to Montresor's heartsickness and ultimately to his need to confess: there is no way his code of revenge is compatible with the love of God.

Placing the analysis of the ending I offered earlier within this context provided by an attention to judgment and progression allows us to recognize that, when Montresor states, "My heart grew sick – on account of the dampness of the catacombs" (366), his unreliability effects a significant alteration in the progression. First, as noted above, it brings about a last-minute reversal in that strand of the progression associated with Montresor's ability to conform to the code of revenge. Second, it sets up a new ethical relation among Poe, Montresor, and the authorial audience. Prior to this point Poe has portrayed Montresor as an unreliable evaluator because he is beyond the pale of normal human feeling. Now, however, the unreliability consists in his maintaining that pretense in face of real evidence to the contrary. Consequently, we add new shadings to our ethical judgment of Montresor. He remains monstrous for what he has done and how he has done it, but his getting heartsick humanizes him. In addition, his need as narrator to hide his confession under the guise of boasting highlights the way his pride affects his telling, even as the confession itself is a remarkable acknowledgment of guilt.

We can move now to summarize Poe's purposes and to reflect on the ethics of his telling. In "The Cask of Amontillado" Poe invites us to contemplate one end of the spectrum of human behavior and uses his ending to insist on both the extremity and the humanness of that behavior. More specifically, he invites us to engage, through our initial fascination with, and repulsion from,

Montresor and our more nuanced final response, in a meditation on pride, guilt, and the powers and limits of confessional narrative. Furthermore, the rhetorical analysis also shows that Poe has admirably succeeded in making the single text of "The Cask" serve both Montresor's purposes and his own. In that sense, we can say that Poe has brilliantly managed to hold himself to a "code of telling" that is as rigorous in its way as Montresor's code of revenge. Unlike Montresor's code, it is both aesthetically and ethically sound, because it provides the basis for a moving story told with respect for his character narrator and his audience.

But if I were to end the rhetorical analysis here, I would end it too soon. Since the rhetorical approach recognizes that different flesh and blood readers bring different hierarchies of value to their reading, I welcome objections from readers who find Poe's subject-matter only repulsive or his attitude toward Montresor and/or Fortunato overly manipulative or otherwise problematic. These objections will not necessarily alter my own ethical assessment of the story, but they have the potential to – just as I hope my assessment above has the potential to alter these objections. Part of the value of narrative is precisely that it invites such debate about its own ethics. Part of the value of rhetorical ethics is that it insists that the debate be carried on in a way that is itself ethically sound.

NOTES

1. Edgar Allan Poe, "The Cask of Amontillado." In *The Fall of the House of Usher and Other Writings* (New York: Penguin Books, 1985), pp. 360–6.
2. Gerald Prince, "Introduction to the Study of the Narratee." In Jane Tompkins (ed.) *Reader-Response Criticism: From Formalism to Post-Structuralism* (Baltimore: Johns Hopkins University Press, 1980), pp. 7–25.
3. James Phelan, *Living to Tell about It: A Rhetoric and Ethics of Character Narration* (Ithaca: Cornell University Press, 2005).
4. Aristotle, *Poetics*. Translated by George Whalley (Montreal: McGill-Queen's University Press, 1997).
5. R. S. Crane (ed.) *Critics and Criticism: Ancient and Modern* (Chicago: University of Chicago Press, 1953).
6. R. S. Crane, "The Concept of Plot and the Plot of Tom Jones." In Crane (ed.) *Critics and Criticism: Ancient and Modern*, pp. 616–47.
7. Wayne C. Booth, *The Rhetoric of Fiction* (Chicago: University of Chicago Press, 1961, 2nd edition, 1983).
8. Wayne C. Booth, *The Company We Keep: An Ethics of Fiction* (Berkeley: University of California Press, 1988).
9. Martha Nussbaum, *Love's Knowledge* (New York: Oxford University Press, 1990).
10. J. Hillis Miller, *The Ethics of Reading* (New York: Columbia University Press, 1987).

11. Lisbeth Korthals Altes, "Ethical Turn." In David Herman, Manfred Jahn, and Marie-Laure Ryan (eds.) *Routledge Encyclopedia of Narrative Theory* (New York; Routledge, 2005), pp. 142–6.

12. Sheldon Sacks, *Fiction and the Shape of Belief* (Berkeley: University of California Press, 1966).

13. Ralph W. Rader, "Fact, Theory, and Literary Interpretation." *Critical Inquiry* 1 (1974), pp. 245–72.

14. David H. Richter, *Fable's End: Completeness and Closure in Rhetorical Fiction* (Chicago: University of Chicago Press, 1974).

15. Peter J. Rabinowitz, *Before Reading: Narrative Conventions and the Politics of Interpretation* (Columbus: Ohio State University Press, 1998 [1987]).

16. James Phelan, *Reading People, Reading Plots: Character, Progression, and the Interpretation of Narrative* (Chicago: University of Chicago Press, 1989).

17. Gérard Genette, *Narrative Discourse: An Essay in Method*. Translated by Jane Lewin (Ithaca: Cornell University Press, 1980).

18. Mikhail Bakhtin, "Discourse in the Novel." *The Dialogic Imagination*. Edited by Michael Holquist, translated by Caryl Emerson and Michael Holquist. (Austin: University of Texas Press, 1981).

19. Peter J. Rabinowitz, "Truth in Fiction: A Re-examination of Audiences." *Critical Inquiry* 4 (1977), pp. 121–41.

20. James Phelan, "Narratee, Narrative Audience, and Second-Person Narration: How I – and You? – Read 'How.'" In *Narrative as Rhetoric* (Columbus: Ohio State University Press, 1996), pp. 135–53.

15

LUC HERMAN AND BART VERVAECK

Ideology

Ideology and narratology

Although early work in narratology focused mainly on the structures of stories rather than the contexts in which stories were told and interpreted, narrative theorists such as Roland Barthes indicated ways in which the study of narrative could be fruitfully combined with the study of the beliefs, norms, and values that constitute what has come to be termed *ideology*. For example, Barthes's 1966 essay "Introduction to the Structuralist Analysis of Narratives"[1] pointed to the way a certain ideological conception of identity or personhood influenced previous understandings of the concept of "character" in narrative. Specifically, Barthes argued that a bourgeois conception of personhood had influenced literary critics to view characters as beings with a psychological essence rather than agents in narrated worlds that are defined by what they do or how they act. In this chapter, we extend Barthes's and others' suggestions to examine ways in which narrative procedures intersect with ideological issues. Building on the work of Karl Marx, Louis Althusser, and Antonio Gramsci, we define ideology as a body of norms and ideas that appear natural as a result of their continuous and mostly tacit promotion by the dominant forces in society. On the basis of this working definition, we investigate how research on stories can profit from greater attention to matters of ideology. Then we use F. Scott Fitzgerald's 1925 novel *The Great Gatsby* to show how the various connections between narrative and ideology can be developed in interpretation.

In its abstract form, ideology is a more or less coherent system of norms and ideas and therefore thrives on clear-cut oppositions, for instance between good and bad. In a specific context, however, these norms and ideas are never completely systematized or made explicit. For Marx, this "common sense" often implies the tacit adherence to norms and ideas imposed by the dominant forces in society and can therefore be branded as false consciousness.[2] Ideology understood as false consciousness thus translates power relations into natural, self-evident structures through which we experience and interpret the world. The post-Marxist Louis Althusser details the societal mechanisms that bring about this adherence to norms and values – mechanisms which literature, according to Pierre Macherey, helps throw into relief.[3]

For Antonio Gramsci, earlier in the twentieth century, narrative is the main form of cultural production to embody normality and establish or maintain what Gramsci termed *hegemony* – that is, the absolute and unquestioned dominance of a particular view or group.[4] If a narrative is convincing, the ideology it both conveys and helps reproduce stands a good chance of being accepted tacitly by the reader. Here the study of ideology meets the study of verisimilitude or *vraisemblance*. Narratives that seem plausible, trustworthy, and truthful bear the stamp of verisimilitude, or lifelikeness. In his seminal essay "Vraisemblance et motivation" ("Verisimilitude and Motivation"), the French narratologist Gérard Genette analyzes verisimilitude on the basis of the linguistic distinction between motivated and arbitrary signs.[5] Story elements are arbitrary because they derive their meaning from their links with the other elements, and not from a connection with the logic of the real world – one that goes without saying. In that sense, they are not motivated. Yet stories regarded as verisimilar succeed in passing off this arbitrary literary logic as real-world logic. The artificial construction seems natural because it is implicitly translated into the common-sense logic that people accept without asking for motivation. The story logic is accepted as common-sensical logic, and vice versa. This is the essence of the naturalization process that is central to ideology if the latter is regarded as the constant transformation of artificial constructs into natural givens.

The naturalization of ideology is an effect on the reader, but early structuralist narratology has little to say about how this reader contributes to the whole process. It seems as if the text does all the work and imposes its ideology on the audience. More recent narratologies have a more active view of the reader. This recognition of the reader's activity and ideology takes a variety of forms. Those who study literature as a form of communication stress the activity while not necessarily underscoring the ideological bias involved in this activity. Peter Rabinowitz is a good example.[6] His "rules of reading" show how the reader organizes a text, for instance into a coherent whole. Organization obviously implies choices and preferences, but Rabinowitz does not discuss their social, political, and ideological background. At the other end of the scale, there are explicitly ideological reader theories, such as those advanced by gender-conscious narratologists, who explicitly link the reader's interpretive preferences with the social and political system and with patriarchal ideology.[7]

In between these two extremes, there are several more or less ideologically conscious reader-oriented narratologies. The cognitive approach can be located quite close to the implicit pole in that ideology is not foregrounded.[8] This approach studies the reader's activity through the frames and scripts activated during the act of reading. Frames are prototypical structures in the mind of the reader; scripts are prototypical sequences. They both function as models through which the reader adapts the text to his or her habitual modes of thinking. Monika Fludernik's constructivist approach stands much closer to the explicit pole, since it is so broad as to include all experiences that the reader brings to his or her reading.[9] She contends that readers naturalize literary stories by linking them to ideologically charged "natural narratives" they encounter in everyday life.

Somewhere in the middle on the sliding scale of combined attention to reader and ideology, one might encounter narrative ethics, as exemplified in Wayne Booth's *The Company We Keep* or Adam Newton's *Narrative Ethics*.[10] Theorists like Booth and Newton are concerned with ideology but study its ethical dimension, not its socio-political context. Booth and Newton see an ethical reading as a reading that does justice to the appeal made by the text. For Booth a text is like a gift from a friend. The reader's reaction is ethical if it honors the friendship in all its aspects. Newton follows the French philosopher Emmanuel Levinas in regarding a text as an appeal to understanding, which the reader should respond to as intensely as possible. Booth and Newton greatly differ from a deconstructionist such as J. Hillis Miller, who, in *The Ethics of Reading,* underscores that one can follow an appeal only by deviating from it. For our purposes, this means that there can be no perfect reconstruction of a text's ideology, as it is always informed by the reader's ideology, which can never be fully spelled out. This may be regrettable, but, on the other hand, it may be one of the reasons why literary texts continue to fascinate readers.

Ideology and *The Great Gatsby*

Influenced by post-Marxism and reader-response criticism, recent narratology has sought to uncover the (political) values informing a narrative and its interpretation. In order to present the whole range of links between narrative theory and ideology as it may affect the reading of *The Great Gatsby* (1925) by F. Scott Fitzgerald, we will enhance a traditional approach to the novel with a variety of more recent suggestions. The traditional, structuralist approach is based on the conventional narratological distinction between "story" (the chronological sequence of events); "narrative" (the way in which these events are presented, e.g., using the perspective of one or more characters); and "narration" (the verbal rendition of this presentation, e.g., by a first-person narrator). In *The Great Gatsby*, Nick Carraway narrates the downfall of his neighbor, the self-made millionaire and suspected con-man Jay Gatsby, whose desperate love for Daisy Buchanan eventually leads to the tragic death of Myrtle Wilson, the girlfriend of Daisy's husband, Tom. Gatsby's noble behavior after this accident seems to redeem him and thus to save the American Dream he personifies. In the end, he is shot by Myrtle's husband.

Ideology and the "story" level

The structuralists call the most abstract level of a narrative the story or *fabula*. It consists of three basic story-elements: actions or events; actants (roles performed by characters); and setting in time and space. These are all studied through binary oppositions. Thus A. J. Greimas[11] distinguishes between six actants divided into three binary pairs: subject versus object; sender (the one initializing the activity of the subject) versus receiver (the one benefiting from the activity of the subject); helper versus opponent. This model splits up roles into clearly delineated unities and therefore has its own ideological leanings, but it also enables the narratologist to see the ideological workings of a story. For instance, if female characters are always assigned the object role, and male characters get to play the subject part, this gives an unmistakable indication of gendered ideas and values.

If the title of *The Great Gatsby* is any indication of what this story is all about, then Gatsby might be assigned the subject role. The object he strives for would be Daisy; he himself would be the receiver. The sender might be considered to be an emotion such as desire or love, but it might also be Daisy herself, who lives across the bay and who induces love in Gatsby, indirectly compelling him to declare this love. The helper would be the I-narrator, Nick Carraway; the opponent would be Tom Buchanan, Daisy's husband. This actantial network puts the woman in the object position, the man in the subject position. This general slant of the story may also be seen in some of its details, such as Tom's extra-marital affairs. Society accepts them, whereas Daisy's extra-marital sympathy for Gatsby is said to be completely unacceptable.[12]

Time and space on the story level are usually studied in terms of dualisms such as light versus dark, high versus low, open versus closed.[13] These divisions may have ideological implications of their own (high, light, and open probably being preferred to dark, low, and closed), but, as far as the story goes, these implications only become obvious when they are combined with the actants and the actions. For instance, actions and actants associated with dark and closed spaces may be more negative than those in open and light spaces. *The Great Gatsby* has clear-cut spatial and temporal borders. For space, the central distinction is between East and West. As the narrator says at the end: "This has been a story of the West" (*Gatsby*, 167). At the beginning he clearly differentiates the two regions. In Long Island, where he lives, there is West and East Egg: "I lived at West Egg, the – well, the less fashionable of the two" (*Gatsby*, 10). West is for the middle class, East for the high class. Being spectacularly rich, Gatsby should be living in the East, but he isn't. He wants to be close to Daisy, whose house on the East side he can see from where he lives, and he wants to go back to the days in the West when he, as a poor man, knew Daisy. When Nick tells him: "'I wouldn't ask too much of her . . . . You can't repeat the past,'" he cries out: "'Can't repeat the past? . . . Why of course you can!'" (*Gatsby*, 106). This longing for the past combines space and time: Gatsby wants to go back to the West and the past, whereas he seems to belong to the East. As a successful businessman he should be oriented towards the future. His ideology should be faithful to the American dream: from rags to riches, and no looking back. Parts of him follow that model, but once he has reached the top, his former place and time seem preferable.

Nick, the narrator, is strictly middle-class and, like Gatsby, he comes from the West and longs to go back there: "So we beat on, boats against the current, borne back ceaselessly into the past" (*Gatsby*, 172). You cannot escape your past or your social background. Since they express a general truth, these lines may be regarded by some readers as an indication of Fitzgerald's ideology.

In addition to actants and setting, the actions and events – the third aspect of the "story" – have ideological implications as well. The grammar of actions is studied by Roland Barthes in *S/Z*.[14] He enumerates five codes through which story elements can be linked together. One of these is the action code, which is used to combine actions and thus reveals the ideology of the story. Obviously, a story that establishes traditional, common-sensical links between actions (such as cause and effect) has a different ideology from a story that seems to link actions in an incomprehensible and illogical way. A story that tends to blur distinctions between actions undertaken by subjects and events befalling these subjects may very well bear witness to a fatalistic ideology; anything man does is in reality ordained by fate. The outcome of actions and events implies a form of ideology, too. Nancy Miller shows that in many eighteenth-century novels the actions of female characters are dictated by the "logic of the faux pas."[15] A woman does something wrong, which may lead to disaster or to correction. This hangs together with an ideology viewing women as vulnerable creatures who are prone to irrational and dangerous actions.

In his "Introduction to the Structural Analysis of Narrative," Barthes specifies actions and events in terms of functions and indexes. A function is a minimal unit that moves the story onward. Thus killing someone is a function, and so is buying a gun. Combinations between functions can take all sorts of forms, such as cause and effect or pole and opposite pole. These forms are part of the action code and thus give away some aspects of the story's ideology. By contrast, indexes do not ensure movement or change; instead, they provide information, for instance about time and place. A "pure" index asks for interpretation and symbolic deciphering. For instance, the Martinis James Bond drinks, the sports car he drives, and the fashionable clothes he wears are all indexes of his worldly manner and his desirability for women. This symbolization bears traces of ideology, in this case a male-oriented worldview that is uncritical of capitalist values and norms.

In *The Great Gatsby*, actions do not seem to lead anywhere. Characters from West Egg remain stuck in their background. Not even love can go against this tragic logic of actions. Moreover, there seems to be little action in the story. If one thinks of actions as important and life-changing, there seems to be only one of those in the book: the killing of Tom's mistress, Myrtle Wilson. But even this is not the result of a premeditated action or a free choice; rather, it is an accident. Gatsby and Daisy are in their car, Daisy is driving (at least according to Gatsby), and suddenly Myrtle runs in front of the car. Accidents will happen, and there is very little people can do about that. Indeed, the whole story underlines how little we can do, which suggests a defeatist view of human existence and coincides with Gatsby's desire to make a continuous return to the past.

If there are few actions that move the story onward, this means, in Barthes's terminology, that there are few functions. By contrast, there is an overload of indexes in *The Great Gatsby*. Every page contains details that are to be interpreted symbolically as indications of the characters' status. Gatsby's house and cars are among them, and so is his artificial way of speaking, his over-correct way of dressing, and, more generally, his "punctilious manner" (*Gatsby*, 63). All these indexes seem to present a man who is in complete control, both of himself and his destiny. But that is mere semblance. Small indexes give away that Gatsby's stately manner is purely make-believe. For instance, he does not seem able to keep still: "This quality was continually breaking through his punctilious manner in the shape of restlessness. He was never quite still" (*Gatsby*, 62–3). For the perceptive reader, these cracks in Gatsby's posture show the ideological bias of the story: although Gatsby may pretend to be in control, in reality man is always controlled – by his own urges and restlessness, and definitely by fate.

Ideology and the "narrative" level

Narrative, the second level in structuralist analysis, is more concrete than the story. It concerns the actual way in which events and characters are presented. This involves three dimensions, namely temporal organization, characterization, and focalization. These three aspects, which are treated in more detail in chapters 4, 5, and 7 in this volume, are more explicit carriers of ideology than the aspects of the story level reviewed in our previous section.[16]

The temporal organization of narrative concerns the actual presentation of the events, whereas the temporal dimension of the story referred to the abstract and chronological sequence constructed by interpreters of the narrative. The difference between the two is significant for the study of ideology. For instance, an event that was important and took a long time on the level of the story may go unmentioned in the narrative. This is called an ellipsis, and it may have various ideological meanings. It may indicate a narrator's hypocrisy or alternatively his or her reticence. The Great Gatsby contains many ellipses. How exactly did Gatsby become rich? What was his precise relation with his supposed benefactor Dan Cody? And what (shady) business with bonds is he involved in when he meets the narrator? Such omissions in the narrative may give the impression that much about Gatsby is ethically dubious. They may also lead to the conclusion that this novel about social and economic inequalities does not present the actual processes that are responsible for these inequalities, namely the processes of production as a Marxist might analyze them. Interestingly, the narrator comments on his omissions. After dwelling on three consecutive meetings (with Tom and Daisy, Tom and Myrtle, and Gatsby), Nick corrects himself: "I see I have given the impression that the events of three nights several weeks apart were all that absorbed me. On the contrary, they were merely casual events . . . Most of the time I worked" (Gatsby, 56). There follows a very brief description of his work. In narratological terms, this is not an ellipsis but a summary. Working and making money are actions that take a long time on the level of the story, but that are only briefly mentioned in the narrative, as if they are not proper subjects for a story about love in the upper classes.

In The Great Gatsby the temporal order is largely chronological, but sometimes the narrator admits that he has altered the chronology in order to clarify certain points. The chronology is further broken up by flashbacks, all of which suggest that the onward movement is just an illusion, and that the past crops up time and again, thus imposing itself on the present in the form of fate. The story is set in 1922 but it looks back on crucial events taking place in 1917 (Gatsby's love affair with Daisy) and 1919 (Gatsby's alleged fixing of the World Series). Not surprisingly these two flashbacks relate to love and money. There is also the First World War, in which Gatsby "did extraordinarily well" (*Gatsby*, 143) – which may be regarded as an indication of Gatsby's fighting capacities. But after the war, he could not find a decent job, until Dan Cody came along – and then the two got into jobs whose ethical propriety remains in question. There are only a few flashforwards in the novel, e.g., when Gatsby tries to get Daisy to leave Tom, so that he will be able to marry her. But this dream about the future is really an attempt to repeat the past, namely the love he had experienced in 1917. "He talked a lot about the past," says Nick about Gatsby, "and I gathered that he wanted to recover something" (*Gatsby*, 106). The future is not some American dream, but a rekindling of the past. This, again, suggests that the novel is relatively critical of dominant contemporary ideologies.

As to characterization, the second aspect on the level of narrative, it is immediately obvious that Gatsby is a continual presence. Even when he is not actually on the scene, he hovers above the events and is talked about very often, both by Nick and by the other characters. He is characterized explicitly by all sorts of statements about him, and implicitly by means of symbolic elements such as his library, which shows him off as a man of education. A visitor compares Gatsby to David Belasco, who wrote, produced, and directed realistic plays. This suggests that Gatsby's reality is stage-managed: the real is in fact theatrical; the natural artificial.

Gatsby is literally and figuratively a character who is perceived as a real person. Literally, he is a character in the book, perceived by the reader as if he were a real human being; figuratively, he is an actor who succeeds in turning his artifice into nature. Sometimes, he does not succeed, for instance when he tells about his Oxford years in phrases Nick calls theatrical. The theatrical nature of Gatsby's reality is underscored by other characters, such as his visitors, who all seem to be "connected with the movies in one way or another" (*Gatsby*, 61). Life is a show turned into reality by the ideological process of naturalization.

At the end of the novel, Gatsby remains a mystery. Though he is continually talked about in gossip and speculation, there seems to be no definitive narrative that captures his real character. After his death, the newspapers publish their stories, but "[m]ost of those reports were a nightmare – grotesque, circumstantial, eager, and untrue" (*Gatsby*, 155). This may be read as an implicit denunciation of narratives; it is impossible to tell the truth about a person. Such a conviction casts a shadow over the reliability of Nick Carraway as narrator. Alternatively, the gossip and newspaper reports may be read as false stories providing the necessary contrast with the true story told by Nick. The options remain open.

Focalization, the final aspect of the level of narrative we will discuss here, refers to the way the events, characters, and objects of the story are perceived. More specifically it involves a focalizer – a center of perception – and a focalized object. Perception should be taken in the broadest possible sense; it encompasses not only sensory perception but also cognitive functions like thinking and evaluating. As such, focalization is directly linked to ideology and has received due attention in the investigation of ideology *vis-à-vis* narrative. Feminist narratology, for instance, has focused on the difference between male and female focalizers and focalized subjects. Nick Carraway is the focalizer in *The Great Gatsby*. Everything is seen through his eyes and filtered through his perceptions. He is a character participating in the story, and as such he is an internal focalizer. As a consequence, his perception is limited; he cannot see inside the heads of the other characters. That is part of his problem, because he wants to see through everything and everyone. Not only does he want to find out what Gatsby is hiding in his vague stories about the past, he also wants to unmask Jordan Baker, though he never really fathoms this girl who becomes his girlfriend. Indeed, in so far as Nick does not really know what to feel or think about Gatsby, the former cannot even see clearly into his own mind and heart.

At the same time, Nick is not just a character but also the writer of the story, and explicitly describes himself as such: "Reading over what I have written so far . . ." (*Gatsby*, 56). At that moment, he becomes an external focalizer. He no longer participates, but looks back and remains outside. External focalization, however, occurs rarely in this novel. In the quoted example, it introduces the statement about work mentioned earlier. As one of the few externally focalized fragments, it may suggest that the deeper reasons for the impossible love affair (the social and economic inequality) are not visible to someone who participates (the internal focalizer), but only to someone who has achieved a certain distance from the narrated events. Even so, the external focalizer remains a rarity and his few appearances never give a definitive view or interpretation of the events. The already mentioned last sentence of the book could be the perception of Nick-the-character, but most readers are likely to see it as externally focalized by Nick-the-writer. Indeed, its position seems to give it a certain weight as an encompassing ideological statement, but then there's very little external focalization to back it up in the rest of the text. A traditional external focalizer would at this point probably resolve all the obscure parts of the story, but *The Great Gatsby* opts for a degree of openness and ambiguity instead of closure and clear-cut explanations.

Ideology and the level of "narration"

Narration, the third level of structuralist analysis, deals with the narrator and with speech representation. As the agent that relates and creates the story, the narrator exerts power and authority, which may turn him or her into an essential component of what Wayne Booth calls the "implied author," the source of values and norms in a text.[17] Most ideologically conscious analyses of the narrator underscore the many-sided ideology narrators regularly exhibit. A traditional narrator may sometimes be seen as "the voice of prevailing orthodoxy"[18] and as the echo of the ideology implicitly accepted as common sense, but even so, he or she can voice different, sometimes contradictory, views on humankind and on life. In line with Bakhtin's analysis of the novel as a polyphonic genre that always allows for multiple voices and registers,[19] many narratologists have paid attention to the multi-stranded ideology involved in this mixture of voices. According to feminist narratologists such as Susan Lanser, this polyphony is "more pronounced and more consequential in women's narratives and in the narratives of other dominated peoples,"[20] but that claim remains open to debate. Even a traditional, male narrator who is not narrated by a higher authority and who has witnessed the things he talks about often tells the story in a way that reveals the effects of conflicting ideological forces. His sympathies may vary, and this may endanger his reliability.

This is clearly the case in *The Great Gatsby*. Nick Carraway is in charge of the entire narration, and he has also been part of the action as a witness. This does not mean that he can be called an unequivocal or fully reliable narrator. For example, Nick's anti-Semitism comes through in his portrait of the Jewish gambler, Meyer Wolfshiem (*Gatsby*, 68–72). In his evaluations of Gatsby, however, Nick fails to decide whether he likes or dislikes his protagonist. The first words Nick utters about Gatsby set the scene. Gatsby "represented everything for which I have an unaffected scorn," but a minute later Nick says: "Gatsby turned out all right at the end" (*Gatsby*, 8). His seemingly final judgment is equally ambiguous. As he is leaving, he shouts to Gatsby: "They're a rotten crowd . . . You're worth the whole damn bunch put together." And then he proceeds: "I've always been glad I said that. It was the only compliment I ever gave him, because I disapproved of him from beginning to end" (*Gatsby*, 146–7). The narrator is ideologically conflicted: he cannot embrace the one-sided critical view that the middle class has of the higher classes, but neither can he align himself with the admiration that the poor might feel for the rich.

This vacillation casts a shadow over Nick's reliability. In the beginning of his narration, he may call himself "one of the few honest people that I have ever known" (*Gatsby*, 59), but at the end his supposed girlfriend, Jordan Baker, tells him that she misjudged him when she thought he was "an honest, straightforward person." He answers: "I'm thirty . . . I'm five years too old to lie to myself and call it honor" (*Gatsby*, 168). This sentence may imply that he used to be a liar, but also that he no longer cares to be perceived as an honest man. How honest is Nick's report? Is he not too involved to be able to give a reliable presentation of what happened? In an interesting analysis, James Phelan shows that Nick's narration hesitates between omniscience and unreliability, a hesitation which Phelan traces to the in-between stature of Nick: he is both a narrator and a character, and this affects his narration.[21] As Nick puts it himself: "I was within and without" (*Gatsby*, 37).

Speech representation forms the second dimension of narration. In so far as this concerns the way the narrator represents the thoughts, feelings, and words of the characters, it always involves a selection and manipulation of the represented elements. The narrator's ideology plays a major part in this operation. It is therefore no surprise that the ideological implications of speech representation have been studied at some length by narratologists. In *Texte et idéologie* (*Text and Ideology*), Philippe Hamon shows how every form of (speech) representation entails an evaluation.[22] The language that characters use shows their ideology, while at the same time this language is colored by the narrator since he or she is the agent putting words into the characters' mouths.

This coloring can take all sorts of shades. A narrator may openly criticize his characters' thoughts. Following *Transparent Minds* by Dorrit Cohn, this can be called dissonant psycho-narration.[23] If, on the other hand, a narrator seems to disappear behind the words and thoughts of his character, Cohn talks about consonant psycho-narration. Ideologically speaking, consonance is more complicated than dissonance. For one thing, the narrator's empathic rendition of the character's thoughts may be just an impression. You can never tell what the character actually thought, since you only see what the narrator allows you to see. Even here, the narrator colors the scene. Maybe he has the same ideas as the character, but maybe he violently disapproves of them, and maybe this becomes clear in the outcome of the story. For instance, a character might meet a terrible end, and at that point the narrator may show the evaluation he has hidden so long and so well.

If the narrator and the character are the same, as in first-person narratives, things get even more complicated. The narrating-I may disagree with the acting and experiencing-I. This often occurs in autobiographical fiction, where the older narrator reflects upon his life as a young man. He might be critical about what he thought as a young man, and this criticism might give the impression that the narrator is wise and trustworthy. Cohn would call this dissonant self-narration. Again, the case of consonant self-narration is ideologically much less clear, since the distinction between I-character and I-narrator is blurred.

The Great Gatsby falls into this last category. Nick talks about things that happened to him in the past, but there are very few instances in which the narrator, living in the present of the narration, shows himself as different from the character living in the past of the narrative. We discussed these instances in connection with temporal organization and ambiguous focalization. Arguably, the fragments in which the narrator comes to the fore never imply a clear criticism (ideological dissonance) or a final statement of ideological stance. As such, character and narrator, past and present seem to be continually interwoven. This ties in with the main theme and ideological focus of the novel, namely, the inescapability of the past.

In psycho-narration and self-narration the narrator summarizes the thoughts of the characters. In linguistic terms, that would be the equivalent of indirect speech, or a summary report of someone else's words. But a narrator may also quote the character's thoughts. This narrative equivalent to direct speech, where someone's words are literally cited, is called quoted monologue by Cohn. The two forms of speech representation may be combined in free indirect speech, which Cohn calls narrated monologue. This situation is quite problematic, since it mixes the words of the character with those of the narrator, and you cannot really tell them apart. Significantly, this happens in *The Great Gatsby* when Gatsby is talking about the past. The relevant passage begins with a sentence spoken by the narrator: "He [Gatsby] talked a lot about the past" (*Gatsby*, 106). This is indirect speech, i.e., psycho-narration. Then the speech representation shifts: "His life had been confused and disordered since then, but if he could once return to a certain starting place and go over it all slowly, he could find out what that thing was . . ." (*Gatsby*, 106). The first part may be a summary of Gatsby's words by Nick. In that case, "confused and disordered" might very well be Nick's words, betraying his view of Gatsby's life. But maybe Gatsby said: "My life has been confused and disordered since then, and if I can once return to a certain starting place . . ." Then his utterance is rendered through free indirect speech and Nick's stance toward events recedes into the background. There are quite a few instances of free indirect speech in the novel. If they relate to Gatsby, they complicate the ideological split between Nick and the title-character; if they relate to the I-figure, they complicate the interaction between past and present. In both cases, they are indications of a complicated and ambiguous ideology that demands careful narratological scrutiny.

NOTES

1. Barthes, "Introduction to the Structural Analysis of Narratives." *Image-Music-Text*. Translated by Stephen Heath (Glasgow: Fontana/Collins, 1977), pp. 79–124.
2. For an excellent exposition of Marx's ideas on ideology see Jorge Larrain, *The Concept of Ideology* (London: Hutchinson, 1979), pp. 35–67.
3. See Louis Althusser's *For Marx*. Translated by Ben Brewster (New York: Pantheon Books, 1969), and *Lenin and Philosophy and Other Essays*. Translated by Ben Brewster (New York: Monthly Review Press, 1971); see also Pierre Macherey, *A Theory of Literary Production*. Translated by Geoffrey Wall (London, Routledge, 1978).
4. Antonio Gramsci, *Selections from the Prison Notebooks*. Edited and translated by Quintin Hoare and Geoffrey Nowell-Smith (New York: International Publishers, 1971). For a more recent treatment of concepts of hegemony see Ernesto Laclau and Chantal Mouffe, *Hegemony and Socialist Strategy: Towards a Radical Democratic Politics*. Translated by Winston Moore and Paul Cammack (London: Verso, 1985).
5. Gérard Genette, "Vraisemblance et motivation." *Communications* 11 (1968), pp. 5–21.
6. Peter Rabinowitz, *Before Reading: Narrative Conventions and the Politics of Interpretation* (Columbus: Ohio State University Press, 1998).
7. See e.g. Teresa de Lauretis (ed.) *Feminist Studies/Critical Studies* (London: Macmillan, 1986); Elaine Showalter (ed.) *Speaking of Gender* (New York: Routledge, 1989).
8. See e.g. Manfred Jahn, "Frames, Preferences, and the Reading of Third-Person Narratives: Towards a Cognitive Narratology." *Poetics Today* 18 (1997), pp. 441–68; David Herman, "Scripts, Sequences, and Stories: Elements of a Postclassical Narratology." *PMLA* 112 (1997), pp. 1046–59.
9. Monika Fludernik, *Towards a "Natural" Narratology* (London: Routledge, 1996).
10. Wayne Booth, *The Company We Keep* (Berkeley: University of California Press, 1988); Adam Zachary Newton, *Narrative Ethics* (Cambridge: Harvard University Press, 1995).
11. Greimas, *Structural Semantics: An Attempt at Method*. Translated by Danielle McDowell, Ronald Schleifer, and Alan Velie (Lincoln: University of Nebraska Press, 1983).
12. F. Scott Fitzgerald, *The Great Gatsby* (London: Penguin Books, 1950), p. 125.
13. Mieke Bal, *Narratology: Introduction to the Theory of Narrative*, 2nd edition (Toronto: Toronto University Press, 1997), pp. 214–17.
14. Roland Barthes, *S/Z: An Essay*. Translated by Richard Miller (New York: Hill & Wang, 1974).
15. Nancy Miller, *The Heroine's Text: Readings in the French and English Novel 1722–1782* (New York: Columbia University Press, 1980), p. x.
16. In the following discussion we are indebted to Gérard Genette's *Narrative Discourse*. Translated by Jane E. Lewin (Ithaca: Cornell University Press, 1980), and *Narrative Discourse Revisited*. Translated by Jane E. Lewin (Ithaca: Cornell University Press, 1988), and also to Mieke Bal's *Narratology*.

17. Wayne Booth, *The Rhetoric of Fiction* (Chicago: University of Chicago Press, 1961).
18. Jeremy Tambling, *Narrative and Ideology* (Bristol: Open University Press, 1991), p. 23.
19. Mikhail Bakhtin, *The Dialogic Imagination: Four Essays by M. M. Bakhtin.* Edited by Michael Holquist, translated by Caryl Emerson and Michael Holquist (Austin, University of Texas Press, 1981).
20. Susan S. Lanser, "Toward a Feminist Narratology." *Style* 20:3 (1986), pp. 341–63.
21. James Phelan, "Reexamining Reliability: The Multiple Functions of Nick Carraway." In *Narrative as Rhetoric: Technique, Audiences, Ethics, Ideology* (Columbus: Ohio State University Press, 1996), pp. 105–18.
22. Philippe Hamon, *Texte et idéologie: Valeurs, hiérarchies et évaluations dans l'œuvre littéraire* (Paris: PUF, 1984).
23. Dorrit Cohn, *Transparent Minds: Narrative Modes for Presenting Consciousness in Fiction* (Princeton: Princeton University Press, 1978).

16

MICHAEL TOOLAN

Language

The language of a narrative: different wordings, different stories

The focus in this chapter is on the verbal detail that linguistic categories and distinctions can help us to pinpoint in the composition of literary narratives. My example text is Joyce's "Two Gallants." Linguistic descriptions may not always be able to *explain* what it is in a passage of literary narrative that makes it particularly effective or striking or moving, but such descriptions can help to make us more aware of the kinds of distinct, even unique, verbal texture a text may have, and more aware of how if a story was narrated – worded – otherwise, it would have created a very different effect. It would, in fact, be a different story.

What happens in "Two Gallants"?

The following is a synopsis of James Joyce's short story "Two Gallants," which was published in 1914 as part of *Dubliners*:

> Two young men, Corley and Lenehan, stroll around the twilight streets talking about women, Corley agreeing to extract money from his woman-friend at the end of his evening with her, this money to be loaned to the impecunious Lenehan. Thereafter we follow the latter as he walks the streets, reflecting on his own miserable condition, until the couple return and Corley is given a sovereign by the woman who departs and, after a brief delay, Corley displays this "tribute" to the anxiously waiting Lenehan.

Does this, should this, make a good story? It is not, on the face of it, the stuff of high drama, life-threatening conflict, heroics, pity, terror, or passion. And yet somehow Joyce creates interest, narrative dynamism, so that any attentive reader is rapidly caught up in the story, and eager by its final paragraphs to find out how matters conclude. In the following sections I will look at what language commentary can help pinpoint about the narrative work done, and the texture used to do it, in the story's opening two paragraphs; then at how

Halliday's analysis of clause transitivity gives insight into the language with which the central character Lenehan – what he is and does – is represented; then finish with some discussion of how the second half of the story uses the technique known as Free Indirect Thought to bring us close, perhaps unpleasantly close, to Lenehan and his narrow, self-enclosed preoccupations.

The opening: setting and character introduction

It is nearly always rewarding to look carefully at the language of a story's opening – texture and expectations are created there that, in a sense, persist and prevail through the remainder of the narrative. Here is the opening of "Two Gallants":

> The grey warm evening of August had descended upon the city and a mild warm air, a memory of summer, circulated in the streets. The streets, shuttered for the repose of Sunday, swarmed with a gaily coloured crowd. Like illumined pearls the lamps shone from the summits of their tall poles upon the living texture below which, changing shape and hue unceasingly, sent up into the warm grey evening air an unchanging unceasing murmur.
>
> Two young men came down the hill of Rutland Square. One of them was just bringing a long monologue to a close. The other, who walked on the verge of the path and was at times obliged to step on to the road, owing to his companion's rudeness, wore an amused listening face. He was squat and ruddy. A yachting cap was shoved far back from his forehead and the narrative to which he listened made constant waves of expression break forth over his face from the corners of his nose and eyes and mouth. Little jets of wheezing laughter followed one another out of his convulsed body. His eyes, twinkling with cunning enjoyment, glanced at every moment towards his companion's face. Once or twice he rearranged the light waterproof which he had slung over one shoulder in toreador fashion. His breeches, his white rubber shoes and his jauntily slung waterproof expressed youth. But his figure fell into rotundity at the waist, his hair was scant and grey and his face, when the waves of expression had passed over it, had a ravaged look.[1]

We see at once that the opening paragraph is general, the second paragraph more particular (introducing and giving a good deal of preliminary information about "two young men"). We infer that the two young men in Rutland Square are *within* the city described very generally in the short first paragraph, although this is not explicitly stated. But we can draw on ideas from language description to provide a closer analysis of the story's opening. Consider first the grammatical Subjects, and hence the sentence constituent a reader is inclined – in normal circumstances – to interpret as the actor or "doer." In each sentence here, and by extension in the scene depicted, the Subjects are not human individuals but the following: *the grey warm evening of August* (which "descends"), *a mild warm air* (which "circulates"), *the streets* (which "swarm"), *the lamps* (which shine), and *the living texture* (which "sends up a murmur"). There seems to be an avoidance of any suggestion of human particularity, this being furthered by the representation of evening, month, air, and streets as if they, and not any particular human beings, were the chief sources and causes of action and movement, and also by the references to "crowds" and "lamps."

But perhaps the most striking avoidance of human particularity comes in the use of the phrase "the living texture," evidently to denote the people who are presumably walking and conversing, perhaps buying sweets from street-vendors, perhaps listening to a brass band. We cannot be sure because at this early stage we are denied detail; we are simply told of the living texture's unceasing changes of shape and hue, and its steady murmur. This is a remarkably removed, generalized, or telescoped view of people in a city thoroughfare, represented in their vague collectivity as if they were ants, or coins – constantly in movement, busy, but each indistinguishable from the next. Joyce is much too subtle to use the metaphor of ants or bees at all directly; the verb *swarmed* is used and this may evoke its conventional association with bees, but notice that what is reported as swarming is not a crowd but the streets. What does Joyce gain by telling that *the streets swarmed with a gaily coloured crowd* rather than that *a gaily coloured crowd swarmed (in) the streets*? The logical doer of the swarming is displaced as Subject by the setting in which the swarming is done. Nor is it the only displacement in the paragraph: the streets are said to be "shuttered" for the repose of Sunday, but we can assume that strictly it is the shopfronts facing onto the streets that are shuttered.

For the grammarian, verbs like *swarm* and *shine* as used in this highly wrought opening are immensely interesting. Unlike most English verbs that can take an Object and are called transitive (like *eat* and *kick*), *swarm* and *shine* allow the Object to serve as Subject in an alternative construction which is still Active voice. So alongside *Someone shone the lamp (upon the living texture)* you can have *The lamp shone (upon the living texture)*, with the original causer, the someone, entirely removed from the representation. Similarly you can have *A crowd swarmed the streets* but also *The streets swarmed*. By contrast most transitive verbs are like *eat*: *He ate his food (greedily)* cannot easily be recast as *His food ate*. Some linguists call verbs like these "ergative" verbs,[2] and the canonical examples in English include *break* and *move* and *change*. These ergative verbs are important in the linguistic study of narratives; at the level of the single sentence, they allow a reporter of an event to use a grammar which conceals a level of causation and agency that would otherwise be overt or easily recovered: not: *Patrick threw the jug and covered the carpet with milk* (where you cannot rephrase as *The jug threw etc.*); or even: *The jug was broken and the milk got spilt* (where someone can immediately wonder "broken by whom?"); but simply *The jug broke and the milk spilt on the carpet*. Looking at the verbs a narrative uses (including the ergative ones) can be crucial to a full sense of what the text represents as having happened, and having been caused by whom. The "ergative" intransitives are representing that things happen here, things "circulate," in a seductively irresponsible way: people are not fully individual or agentive, but only a swarm, or herd, or mob.

There are other clearly "poetic" or rhetorical effects here, notably of chiastic repetition, where a wording is followed by the same words used a second time soon after, but with some inversion of word order, so that that second use seems a reinforcement or reply or even a completion of the first use. Here the paragraph begins with *the grey warm evening* and ends with *the warm grey evening*, thereby enacting the idea of circulation and exchange (of words, at least). In fact the recyclings are more complicated, because while the opening sentence represents *the grey warm evening* and *a mild warm air* as distinct but complementary, these two elements are integrated in the final sentence: *the warm grey evening air*. Similarly, in the final sentence, the *changing shape and hue unceasingly* is interestingly modulated in the final phrase to *an unchanging unceasing murmur*. It is worth thinking carefully about such effects, especially here at the opening, as they can carry importance guidance as to how the narrative that follows should be understood.

If the first paragraph is thematic and conspectual, analogous to the overture that precedes a classical opera, the second paragraph introduces the protagonists and launches the action. Throughout the paragraph, there is clearly some defamiliarization in the way Lenehan (as, we later learn, he is named) is described. Consider, for instance:

> Little jets of wheezing laughter followed one another out of his convulsed body.

The laughter and the body are endowed with human-like animation, as if they were sentient and had intentions. Thus the laughter is wheezing, and his body is convulsed, and these are related in that the spasms of laughter (in the form of mechanical-sounding "little jets") "follow one another" out of the body. This is a striking effort to report the laughter without suggesting that it emanates, naturally or spontaneously, from Lenehan the person. One can sense this the more if we contrast *followed one another* with a more routine verb, such as *came*. The "follow one another" construction even hints (without asserting) that the causation of one jet of laughter emerging is simply the fact that a previous jet has just emerged.

A similar estrangement is suggested by the preceding sentence, which describes Lenehan's reaction to Corley's monologue as follows:

> . . . the narrative to which he listened made constant waves of expression break forth over his face . . .

The wording, I suggest, implies that Lenehan did not *really* listen with genuine animated interest to Corley's story – which is why Joyce has not written more straightforwardly that he did. Outward signs and shows of interest and amusement conceal dishonesty in this interaction between Lenehan and Corley, just as dishonesty structures all the exchanges between them, and between Corley and the young woman. The story does not tell this explicitly, only showing it in these oblique ways, but it is a major point of the entire telling. As Margot Norris says, the effect is to present the entire scene as mime or pantomime – especially on Lenehan's part – rather than authentic and "felt."[3] Our sense that Lenehan is faking things is rooted in the phrase "constant waves of expression," which in linguistic terms is a nominalization, that is, a grammatical casting as a "thing" (a noun phrase) that which is implicitly a process (a clause), with an Actor and a Goal (see the next section for further explanation of these terms). Describing Lenehan's reaction in process terms, we might expect a clause like "he expressed his reactions," or "he reacted expressively." But you can take the person and the immediacy of the process out of the picture, out of the representation, if you nominalize: instead of "the narrative made him repeatedly react expressively" or something similar, Lenehan's reacting can be can be cast as a thing, "waves of expression."

There are other things to be said about the construction *made constant waves of expression break forth* that might prompt one to suspect that it is somewhat strained, relative to standard written English. For me, the core idea of "waves breaking (over something)," is perfectly normal; but less normal is the idea of "waves breaking forth" and even less so is that of something "making constant waves break forth." But these of course are only my own judgments (confirmed with other readers), rooted in the English I am familiar with and regard as standard, and some readers may find the cited wording unremarkable. I would hesitate to call the wording "ungrammatical," but rather a usage so awkward as to create a meaning-clash (waves cannot be "constant," so the presumed sense is that the waves constantly break forth, not in the sense of continuously but only repeatedly; but isn't it in the nature of waves – of anything – that they occur repeatedly?). My argument then is that linguistic analysis confirms that the phrasing relating to

Lenehan is strained and artificial, and that this is a tacit showing to us that Lenehan himself is under strain, dissembling, and maintaining a "front." This is matched by the calculatedness of the description of Lenehan's self-presentation, who wears his clothes with sea-dog jauntiness and in "toreador fashion." Lenehan, we sense, is anything but seadog or toreador, and the narrative itself seems to mock his threadbare pretences; compare, also, Corley's woman friend, no genuine sailor either, although she too evokes the latter with her "white sailor hat" (*Dubliners*, 54).

Transitivity analysis: trends in characters' semantic processes and roles

In the above discussion of the opening two paragraphs, a number of informal comments have been made about the kinds of activity each verb implies, and about who or what is the agent and the patient in the reported activities. But the semantic parsing and labeling system devised by the linguist Michael Halliday[4] enables us to make a more systematic and comprehensive classification of the clauses in a text, specifying the basic process of each clause and the semantic roles filled by the phrases in that clause. This is also known as transitivity analysis. We can use Hallidayan transitivity analysis to identify all the clauses that involve a particular character, noting what kind of *process* is involved (from among the Hallidayan array of six options: Material, Mental, Relational, Behavioral, Existential, and Verbal), and what kind of *role* in the process that the character fills. The idea is that in a revealing sense all conceivable clauses of English amount to a representation of the world's processes as one of these six core types. To refer just to the four main types (the Behavioral and Existential are relatively minor), all reports of physical actions and happenings are Material processes; all forms of thinking, perceiving, and reacting are Mental processes; all static descriptions and identifications are Relational processes; and all acts of communication are Verbal ones. A Hallidayan transitivity analysis throws into relief the core semantic framework of a text, and is often useful on narrative texts; it answers certain fundamental questions we might have about a narrative: which characters are, in this narrative, prominently occupying which of a very limited set of participant roles (most basically the "doer" roles – such as Actor, Senser, or Sayer – and the "done-to" roles – such as Goal, or Addressee); and which of the four basic processes mainly occur. Most of these labels will become clear in the following discussion, but it may be worth defining Goal at the outset. The Goal in a Material process is the person or entity that is acted upon or affected; in Active-voice sentences, the Goal is usually the grammatical Object. A narrative overwhelmingly consisting of Material processes in which the main character is repeatedly the Goal participant is immediately but foundationally different from one where Mental ones predominate, with the main character as Senser.

In addition to identifying the kinds of process involved in different parts of the story, we can go on to identify which of a small number of types of role is occupied by such main figures as Lenehan and Corley. In the following four examples (which are all Material process clauses), the grammatical Subject is Lenehan and he is the Actor in these Material processes. But a further distinction can be made between those Material processes which involve a Goal, as in

> He ate his food greedily . . . He paid twopence halfpenny to the slatternly girl.
> (*Dubliners*, 57–8)

and ones which are, significantly, Goal-less, as in

> Lenehan walked as far as the Shelbourne Hotel . . . He paused at last before the window of a poor-looking shop. (*Dubliners*, 56)

We can also go on to discriminate degrees or kinds of Goal-oriented material process clause: we can distinguish, for example, between Goals which are in fact part of the denoted Actor (as in *He strained his eyes as each tram stopped*) and Goals which are a quite separate person or thing (as in *The other . . . was at times obliged to step on to the road, owing to his companion's rudeness*, where Corley's rudeness is Actor, and Lenehan is Goal). The latter representation or "construal" (as it is sometimes called in Hallidayan linguistics) treats any human Actor involved as most dynamic and powerful, and any separate human Goal as almost reciprocally passive and powerless. An example of a Mental process clause also demonstrates how one process can be embedded within another. For instance, in the sentence:

> He found trivial all that was meant to charm him

there is a Mental process of finding or judging, with *He* as the Senser and *all that was meant to charm him [was] trivial* as the Phenomenon; but this Phenomenon is itself a process, of the Relational kind, those processes that identify or characterize with an intensive verb like *be*, *seem*, or *appear*. In some of the following commentary I have drawn on Nina Nørgaard's invaluable stylistic study of the story which uses the systemic linguistic transitivity classification in the course of a full and insightful analysis.[5]

Using even a quite simple version of the Hallidayan repertoire of the language's most fundamental roles and processes, a detailed profile can be prepared, noting that Lenehan is Carrier in so many Relational processes, Actor in so many Goal-less material processes and this many Goal-implying ones, and so on. If we think of each clause in which Lenehan is referred to as a "scenario" or a snapshot from Lenehan's life, his ways of being, we can treat the fact that Lenehan is so rarely a Goal-oriented Actor, so often a Goal-less one or occupying some other less dynamic role, as not only symptomatic but an articulation of his aimlessness and his self-pitying dependency, his chief resource being his (flagging) ability to put on an act, to keep up a façade. In this way a quite useful semantic/experiential "map" of a story or novel can be prepared – and depending on how the information is presented, some display of the narrative extension or progression can also be achieved. For example, if a novel is divided into sections, does the transitivity mapping show any interesting shifts in the representation options for particular characters, from the opening to the final section? In shorter and more unitary texts such as "Two Gallants" such shifts are likely to be slight, and it is often more useful simply to note the transitivity *trends* in a passage of narration, rather than embarking on an exhaustive parsing, labeling, and counting of types of process and types of participant role, all tabulated for each character. In other words, you don't have to be an expert grammarian to apply transitivity insights. You can simply look at passages such as the following in the round, and consider how it represents or construes Lenehan. I have highlighted phrases referring to Lenehan by using italics, and put the verbal core of each associated process in bold:

> *He* **walked** listlessly round Stephen's Green and then down Grafton Street. Though *his eyes* **took note of** many elements of the crowd through which *he* **passed** *they* **did** so morosely. *He* **found** trivial all that was meant to **charm** *him* and **did not answer** the glances which **invited** *him* to be bold. *He* **knew** that *he* **would have to speak** a great deal, to **invent** and to **amuse** and *his brain and throat* **were** too dry for such a task. The problem of how *he* **could pass** the hours till *he* **met** Corley again **troubled** *him* a little. *He* **could think** of no way of passing them but to **keep on walking**. *He* **turned** to the left when *he* **came** to the corner of Rutland Square and **felt** more at ease in the dark quiet street, the sombre look of which **suited** *his mood*. (*Dubliners*, 56)

Here we can see that while Lenehan is entirely the focus of attention, he is almost never represented as an agent (the Actor role) acting upon another person (the one – partial – exception is the still-in-the-future "till he met Corley again"). Instead, Lenehan is often the acted upon (the Goal role), or the performer of Goal-less movements, or recurrently the thinker of negative or defensive thoughts (Senser), and sometimes seemingly subject to the reactions of parts of his body (his eyes, his brain, and his throat).

If we study the passages describing Lenehan walking the streets of Dublin, between his initial encounter with Corley and the latter's return, we find a high proportion of the clauses have intransitive (Goal-less) verbs with Lenehan as Actor. But, as Nørgaard comments, the effect of "ineffectuality" which is noted by many readers stems not simply from the intransitivity of the clauses but also from the typical semantic associations of the particular verbs used here: *walked, halted, turned, went, came, passed, paused, stopped, set off*. Granted, there may be nothing ineffectual or purposeless associated with these verbs taken individually: *halted, went, set off*, etc. Rather it is their collective use in close proximity to each other to describe Lenehan's actions, ones lacking any stated Goal, that promotes the interpretation of him as purposeless, frustrated, or trapped. A good way to get a sense of this is to ask yourself, "What sort of scenario might it be in which an entity walked, then halted, then turned, then went, then came, then passed, and so on?" You might conceivably say, well, this could be someone working in a stockroom, or a shop, fetching and carrying things; but if you restrict the picture further by stipulating the lack of stated Goals, i.e., that this is halting, turning, coming and going without particular affected entities, then only a few scenarios would seem plausible: one of trapped or imprisoned movement, such as that of a prisoner exercising or an animal in the zoo; or one of free but aimless movement, such as that of someone lost in alien territory. Which of these is Lenehan? How different are they anyway?

And what semantic roles does Corley fill? Corley is of course much less "narrated" than Lenehan, so that there's less semantic representation to inspect; but by contrast with Lenehan he is as frequently the Actor in Goal-directed material processes as Goal-less ones. Further, he is rarely the Senser of perception-related Mental processes (only four, as Nørgaard notes,[6] in comparison to the twenty to which Lenehan is linked). Equally importantly Corley's few perception acts are straightforward and his own – he *stares* or he *gazes* – while Lenehan's, as I will explain below, are oblique or refracted, done by his eyes or his gaze, not by the man himself.

With so much of the story about Lenehan and what he sees and thinks (Lenehan as focalized and focalizer), the precise wording of the narrative reports of Lenehan's watching, seeing, and looking repay scrutiny. In general, the text declares, it is not Lenehan who sees but only his eyes, represented as a distinct organ or tool dissociated from Lenehan as a person, with a mind, body, and will. Nørgaard usefully cites a number of instances in which Lenehan's eyes do the looking, and she sensitizes us to the alternative and less appropriate effect that an alternative wording might have given.[7] Here are just two examples:

Actual wording:
His eyes . . . glanced at every moment towards his companion's face.

Alternative wording:
He glanced at every moment towards his companion's face [or even: towards his companion].

Actual wording:
His eyes made a swift anxious scrutiny of the young woman's appearance.

Alternative wording:
He made a swift anxious scrutiny of the young woman's appearance.
(Dubliners, 49, 55)

In all these cases, where a simple *He* has been displaced by a phrase such as *His eyes*, a kind of markedness also operates. Here, the use of a longer construction – *His eyes* – where a shorter one would ordinarily have sufficed, implies that the longer phrase has been used in order to communicate something extra. To report continually that not Lenehan the person but only "his eyes" *glanced, searched*, and *made a swift scrutiny* is to imply a distance between Lenehan and his sense organs, his body. It may suggest dissociation or alienation. In these sentences Lenehan's eyes are reported as if functioning at a remove from the man himself, and not as a tool that he controllingly uses. The latter interpretation might be prompted by sentences like *He used his eyes to make a swift anxious scrutiny* or *With his eyes he glanced . . .* but neither of these occurs in the text. We might even claim that neither invented sentence is likely or "suitable" in the narrative style that depicts Lenehan, being much too purposive as distinct from reactive. Whatever the eyes see, glance at, or scrutinize, Lenehan himself, as a person with free will, is unable to absorb what they perceive, let alone act upon it. The careful reader may notice these things, but a transitivity analysis lays bare how systematic the representation is, marked and systematic enough to be an important contribution to the narrative point of the story.

To what extent are reading and the reader "directed" by the patterns uncovered in the semantic analyses of clause processes proposed here? I think it is more a matter of prompting than compulsion: the particular patterns *foster* an interpretation that fits them, rather than insisting. The linguistic detail of a narrative text guides its uptake, and the grammar of the language is a kind of "baggage" that we come to any new text equipped with and constrained by. So particular kinds of language analysis and language attentiveness may help our reading (in a sense, they must help!), but there are few guarantees, few certainties, and no "master linguistic code" that tells a reader how a text must be interpreted. A linguistic orientation can only contribute to interpretation and understanding, not impose them. We see this again in relation to my final topic, Free Indirect Thought, which is all to do with the strange feeling we sometimes have, as we read a passage of narrative, that the narrator's "voice" has been supplanted by some character's, even though the character is still being referred to as a *she* (or *he*) and the "voicing" is still in the narrative tense. It's almost as if we are reading two "voices" at once, even though that sounds unnatural, and impossible to prove.

Free Indirect Thought

The kind of narration known as Free Indirect Thought (henceforth FIT; it is known by many other names besides) has been widely used in literary fiction of the last hundred years or so, and Joyce was a skilled exponent. A stylistic analysis of this narrative technique further underscores the relevance of linguistic concepts to methods of narrative study; in addition, my analysis complements the discussions of dialogue and consciousness representation by Bronwen Thomas and David Herman in their respective chapters in this volume.

Essentially, FIT affords the reader the impression of encountering a character's ordered thoughts very much in that character's own words, and from that reflecting character's current perspective (via deictic or orientating words and phrases, the commonest of which include words such as *here, now, this, today*, and so on). FIT does this despite the fact that no quotation marks are present, there isn't the intrusion of a reporting clause (such as *he thought* or *she realized*), the narrative tense is unchanged (e.g., it remains past tense if that has been the one used for normal narration in the story), and there is no switch away from third-person pronouns to first-person ones. In a story like "Two Gallants," for example, the narrative appears to proceed smoothly, in the past tense and referring to Lenehan in the third person. But a point comes where the narration is no longer detached and external: it adopts the character's viewpoint, revealing what Lenehan alone (and not "the narrator") is thinking, in Lenehan's language. This modulation from external narration to FIT can be seen fairly clearly if we compare the following two extracts. Both extracts involve Lenehan's thoughts and reactions, but they represent them by different formal means. The first extract uses "external narration," the second uses the technique of Free Indirect Thought:

1. The problem of how he could pass the hours till he met Corley again troubled him a little. He could think of no way of passing them but to keep on walking. He turned to the left when he came to the corner of

Rutland Square and felt more at ease in the dark quiet street, the sombre look of which suited his mood. (*Dubliners*, 56)

2. He was tired of knocking about, of pulling the devil by the tail, of shifts and intrigues. He would be thirty-one in November. Would he never get a good job? Would he never have a home of his own? He thought how pleasant it would be to have a warm fire to sit by and a good dinner to sit down to. (*Dubliners*, 57)

In the first extract, there is little sense that any of these words are Lenehan's words: they are the narrator's, about Lenehan. (And they tell us things that Lenehan himself would surely not "think into words": "now that I've reached the corner of Rutland Square I am turning to the left . . .") In the second extract, despite the past tense and third-person pronoun, much of the first four sentences feels to us to be Lenehan's words, shadowed by an implicit "he thought to himself" or something similar. Lenehan might well have thought: "I'm tired of knocking about . . . will I never have a home of my own?" The questions, for example, are Lenehan's addressed to himself – certainly not ones from the narrator to the reader. As for the final sentence, this might equally have been cast as FIT, if Joyce had deleted its initial *He thought* and began with *How pleasant*. But he has chosen to use Indirect Thought, making the teller a little more prominent and Lenehan's "voice" a little more distant. In the second passage it is *as if* the text had moved from the externality of third person and past tense to the inwardness of first person and present tense, in relating Lenehan's thoughts, but without the jarring effect that such a move in actuality would have caused. This may be confirmed if we imagine 2* appearing instead of 2, in the relevant context:

2*. In his imagination . . . he heard Corley's voice in deep energetic gallantries and saw again the leer of the young woman's mouth. This vision made him feel keenly his own poverty of purse and spirit. He thought to himself: I am tired of knocking about, of pulling the devil by the tail, of shifts and intrigues. I'll be thirty-one in November. Will I never get a good job? Will I never have a home of my own? He thought how pleasant it would be to have a warm fire to sit by and a good dinner to sit down to.

In the first person parts of 2*, given the detached and occasionally ironic tone of the narration of the story, there is just "too much" hand-over of voice and viewpoint to Lenehan; by comparison, the version using FIT has just the right amount.

As will be apparent, FIT is a subtle way of dramatizing a character's thoughts; in a story where the narration is largely detached and external, chiefly reporting information about what happened that August evening that any of Lenehan's more observant acquaintances might have been able to relay, FIT enables departures from that norm, so as to convey most of the content (but not all the form: not the pronouns or tenses) of a character's thoughts about important or revealing matters. Or what in the character's own view are important matters: FIT is used in the final paragraphs to dramatize Lenehan, wracked by anxiety and petty suspense, embittered and suspicious that Corley has already seen the woman home or will fail to obtain money from her – expectations that, happily or otherwise, prove false. More generally, tools from linguistics here help us to recognize those sentences or fragments that are or may be FIT, and help us to think more clearly about why they are strange and ambivalent, and why so many critics have found FIT to be such a powerful means of dramatizing the conflict of voices and values, or dialogism, within the subtlest narrative fiction.

Final remarks

In this chapter I have briefly introduced a handful of language-based elements that are deployed extensively in "Two Gallants" and are central to the story's quality. I hope to have shown that the specificity of the texture of literary narratives (perhaps especially in modern short stories) is crucial to how and why we value them. And that in turn is why commentary on the narrative's language is worth attempting. By means of unorthodox or "weighted" choices of grammar and wording in the story's first two scene-setting paragraphs, the foregrounding of particular transitivity patterns in the representation of Lenehan, and the modulation from neutral narration into Free Indirect Thought to suggest Lenehan's growing frustration and anxiety, the language itself "tells" important themes of this story. Most of the linguistic patterns discussed here, for example, point to Lenehan as not merely selfish or self-centered, but what we might call Self-enclosed: dispositionally unable to give, unable to connect with others as a responsible agent, caught up in an instinctual herd-like circulation and exchange. It is a commonplace to say that a classic story like "Two Gallants" cannot be replaced by a paraphrase version without enormous loss; looking systematically at Joyce's language choices helps us pinpoint what we might lose.

NOTES

1. James Joyce, "Two Gallants." *Dubliners* (Harmondsworth: Penguin, 1968), p. 49.
2. See e.g. M. A. K. Halliday, *An Introduction to Functional Grammar*, 2nd edition (London: Edward Arnold, 1994).

3. Margot Norris, "Gambling with Gambles in 'Two Gallants.'" *Novel: A Forum on Fiction* 29:1 (1995), p. 35.
4. Halliday, *An Introduction to Functional Grammar*.
5. Nina Nørgaard, *Systemic Functional Linguistics and Literary Analysis: A Hallidayan Approach to Joyce – A Joycean Approach to Halliday* (Odense: University of Southern Denmark Press, 2003).
6. Nina Nørgaard, *Systemic Functional Linguistics and Literary Analysis*, p. 77.
7. Nørgaard, *Systemic Functional Linguistics and Literary Analysis*, p. 83.

17

DAVID HERMAN

Cognition, emotion, and consciousness

When he saw Freddy Malins coming across the room to visit his mother Gabriel left the chair free for him and retired into the embrasure of the window. The room had already cleared and from the back room came the clatter of plates and knives. Those who still remained in the drawing-room seemed tired of dancing and were conversing quietly in little groups. Gabriel's warm trembling fingers tapped the cold pane of the window. How cool it must be outside! How pleasant it would be to walk out alone, first along by the river and then through the park! The snow would be lying on the branches of the trees and forming a bright cap on the top of the Wellington Monument. How much more pleasant it would be there than at the supper-table![1]

At this point in "The Dead," the last short story included in James Joyce's 1914 collection *Dubliners*, Gabriel Conroy is taking a moment by himself just before dinner is served at the holiday party hosted annually by Gabriel's two aunts, Kate and Julia Morkan, and by their niece, Mary Jane. Gabriel is trying to prepare himself for the speech he is to deliver after dinner. This moment is followed in turn by a life-changing revelation by his wife, Gretta, who tells Gabriel about how a young man named Michael Furey in effect chose her over life itself, standing out in a cold rain in ill-health for one last chance to see her. Below I provide a fuller synopsis of "The Dead" as a basis for exploring the crucial role that representations of consciousness play in the narrative as a whole; but let me dwell for a moment on the many manifestations of Gabriel's mind in just these few lines. Building on work by narrative scholars such as Alan Palmer and Ralf Schneider, my preliminary discussion suggests that analyzing fictional minds like Gabriel's entails giving an account of readers' minds, too – of how readers interpret particular textual details as information about characters' attempts to make sense of the world around them.[2]

As he does throughout the story, Gabriel functions in the quoted passage as what narratologists, borrowing from the critical writings of Henry James, call a "reflector" – that is, a center of consciousness through whom situations and events told about by a heterodiegetic or third-person narrator are refracted.[3] Accordingly, although the narrator remains distinct from Gabriel (hence the use of the third-person pronoun *he*), the narration is filtered through Gabriel's vantage-point on the scenes he encounters over the course of the story.[4] Likewise, as the passage suggests, the story concerns Gabriel's perceptions of his current surroundings, memories of past events, and inferences about others' (as well as his own) mental states and dispositions. It may seem strange to say that Gabriel has to formulate inferences about (the contents of) his own mind; but we see him doing just that in the passage, when he speculates about how pleasant he himself would find it to be outside at this moment. Similarly, though in a more far-reaching way, Gretta's story about Michael Furey at the end of "The Dead" prompts Gabriel to re-evaluate his motives and values and to construct a new profile of his own emotional make-up.[5]

Meanwhile, in the first sentence of the passage the verb *saw* indexes Gabriel's perceptual activity, whereas the subsequent participial phrase (*coming across the room to visit his mother*) marks an inference that Gabriel has drawn about Freddy's motives in moving across the room. Note, too, that the participle itself – *coming* – suggests movement toward Gabriel's vantage-point. *Come* and *go* are verbs of motion, and forms based on them (gerunds, participles) can be used to suggest movement toward or away from, respectively, an orienting viewpoint.[6] In the second sentence the temporal adverb *already* suggests another inference: namely, that there is an expected time-line for events associated with the party, with one phase of the party giving way to the next according to a regular process, and that at this moment in the storyworld the pre-dinner-dancing phase is giving way to the mealtime phase, whose onset is marked by the clatter of cutlery issuing from the back room. Again, since Gabriel's is the orienting perspective on unfolding events, readers are likely to interpret *already* as an index of Gabriel's understanding of how the present moment relates to previous and upcoming stages of the party. Next, in the following sentence it is the word *warm* that is freighted with Gabriel's consciousness, more specifically, his felt subjective awareness of the difference between the temperature of his finger and that of the window.

Finally, the last four sentences of the passage feature imaginative projections by Gabriel – hypothetical forays into the way it is or would be like outside the house where the party is taking place. Once more, the verbal texture of the passage reflects the operations of Gabriel's consciousness. For one thing, the exclamation marks suggest sentiments or thoughts that have forcibly struck Gabriel, and that are therefore linked to his subjectivity rather than the neutral, non-exclamatory discourse of the narrator. Further, the sequence of clauses containing verbs with modal auxiliaries ("How cool it *must be* . . . ," "The snow *would be* lying . . . ," "How pleasant it *would be* . . . ," etc.) exemplifies a process that linguists have termed the *irrealis* modality. This modality encompasses all the semantic resources that enable language users to signal that they that are not fully committed to the truth of a proposition about the world.[7] In this case the main resource is the subjunctive mood signaled by the auxiliary verbs. Coupled with the exclamation marks that express Gabriel's subjectivity, the subjunctive indicates that Gabriel is again framing inferences about the storyworld, but in this case inferences based on probabilistic reasoning rather than on evidence to which he has direct, perceptual access. At the same time, Gabriel's inferences concerning the outside environment are themselves second-order cues: they prompt readers to build a working model of the character's current emotional state and his larger frame of mind. Given what Gabriel infers, I myself conclude that he is feeling trepidatious about delivering his speech, and that he would prefer to be alone in a wintry world whose very inhospitableness affords for him at this moment a sense of relief from the social pressures bound up with the party.

As I have tried to suggest thus far, a fine-grained textual analysis can illuminate how narratives represent the moment-by-moment experiences of fictional minds, as well as the coloration that those experiences acquire from the characters' broader cognitive and emotional stances toward situations and events. I would now like to move from looking at individual sentences to outlining some general parameters for building models of characters' minds, using "The Dead" as my case study. I begin by reviewing the classical "speech-category" approach to consciousness representation in narrative – this being Alan Palmer's term for the approach developed by Dorrit Cohn and other narrative scholars, in which strategies for representing characters' verbal utterances furnish a paradigm for understanding the means by which narratives represent their minds (Palmer, *Fictional Minds*, 53–86).[8] Then I discuss how more recent work in narrative theory (and other fields) provides new ways of studying the nexus between narrative and consciousness, new insights into the guiding principles on which readers rely when converting words on the page into information about fictional minds. To furnish context for my discussion, as well as a sense of the complexity of all the factors impinging on readers' (re)construction of Gabriel's and the other characters' minds, I give a more detailed paraphrase of Joyce's story. My claim is that any attempt to paraphrase Joyce's story must take into account the cognitive and emotional states and processes of the characters as they act and interact in the storyworld; these states and processes must be construed as integral to the core events or "gist" of the narrative, not as optional or peripheral elements that can be safely omitted from the story-paraphrase.[9]

In particular, I highlight four dimensions of mind thrown into relief by my own paraphrase of the narrative: the construal or conceptualization of events from one or more perspectives in the storyworld; characters' inferences about their own and one another's minds; the use of discourse pertaining to emotions; and "qualia," a term used by philosophers of mind to refer to the felt, subjective character of conscious experience. These four dimensions constitute crucial concerns for postclassical approaches to the study of consciousness representation.

The speech-category approach – and beyond

In her foundational study of strategies for representing consciousness in narrative fiction, Dorrit Cohn draws on theories of speech representation as the basis for her account of how narrative texts afford access to fictional minds. Just as narratives can use direct discourse, indirect discourse, and free indirect discourse to present the utterances of characters, fictional texts can use what Cohn calls quoted monologue, psycho-narration, and narrated monologue to represent the thought processes of fictional minds. Subsequent theorists, seeking to underscore even more clearly the assumed analogy between modes of speech and thought representation, have renamed Cohn's three modes as direct thought, indirect thought, and free indirect thought, respectively.[10]

Before I turn to the possibilities and limitations of this speech-category approach to consciousness representation, let me provide some instances of speech representation in Joyce's text. (1)–(3) exemplify direct, indirect, and free indirect speech:

(1) –Gretta dear, what are you thinking about?　　　　　("The Dead," 218)

(2) Mrs Malins, who had been silent all through the supper, said that her son was going down to Mount Melleray in a week or so.　　　　　(200)

(3) On the landing outside the drawing-room Gabriel found his wife and Mary Jane trying to persuade Miss Ivors to stay for supper. But Miss Ivors, who had put on her hat and was buttoning her cloak, would not stay. *She did not feel in the least hungry and she had already overstayed her time.*

(195, emphasis added)

In (1), readers can assume that the narrator reproduces Gabriel's vocalized utterance such that it mirrors the way it was performed in the storyworld,[11] whereas in (2) the narrator reports rather than reproduces Mrs Malins's utterances. Meanwhile, the italicized segment of (3) is free indirect speech: although it is couched as a third-person report given by the narrator, it also contains expressivity markers that point to the speech patterns of a particular character (here, Miss Ivors). Falling into this category is the formulaic locution *feel in the least hungry* and the evaluative appraisal implied by *had already overstayed* – an appraisal that can be assumed to emanate from Miss Ivors herself rather than from the narrator. Given that the characters are engaged in conversation at this point in the narrative, the forms just mentioned can be taken as insinuations of Miss Ivors's voice into the narrator's discourse, rather than as transcriptions of her unspoken thoughts.[12]

The grounding assumption of the speech-category approach to consciousness is that the same categories used to analyze speech representations such as (1)–(3) can be mapped on to narrative strategies used to present the thought processes of fictional minds. Analysts using this approach would search Joyce's text for passages that can be read as mind-presenting corollaries of the above styles of speech representation, that is, as instances of direct thought, indirect thought, and free indirect thought. These modes are exemplified in (4)–(6):

(4) [Gabriel] repeated to himself a phrase he had written in his review: *One feels that one is listening to a thought-tormented music.* (192)

(5) He thought of how she who lay beside him had locked in her heart for so many years that image of her lover's eyes when he had told her that he did not wish to live. (223)

(6) The indelicate clacking of the men's heels and the shuffling of their soles reminded him that their grade of culture differed from his. *He would only make himself ridiculous by quoting poetry to them which they could not understand . . . His whole speech was a mistake from first to last, an utter failure.* (179, emphasis added)

In (4), the first sentence reports a mental action that Gabriel performs (silently repeating words to himself), while the second sentence directly reports the contents of that action. By contrast, (5) presents Gabriel's thoughts in a summary rather than direct way. (6), finally, can be interpreted as an instance of free indirect thought. The third-person report, in the first sentence, gives way in the subsequent sentences to narration suffused with Gabriel's subjectivity. In these sentences, Joyce continues to use third-person pronouns along with past-tense verbs, although these can be read as "backshifted" from the present tense that would have been used in a direct thought quotation (along the lines of "I will only make myself ridiculous . . ."). At the same time, the evaluative appraisals expressed through word choices (*ridiculous, mistake, utter failure*) can be assumed to reflect Gabriel's own tacit construal of the situation.

Even this cursory discussion should suggest how the speech category approach to fictional minds has yielded important insights into the interface between narrative and consciousness. In particular, it illuminates how specific textual cues can be used to indicate a more or less mediated relationship between narrators' discourse and the subjective awareness of particular characters. As Alan Palmer argues, however, this classical approach captures only some of the phenomena relevant for research on narrative representations of consciousness. For Palmer, the speech category approach has induced analysts to focus solely on inner speech, with the result that theories of consciousness representation in narrative have been "distorted by the grip of the verbal norm" (*Fictional Minds*, 53). Building on Palmer's claims, the following sections explore aspects of consciousness representation in "The Dead" that are not reducible to techniques for presenting inner speech. Indeed, paraphrasing the story serves to emphasize the extent to which narrative understanding hinges on a wide variety of inferences about the states and processes of fictional minds – including inferences about what they infer is going on in their own and others' minds.

Paraphrasing the "The Dead": or, the irreducibility of consciousness

Gabriel Conroy is Aunt Kate and Aunt Julia's favorite nephew. True, his dead mother's sisters have made a standing joke of Gabriel's solicitude toward his wife, Gretta, as exemplified by his insistence that she wear galoshes in inclement weather (178). Yet they also count on Gabriel to carve the goose for the assembled guests, to make an appropriate speech after dinner to commemorate the occasion, and to ensure that Freddy Malins isn't too drunk to come upstairs, despite (or perhaps because of) his having been compelled by his mother to pledge temperance just a few days previously (185). For his part, Gabriel leads a rich inner life during the few hours traced in the main action of the story. In his role as the reflector or orienting consciousness, Gabriel reveals himself to be a patchwork of traits, dispositions, and attitudes, ranging from self-superiority, obtuseness, jealousy, and romantic idealization, to self-doubt, perceptiveness, generosity, and an ability to come to terms with the complexity of his own and others' experiences and emotions.

For example, although Gabriel is initially seized by a "vague terror" when Gretta tells him that she thinks Furey died for her, feeling that "at the hour when he had hoped to triumph, some impalpable and vindictive being was coming against him, gathering forces against him in its vague world" (220), as he considers further the circumstances and implications of Furey's death, "a strange friendly pity for her entered his soul" (222). Indeed, Gabriel has by story's end undergone a major personal transformation. The extent of that transformation is evident in the contrast between Gabriel's afterdinner speech, which downplays the sad memories of lost loved ones and emphasizes the importance of "our work among the living" (204), and his reflections at the end of the story. His mind turning to thoughts of Aunt Julia's imminent death, and more generally of how "[o]ne by one they were all becoming shades" (222), Gabriel considers the undying legacy of Furey's love for Gretta and concludes that living passionately in the moment is to be preferred to longevity bought at the price of cautious circumspection, and ultimately fading away anyway (222–3). At the same time, Gabriel in effect abolishes the sharp boundary he tried to draw in his speech between death and life, the past and the present, absence and presence. The snow is indeed general all over Ireland (211, 223), suggesting the connectedness rather than the separation of the living and the dead, those attending the party and those buried in lonely churchyards like the one in which Furey is now interred.

This global paraphrase of the story encompasses many propositions about fictional minds; the rest of my chapter identifies some categories into which those propositions can be grouped. In other words, by breaking down my own interpretation of the story into several types of mind-related propositions, my discussion reverses the path followed by readers as they build up a model of the characters' minds on the basis of textual cues. I suggest that, as they create models of this sort, readers use heuristics or guiding principles like the ones outlined below to sift through the textual data and organize them into different (but interrelated) kinds of information about consciousness.

Consciousness representation in narrative: postclassical approaches

Perspective and the conceptualization of events

In a way that complements Manfred Jahn's discussion of classical accounts of narrative perspective in chapter 7, perspective can be interpreted as a reflex of the mind or minds conceptualizing scenes represented in narrative texts.[13] To develop this interpretation I draw on work in cognitive linguistics, which examines how language structure and use reflect more general cognitive abilities of embodied human minds.

The basic idea behind what cognitive linguists call *conceptualization* or *construal* is that one and the same situation or event can be linguistically encoded in different ways – ways that reflect different possibilities for mentally construing the world.[14] I can say *The rabbit ate the tomato plant*, but also *The tomato plant was eaten by the rabbit*, with my choice of the active or passive voice corresponding to different conceptualizations of the scene. These construals select a different element of the scene as the focal participant: the active voice selects the rabbit; the passive voice selects the tomato plant. More generally, cognitive linguists such as Ronald W. Langacker and Leonard Talmy suggest that a range of cognitive abilities support the processes of conceptualization that surface in linguistic choices of this kind. My specific concern here is with what Langacker calls *focal adjustment*, or the ways in which construals are affected by language users having an embodied, spatio-temporally situated perspective on events; Talmy likewise explores this process, characterizing perspective as a "conceptual structuring system."[15] Langacker's and Talmy's ideas, taken together, yield a rich framework for studying how narrative perspective affords information about minds.

Drawing on this framework, theorists can ask questions about narrative perspective that could not even be formulated within the classical models, while still preserving the (important) insights afforded by earlier theories. Analysts can explore how narratives may represent scenes that are either **statically** (synoptically) or **dynamically** (sequentially) scanned by the perceptual agents construing them. Scenes will have a relatively wide or narrow **scope, focal participants**, and **backgrounded elements**, and an **orientation** within a horizontal/vertical dimensional grid. Scenes are also **"sighted"** from particular temporal and spatial directions, and viewpoints on scenes can be **distal, medial**, or **proximal**, that is, range from being far away to being up close. Each such distance increment, further, may carry a default expectation about the **degree of granularity** (or level of detail) of the construal. Closer perspectives on scenes generally yield finer-grained (= more granular, more detailed) representations; more distant perspectives generally yield coarser-grained (= less granular, less detailed) representations.[16]

This approach affords a more unified, systematic treatment of the perspective-related markers of Gabriel's mind that I discussed in the opening section of my chapter. The passage reveals how Gabriel's perspective constitutes a conceptual structuring system, in which Freddy Malins and his mother are, initially, the focal participants in a sequentially scanned scene. The past-tense indicative verbs indicate that the scene is sighted from a temporal viewpoint located later on the time-line than the point occupied by the represented events. Spatially, the scene is sighted from a viewpoint situated on the same plane as the represented action: Gabriel is not observing the scene from below, for example, as is the case when he construes Gretta as "a symbol of something" at the top of the stairs (210). Further, Gabriel's initial medium-distance viewpoint on the scene (from the chair next to Mrs. Malins) affords a medium-scope representation with a corresponding, mid-level degree of granularity or detail.

Then, when Gabriel takes up his new position in the embrasure of the window, his distance from the scene increases, producing a wider-scope conceptualization of the scene that has a correspondingly lower degree of granularity: Gabriel construes the scene in terms of groups rather than individuals. The factors of distance, scope, and granularity of construal thus co-vary systematically: as you get farther away from something, you see more of the context that surrounds it but with less overall detail, and these perspectival constraints on people's mental lives also shape how they use language – for example, how they produce and interpret narratives. Meanwhile, Gabriel has now moved much closer to the window, his position affording a proximal, narrow-scope, and highly granular, detailed representation of his own fingers tapping the cold pane. The shift to free indirect thought in "How cool it must be outside!" marks the onset of a new conceptualization – this time of an imagined scene outside. As the new construal gets underway, distance, scope, and granularity again co-vary: the hypothetical scene is farther away than the window, encompasses the whole area by the river and through the park, and is not envisioned in any detailed way. But then Gabriel imagines specific features of the scene, the degree of granularity increasing dramatically to the point where the snow on the branches of trees and on the top of the Wellington monument comes into focus. Working against default expectations about how much granularity is available from what perspectival distance, Joyce's text evokes the power of the imagination to transcend the constraints of space and time. Gabriel's construal of the scene in the park thus emulates the ability of Joyce's own fictional discourse to transport readers to another time and place.

Inferences about one's own and other minds

Other mind-relevant propositions contained in my paraphrase of Joyce's story can be grouped together to form a different category: namely, those describing the characters' inferences about their own and other minds. Relevant in this context are fundamental, generic processes by which humans attribute mental states, properties, and dispositions both to themselves and to their social cohorts. These processes are part of what psychologists refer to as the native "Theory of Mind" in terms of which people make sense of their own behavior and that of the people they observe and interact with. Philosophers tend to refer to the same native inference-yielding resources as "folk psychology."[17] At issue is people's everyday understanding of how thinking works, the rough-and-ready heuristics to which they resort in thinking about thinking itself. We use these heuristics to impute motives or goals to others, to evaluate the bases of our own conduct, and to make predictions about future reactions to events. Such thinking about thinking points beyond inner speech and solitary self-communings to the "social mind in action" that Palmer identifies as the object of study for postclassical approaches to consciousness representation (*Fictional Minds*, 130–69).

Although my paraphrase of the story does not purport to be exhaustive, nor the only defensible interpretation of Joyce's narrative, it does feature inferences by the characters concerning their own and others' minds that could not be deleted or modified without changing the gist of the story itself. For example, the solicitousness that Aunt Julia and Aunt Kate impute to Gabriel is part of a larger constellation of traits that they ascribe to him; this ascription in turn licenses their assumption that he will be able to take the measure of Freddy and judge whether he is too drunk to attend the party. Hence, to interpret Aunt Kate's and Aunt Julia's words and comportment as evidence of their distrust or dislike of Gabriel would be to misinterpret the narrative.

More than this, however, "The Dead" turns on Gabriel's recognition that he has framed mistaken inferences concerning Gretta's thoughts, emotions, and intentions during the scene in their room at the Gresham hotel. "While he had been full of memories of their secret life together" (219), hypothesizing that "[p]erhaps she had felt the impetuous desire that was in him and then the yielding mood had come upon her" (217), Gretta is in fact grieving Furey's death all over again. Made painfully aware of how disparate their memories and emotions are at this moment, Gabriel stands stock-still in astonishment at Gretta's tearful reaction to his attempt to draw her near to him. What causes Gabriel the greatest distress is Gretta's own inference that Michael Furey died for her sake. Further, by using an embedded narrative told by Gretta to convey the supposed cause of Furey's death, the text suggests that the process of ascribing beliefs, desires, and intentions to oneself and others goes all the way down, so to speak. Rather than conveying bedrock facts about Furey, the story represents Gretta making her best effort to understand what happened, and during their interaction her attempt informs Gabriel's inferences about Gretta's mind. That process in turn shapes Gabriel's self-understanding, generating new inferences about his own long-held assumptions and beliefs – about the bearing of the past on the present, about Gretta's and his relationship, about his capacity to love.

Emotions and emotion discourse

As Peter Stearns points out, there is a basic tension between naturalist and constructionist approaches to emotion. Whereas naturalists argue for the existence of innate, biologically grounded, emotions that are more or less uniform across cultures and sub-cultures, constructionists argue that emotions are culturally specific.[18] To study the cultural and rhetorical grounding of emotion discourse, constructionists have developed the concept of "emotionology," which concerns the collective emotional standards of a culture as opposed to the experience of emotion itself.[19] Emotionologies are frameworks for conceptualizing emotions, their causes, and how participants in discourse are likely to display them. Narratives, which at once ground themselves in, and help build, frameworks of this sort, provide insight into a culture's or sub-culture's emotionology – and also into how members of those (sub)-cultures use these systems to make sense of minds.

Any paraphrase of Joyce's text would have to take into account the emotional valences that particular situations and events have for the characters in the storyworld. For example, a paraphrase of "The Dead" would not be adequate if it failed to mention that Gretta was upset by her memories of Furey, and that her non-responsiveness to Gabriel's sexual overtures in their hotel room stems from this emotional disturbance. What is more, mutually consistent paraphrases can differ in the degree of emotionological detail that they include. The global paraphrase provided earlier is relatively coarse-grained: it traces in broad terms the emotional arc corresponding to Gabriel's and Gretta's divergent paths through the storyworld, but it leaves out other details that would be included in a finer-grained paraphrase – for example, the resentment Gabriel feels when he remembers his mother's sullen opposition to his marriage with Gretta (187). The system of emotion terms and concepts in which Joyce and his readers participate makes such ascriptions of emotion legible. To put the same point another way, emotionology allows readers to interpret characters' utterances and actions as coherent *classes* of behaviors rather than as random assemblages of words and deeds; what the characters say and do can be sorted into classes of behaviors in which one is likely to engage when motivated by happiness, resentment, fear, sadness, etc.

More than indicating how emotionology provides resources for narrative understanding, however, Joyce's text also suggests how stories have the power to (re)shape emotionology itself. As "The Dead" reveals, narrative provides a means for reassessing the emotion potential of whole sectors of experience, binding or detaching emotional responses to or from aspects of experience. Prior to the process of storytelling, these dimensions of experience may be uninvested or else overly saturated with the emotions at issue. Thus, using Gretta's narrative to make sense of Furey's role in her life, Gabriel experiences emotions progressing from jealousy and fear through empathy and resignation, along the way building a new emotional vocabulary with which to understand Gretta, the past, and himself. Stories do not just emanate from cultural understandings of emotion but also constitute a primary instrument for adjusting those systems of emotion terms and concepts to lived experience.

Narrative, experientiality, and qualia

Qualia is the (controversial) term that I will use for the fourth guiding principle on which readers rely to assemble textual data into categories or kinds of information relevant to consciousness. As Janet Levin notes, "[t]he terms *quale* and *qualia* (pl.) are most commonly used to characterize the qualitative, experiential, or felt properties of mental states" – what Thomas Nagel characterized as the sense or feeling of "what it is like" for someone or something to undergo conscious experiences.[20] In the philosophy of mind, the notion of qualia continues to be debated among scholars who have adopted a range of positions on their status. Some philosophers have drawn on Nagel's study to argue for the irreducibly subjective or "first-person" nature of consciousness, its fundamental incompatibility with the "third-person" orientation of scientific discourse. Others, such as Daniel Dennett, have suggested that conscious experience only seems to have an irreducibly subjective character, and that consciousness is therefore susceptible of description and explanation in third-person terms. For his part, David Lodge has pursued a middle way by suggesting that narrative fiction, and more specifically the use of free indirect discourse/thought, makes it possible to combine "the realism of assessment that belongs to third-person narration with the realism of presentation that comes from first-person narration."[21] Analysts can build on Lodge's argument by exploring whether narrative in general not only encapsulates but also provides access to qualia. Is it the case that narratives, by virtue of their very structure and dynamics, in fact enable us to know "what it is like" to be someone else, and maybe also ourselves?

Monika Fludernik has made *experientiality*, or the impact of narrated situations and events on an experiencing consciousness, a core property of narrative itself.[22] Fludernik's account suggests that unless a text or a discourse registers the pressure of events on a embodied human or at least human-like consciousness, then that text or discourse will not be construed by interpreters as a full-fledged narrative, but rather as (at best) a report or chronicle. From this perspective, what makes Joyce's text a narrative is not only its tracing of a sequence of events unfolding within a particularized storyworld but also its representation of what it is like for Gabriel to live through those events as an embodied human experiencer – an experiencing consciousness for which the touch of warm fingers against the cold panes of the window has a distinctive, irreducibly first-person feel, as does the sense of fear that overwhelms Gabriel, at first, when Gretta tells him that Michael Furey died for her.

Joyce's text might also be used, however, to substantiate the converse claim, which is a more radical one: that we cannot even have a notion of the felt quality of experience without narrative. On this account, it is only by telling a story that Gretta can convey to Gabriel a sense of what it was like to have experienced Furey's death, and what it is like to remember it so vividly and so painfully in the here and now. In turn, the felt, subjective character of Gretta's encounter with the dying Furey derives from, or is at least inextricably interlinked with, the process of constructing a narrative about that encounter. Hence the experiential profile of events emerges from the situated narrative practices that Gretta and Gabriel use to make sense of them. The act of storytelling represented in the text thus mirrors how, at another level, Joyce's narrative gives readers access to what it is like for these characters to experience the life-changing events that unfold over the course of "The Dead" as a whole.

Conclusion

This chapter has outlined directions for the study of consciousness representation in narrative. But the program for inquiry sketched here constitutes only a beginning. Other aspects of the nexus between narrative and mind will need to be brought within the scope of investigation, and additional tools, from multiple disciplines, will be needed to investigate them. Also, given that representations of minds are fundamental to stories, and can be found in cinematic narratives, instances of face-to-face storytelling, written literary texts, and other narrative modes, the ideas discussed in this chapter need to be brought into dialogue with those developed by the contributors to Part III of the present volume. The study of narrative across media, by focusing on the mind-relevance of storytelling processes in a variety of semiotic systems, promises to illuminate further the dialectical interplay between narrative and consciousness. Caught up in that interplay, stories both shape and are shaped by what minds perceive, infer, remember, and feel.[23]

NOTES

1. James Joyce, "The Dead." In *Dubliners* (New York: Penguin Books, 1967), p. 192.
2. See Alan Palmer, *Fictional Minds* (Lincoln: University of Nebraska Press, 2004) and Ralf Schneider, "Toward a Cognitive Theory of Literary Character: The Dynamics of Mental-Model Construction." *Style* 35:4 (2001), pp. 607–40. See

also Uri Margolin's discussion of cognitive approaches to character in the final section of chapter 5 of this volume.

3. See F. K. Stanzel, *A Theory of Narrative*. Translated by Charlotte Goedsche (Cambridge: Cambridge University Press, 1984).

4. As Manfred Jahn discusses in chapter 7 of the present volume, this technique can be characterized as *internal focalization*.

5. Joyce's portrayal of Gabriel thus harmonizes with the research on "Theory of Mind" that I discuss below. This work suggests that people's knowledge of their own minds is as theoretical as their knowledge of the minds of others. See Alison Gopnik, "How We Know Our Minds: The Illusion of First-Person Knowledge of Intentionality." *Behavioral and Brain Sciences* 16 (1993), pp. 1–14.

6. See Gillian Brown, *Speakers, Listeners and Communication: Explorations in Discourse Analysis* (Cambridge: Cambridge University Press, 1995), pp. 108–24.

7. See William Frawley, *Linguistic Semantics* (Malwah, N.J.: Lawrence Erlbaum, 1992), pp. 387–90.

8. For fuller discussion of the distinction between classical, structuralist theories of narrative and the postclassical approaches that build on those theories but supplement them with ideas unavailable to the early narratologists see David Herman, "Introduction." In David Herman (ed.) *Narratologies: New Perspectives on Narrative Analysis* (Columbus: Ohio State University Press, 1999), pp. 1–30.

9. Similar arguments are made by Claude Bremond in "The Logic of Narrative Possibilities." Translated by Elaine D. Cancalon, *New Literary History* 11 (1980), pp. 387–411; Marie-Laure Ryan in *Artificial Intelligence, Possible Worlds and Narrative Theory* (Bloomington: Indiana University Press, 1991), pp. 109–47; David Herman in *Story Logic: Problems and Possibilities of Narrative* (Lincoln: University of Nebraska Press, 2002), pp. 115–69; and Alan Palmer in *Fictional Minds*, pp. 170–239.

10. Cohn's foundational study is titled *Transparent Minds: Narrative Modes for Presenting Consciousness in Fiction* (Princeton: Princeton University Press, 1978). Later work that seeks to extend the speech-category approach includes Geoffrey Leech and Michael Short, *Style in Fiction* (London: Routledge, 1981), pp. 336–50; Monika Fludernik, *The Fictions of Language and the Languages of Fiction* (London: Routledge, 1993); and Michael Toolan, *Narrative: A Critical Linguistic Introduction*, 2nd edition (London: Longman, 2001), pp. 116–42. See also Michael Toolan's discussion, in chapter 16 of this volume, of the use of free indirect thought in "Two Gallants," another story from *Dubliners*.

11. Joyce used dashes rather than quotation marks to indicate utterances spoken directly by characters, that is, to signal direct discourse.

12. Here I follow other commentators in acknowledging the role of context in decisions about what counts as an instance of this narrative mode. See Monika Fludernik, *The Fictions of Language and the Languages of Fiction*, pp. 227–79; Brian McHale, "Free Indirect Discourse: A Survey of Recent Accounts." *Poetics and Theory of Literature* 3 (1978), pp. 249–87; and Michael Toolan, *Narrative: A Critical Linguistic Introduction*, pp. 130–40. Also, I should note that the "dual-voice hypothesis" on which I rely in my account – that is, the hypothesis that free indirect discourse marks a fusion between the narrator's voice and a character's

voice – has been disputed by Ann Banfield in her influential book, *Unspeakable Sentences* (London: Routledge, 1982).

13. See also Teresa Bridgeman's account, in chapter 4, of how characters' perspectives shape the spatial configuration of narrative worlds.

14. For a detailed overview see William Croft and D. Alan Cruse, *Cognitive Linguistics* (Cambridge: Cambridge University Press, 2004), pp. 40–73.

15. See Ronald W. Langacker, *Foundations of Cognitive Grammar*, Vol. I (Stanford: Stanford University Press, 1987), pp. 116–37; and Leonard Talmy, *Toward a Cognitive Semantics*, Vol. I (Cambridge, MA: MIT Press, 2000), pp. 68–76.

16. This overview is distilled from a more detailed account provided in David Herman, "Cognitive Approaches to Narrative Analysis." In Geert Brône and Jeroen Vandaele (eds.) *Foundations for Cognitive Poetics* (Berlin: Mouton de Gruyter, forthcoming).

17. See, for example, Alison Gopnik and Henry Wellman, "Why the Child's Theory of Mind Really Is a Theory." *Mind and Language* 7 (1992), pp. 145–71, and Alvin Goldman, "The Psychology of Folk Psychology." *Behavioral and Brain Sciences* 16 (1993), pp. 15–28. Also, see Lisa Zunshine's *Why We Read Fiction* (Columbus: Ohio State University Press, 2006) for a discussion of how ideas concerning Theory of Mind can be brought into dialogue with research on the evolution and formal properties of the novel.

18. Peter Stearns, "Emotion." In Rom Harré and Peter Stearns (eds.) *Discursive Psychology in Practice* (Thousand Oaks, CA: Sage, 1995), pp. 37–54. For an account of emotions as innate and universal see Patrick Colm Hogan, *The Mind and Its Stories* (Cambridge: Cambridge University Press, 2003).

19. See Peter Stearns and Carol Stearns, "Emotionology: Clarifying the History of Emotions and Emotional Standards." *American Historical Review* 90 (1985), pp. 13–36; and Rom Harré and Grant Gillett, *The Discursive Mind* (London: Sage, 1994), pp. 144–61.

20. Janet Levin, "Qualia." In Robert A. Wilson and Frank C. Keil (eds.) *The MIT Encyclopedia of the Cognitive Sciences* (Cambridge, MA: MIT Press, 1999), p. 693; Thomas Nagel, "What Is It Like to be a Bat?" *The Philosophical Review* 83:4 (1974), pp. 435–50.

21. David Lodge, *Consciousness and the Novel* (Cambridge, MA: Harvard University Press, 2002), p. 45.

22. See Fludernik, *Towards a "Natural" Narratology* (London: Routledge, 1996), pp. 48–50.

23. I am grateful to Manfred Jahn and James Phelan for their insightful comments on earlier drafts of this chapter.

18

MONIKA FLUDERNIK

Identity/alterity

Identity and alterity (or otherness) are key concerns in the context of post-colonial studies, which focuses on the power relations between colonizer and colonized. Until recently, however, the centrality of identity and alterity for narrative theory has not been sufficiently recognized. While the final part of my chapter will focus on identity and alterity in postcolonial narratives, I will begin by considering two more general questions; namely (1) the status of identity in narrative and narrating (outside a postcolonial framework); and (2) the importance of alterity, difference, or deviation from cultural, societal, narrative, and stylistic norms that are constitutive of storytelling. The basic argument of the chapter is that issues of identity and alterity are relevant to *all* narratives, even though – for thematic and ideological reasons – they seem to be more prominently addressed in postcolonial texts.[1]

Identity, empathy, and narration

In conversational narratives, or "natural" narratives, as William Labov calls them, narration does not necessarily only serve the purpose of telling a good story; it additionally – and often primarily – has the function of protecting "face."[2] The narrator wants to demonstrate that he or she is courageous, a tough guy, a really shrewd person, astute in judging others, able to fend for herself, adept at repartee, and generally a good person. Such a narrative, then, does not simply project a referential identity ("I am John and not Thomas") – the narrator's identity in this sense is either a given, or quite irrelevant. Instead, natural narrative creates and elaborates an image of the self which the narrator wants others to recognize as his or her character or personhood. Narratives construct selfhood as individuality and functional role.

Such identities are imaginary in much the same way as Benedict Anderson's imaginary homelands of national and/or ethnic origin.[3] They do not really "exist" independently of a conversational context since they are constituted in interaction with others, in fluid self-presentation. They also deliberately elide or camouflage possible negative facets of the self. One will tend to present oneself as frugal and not miserly; as astute in financial matters and not grasping; as loving and caring but not clinging. You do not on your first date mention that you are an appallingly bad cook, but will maybe dwell on your expertise as a good organizer. Images projected in conversational narrative, like images of one's self that one tries to live up to in one's behavior ("I am a responsible person"; "I understand and forgive"), are fictions/fantasies that the narrator is at pains to uphold narratively, self-images to emulate and realize. Many such versions of the self, even if not downright fraudulent, are nevertheless prone to the self's self-deceptive inclinations – one would like to believe that one is a nice person and tends to throw a veil over one's less likeable traits.

Narrative identity, therefore, is part of a general performative identity which we create inside our social roles – as teachers, as wives, as parents, as drivers, etc. These roles do not necessarily cohere, so somebody can be an irresponsible driver but a caring son to his or her aged parents. We also define ourselves through these roles – a person may like to think of himself as a superb gardener and define himself less as a competent salesperson, which he is for his customers, colleagues, and employers. Identity should therefore be used in the plural – identities – to acknowledge the multiplicity of roles and their contextual relevance. None of these roles allows one to establish a real self, a definite identity. Rather, identities are constituted in the interplay of individuals with other people in social contexts of family, work, study, leisure activities, etc. Although narrators generally believe they have a clear identity, that identity is an accumulation of performative stances and memories of past experiences which creates a continuity of self-understanding between roles and between contexts.

Identities cannot be upheld without the co-operation of others. The continuity between present and past self that subjectively exists for individuals relies to a significant extent on the support that identity construction receives from the other, especially because – as Jacques Lacan argues – we see ourselves as other and as others see us.[4] The best face-preserving techniques turn into failures if the addressees – those interacting with us – do not believe in the projected self. Even more importantly, the self is projected in the first place in order to answer the glance of the other. Consequently, identity is not merely differentiated from alterity, the other, by singling itself out from a multiplicity of others; it is itself constituted in a dialectic process that interacts with the other. In this sense, the psychological dynamics that Homi Bhabha describes for the relationship between colonizer and colonized (already noted by Albert Memmi and Frantz Fanon) derives from the constitutive process of identity construction, and goes back to what Lacan characterizes as the imaginary mirror phase in our development and to the child's fixation on the mother as primal o/Other.[5]

Identity, moreover, is (re)constituted continuously in our self-narrations. We do not merely tell stories about our recent experience in which we try to make ourselves look good; we also narrate and retell our lives to ourselves. In order to create continuity between past and present, in order to lend meaning to the experiences that we have undergone, we construct a story of our life. In this story we may be the victim of external forces that keep intruding on us; we may also project ourselves as the shrewd manipulator who is in control of everything: the sociable guy who has innumerable friends; the ugly duckling who is unable to attract the right partner; and so on. Again, in these stories it is less the plot that counts than the evaluation that is given to (often recurring) events. As psychologists have shown, the point of much therapy is not to find the truth (there is no truth about the self, just as there is no core self), but to create a story of one's life with which one can live, a story of success, or of hope. By putting a different construction on the same occurrences, one can convert failure, depression, or anxiety into placid confidence in the future.

Telling one's own life, however, is not the only way of constituting self. Telling *other people's* lives similarly works by constructing uniformity and consistency on the basis of a mass of recalcitrant material. Just as autobiographies (whether literary or non-literary) often open up interpretative gaps that allow one to read between the lines and uncover unintended or veiled meanings in the account, biographies likewise do not always manage to shut out all inconsistencies regarding the actions of their subjects. Eighteenth-century criminal biographies are especially notorious for projecting a didactic, moralizing stance that is however undercut by the logic of the narrated events. Thus, Daniel Defoe's "The True and Genuine Account of the Life and Actions of the Late Jonathan Wild" (1725) in the "Preface" presents the eponymous subject of the text as "this famous, or if you please, infamous creature."[6] In the subsequent "Introduction" we get a lengthy moralizing paragraph on Wild's personality:

> Take him as a man, only he had a kind of brutal courage which fitted him to be an instrument in attacking some of the most desperate of the several gangs of rogues he had to do with. But as his courage also served to make him audacious in the other wicked things he undertook, he was rather bold than courageous, and might be called impudent, but we cannot say he was brave, as appeared in a more particular manner in his stupid and confused behaviour, during his lying in Newgate, and at his execution, of which in its place. ("Wild," 226)

The real story, titled "An Account of the Life and *Eminent* Actions &c." ("Wild," 229, my emphasis) opens with the characterization of the hero as

"JONATHAN WILD, the wretched subject of this history" (229). These images of Wild – bold, eminent, wretched – do not cohere, and the account of his exploits foregrounds in turn one or the other of Wild's traits without being able to connect them into a unified whole:

> But he knew no bounds to his gain, and therefore knew no restraint of laws, or at least considered of none, till he involved himself in a mass of crimes, out of which it was impossible he should recover. ("Wild," 235)

> It must be allowed to Jonathan's fame, that as he steered among rocks and dangerous shoals, so he was a bold pilot. He ventured in, and always got out in a manner equally surprising. No man ever did the like before him, and I dare say, no man will attempt to do the like after him. ("Wild," 240)

> Thus ended the tragedy, and thus was a life of horrid and inimitable wickedness finished at the gallows, the very same place where, according to some, above 120 miserable creatures had been hanged whose blood in great measure may be said to lie at his door . . . ("Wild," 257)

The lack of consistency is particularly obvious in the following passage: "It is time now to enter into a particular account of the conclusion of this life of crime. It has been a kind of comedy, or a farce rather, all along, but it proved a tragedy at last" ("Wild," 250). Wild's eminent fame perhaps corresponds to the tragic genre; his boldness to the comic aspects of his life; his wretched end to the farcical element. These three views are never entirely reconciled; in fact, they are placed one beside the other and open up evaluative and ideological rifts in the story. Just as all happy families are alike and only unhappy ones yield material that provides interest for novels,[7] the story of a person's life that fits too neatly into one pattern becomes boring. It is when a text gives expression to conflicting accounts of a protagonist's actions or motives, when speculations about his or her state of mind are encouraged, that the story becomes interesting and in the plenitude of life defeats the uniform banality of moralistic judgment.

Having argued for the constitutive function of identity creation in narrative, even though these constructions can never do justice to their tellers or the "reality" of life, let us now turn to the functions of alterity, i.e., of difference or otherness, in narrative.

Narrative othering

Even before the advent of postcolonial studies, and even outside colonial or postcolonial contexts, narrative has always dealt with the other, with alterity. I have argued above that the construction of identity psychologically depends on a differentiation of self and other, and perhaps even an imagining of the self *as* other. In this section, by contrast, I will focus on the functions of alterity in narratives that do not directly align with identity construction.

Formulating the point in a very general manner, one could argue that narrative is, basically, about the depiction and recuperation of alterity. This is true even for autobiography, in which the writing of one's life attempts to reintegrate centrifugal material of the past and of memory into the fold of recognized continuity and identity. For non-autobiographical narrative, the past is "a different country," and in heterodiegetic or third-person fiction, the storyworld by definition functions as the realm of the unfamiliar, the strange and the alluring that seduces us with its charms and secrets.

As we know from conversational narrative, stories need to have reportability, they need to provide an interest, some news, something that thrills or excites the audience. Happy couples are not storyworthy – their lives are a routine of placidity that withers in the mouth of the storyteller. Likewise, what we already know well does not have any news value or interest to the reader or listener. It is therefore only logical that narrative mostly deals with the unfamiliar, the long ago, the far away; or with the dangerous, the secret, and the prohibited. Narratives traditionally deal with the Gods, with superhuman heroes performing feats of unbelievable bravery, with magicians who can make the impossible happen, and with travels into nearly inaccessible territories and dangerous zones.

In a literal reading of the romance quest motif – the perhaps most basic narrative plot, for instance for Propp and Bremond – the other is a space of alterity: strange countries, forests or seas, peopled by foreigners, enemies, and monsters. The excitement of penetrating into the unknown is fraught with the dangers of incorporation and death. (The sexual puns rampant in travelogues and other colonial texts are, therefore, merely a continuation of the phallocentric patterns of romance, that is, of the imposition of male sexuality on the way in which we perceive action.) From a psychoanalytic point of view, these uncanny spaces of alterity symbolize the unconscious or *id* which, it could be argued, the protagonist (and, empathetically, the reader) confronts in the storyworld. The psychological processes involved in the confrontation with the other (or, more correctly: the Other, in Lacanian terms) consist in an acknowledgment of the *id* and its drives, but also – by helping the subject to enact in fantasy what is prohibited in reality – serve to expel the Other more successfully from the self (*moi*). In other words, the protagonist and reader confront, and therefore come to terms with, the Other, but they end up by reasserting themselves against this alterity, continuing to repress and repulse the o/Other.[8]

There are several additional levels on which narrative is involved in othering. One very obvious level is that of the medium of storytelling. Most audiences and readers encounter narrative not merely as representing the other place or other person; they additionally encounter it in the voice of a storyteller, a book (words on the page), a movie screen, or a dramatic performance in which the actors iconically signify the otherness of the fictional world and their inhabitants. Not only the subject but also the medium of narrative therefore relates to a process of othering.

Yet another level of alterity emerges from the perspective of the reader/audience. One of the key accusations against belles lettres or imaginative forms of writing has always been that they lie; that literature represents fictive worlds, and that it morally corrupts the reader. One way in which the reader is supposedly corrupted is through his/her indulgence in escapism. Readers like to immerse themselves in the worlds of fiction and in the lives of characters that are very different from their own situations. Not all literature is of course escapist in this sense. Courtly literature often deals with love intrigues at court that may owe their popularity to the reader's familiarity with the setting. Nevertheless, much English courtly literature, even if interested in providing parables of contemporary politics, places the plot of its narratives elsewhere – in Italy, France, or Spain; in a pastoral world, a utopian island, or in the New World; or among the lower levels of society (the picaresque novel). Despite the novel's much-discussed realism and thematization of contemporary life (Ian Watt),[9] the novel as a genre – if seen from the perspective of its authors and readers – has rarely engaged in a description of the familiar. Criminal biography, Gothic romance, the historical novel, naturalistic writing about the working class – these genres all concern themselves with other settings and characters than those familiar to the reader. Even the highlights of realism in British fiction, such as Richardson's *Clarissa*, the work of George Eliot, and, to some extent, Dickens's œuvre, can be argued to compensate for the deliberate familiarity of the setting with the excessive individuality of their protagonists, who are clearly "other" selves into whose mind's thinking the reader starts to immerse her/himself empathetically. For their part, many figures from twentieth-century novels are outsiders, freaks, or weirdos.

In this connection we might refer to Käte Hamburger's dictum that fiction is the only place where another's consciousness can be represented.[10] The alterity of much third-person literary narrative consists, precisely, in the fabulous access that it affords to another person's (the protagonist's) mind. In fact, besides access to consciousness, fictional narrative has started to deploy a whole panorama of non-natural storytelling situations whose allure, at least initially, consists precisely in the impossible scenarios that they enact.

Examples of this type of writing are we-narratives, second-person narratives, present-tense first-person narratives, in which we focus on the narrator's current experiences simultaneous with the telling of them, or narratives playing with pronouns and tenses.[11]

Alterity plays a role even formally in narratives. This is the case most strikingly in paratextual formats and framing techniques. Paratexts such as title pages and chapter headings, marginalia and annotations or footnotes provide a frame that gives access to, or mediates between, the world of the reader and the interior of the (fictional) world. Frames, editorial introductions, and critical comments in appendices likewise ease the reader into or out of the text. In particular, the deployment of framing techniques often serves to prevaricate on the truth conditions of the tale, thereby thematizing the alterity of the narrative. Thus, in Jonathan Swift's *Gulliver's Travels* (1726), the editor's account of Gulliver tends to put the story into ironic perspective. Moreover, the frame narrative, as a narrative in its own right, is already a fiction within whose fold the embedded narrative, twice removed from the "real" world, is distanced at a double remove and therefore an other of the other world. For instance, in Shakespeare's *The Taming of the Shrew*, the initial frame of Sly, the tinker, being put to bed and wakened as if he were a lord already constitutes a different world from that of the spectators; Sly then starts to watch the play about Petruchio and Katherina which is at a double remove from the audience of the play.

Although there has not been sufficient space to provide an in-depth analysis of the many ways in which narrative, especially fiction, engages with, indeed depends on, alterity, I hope to have demonstrated that otherness is at least as important for narrative as identity. Othering processes are in fact constitutive of narration.

Colonial and postcolonial alterity in narrative

I now return to the area in which the term alterity has become most important in recent years, postcolonial studies. The "other" in this framework is primarily the native; the implied self the colonizer or Western subject. As a consequence, the othering processes analyzed in postcolonial theory are, at bottom, a reflection of the *colonial* scenario in which imperial power and knowledge impact on the native population. Since postcolonial approaches discuss the continued subjection of the non-Western subject to Western domination, postcoloniality can be argued to affect the home country as much as the former colonies.

The other of colonialism has been described in complementary ways by the three leading theorists of postcolonial studies: Edward Said, Gayatri Spivak, and Homi Bhabha. Clearly, in the space of this chapter I could not possibly do justice to the complexity of these critics' ideas, but will merely focus on a few major concepts proposed by Said and Bhabha.

Edward Said's major insights center on the concept of orientalism which one could describe as the West's othering of the East in terms of knowledge, power, and status.[12] Leaving aside the problems that Said's uniform reference to "a" West and "an" East involves, the major point of his theory is to demonstrate that the Near East (and, by implication also, the Far East) has been subjected to a totalizing and disempowering glance by European scholars and politicians. Within an orientalist framework, people living in the East were taken to be all the same ("East" as a label that spans everything from Egypt and Arabia to Iran, India, and Japan). Colonial knowledge saw them as racially, morally, intellectually, and culturally inferior. This belief in the inferiority of the native other served as an excuse for disregarding these peoples' cultural achievements and for violating their civilizations by imposing British (or French) culture and language on them, subjecting them by military force and keeping them in the position of colonies dependent on their supposedly wiser and benevolent mother countries. A typical example of these tenets of high imperialism is Thomas Babington Macaulay's infamous pamphlet *Minutes on Education* (1835), in which he claimed that oriental civilisation had nothing to offer that was comparable to Shakespeare as a pretext for imposing British education on India.

Said added to the major tenets of his book by distinguishing between *manifest* and *latent* orientalism. Whereas manifest orientalism focuses on the discriminating clichés used against natives from the East (e.g., the sly, idle, and cowardly native), latent orientalism emerged in what seemed to be very positive images of the oriental other (the East as exotic, alluring, resplendently wealthy, and martial). Said shrewdly shows that these images correlate with the secret desires of Western subjects for that which is forbidden (wealth, violence, tyrannical power, promiscuity, lust). As a consequence, many Eastern institutions are fraught with ambivalence in Western eyes: e.g., the harem as a site of unlimited male promiscuity yet also as an institution of illicit male tyranny over women.

Homi Bhabha's *The Location of Culture* is likewise a key text which has provided a crucial set of terms for the analysis of the colonial scenario.[13] Following theorists such as Frantz Fanon and Albert Memmi, Bhabha focuses on the imaginary relationship between colonizer and colonized. In Memmi's and Bhabha's scenario the (male) colonizer and the (male) native exchange glances. The native would like to be accepted as an equal by the colonizer – he engages in what Bhabha calls mimicry: he wants to become the same, but is never accepted as quite the same even if (or precisely because) he tries to be more British than the British. Since the colonizer cannot see the native as his equal but wants to keep him in a position of inferiority, the mimicry of the native is doomed to failure. Conversely, the colonizer feels a radical ambivalence towards the native. On the one hand, the native appears to be his friend, faithful servant, admiring inferior; on the other, he threatens the colonizer with insurrection, only pretends to be reliable, and appears to be the cunning, sly native of orientalist stereotypes.

Summarizing the status of the other in postcolonial theory, one can clearly see the other as the constitutive or focal point in postcolonial theory. The question that most concerns us in the present context, however, is to what extent (post)colonial othering impacts on narrative or narrative theory. To what extent do postcolonial narratives textualize the alterity of the (post)colonial setting and the theme of the self–other dialectic?

The conflict between colonizer and colonized consists in a clash of ideologies. The handling of this clash can be managed in an ideologically significant manner, emphasizing one worldview to the exclusion of the other or illustrating the irresolvable conflict between them. There are texts with a clearly colonial orientation; texts with a clearly anti-colonial or postcolonial framework; and texts that focus on the hybridity of self-versus-other or us-versus-them constellations. The boundaries between these groups overlap. In the key example text that I will be discussing below, Hari Kunzru's *The Impressionist* (2002),[14] all of these categories can be illustrated.[15] The novel describes several stages in the life of a young Indian boy, Pran Nath, who finds out he is of mixed blood, is evicted from his home, kidnapped to serve as hijra in the harem of the Nawab of Fatehpur, and ends up passing as a white person, taking over the identity of the murdered Jonathan Bridgeman. As we will see, this step is only the beginning of Pran's problems of identity.

Colonial narratives present a Western view on the native other and the native's country. Most travelogues belong to this category. A Western (usually male) explorer or traveller enters foreign territory and judges the natives from a superior white perspective. This attitude of denigration is sometimes complemented by elements of manifest orientalism, as when the traveller praises the courage of the native warriors, or the beauty of the women. Kunzru's novel opens with Ronald Forrester encountering the palanquin of Amrita and falling prey to her exotic charms. Colonial texts employ many exotic descriptions of the indigenous scene ("The native mother goddess stands before him in the firelight, elemental and ferocious. Her body is smeared with mud. A wild tangle of hair hangs over her face: She is entirely naked," *Impressionist*, 13).

In colonial texts interaction with the natives is frequently presented as difficult owing to the natives' failure to speak English and understand British customs. Narratologically, the native other is presented as a βάρβαρος, a stammerer, whose maltreatment of the English language causes hilarity, frustration, or disgust (e.g., Pran's "treacle-thick bazaar English," *Impressionist*, 48). Frequently the native other – like the peasant or working-class subject in British fiction – remains speechless, or is represented in the words of a translator. Joyce Cary's *Mister Johnson* (1939) is a good example of this denigrating strategy. By these means, the natives function as flat characters and never acquire the scope for agency, articulation, and intellectual or emotional expression that are necessary for a protagonist. Like the landscape, the natives remain props until they turn into the enemy and then become antagonists who are eventually conquered and cruelly punished for their criminal attacks on the European invaders.

Narratives critical of colonialism tend to present the situation outlined above with consummate irony and implicitly (or, more rarely, explicitly) condemn the imperial system. There are two main strategies employed in this context: the deconstruction of British superiority; and the enhancement of the native position as just. Many anti-colonial texts present the British in India (for example) as ridiculous, pompous, and arrogant. Thus Rushdie's Mr. Methwold, into whose estate Saleem's parents move in *Midnight's Children* (1981), is presented as a figure of fun; in Farrell's *The Siege of Krishnapur* (1973), likewise, the depiction of the men and women in the garrison is overwhelmingly that of incompetence, quirkiness, and social hubris.

In Kunzru's novel, the debunking of the British is even more abrasive. Here the native citizens of Agra make fun of the Anglo-Indians aping British mores: "The women wear hats. So do the men. Even when it is cloudy. Even (some people joke) indoors . . . The wife of the Political Resident in Bharatpur swears she once saw a party of them . . . playing a hand of bridge in their hats. Indoors. *After dark* . . . What a chee-chee thing to do, to wear one's hat at night!" (45–6). The irony here cuts both against the British colonizers and the Anglo-Indian mimic men.

By contrast, Indians in anti-colonial texts are presented as fully endowed protagonists who are able to speak English correctly, have a wide scope of agency, and are morally and intellectually superior to the colonizers, even if the story ends tragically with their defeat, death, or captivity. Toni Morrison's *Beloved* (1987) is such a text, as is Rudy Wiebe's *The Temptations of Big Bear* (1973). The enhancement of the non-Western subject in this fiction follows well-known patterns of giving more agency to the native subject in the plot, allowing for positive options at the end of the novel, and extensively presenting the protagonist's mind in order to enhance the reader's empathy and understanding for the native hero or heroine. For example, in Amitav Gosh's *The Glass Palace* (2000), the Burmese protagonists are plantation owners.

More radical postcolonial texts have proceeded to demonstrate their independence from the West by choosing to militate against the patterns of colonial literature in more basic ways. One avenue of revolt has been the choice to write not in English but in one of the native languages (Ngugi wa Thiong'o's Gikuyu, for instance). Another strategy which is quite common in the Indian novel in England is simply to elide any contact with Westerners. By focusing on Indian protagonists exclusively, these texts make the point that, for India today, only Indians are important. This strategy is used in such texts as Rohinton Mistry's novel *A Fine Balance* (1995) and Vikram Seth's *A Suitable Boy* (1993).

Concerning hybrid or multi-ironic texts, there are some key examples of this type among colonial fiction, such as Kipling's Indian short stories and Conrad's *Heart of Darkness* (1902), but also some recent postcolonial texts such as Kunzru's *The Impressionist*. In these narratives, the irony cuts both ways – there is criticism of the colonizer but also an ironical portrayal of native aspirations. For example, in Manjula Padmanabhan's story "Hot-Death, Cold Soup," the status of the two main women characters is inverted in comparison to the typical situation in the colonial novel: the Indian protagonist is a journalist, whereas the woman whose self-immolation as a sati is the topic of the story is a white woman married to an Indian man.

Hari Kunzru's *Impressionist* also radicalizes the use of ironic ambivalence. As we saw above, we first get a view of the Anglo-Indians as behaving ridiculously like the funny Englishmen; then we encounter the Anglo-Indian view of the natives from their perspective. Having internalized British colonial stereotypes, the Anglo-Indians repress their own Indian blood and allegiance entirely and pretend that their one European parent constitutes their entire identity.

> In the Agra Post and Telephone Club, the horrid blackie-whites [term used by the natives for Anglo-Indians] gather together to swap their own stories of disgustingness, the disgustingness of the natives, the foul Indian-ness of native ways . . . The natives are devious, untrustworthy and prone to crime. Their lasciviousness is proverbial. What a contrast to Home, to the Northern rectitude of English ways and manners. (*Impressionist*, 46–7)

This reference to "Home" has already been debunked by the natives: "Home home home! Everyone knows none of them has been anywhere near

England" (*Impressionist*, 46). The protagonist, Pran Nath, in his role as Jonathan Bridgeman, actually travels to Britain and attends school and college. His attempts to understand British life find their way into a notebook that contains hilarious insights into English customs from an outsider's point of view:

> Everywhere Jonathan finds the originals of copies he has grown up with, all the absurdities of British India restored to sense by their natural environment . . . The parks yield expanses of rich green lawn, and for the first time he understands what the British have tried unsuccessfully to replicate in India. Velvet green . . . In their London you can shake the rainwater from your umbrella and step into a Lyons tearoom where pale girls in black and white uniforms serve cake as heavy and moist as the lawns.
>
> (*Impressionist*, 299, 298–9)

The ironies of the novel climax in Jonathan's futile love for Miss Astarte ("Starr") Chapel, who finds him lacking in attractiveness precisely because he has worked so hard to be a typical Englishman: "You're the most conventional person I know, Johnny. I think that's all right, but it's not for me . . . It's stifling . . . I want passion, primitive emotions" (*Impressionist*, 415). When Jonathan achieves perfect Britishness, adopting the career of an anthropologist, he loses what he most cares for, the exotic Starr. The ending of the novel underlines these ironies even further when Starr ends up marrying the new Nawab of Fatehpur, in whose palace Pran was formerly imprisoned in the harem; Jonathan himself undergoes another change of identity back to the ultraprimitive, surviving the massacre of an anthropological expedition at the hands of the Fotse tribe by allowing himself to be turned into a Fotse. The novel therefore criticizes the colonized's mimicry of the colonizer, demonstrating Pran's attempts to "become" British to be thoroughly ridiculous and counterproductive; it also illustrates the psychic costs of having no identity of one's own.

To summarize, how do identity and alterity impinge on narrative? All narratives manifest subjecthood and subjectivity, and these interrelate with the construction of identity. Yet identity becomes notable only where set into relief against one or more others: others that can be non-human (landscape, nature, the city, society); or human subjects (the mother or father, one's partner, one's friend, one's master, one's son or daughter, a stranger). In our relationships with human others, as psychoanalysis has shown, complex processes of transference take place, with the concept of the self a product of this exchange on either side. The imaginary relationship of self and other is enabling but also fraught with ambivalence towards the threatening qualities of other people, a situation that is typical of the colonial scenario where colonizer and colonized face one another. Colonial confrontation leads to neurotic denigration of the native, on the one hand, and unacknowledged desire for the other on the colonizer's side; to internalization of inferiority as imposed by the colonizer and to hysteric mimicry of Western patterns of behavior on the side of the colonized. In postcolonial fiction, these processes of transference are often highlighted by complex and multi-layered ironies that subversively invert orientalist stereotypes, present the former colonizer as the inferior party, and foreground the agency of the native subject. Just as the colonial scenario constitutes a radicalization of self–other relations, its fictional representation exploits to the full narrative's potential for formal as well thematic exploration of identities and alterities.

NOTES

1. Insights articulated in this essay have developed over the seven-year span during which I (co)directed an interdisciplinary research project "Identities and Alterities" (SFB 541) funded by the Deutsche Forschungsgemeinschaft (German Research Council). Financial support is here gratefully acknowledged.

2. Cf. William Labov, *Language in the Inner City: Studies in the Black English Vernacular* (Philadelphia: University of Pennsylvania Press, 1972). As used by Erving Goffman in *Interaction Ritual* (Garden City, N.J.: Doubleday, 1967), *face* refers to the positive self-image that interlocutors seek to maintain for themselves and others in a conversational exchange. Politeness theory, originally developed by anthropologists (see Penelope Brown and Stephen C. Levinson, *Politeness: Some Universals in Language Usage* [Cambridge: Cambridge University Press, 1987]), extends Goffman's insights to explore both positive politeness, which involves showing solidarity with another, and negative politeness, which involves not trespassing on another's wants or interactional goals.

3. Benedict Anderson, *Imagined Communities: Reflections on the Origin and Spread of Nationalism* (London: Verso, 1991).

4. For Jacques Lacan see Sean Homer, *Jacques Lacan* (London and New York: Routledge, 2005). Briefly, in Lacan's model, the "I" is constituted in the mirror stage by the perception of itself as other (small o, *petit a*), the other person whose regard reinforces the identity construction of the self. Lacan describes the relationship between self and other under the label of the Imaginary. By contrast, the Other in Lacan's theory refers to the Real, that which lies outside symbolization and imaginary access. On the mirror stage see Lacan, *Écrits: A Selection*. Translated by Alan Sheridan (New York: Norton, 1977).

5. The mother is both an other, a person with whom the child enters into an imaginary relationship, for instance when learning to apply personal pronouns correctly (mother says *you*, the child needs to learn to say *I*, and vice versa), and – according to the dynamics described by Freud in the *fort/da* ("away"/"here") game – an unreachable Other. The baby has to learn that the mother is not continually available to him/her. See Sigmund Freud, *Beyond the Pleasure Principle*. Edited and translated by James Strachey (London: Hogarth Press, 1974).

6. Daniel Defoe, "The True and Genuine Account of the Life and Actions of the late Jonathan Wild" [1725]. In Henry Fielding, *Jonathan Wild*. Edited by David Nokes (London: Penguin, 1986), p. 223.
7. Compare the opening sentence of Lev Tolstoi's *Anna Karenina* (1877/8).
8. As with the child and mother, the relationship between explorer and the wilderness or native partakes both in the imaginary relationship (the native as other, i.e., as a mirror image of the self) and a relationship of complete othering as in the Real. The term *id* derives from Freud and refers to a person's sexual drives. Compare Sean Homer, *Jacques Lacan*.
9. Ian Watt, in *The Rise of the Novel* (London: Chatto & Windus, 1957), attributed the novelty of Defoe's work to its representation of the details of ordinary life.
10. Käte Hamburger, *The Logic of Literature* [1957], 2nd edition. Translated by Marilynn J. Rose (Bloomington: Indiana University Press, 1983).
11. On *we*-narratives see Uri Margolin, "Person." In David Herman, Manfred Jahn, and Marie-Laure Ryan (eds.) *The Routledge Encyclopedia of Narrative Theory* (London: Routledge, 2005), pp. 422–3; and Uri Margolin, "Telling in the Plural: From Grammar to Ideology." *Poetics Today* 21:3 (2000), pp. 591–618. See also Monika Fludernik, *Towards a "Natural" Narratology* (London: Routledge, 1996), pp. 178–221.
12. Edward Said, *Orientalism* (New York: Vintage, 1979).
13. Homi Bhabha's *The Location of Culture* (London: Routledge, 1994).
14. Hari Kunzru, *The Impressionist* (London: Hamish Hamilton, 2002).
15. My examples are mainly taken from Anglophone literatures, and include British colonial texts and British texts critical of colonialism, as well as texts usually included among anti-colonial and postcolonial literature from India, Africa, and North America. Although there are salient differences among postcolonial cultures, it can be argued that the structures of colonial and postcolonial discourse remain the same cross-culturally.

GLOSSARY

The following is a glossary of key terms for narrative study. Each term is followed by the numbers of the chapter or chapters where fuller discussion of relevant issues may be found. If a term is capitalized within a definition, that term has its own glossary entry. Readers should also consult the index for pointers to discussions (elsewhere in the volume) of terms not listed here.

Glossary definitions that refer to "the Labovian model" allude to the research on storytelling in face-to-face interaction that was pioneered by William Labov and Joshua Waletzky, and further developed in later work by Labov and other narrative scholars influenced by him. See chapters 1 and 9 of this volume for further discussion and bibliographic references.

For additional information about these and other relevant terms and concepts, readers are encouraged to consult other recently published guides to the field. The following works provide foundations for further study:

Abbott, H. Porter. *The Cambridge Introduction to Narrative*, 2nd edition (Cambridge: Cambridge University Press, 2008).

Herman, David, Manfred Jahn, and Marie-Laure Ryan (eds.) *Routledge Encyclopedia of Narrative Theory* (London: Routledge, 2005).

Herman, Luc, and Bart Vervaeck. *Handbook of Narrative Analysis* (Lincoln: University of Nebraska Press, 2005).

Jahn, Manfred. *Narratology: A Guide to the Theory of Narrative* (www.uni-koeln.de/~ame02/pppn.htm)

Keen, Suzanne. *Narrative Form* (London: Palgrave Macmillan, 2004).

Phelan, James, and Peter J. Rabinowitz (eds.) *A Companion to Narrative Theory* (Malden, MA: Blackwell, 2005).

Prince, Gerald. *A Dictionary of Narratology*, 2nd edition (Lincoln: University of Nebraska Press, 2003).

Riessman, Catherine Kohler. *Narrative Analysis* (Thousand Oaks, CA: Sage, 1993).

Rimmon-Kenan, Shlomith. *Narrative Fiction: Contemporary Poetics*, 2nd edition (London: Routledge, 2002).

ABSTRACT In the Labovian model, the abstract is a pre-announcement of the gist of a story about to be told, used to clear the floor for the more or less extended turn at talk required to convey the narrative. (9)

ACTANT A term used by structuralist NARRATOLOGISTS to designate general roles fulfilled by particularized actors or characters. One such role is Opponent, which is fulfilled by characters as diverse as Claudius in *Hamlet* and Lex Luther in *Superman*. (1, 13, 15)

ADDRESSEE. See AUDIENCE

ADDRESSOR. See NARRATOR

AGENCY At the level of the STORY, agency concerns characters' ability to bring about deliberately initiated EVENTS, or actions, within a STORYWORLD. But agency is also a pertinent concern at the level of storytelling or NARRATION, affecting who gets to tell what kind of story in what contexts. FEMINIST NARRATOLOGY explores differences in the sorts of agency available to male versus female characters and NARRATORS. (5, 13)

ANACHRONY Nonchronological NARRATION, where EVENTS are told in an ORDER other than that in which they can be presumed to have occurred in the STORYWORLD. (3, 4, 10)

ANALEPSIS The equivalent of a flashback in film. Analepsis occurs when EVENTS that occur in the ORDER ABC are told in the order BCA or BAC. (3, 4, 10)

ANTHOLOGY SERIES A television series that, unlike an EPISODIC SERIES, presents a new, stand-alone STORYWORLD with each new EPISODE, as in *Tales from the Crypt*. (11)

AUDIENCE[1] In contexts of narrative study, the audience can be defined as real or imagined addressees of (multi-layered) acts of narrative communication. One influential way of analyzing such communicative acts distinguishes among actual authors, IMPLIED AUTHORS, and NARRATORS on the production side of the storytelling process, and, on the interpretation side, the corresponding roles of actual readers, IMPLIED READERS, and NARRATEES (the audience implicitly or explicitly addressed by the narrator in the text). For their part, rhetorical theorists of narrative have refined this model by retaining the distinction between actual readers and narratees and dividing implied readers into two kinds, the authorial audience and the narrative audience. The authorial audience is the hypothetical reader for whom the author intends every signal in the text. The narrative audience can be described as an observer role within the STORYWORLD. To engage fully with FICTIONAL texts, actual readers have to enter both audiences simultaneously so that they both view fictional characters as if they were real people and remain tacitly aware that they are artificial constructs. This model explains why actual readers can be "taken in" enough to empathize with the characters and experience curiosity, suspense, and surprise on the characters' behalf, but not so taken in that they jump onto the stage during the performance of a play to "rescue" a character being threatened by a villain, say. (8, 14)

AUTODIEGETIC NARRATION First-person or HOMODIEGETIC narration in which the NARRATOR is also the main character in the STORYWORLD. (3)

BACKSTORY A type of EXPOSITION often involving ANALEPSIS or flashback; a filling in of the circumstances and events that have led to the present moment in a STORYWORLD, and that illuminate the larger implications of actual or potential behaviors by characters occupying a particular narrative "now." (3, 4, 11)

COMPLICATING ACTION In the Labovian model, this is the interest-bearing element of the narrative, involving unexpected or non-canonical, and thus TELLABLE, situations and events. (9)

CODA In the Labovian model, the coda serves a "bridging" function at the end of a story told in face-to-face interaction, returning the focus of attention from the world of the story to the world of the here and now, in which the current discourse is unfolding. (9)

CONFLICT A process whereby an initial state of equilibrium in a STORYWORLD is upset by a more or less disruptive EVENT or chain of events. Alternatively, a clash between the beliefs, desires, and intentions of two characters in a narrative, or between dissonant aspects of a single character. For many theorists, conflict is a core aspect of NARRATIVE, whether it originates from within the characters themselves or from an external AGENT or impeding force. (1, 2, 5)

DESCRIPTION A kind of text or discourse core instances of which ascribe properties to situations, objects, and events, whether statically or dynamically (as in *That cat is elegant* versus *Tuesdays and Thursdays I eat cereal for breakfast and on other days I eat toast and jelly*). (1, 2, 4, 8)

DIALECT REPRESENTATION The representation of a speech variety used by one or more characters in a narrative text; such speech representations can be used to position and identify characters within regional, class-based, ethnic, and gender-related coordinates, suggesting alterity or otherness. (6, 16, 18)

DIRECT DISCOURSE A technique for representing characters' speech. In DD, a NARRATOR reproduces a character's utterance in a manner that (one can assume) mirrors the way it was performed in the STORYWORLD. (3, 6, 16, 17)

DIEGESIS In one sense, the term *diegesis* corresponds to what NARRATOLOGISTS call STORY; in this usage, it refers to the STORYWORLD evoked by the narrative text and inhabited by the characters. In a second usage, *diegesis* (along with cognate terms such as *diegetic*) refers to one pole on the continuum stretching between modes of speech presentation in narrative texts. In this second usage, techniques for presenting speech that are relatively diegetic are those in which a NARRATOR's mediation is evident, as in INDIRECT DISCOURSE. By contrast, modes that are relatively MIMETIC background the narrator's mediating role, as in DIRECT DISCOURSE or free direct discourse, where speech tags like *she said* are omitted to produce the sense of unfiltered access to characters' utterances. (6, 10, 11, 16, 17)

DISCOURSE In NARRATOLOGY, the "discourse" level of narrative (in French, *discours*) corresponds to what Russian Formalist theorists called the "sjuzhet"; it contrasts with the "STORY" (*histoire*) level. In this usage, *discourse* refers to the disposition of the SEMIOTIC cues used by interpreters to reconstruct a STORYWORLD. (1, 3, 4, 10, 15)

DURATION The ratio between how long situations and events take to unfold in the STORYWORLD and how much text is devoted to their NARRATION. Variations in this ratio correspond to different narrative speeds; in order of increasing speed, these are PAUSE, STRETCH, SCENE, SUMMARY, and ELLIPSIS (4, 10)

ELLIPSIS The omission of STORYWORLD events during the process of NARRATION; in ellipsis, narrative speed reaches infinity. (3, 4)

EMOTIONOLOGY A system of terms and concepts used to understand and produce discourse about emotions. Such systems can vary across cultures and subcultures, affording different ways of conceptualizing emotions, their causes, and how they are likely to be displayed. (17)

EMPLOTMENT The process by which situations and events are linked together to produce a PLOT. The more overtly or reflexively a narrative emplots the events it recounts, and thereby draws attention to its status as a constructed artifact, the less immersed interpreters will be in the STORYWORLD evoked by the text. (3, 4, 10)

EPISODE A bounded, internally coherent sequence of situations and EVENTS that can be chained together with other such narrative units to form larger narrative structures. (11)

EPISODIC SERIES A kind of television series that, unlike the ANTHOLOGY SERIES, presents in relatively independent installments phases of a STORY-WORLD assumed to be continuous over the course of the series, as in shows like *Combat* and *Law & Order*. (11)

EVALUATION In the Labovian model, evaluation refers to the expressive resources used by storytellers to signal the point of a narrative, or why it is worth telling in the first place. Evaluation, in this sense, helps ward off the question that every storyteller dreads: "So what?" (9)

EVENT A change of state, creating a more or less salient and lasting alteration in the STORYWORLD. Events can be subdivided into temporally extended processes, deliberately initiated actions, and happenings not brought about intentionally by any AGENT. (1, 2)

EXPERIENCING-I In retrospective first-person or HOMODIEGETIC (or AUTO-DIEGETIC) NARRATION, the younger self who lived through the experiences recounted by the older, NARRATING-I. (3, 7)

EXPERIENTIALITY The dimension of NARRATIVE by which it conveys what philosophers of mind term QUALIA, or the sense of what it is like for an embodied human or human-like consciousness to experience the situations and EVENTS recounted in the story. According to Monika Fludernik, experientiality is an essential condition for NARRATIVITY. (1, 17)

EXPOSITION A presentation, sometimes given in the form of BACKSTORY, of the circumstances and EVENTS that form a context or background for understanding the main action in a narrative. (3, 4, 10)

EXTRADIEGETIC NARRATOR A NARRATOR who does not inhabit the STORYWORLD evoked by a narrative. Narrators can be extradiegetic-HOMODIEGETIC, like the older Pip who narrates his life experiences in Charles Dickens's *Great Expectations*, or extradiegetic-HETERODIEGETIC, like Henry Fielding's narrator in *Tom Jones*. (3)

FEMINIST NARRATOLOGY An approach to narrative inquiry that explores how issues of gender bear on the production and interpretation of stories. (13)

FICTION Negatively, fiction can be defined as a type of discourse or communicative practice for which questions of truth-value do not apply in the way that they do for factual discourse. Thus, whereas journalists and police detectives attempt to verify a witness's account of events by comparing the account with those given by other witnesses, it would be a category mistake to try to ascertain the truth status of the events represented in Charlotte Brontë's *Jane Eyre* by comparing the novel with newspaper articles or historical records originating from the same period. Likewise, a subsequent fictional text that rewrites the novel, such as Jean Rhys's *Wide Sargasso Sea*, cannot validate or invalidate Brontë's text, but rather constitutes another, autonomous fiction. Positively, fiction can be defined as type of discourse or communicative practice in which participants are transported, through a more or less immersive experience, to a STORYWORLD assumed to be imaginary rather than actual. (2)

FREE INDIRECT DISCOURSE A technique for representing characters' speech. Couched as a report given by a NARRATOR, FID also contains expressivity markers (for example, DIALECT REPRESENTATIONS) that point to the speech patterns of a particular character. (6, 7, 16, 17)

FREQUENCY The ratio between the number of times something is told and the number of times it can be assumed to have occurred in the STORYWORLD. In singulative NARRATION, there is a one-to-one match between how many times an EVENT occurred and how many times it is told; in iterative narration, something that happened more than once is told once; and in repetitive narration, the number of times something is told exceeds the frequency with which it occurred in the STORYWORLD. (3, 4, 10)

GAPS Lacunae or omissions in what is told or in the process of telling. Omissions in the telling constitute ELLIPSES; those in the told underscore the radical incompleteness of fictional worlds (how many siblings did Captain Kirk of *Star Trek* have? In *The Incredible Hulk*, where was Bruce Banner's maternal grandfather born?). (3, 4, 11, 14)

HEGEMONY The dominance of a particular view or group over other views or groups, often through a process of manufactured consent, whereby those in a subordinate role are induced to participate in their own domination. A key question for narrative study is how stories can both shore up hegemony, in the form of "master narratives," but also critique such domination, by way of "counter narratives" that contest entrenched accounts of how the world is. (15)

HETERODIEGETIC NARRATOR A NARRATOR who has not participated in the circumstances and events about which he or she tells a story. (3)

HOMODIEGETIC NARRATOR A NARRATOR who has participated (more or less centrally) in the circumstances and events about which he or she tells a story. At the limit, homodiegetic narration shades off into AUTODIEGETIC narration. (3)

HYPODIEGETIC NARRATIVE A story within a story. In Conrad's *Heart of Darkness*, Marlow's tale about his trip to the Belgian Congo is a hypodiegetic narrative. (3, 12)

IMPLIED AUTHOR In the pathbreaking account outlined by Wayne Booth, the implied author is a role or persona assumed by an actual author. That role can described as a set of norms and values that flesh-and-blood authors adopt for the purpose of producing a given narrative. Interpreting a narrative entails searching the text for clues about these norms and values, which in turn enable the AUDIENCE to detect favored versus disfavored character traits, modes and degrees of UNRELIABLE NARRATION, etc. (14)

IMPLIED READER The intended addressee or AUDIENCE of the IMPLIED AUTHOR; another term for what rhetorical narrative theorists of narrative call the authorial audience. The implied reader of Conrad's *Heart of Darkness* will know, for example, that Brussels is a city in Belgium and the Thames a river that runs through London – though an actual reader unschooled in geography may not know these details. (14)

INDIRECT DISCOURSE A technique for representing characters' speech. In contrast to DIRECT DISCOURSE, in ID a NARRATOR reports in a more or less summary fashion characters' utterance(s), rather than reproducing them verbatim. (6, 16, 17)

INTERACTIVE FICTION A digitally produced narrative that involves textual exchange between a user or interactor and a computer program. The computer generates a text that situates existents and events in the simulated world, while input from the user (commands to a character or avatar) influences the unfolding of those events. (12)

INTRADIEGETIC NARRATOR A character NARRATOR, like Marlow in Conrad's *Heart of Darkness*; in other words, a character in a STORYWORLD who in turn narrates a story within the story, that is, a HYPODIEGETIC NARRATIVE. (3, 12)

MIMESIS An ancient Greek word meaning "imitation." In the study of FICTIONAL narrative, the concept of mimesis is relevant both for the analysis of character (the mimetic dimension of a character accounts for the tendency of the AUDIENCE to treat him or her as a real person) and for the analysis of speech representation (in contrast with more DIEGETIC techniques for representing characters' utterances, such as INDIRECT DISCOURSE, more mimetic techniques, such as DIRECT DISCOURSE, background the narrator's mediating role). (5, 8, 10, 14, 15)

METALEPSIS A confusion or entanglement of narrative levels, as when characters situated in a story within a story (or HYPODIEGETIC NARRATIVE) migrate into the DIEGESIS or main narrative level. In Flann O'Brien's *At Swim-Two-Birds*, for example, the protagonist writes a novel whose characters then jump up one narrative level and attack the novelist who created them. (10)

NARRATED MONOLOGUE Dorrit Cohn's term for the mode of thought representation that is equivalent to FREE INDIRECT DISCOURSE in the realm of speech representation. (17)

NARRATEE The AUDIENCE of the NARRATOR, like those who listen to Marlow on board the Nellie in Conrad's *Heart of Darkness*. In so far as the narratee is an AUDIENCE role more or less explicitly inscribed in a narrative text, it is distinct from both the actual reader, the IMPLIED READER, and the narrative audience. (14)

NARRATING-I In retrospective first-person or HOMODIEGETIC (or AUTODIEGETIC) NARRATION, the older, narrating self who tells about the situations and events experienced by the younger, experiencing-I. (3)

NARRATION The process by which a NARRATIVE is conveyed; depending on the SEMIOTIC medium used, this process can involve complex combinations of cues in different channels (visual, auditory, tactile, etc.). Also, some theorists of NARRATIVE make narration the third term in a tripartite model that includes the STORY level, the DISCOURSE or text level on the basis of which the story can be reconstructed, and the narration as the communicative act that produces the discourse. (3, 7, 15)

NARRATIVE In informal usage, *narrative* is a synonym for STORY. More technically, as defined in chapter 1 of this volume, a narrative is a representation of (i) a structured time-course of particularized EVENTS that (ii) introduces CONFLICT (disruption or disequilibrium) into a STORYWORLD (whether that world is presented as actual, FICTIONAL, dreamed, etc.), conveying (iii) what it's like to live through that disruption, that is, the "QUALIA" (or felt, subjective awareness) of real or imagined consciousnesses undergoing the disruptive experience. See chapter 2 for other definitions. (1, 2, 8)

NARRATIVE ARCS Plot-lines that run across multiple EPISODES within an EPISODIC SERIES, but that eventually are resolved. (11)

NARRATIVE DISCOURSE. See DISCOURSE

NARRATIVE SITUATIONS The Austrian narrative theorist Franz Karl Stanzel, developing a nomenclature that has been especially influential in German-language traditions of narrative inquiry, distinguished among three main narrative situations: first-person, third-person or authorial, and figural, which combines a third-person narrative voice with a REFLECTOR figure or particularized center of consciousness. (3, 7)

NARRATIVITY That which makes a story a story; a property that a text or discourse will have in greater proportion the more readily it lends itself to being interpreted as a NARRATIVE. (1, 2)

NARRATOLOGY An approach to narrative inquiry developed during the heyday of STRUCTURALISM in France. Instead of working to develop interpretations of individual narratives, narratologists focused on how to describe NARRATIVE viewed as a SEMIOTIC system – that is, as a system by virtue of which people are able to produce and understand stories. (1)

NARRATOR The AGENT who produces a NARRATIVE. Some story analysts distinguish among AUTODIEGETIC, EXTRADIEGETIC, HETERODIEGETIC, HOMODIEGETIC, and INTRADIEGETIC narrators. (3, 12, 15)

ORAL NARRATIVE Storytelling in contexts of face-to-face communicative interaction. Oral narrative is a broader category than conversational storytelling, since oral narratives can be told during research interviews and not just informal conversations among peers. (9)

ORDER A way of describing the relation between two temporal sequences: the sequence of events that can be assumed to have unfolded in the STORYWORLD, and the unfolding of the DISCOURSE used to recount that sequence. When these two sequences are aligned, the result is chronological narration. ANACHRONY results when the sequences are dis-aligned, yielding ANALEPSES (or flashbacks), PROLEPSES (or flashforwards), and sometimes complex combinations and embeddings of the two. (4, 10)

ORIENTALISM The practice of representing non-Western people and cultures in stereotypic terms, as exotic, passive, etc. (18)

ORIENTATION In the Labovian model, the term *orientation* refers to the part of the NARRATIVE in which storytellers provide information about the context in which the COMPLICATING ACTION occurs, including time, place, characters, etc. (9)

PAUSE The slowest possible narrative speed; a type of DURATION in which the NARRATOR's DISCOURSE continues to unfold, even though the action has come to a stand-still. (4, 10)

PERSPECTIVE/POINT OF VIEW Issues of perspective and point of view are now most often treated under the heading of focalization, a term coined by the NARRATOLOGIST Gérard Genette. Genette drew a contrast between focalization and NARRATION to distinguish between who sees or perceives and who speaks in a narrative, respectively. See chapter 7 for a full discussion. (4, 7, 17)

PLOT In chapter 3 of this volume, H. Porter Abbott distinguishes between three senses of the term *plot*: a type of story; the combination and sequencing of EVENTS that makes a story a story and not just an assemblage of events; and a sense similar to that of DISCOURSE, by which theorists emphasize how the plot rearranges and otherwise manipulates the events of the story. (3, 4)

POSTCOLONIAL STUDIES A framework for inquiry that focuses on the power relations between colonizer and colonized. (18)

PROLEPSIS The equivalent of a flashforward in film. Prolepsis occurs when events that occur in the order ABC are told in the order ACB or CAB. (4, 10)

PSYCHO-NARRATION Dorrit Cohn's term for the mode of thought representation that is equivalent to INDIRECT DISCOURSE in the realm of speech representation. (17)

QUALIA Term used by philosophers of mind to refer to the sense or feeling of *what it is like* for someone or something to have a given experience. (1, 17)

QUOTED MONOLOGUE Dorrit Cohn's term for the mode of thought representation that is equivalent to DIRECT DISCOURSE in the realm of speech representation. (17)

REFLECTOR A term coined by the novelist Henry James to designate the center of consciousness through whose perceptions events are filtered in a narrative using third-person or HETERODIEGETIC narration. A paradigm case would be Gregor Samsa in Franz Kafka's *Metamorphosis*. (7)

RESOLUTION In the Labovian model, the resolution of a story marks the point past which it no longer makes sense to ask "And then what happened?" (9)

SCENE Scenic presentation is a narrative speed or mode of DURATION in which one can assume a direct equivalence between how long it takes for things to happen in the STORYWORLD and how long it takes the NARRATOR to recount those happenings. (4, 10)

SEMIOTICS The study of signs. C. S. Peirce divided signs into three main types: *icon*, where there is a resemblance between signifier and signified (as when big eyeglasses are placed in front of an optometrist's office); *index*, where there is a causal relation between signifier and signified (as when smoke signifies fire); and *symbol*, where there is a conventional relation between signifier and signified (as with verbal language). (2)

SERIAL NARRATION Narration across multiple EPISODES, such that any individual episode must be situated in the larger history of the storyworld. (11)

SHOT/REVERSE SHOT A sequence of shots in a film that alternates between (a) the viewpoint assumed to correspond to a character's angle of vision and (b) a viewpoint from which that character's facial reactions can be seen. (11)

STORY In informal usage, *story* is a synonym for NARRATIVE. In NARRATOLOGY, the "story" level of narrative (in French, *histoire*) corresponds to what Russian Formalist theorists called the "fabula"; it contrasts with the "DISCOURSE" (*discours*) level. In this sense, *story* refers to the chronological sequence of situations and events that can be reconstructed on the basis of cues provided in a narrative text. (1, 3, 4, 10, 15)

STORYWORLD The world evoked by a NARRATIVE text or DISCOURSE; a mental representation of who did what to and with whom, when, where, why, and in what fashion in the world for whose reconstruction a narrative artifact (text, film, etc.) provides a blueprint. (1, 2, 3, 4, 8, 10, 11, 17)

STRETCH A narrative speed or mode of DURATION faster than PAUSE but slower than SCENE, in which both NARRATION and action progress but what is told transpires more rapidly than the telling. (4, 10)

STRUCTURALISM An approach to literary and cultural analysis, especially prominent in the 1960s and 1970s, that used linguistics as a "pilot-science" to study diverse forms of cultural expression as rule-governed signifying practices or "languages" in their own right. NARRATOLOGY was an outgrowth of this general approach. (1)

STYLISTICS A field of study that draws on tools from linguistics to analyze how language is used (sometimes in transgressive or defamiliarizing ways) in literary works, including narratives. (16)

SUMMARY A narrative speed or mode of DURATION faster than SCENE but slower than ELLIPSIS; summaries are more or less compressed accounts of STORYWORLD occurrences. (4, 10)

TELLABILITY To be tellable, situations and EVENTS must in some way stand out against the backdrop formed by everyday expectations and norms, and thus be worth reporting. (9)

UNRELIABLE NARRATION A mode of NARRATION in which the teller of a story cannot be taken at his or her word, compelling the audience to "read between the lines" – in other words, to scan the text for clues about how the STORYWORLD really is, as opposed to how the narrator says it is. (14)

NOTE

1. I am grateful to my colleague Jim Phelan for his assistance with this entry.

FURTHER READING

The following texts were suggested by the contributors as sources of additional information about the key concerns addressed in their respective chapters. The sources are thus grouped by chapter; however, particular items are often relevant for issues discussed in other chapters as well. Conversely, in cases where more than one contributor suggested the same item for further reading, I have not listed it twice here. Authors were asked not to duplicate, in their suggestions for further reading, sources cited in their own chapters. Hence readers should consult the endnotes of each chapter in addition to this list.

Introduction

Doležel, Lubomír. *Heterocosmica: Fiction and Possible Worlds* (Baltimore: Johns Hopkins University Press, 1998).

Fleischman, Suzanne. *Tense and Narrativity: From Medieval Performance to Modern Fiction* (Austin: University of Texas Press, 1990).

Herman, Luc, and Bart Vervaeck. *Handbook of Narrative Analysis* (Lincoln: University of Nebraska Press, 2005).

Onega, Susan, and José Angel García Landa (eds.) *Narratology: An Introduction* (London: Longman, 1996.)

Pavel, Thomas. *The Poetics of Plot: The Case of English Renaissance Drama* (Minneapolis: University of Minnesota Press, 1985).

Prince, Gerald. *A Dictionary of Narratology*, 2nd edition (Lincoln: University of Nebraska Press, 2003).

"Narratology." In Raman Selden (ed.) *The Cambridge History of Literary Criticism*, Vol. VIII (Cambridge: Cambridge University Press, 1995), pp. 110–30.

Narratology: The Form and Functioning of Narrative (The Hague: Mouton, 1982).

Polkinghorne, David. *Narrative Knowing and the Human Sciences* (Albany: State University of New York Press, 1988).

Shuman, Amy. *Storytelling Rights* (Cambridge: Cambridge University Press, 1986).

Richardson, Brian (ed.) "Concepts of Narrative," special issue of *Style* 34:2 (2000), pp. 167–349.

(ed.) *Narrative Dynamics: Essays on Time, Plot, Closure, and Frames* (Columbus: Ohio State University Press, 2002).

Sternberg, Meir. "Telling in Time (I): Chronology and Narrative Theory." *Poetics Today* 11:4 (1990), pp. 901–48.
"Telling in Time (II): Chronology, Teleology, Narrativity." *Poetics Today* 13:3 (1992), pp. 463–541.

Toward a definition of narrative

Chatman, Seymour. *Story and Discourse: Narrative Structure in Fiction and Film* (Ithaca, N.Y: Cornell University Press, 1978).
Fludernik, Monika. *Towards a "Natural" Narratology* (London: Routledge, 1996).
Rimmon-Kenan, Shlomith. *Narrative Fiction: Contemporary Poetics*, 2nd edition (London: Routledge, 2002).
Ryan, Marie-Laure (ed.) *Narrative Across Media: The Languages of Storytelling* (Lincoln: University of Nebraska Press, 2004).
Avatars of Story: Narrative Modes in Old and New Media (Minneapolis: University of Minnesota Press, 2006).

Story, plot, and narration

Bal, Mieke. *Narratology: Introduction to the Theory of Narrative* (Toronto: University of Toronto Press, 1997).
Banfield, Ann. *Unspeakable Sentences: Representation and Narration in the Language of Fiction* (Boston: Routledge & Kegan Paul, 1982).
Booth, Wayne. *The Rhetoric of Fiction*, 2nd edition (Chicago: University of Chicago Press, 1983).
Brooks, Peter. *Reading for the Plot* (New York: Random House, 1985).
Cohn, Dorrit. *Transparent Minds: Narrative Modes for Presenting Consciousness in Fiction* (Princeton: Princeton University Press, 1978).
O'Neill, Patrick. *Fictions of Discourse: Reading Narrative Theory* (Toronto: University of Toronto Press, 1994).
Phelan, James. *Living to Tell about It: A Rhetoric and Ethics of Character Narration* (Ithaca: Cornel University Press, 2004).
Phelan, James. *Reading People, Reading Plots: Character, Progression, and the Interpretation of Narrative* (Chicago: University of Chicago Press, 1989).

Time and space

Bachelard, Gaston. *The Poetics of Space: The Classic Look at How We Experience Intimate Places*. Translated by Maria Jolas (Boston: Beacon Press, 1994).
Buchholz, Sabine, and Manfred Jahn. "Space in Narrative." In David Herman, Manfred Jahn, and Marie-Laure Ryan (eds.) *The Routledge Encyclopedia of Narrative Theory* (London and New York: Routledge, 2005), pp. 551–5.
Duchan, Judith F., Gail A. Bruder, and Lynn E. Hewitt (eds.) *Deixis in Narrative: A Cognitive Science Perspective* (Hillsdale, NJ: Erlbaum, 1995).
Fludernik, Monika. "Chronology, Time, Tense and Experientiality in Narrative." *Language and Literature* 12:2 (2003), pp. 117–34.

"Time in Narrative." In David Herman, Manfred Jahn, and Marie-Laure Ryan (eds.) *Routledge Encyclopedia of Narrative Theory* (London and New York: Routledge, 2005), pp. 608–12.

Genette, Gérard. *Narrative Discourse. An Essay on Method.* Translated by Jane E. Lewin (Ithaca: Cornell University Press, 1980).

Kermode, Frank. *The Sense of an Ending* (New York: Oxford University Press, 1967).

Margolin, Uri. "Of What Is Past, Is Passing, or to Come: Temporality, Aspectuality, Modality, and the Nature of Narrative." In David Herman (ed.) *Narratologies: New Perspectives on Narrative Analysis* (Columbus: Ohio State University Press, 1999), pp. 142–66.

Character

Emmott, Catherine. "Constructing Social Space: Sociocognitive Factors in the Interpretation of Character Relations." In David Herman (ed.) *Narrative Theory and the Cognitive Sciences* (Stanford, CA: CSLI Publications, 2003), pp. 295–321.

Garvey, James. "Characterization in Narrative." *Poetics* 7 (1978), pp. 63–78.

Grabes, Herbert. "Turning Words on the Page into 'Real' People." *Style* 38:2 (2004), pp. 221–35.

Hochman, Baruch. *Character in Literature* (Ithaca: Cornell University Press, 1985).

Knapp, John (ed.) "Literary Character." *Style* 24:3 (1990) [special issue].

Margolin, Uri. "Introducing and Sustaining Characters in Literary Narrative." *Style* 21:1 (1987), pp. 107–24.

"Characters and their Versions." In Calin-Andre Mihailescu and Walid Hamarneh (eds.) *Fiction Updated: Theories of Fictionality, Narratology, and Poetics* (Toronto: University of Toronto Press, 1996), pp. 113–32.

"Naming and Believing: Practices of the Proper Name in Narrative Fiction." *Narrative* 10:2 (2002), pp. 107–27.

Dialogue

Bakhtin, Mikhail. *Problems of Dostoyevsky's Poetics.* Edited and translated by Caryl Emerson (Manchester: Manchester University Press, 1984).

Buck, R. A., and T. R. Austin. "Dialogue and Power in E. M. Forster's *Howards End.*" In Peter Verdonk and Jean Jacques Weber (eds.) *Twentieth-century Fiction: From Text to Context* (London: Routledge, 1995), pp. 63–77.

Burton, Deirdre. *A Sociolinguistic Approach to Modern Drama Dialogue and Naturally Occurring Conversation* (London: Routledge, 1980).

Chapman, Raymond. *Forms of Speech in Victorian Fiction* (Harlow: Longman, 1994).

Fludernik, Monika. *The Fictions of Language and the Languages of Fiction* (London: Routledge, 1993).

Hartley, Lucy. "Conflict not Conversation: The Defeat of Dialogue in Bakhtin and de Man." *New Formations* 41 (2002), pp. 71–82.

Herman, David. "The Mutt and Jute Dialogue in Joyce's *Finnegan's Wake*: Some Gricean Perspectives." *Style* 28:2 (1994), pp. 219–41.

Short, Michael. "Understanding Conversational Undercurrents in 'The Ebony Tower' by John Fowles." In Peter Verdonk and Jean Jacques Weber (eds.) *Twentieth-century Fiction: From Text to Context* (London: Routledge, 1995), pp. 45–62.

Sternberg, Meir. "Proteus in Quotation Land: Mimesis and the Forms of Represented Discourse." *Poetics Today* 3:2 (1982), pp. 107–56.

Tannen, Deborah. *Conversational Style: Analyzing Talk Among Friends* (Norwood, N.J.: Ablex, 1984).

Yell, Susan. "Control and Conflict: Dialogue in Prose Fiction." *AUMLA: Journal of the Australasian Universities Language and Literature Associations* 74 (1990), pp. 136–53.

Focalization

Broman, Eva. "Narratological Focalization Models – A Critical Survey." In Göran Rossholm (ed.) *Essays on Fiction and Perspective* (Bern: Peter Lang, 2004), pp. 57–89.

Chatman, Seymour. *Coming to Terms: The Rhetoric of Narrative in Fiction and Film* (Ithaca: Cornell University Press, 1990).

Edmiston, William F. *Hindsight and Insight* (University Park: Pennsylvania State University Press, 1991).

Jost, François. *L'oeil-Caméra: Entre film et roman* (Lyon: Presses Universitaires, 1989).

Nieragden, Göran. "Focalization and Narration: Theoretical and Terminological Refinements." *Poetics Today* 23:4 (2002), pp. 685–97.

Genre

Bakhtin, Mikhail. *The Dialogic Imagination: Four Essays by M. M. Bakhtin.* Edited by Michael Holquist, translated by Caryl Emerson and Michael Holquist (Austin: University of Texas Press, 1981).

Cohen, Ralph. "History and Genre." *New Literary History* 17:2 (1986), pp. 203–18.

Cohen, Ralph. "Genre Theory, Literary History, and Historical Change." In David Perkins (ed.) *Theoretical Issues in Literary History* (Cambridge, MA: Harvard University Press, 1991), pp. 85–113.

Fishelov, David. *Metaphors of Genre: The Role of Analogies in Genre Theory* (University Park: Pennsylvania State University Press, 1993).

Fowler, Alastair. *Kinds of Literature: An Introduction to the Theory of Genre and Modes* (Oxford: Clarendon, 1982).

Fowler, Alastair. "The Future of Genre Theory: Functions and Constructional Types." In Ralph Cohen (ed.) *The Future of Genre Theory* (New York: Routledge, 1989), pp. 291–303.

Gerhart, Mary. *Genre Choices, Gender Questions* (Norman: University of Oklahoma Press, 1992).

Guillén, Claudio. *Literature as System: Essays Toward the Theory of Literary History* (Princeton: Princeton University Press, 1971).

Hernadi, Paul. *Beyond Genre: New Directions in Literary Classification* (Ithaca: Cornell University Press, 1972).

Jauss, Hans Robert. "Theory of Genres and Medieval Literature." Translated by Timothy Bahti. In David Duff (ed.) *Modern Genre Theory* (London: Longman, 2000), pp. 127–48.

Lemon, Lee T., and Marion J. Reis (eds.) *Russian Formalist Criticism: Four Essays* (Lincoln: University of Nebraska Press, 1965).

Lindenberger, Herbert. *The History in Literature: On Value, Genre, Institutions* (New York: Columbia University Press, 1990).

Opacki, Ireneusz. "Royal Genres." Translated by David Malcolm. In David Duff (ed.) *Modern Genre Theory* (London: Longman, 2000), pp. 118–26.

Perloff, Marjorie. *Postmodern Genres* (Norman: University of Oklahoma Press, 1988).

Shklovsky, Victor. *Theory of Prose*. Translated by Benjamin Sher. (Elmwood Park, IL: Dalkey Archive Press, 1990).

Strelka, Joseph P. (ed.) *Theories of Literary Genre*. Yearbook of Comparative Criticism 8 (University Park, PA: Pennsylvania State University Press, 1978).

Conversational storytelling

Bartlett, Frederic C. *Remembering: A Study in Experimental and Social Psychology* (Cambridge: Cambridge University Press, 1932).

Cederborg, Ann-Christin, and Karin Aronson. "Conarration and Voice in Family Therapy: Voicing, Devoicing and Orchestration." *Text* 14 (1994), pp. 345–70.

Chafe, Wallace. "Beyond Bartlett: Narratives and Remembering." *Poetics* 15 (1986), pp. 139–51.

Cheshire, Jenny. "The Telling or the Tale? Narratives and Gender in Adolescent Friendship Networks." *Journal of Sociolinguistics* 4 (2000), pp. 234–62.

Goodwin, Marjorie H. "Towards Families of Stories in Context." *Journal of Narrative and Life History* 7 (1997), pp. 107–12.

Holmes, Janet. "Story-telling in New Zealand Women's and Men's Talk." In Ruth Wodak (ed.) *Gender and Discourse* (London: Sage), pp. 263–93.

Jefferson, Gail. "Sequential Aspects of Storytelling in Conversation." In Jim Schenkein (ed.) *Studies in the Organization of Conversational Interaction* (New York: Academic Press), pp. 219–48.

Labov, William. "Intensity." In Deborah Schiffrin (ed.) *Meaning, Form, and Use in Context* (Washington, D.C.: Georgetown University Press, 1984), pp. 43–70.

Ochs, Elinor, and Lisa Capps. *Living Narrative: Creating Lives in Everyday Storytelling* (Cambridge: Harvard University Press, 2001).

Ryave, Alan L. "On the Achievement of a Series of Stories." In Jim Schenkein (ed.) *Studies in the Organization of Conversational Interaction* (New York: Academic Press, 1978), pp. 113–32.

Sacks, Harvey. "On the Analyzability of Stories by Children." In John J. Gumperz and Dell Hymes (eds.) *Directions in Sociolinguistics* (New York: Holt, Rinehart & Winston, 1972), pp. 325–45.

Schiffrin, Deborah. "Tense Variation in Narrative." *Language* 57 (1981), pp. 45–62.

"How a Story Says What It Means and Does." *Text* 4 (1984), pp. 313–46.

"Narrative as Self-portrait: Sociolinguistic Constructions of Identity." *Language in Society* 25 (1996), pp. 167–203.

Tannen, Deborah. *Talking Voices: Repetition, Dialogue and Imagery in Conversational Discourse* (Cambridge: Cambridge University Press, 1989).

Thornborrow, Joanna, and Jennifer Coates (eds.) *The Sociolinguistics of Narrative* (Amsterdam: Benjamins, 2005).

Quasthoff, Uta M., and Tabea Becker (eds.) *Narrative Interaction* (Amsterdam: Benjamins, 2004).

Drama and narrative

Bristol, Michael D. *Carnival and Theater: Plebian Culture and the Structure of Authority in Renaissance England* (New York: Routledge, 1989).

Carlson, Marvin. *Theories of the Theatre: A Historical and Critical Survey, from the Greeks to the Present* (Ithaca: Cornell University Press, 1986).

Case, Sue-Ellen (ed.) *Performing Feminisms: Feminist Critical Theory and Theatre* (Baltimore: Johns Hopkins University Press, 1990).

Morrison, Kristin. *Canters and Chronicles: The Use of Narrators in the Plays of Beckett and Pinter* (Chicago: University of Chicago Press, 1983).

Pavis, Patrice. *Languages of the Stage* (New York: Performing Arts Journal Publications, 1982).

Robinson, Mark. *The Other American Drama* (Baltimore: Johns Hopkins University Press, 1997).

Sommer, Roy. "Drama and Narrative." *Routledge Encyclopedia of Narrative Theory.* Edited by David Herman, Manfred Jahn, and Marie-Laure Ryan (London: Routledge, 2005), pp. 119–24.

Szondi, Peter. *Theory of the Modern Drama* (Minneapolis: University of Minnesota Press, 1987).

Wilson, Rawdon. *Shakespearean Narrative* (Newark, DE: University of Delaware Press, 1995).

Film and television narrative

Hayward, Jennifer. *Consuming Pleasures: Active Audiences and Serial Fictions from Dickens to Soap Opera* (Lexington: University Press of Kentucky, 1997).

Johnson, Steven. *Everything Bad Is Good for You: How Today's Popular Culture Is Actually Making Us Smarter* (New York: Riverhead Books, 2005).

Kozloff, Sarah. "Narrative Theory and Television." In Robert C. Allen (ed.) *Channels of Discourse, Reassembled* (Chapel Hill: University of North Carolina Press, 1992), pp. 61–100.

Mittell, Jason. *Genre and Television: From Cop Shows to Cartoons in American Culture* (New York: Routledge, 2004).

"Narrative Complexity in Contemporary American Television." *The Velvet Light Trap* 58 (fall 2006), pp. 29–40.

Sconce, Jeffrey. "What If? Charting Television's New Textual Boundaries." In Lynn Spigel and Jan Olsson (eds.) *Television After TV: Essays on a Medium in Transition* (Durham: Duke University Press, 2004), pp. 93–112.

Thompson, Kristin. *Storytelling in Film and Television* (Cambridge, MA: Harvard University Press, 2003).

Warhol, Robyn R. *Having a Good Cry: Effeminate Feelings and Pop-Culture Forms* (Columbus: Ohio State University Press, 2003).

Narrative and digital media

Buckles, Mary Ann. "Interactive Fiction: The Computer Storygame 'Adventure.'" Ph.D. thesis, University of California San Diego, 1985.
Juul, Jesper. *Half-Real: Video Games between Real Rules and Fictional Worlds* (Cambridge: MIT Press, 2005).
Laurel, Brenda. *Computers as Theatre* (Reading, MA: Addison-Wesley, 1991).
Wardrip-Fruin, Noah, and Pat Harrigan (eds.) *First Person: New Media as Story, Performance, and Game* (Cambridge: MIT Press, 2004).
Wardrip-Fruin, Noah, and Nick Montfort. *The New Media Reader* (Cambridge: MIT Press, 2003).

Gender

Abney, L. "Gender Difference in Oral Folklore Narratives." *The SECOL Review* 18:1 (1994), pp. 62–79.
Anderson, Antje S. "Gendered Pleasure, Gendered Plot: Defloration as Climax in *Clarissa* and *Memoirs of a Woman of Pleasure*." *Journal of Narrative Technique* 28:2 (1995), pp. 108–38.
Cazden, Courtney B. "Speakers, Listeners and Speech Events in Issues of Universality." *Journal of Narrative and Life History* 7:1–4 (1997), pp. 185–8.
Coates, Jennifer. *Women Talk* (Oxford: Blackwell, 1996).
DuPlessis, Rachel Blau. *Writing Beyond the Ending: Narrative Strategies of Twentieth-century Women Writers* (Bloomington: Indiana University Press, 1985).
Hirsch, Marianne. *The Mother/Daughter Plot: Narrative, Psychoanalysis, Feminism* (Bloomington: Indiana University Press, 1989).
Lanser, Susan. "Sexing Narratology: Toward a Gendered Poetics of Narrative Voice." In Walter Grünzweig and Andreas Solbach (eds.) *Transcending Boundaries: Narratology in Context* (Tübingen: Gunter Narr Verlag Tübingen, 1999), pp. 167–83.
Meinhof, Ulrike. "'The Most Important Event of my Life!' A Comparison of Male and Female Written Narratives." In Sally Johnson and Ulrike H. Meinhof (eds.) *Language and Masculinity* (Oxford: Blackwell, 1997), pp. 208–28.
Prince, Gerald. "On Narratology: Criteria, Corpus, Context." *Narrative* 3 (1995), pp. 73–84.
Roof, Judith. *Come as You Are: Sexuality and Narrative* (New York: Columbia University Press, 1996).

Rhetoric/ethics

Booth, Wayne C. *A Rhetoric of Irony* (Chicago: University of Chicago Press, 1974).
Case, Alison. *Plotting Women* (Charlottesville: University of Virginia Press, 1999).

Jost, Walter, and Wendy Olmstead (eds.) *A Companion to Rhetoric* (Oxford: Blackwell, 2004).

Kearns, Michael. *Rhetorical Narratology* (Lincoln: University of Nebraska Press, 1999).

Newton, Adam Zachary. *Narrative Ethics* (Cambridge: Harvard University Press, 1995).

Phelan, James, and Peter J. Rabinowitz (eds.) *A Companion to Narrative Theory* (Oxford: Blackwell, 2005).

Womack, Kenneth, and Todd Davis (eds.) *Mapping the Ethical Turn* (Charlottesville: University of Virginia Press, 2001).

Ideology

Eagleton, Terry. *Ideology: An Introduction* (London: Verso, 1991).

Hawkes, David. *Ideology*, 2nd edition (London: Routledge, 2003).

Jameson, Fredric. *The Political Unconscious: Narrative as a Socially Symbolic Act* (Ithaca: Cornell University Press, 1981).

Phelan, James (ed.) *Reading Narrative: Form, Ethics, Ideology* (Columbus: Ohio State Univeristy Press, 1989).

Uspensky, Boris. *A Poetics of Composition: The Structure of the Artistic Text and Typology of a Compositional Form*. Translated by Susan Wittig and Valentina Zavarin (Berkeley: University of California Press, 1973).

Language

Carter, Ronald. *Language and Literature: An Introductory Reader in Stylistics* (London: Routledge, 1992).

Carter, Ronald, and Paul Simpson (eds.) *Language, Discourse and Literature: An Introductory Reader in Discourse Stylistics* (London: Unwin Hyman, 1989).

Leech, Geoffrey, and Michael Short. *Style in Fiction* (London: Longman, 1981).

Simpson, Paul. *Language, Ideology, and Point of View* (London: Routledge, 1993).

Toolan, Michael. *Narrative: A Critical Linguistic Introduction*, 2nd edition (London: Routledge, 2001).

Verdonk, Peter, and Jean Jacques Weber (eds.) *Twentieth-Century Fiction: From Text to Context* (London: Routledge, 1995).

Cognition, emotion, and consciousness

Auerbach, Erich. "The Brown Stocking." In *Mimesis: The Representation of Reality in Western Literature*. Translated by Willard R. Trask (Princeton: Princeton University Press, 1953), pp. 525–53.

Bockting, Ineke. "Mind Style and Characterisation in Faulkner." *Language and Literature* 3:3 (1994), pp. 157–74.

Brinton, Laurel. "Represented Perception: A Study in Narrative Style." *Poetics* 9 (1980), pp. 363–81.

Butte, George. *I Know that You Know that I Know: Narrating Subjects from Moll Flanders to Marnie* (Columbus: Ohio State University Press, 2004).

Damasio, Antonio R. *Descartes' Error: Emotion, Reason, and the Human Brain* (New York: G. P. Putnam, 1994).

Fireman, Gary D., Ted E. McVay, R., and Owen J. Flanagan (eds.) *Narrative and Consciousness: Literature, Psychology, and the Brain* (Oxford: Oxford University Press, 2003).

Freeman, Anthony. *Consciousness: A Guide to the Debates* (Santa Barbara: ABC-Clio, 2003).

Herman, David (ed.) *Narrative Theory and the Cognitive Sciences* (Stanford, CA: Publications of the Center for the Study of Language and Information, 2003).

"Narrative Theory after the Second Cognitive Revolution." In Lisa Zunshine (ed.) *Introduction to Cognitive Cultural Studies* (Baltimore: Johns Hopkins University Press, forthcoming).

Hamburger, Käte. *The Logic of Literature*, 2nd edition. Translated by Marilynn J. Rose (Bloomington: Indiana University Press).

Kahler, Erich. *The Inward Turn of Narrative*. Translated by Richard and Clara Winston (Princeton: Princeton University Press, 1973).

Marshall, Adré. *Turn of the Mind: Constituting Consciousness in Henry James* (Madison, N.J.: Fairleigh Dickinson University Press, 1998).

Palmer, Alan. "Thought and Consciousness Representation (Literature)." In David Herman, Manfred Jahn, and Marie-Laure Ryan (eds.) *The Routledge Encyclopedia of Narrative Theory* (London: Routledge, 2005), pp. 602–7.

Turner, Mark. *Reading Minds: The Study of English in the Age of Cognitive Science* (Princeton: Princeton University Press, 1991).

Identity/alterity

Ashcroft, Bill, Gareth Griffiths, and Helen Tiffin. *The Empire Writes Back: Theory and Practice in Post-Colonial Literatures* (London: Routledge, 1989).

Childs, Peter, and Patrick Williams (eds.) *Post-colonial Theory and English Literature: A Reader* (Edinburgh: Edinburgh University Press, 1999).

Dallery, Arleen B., and Charles E. Scott (eds.) *The Question of the Other: Essays in Contemporary Continental Philosophy* (Albany: State University of New York Press, 1989).

Dirlik, Arif. "The Postcolonial Aura: Third World Criticism in the Age of Global Capitalism." *Critical Inquiry* 20 (1994), pp. 328–56.

Fanon, Frantz. *Black Skin, White Masks*. Translated by Charles Lam Markmann (New York: Grove, 1967).

Fludernik, Monika. "Colonial vs. Cosmopolitan Hybridity: A Comparison of Mulk Raj Anand and R. K. Narayan with Recent British and North American Expatriate Writing." In Monika Fludernik (ed.) *Hybridity and Postcolonialism* (Tübingen: Stauffenberg Verlag, 1998), pp. 261–90.

JanMohamed, Abdul R. "The Economy of Manichean Allegory: The Function of Racial Difference in Colonialist Literature." *Critical Inquiry* 12:1 (1985), pp. 59–87.

Memmi, Albert. *The Colonizer and the Colonized*. Translated by Howard Greenfield (Boston: Beacon Press, 1991).

Pratt, Mary Louise. *Imperial Eyes: Travel Writing and Transculturation* (London: Routledge, 1992).

Rajchman, John (ed.) *The Identity in Question* (New York: Routledge, 1995).

Ricoeur, Paul. *Oneself as Another*. Translated by Kathleen Blarney (Chicago: University of Chicago Press, 1994).

Spivak, Gayatri Chakravorty. "Can the Subaltern Speak" [1988]. In Patrick Williams and Laura Chrisman (eds.) *Colonial Discourse and Post-Colonial Theory: A Reader* (London: Harvester Wheatsheaf, 1993), pp. 66–111.

Spurr, David. *The Rhetoric of Empire: Colonial Discourse in Journalism, Travel Writing, and Imperial Administration* (Durham, NC: Duke University Press, 1993).

West, Cornel. "The New Cultural Politics of Difference." In John Rajchman (ed.) *The Identity in Question* (London: Routledge, 1995), pp. 147–72.

Yeazell, Ruth Bernard. *Harems of the Mind: Passages of Western Art and Literature* (New Haven, CT: Yale University Press, 2000).

Young, Robert J. C. *Colonial Desire: Hybridity in Theory, Culture and Race* (London: Routledge, 1995).

INDEX

space in narrative (*cont.*)
and the positioning of the reader, 62–3
and public vs. private domains, 61
and shifts to characters' private mental
worlds, 62
social and psychological aspects of, 55, 60,
61
and the use of locations to track multiple
plot-lines, 56
and the variable scope or size of
storyworlds, 60. *See also* drama;
narrative; plot; time in narrative
speech act theory. *See* genre
speech and thought representation
and direct discourse, 40–2, 45, 47–9, 80,
82, 132, 228, 248
and dissonant vs. consonant
psychonarration, 227
and the dual-voice hypothesis, 258n.12
as entailing evaluation by the narrator,
227–8
and expressivity markers suggesting
characters' speech patterns, 248
and free indirect discourse, 228, 248
historical development of in the novel,
81–3
and indirect discourse, 228, 248
ideological dimensions of, 227–8
and James Joyce's use of dashes for direct
discourse, 258n.11
and stage dialogue, 81. *See also*
consciousness; dialogue; focalization;
linguistic approaches; narrative;
reliability
Stanzel, Franz K., 95, 258n.3
Stearns, Carol, 259n.19
Stearns, Peter, 254, 259nn.18, 19
Sternberg, Meir, 44, 46, 54, 57, 65n.20, 81,
84
story (= *fabula* or what is narrated)
and Barthes', grammar of actions and
events, 221–3
as composed of actions and characters, 41,
220
vs. discourse, 13, 24, 26, 34n.25, 40, 41,
53, 212
essential vs. expendable components of, 41
as event-sequence that can be presented in
different ways, 39, 40
and functions vs. indexes (Barthes), 222–3
as *histoire* vs. *discours*, 41
ideological dimensions of, 220–3
vs. narration, 40

vs. plot, 39, 40
and setting, 220
as "signified" vs. "signifier," 41. *See also*
action code (Barthes); actions vs. events;
discourse; ideology; narration;
rhetorical approaches; storyworld
story arcs. *See* television
storytelling rights. *See* conversational
storytelling
storyworld
cognitive and emotional immersion in, 170
and the concept of diegesis in film studies,
160
in contrast with sub-worlds of characters,
62, 71
identifying the fact domain of, 71
as mental construction, 168
of postmodern narratives, 63
as spatially and temporally structured, 52,
63
as world evoked by a narrative, 42, 44, 49,
66, 71. *See also* character; fictional
world; story
Strawson, Galen, 19n.13
stream of consciousness, 95, 96. *See also*
consciousness; dialogue; novel of
consciousness; speech and thought
representation
stretch, 58. *See also* duration; time in
narrative
structuralism. *See* narrative; narratology;
Saussure
structuralist narratology. *See* narrative;
narratology; pragmatics
stylistics. *See* linguistic approaches
summary, 58, 59. *See also* duration;
ideology; time in narrative
surprise (as narrative universal). *See* time in
narrative
suspense, 40, 54, 58, 161. *See also* dialogue;
time in narrative
Süskind, Patrick, 106
Sweeney, Susan Elizabeth, 120

TALE-SPIN, 184
Talmy, Leonard, 252
Tambling, Jeremy, 230n.18
Tani, Stefano, 119, 120, 121
Tannen, Deborah, 140n.7, 141n.23
television
as affording greater immersion than films,
171
and commercial breaks, 165

Cambridge Companions to...

AUTHORS

TOPICS

Medieval English Theatre *edited by Richard Beadle*

Medieval Romance *edited by Roberta L. Krueger*

Medieval Women's Writing *edited by Carolyn Dinshaw and David Wallace*

Modern American Culture *edited by Christopher Bigsby*

Modern British Women Playwrights *edited by Elaine Aston and Janelle Reinelt*

Modern French Culture *edited by Nicholas Hewitt*

Modern German Culture *edited by Eva Kolinsky and Wilfried van der Will*

The Modern German Novel *edited by Graham Bartram*

Modern Irish Culture *edited by Joe Cleary and Claire Connolly*

Modernism *edited by Michael Levenson*

The Modernist Novel *edited by Morag Shiach*

Modernist Poetry *edited by Alex Davis and Lee M. Jenkins*

Modern Italian Culture *edited by Zygmunt G. Barański and Rebecca J. West*

Modern Latin American Culture *edited by John King*

Modern Russian Culture *edited by Nicholas Rzhevsky*

Modern Spanish Culture *edited by David T. Gies*

Narrative *edited by David Herman*

Native American Literature *edited by Joy Porter and Kenneth M. Roemer*

Nineteenth-Century American Women's Writing *edited by Dale M. Bauer and Philip Gould*

Old English Literature *edited by Malcolm Godden and Michael Lapidge*

Postcolonial Literary Studies *edited by Neil Lazarus*

Postmodernism *edited by Steven Connor*

Renaissance Humanism *edited by Jill Kraye*

Roman Satire *edited by Kirk Freudenburg*

The Spanish Novel: From 1600 to the Present *edited by Harriet Turner and Adelaida López de Martínez*

Travel Writing *edited by Peter Hulme and Tim Youngs*

Twentieth-Century Irish Drama *edited by Shaun Richards*

Victorian and Edwardian Theatre *edited by Kerry Powell*

The Victorian Novel *edited by Deirdre David*

Victorian Poetry *edited by Joseph Bristow*

Writing of the English Revolution *edited by N. H. Keeble*